Anthony Haden-Guest

Bad Dreams

BALLANTINE BOOKS • NEW YORK

For my mother and father.

Contents

Acknowledgments

This book is an account of an event, the effects of that event on a few people, and the other events that it bred. In writing it, I observed certain natural rules. Every conversation, for instance, represents the recollection of at least one person who took part in it. Where there has been trimming—mainly in the court transcripts—it has been for sense, not for improvement. *Bad Dreams* is as close to the actuality of these extraordinary happenings as human frailties have allowed.

The people in these pages are all real people, though a few go under disguised names. This is true of some of the models—"Tracy," "Ingrid," "Dolly Robertson"—and of the few people—"Dermot," for instance—who made pseudonymy a prerequisite for their cooperation. *Bad Dreams* could not have been written from afar. It depended upon those people who allowed me, for however long or briefly, to share in their lives. Among many, I should like to thank the following.

Melanie Cain herself, of course; the Tupper family, including Jack Tupper, Sr., and his wife, Marie; Kevin and Kathy Tupper; Tom and Dorothy Myers; Ellen Gannon; also various of Jack's friends, including Claire Normandeau, Brian Monaghan, and David Silbergeld. Among those other friends, who were to run afoul of the law and each other, I should like to disregard their internal strife, and thank Donald Brown, Jimmy Leonard, and Billy Sharrocks.

Also, Sarah Hall, who told me much about the track; also, such combative lawyers as Peter Grishman, Bill Hrabsky, Douglas Behm, Bill Kelly, and, despite his attempt to nail me for contempt of court, Jack Evseroff.

Buddy Jacobson was also helpful, but I will not thank him, since he was hoping to help himself.

Some of the people who helped me most do not wish to be thanked. They know who they are.

Some people were no help at all. They know who they are, too.

Finally, I should like to thank Devon for living through so much of this.

- 1 -

The Murder

Certain weekends in high summer, the Upper East Side of Manhattan takes on an oddly subtropical aspect. Sensible natives of New York's richest neighborhood have left for the shores. The tourist tribes, and their predators, are across on Madison Avenue, and Fifth. Farther east, a languor prevails. The air is thick. Old newspapers flap underfoot like rank vegetation, and the macadam moves like flesh, or jellied mud. It is a quiet not of peace, but of exhaustion, and sullen watchfulness.

It was to just such a Sunday in early August that Melanie Cain awoke. It was just before nine. She had slept wretchedly again, and felt tired, muzzy. Beside her, Jack Tupper was still asleep. Melanie got up. She went downstairs to the kitchen and began to boil water for a cup of tea.

She still felt uneasy, even though the worst was over. This had been the last night Melanie was to spend in the duplex at 155 East 84th Street. Before the morning was over, she would have signed a lease on a new apartment, a good thirty blocks from the ramshackle townhouse which was the center of Buddy Jacobson's world. And once, of hers.

Sometime later, Jack and Melanie would be getting out of New York. Going for a week or so to California. Outside, the low sky was heavy with warm rain. Melanie finished her tea and went upstairs for a shower.

The water was cold. She waited, but it got no warmer.

Of *course* the water was cold.

It was one more of Buddy's tricks, those irritating little games that he had been playing since she had at last left him seventeen days before. Like the way that she and Jack had been followed. Like the dire cancer to which Buddy had claimed he was succumbing as recently as last Thursday. Like the hollow hammering sounds that she and Jack had heard on Friday night, apparently coming from the roof. Like those oblongs of masking tape upon which he scrawled *I Love You* with a felt-tip pen, and which she had found sticking to her woolens and underwear. And, mostly, like the telephone calls—incessant, urgent, husky-throated, meandering. Buddy had called Jack and some of Jack's friends, offering $100,000 for Melanie's return. He called her his "wife," which puzzled both Melanie and Jack at the time, though it made a terrible sense to Melanie later. A couple of times Melanie and Jack had called him back from their useless hideaway suite in the Drake Hotel, and taped the conversations, but mostly he had called her, even hauling her to the telephone in the middle of a two-day Clairol commercial, frazzling her nerves.

Buddy's game. Melanie was irate. She marched out of 7C, where she had been staying with Jack, and banged on the door of 7D. Buddy's door, her former door.

Buddy appeared. He was always quick.

"Hi, babe!" he said.

"Buddy, there's no hot water. Why isn't there?"

Melanie was snappish. And later, when it seemed that every moment of that long day could be examined, as though the specks of time were embedded in some crystalline medium, she was to say that his behavior had seemed unusual. His eyes were bloodshot, as though he hadn't slept. He was shaky, hyper. Right then it only fueled her annoyance, especially when Buddy started mumbling something about a broken water main. A typical story; she didn't believe it for one moment.

So Buddy made some sort of to-do about checking his own water, which was hot, and walking into 7B, which was empty this weekend, and where the water was also hot. "Wait half an hour," Buddy advised Melanie. "Knock on my door, and let me know."

Melanie waited. Jack slept on. She tried the tap. It was still cold. So she got properly dressed, which is to say she put on the old gray-blue button-down shirt that she used to wear in the sixth grade and that she felt comfortable in on weekends. Then she pulled on a pair of baggy white painter's pants, the sort with loops for tools, and a pair of hefty green Frye boots. She didn't put on any makeup, making up being something she had to do when modeling, and she pulled her long, dark-blond hair back into a ponytail. Then she picked up a sloppy old raincoat, green like the boots, and knocked on Buddy's door. It was about a quarter to ten.

"Don't worry! It'll come on," Buddy told her. Eyeing her coat, he added, "Where are you going?"

"I've found an apartment," Melanie said. She felt willful, but wary.

"Well, that's *good*. I guess that means you and Jack will be living together?"

"It's none of your business."

"Okay," Buddy agreed. "When are you leaving?"

"I'm going away today. I'm going away *this afternoon*."

Buddy persisted. His manner, Melanie says, was at once intent and casual. "Where are you going now?" he asked.

"I'm going down to sign a lease. But I'm not telling you where. I'm not telling you *anything*." Then she marched back to her apartment.

Melanie was hamming it up a bit, but not entirely. Buddy's game had trespassed beyond the irritating, had become alarming. So much so, in fact, that when she found he knew the whereabouts of the apartment that she had planned to move into the previous week—"Mr. Jacobson called for you," the landlord's secretary had innocently told her—she had become so nervous that she had abandoned the place.

It was absurd, of course. Buddy Jacobson was in his late forties. He was five foot eight, and scrawny. Jack Tupper was much younger, six foot one, and 190 pounds. He worked out zealously, and jogged. Their affair, indeed, had germinated while jogging; truly a modern American romance. A judo enthusiast who sometimes worked out with Jack says that although he had only a brown belt, Jack was not a man to trifle with. "He was one tough piece of work," says the black belt (of the third dan). "You could hit Jack over the head with a chair, and he wouldn't go down."

Melanie's mood was dark all the same. Jack had laughed off Buddy's antics. Others did not. Two weeks ago, Melanie and Jack had been staying with Dorothy, Jack's sister, and her husband, Tom Myers, an FBI agent in Puerto Rico. Dorothy had become so anxious at what she had heard that she had been telephoning from San Juan ever since. Al Seifert, with whom Melanie and Jack had just stayed a couple of days, and who was to be best man at their wedding, knew Buddy well. Buddy had trained a couple of racehorses for him. "Buddy will get even," he told Jack. "He's vicious. You've got to be careful."

The night before, Jack and Melanie had gone for a nightcap to R.W. Bonds, a place on Third Avenue. Dick Leslie, the owner, an old friend of Jack's, had gotten a bad feeling from what he heard, and said so.

"Buddy's not tough," Jack said.

Dick had extended two fingers; a stiff, pointing gesture.

"He's tough as a gun," he had said bleakly, and offered Melanie the use of a room in his own house. It was small, but it would be for only a few days. Jack and Melanie had turned Dick's offer down. It seemed to be taking Buddy Jacobson too seriously, they felt.

Melanie was collecting her bankbooks and paraphernalia when there was a knock on her door. It was Buddy.

Melanie looked at him as though daring him to try something new.

"Melanie," Buddy said. "Something's happened. Cheryl Corey got killed. She's dead."

It was too much. Melanie suddenly remembered Buddy's saying that he had only a month left to live—that "cancer." She had to laugh. "Oh, go on, Buddy," she said, and slammed the door in his face.

Melanie didn't know Cheryl Corey well. Cheryl, a twenty-year-old with wavy hair, came from Cherry Hill, New Jersey, and had joined the model agency My Fair Lady only a few weeks back. My Fair Lady, which was named for Melanie's favorite musical, was on the ground floor of Buddy's building, and Buddy and Melanie were co-owners. Or so Melanie thought.

But there was so much Melanie had thought. Until just a few days ago, for instance, she had thought that David and Douglas Jacobson were Buddy's brothers. That was what they had said, and what he had said. Now she knew for certain that they were, in fact, his sons.

She had been aware that Jacobson had, formerly, been a power on the racetrack. But again it was only recently, and by looking up clippings at the New York Public Library, that she had learned that he had been for five years the nation's principal horse trainer. It was Buddy Jacobson who had led the strike that had attempted to break the power of the New York Racing Association, which is to say the Jockey Club, but this was a period of which he spoke only seldom, and reluctantly.

Melanie knew more about the property empire that Buddy had been laboring to create since leaving the racetrack, and she knew something of the great and glistening schemes that worked their way through his fertile mind; and she knew, at least in bits and pieces, about the pressures under which he was laboring. Right now, for instance, she was aware that the disgruntled owner of one particular horse farm, who was trying to get Buddy to disgorge a quarter of a million dollars, was only one of several insistent creditors.

There was other information in those newspaper files. Buddy Jacobson, who had long said he was in his twenties, now admitted to being in his thirties. And he had numerous IDs—driver's licenses and such—to bear him out. *The New York Times* showed him up to be what he was: a man of forty-eight. It was a final touch, almost pitiful, when she realized that Buddy's disordered black hair and his untrimmed mustache owed their hue to the bottle of Grecian Formula he kept behind the sink.

"It's for the models," he had told her. The models. There was much that Melanie had chosen to ignore, stored in a closed cupboard in her mind. When she and Buddy had launched My Fair Lady in 1974, she had been a rising star in the Ford Agency, to be sure, appearing on the covers of such dissimilar magazines as *Seventeen, Redbook,* and *Cosmopolitan,* and the pictures in her portfolio had been shot in Paris, Italy, and the Caribbean. But at that time she was a young girl, still eighteen, a junior model. She had lived in the city just seven months, and when she spoke of home, she meant Naperville, Illinois.

Four years of rumor and gossip had altered this. She had recently found it less and less possible to ignore the fact that Buddy maintained My Fair Lady in part as a handy source of sexual conquest, his little black book come to life, and that he kept it replenished with fresh young things from places less knowing than Manhattan just as a fisherman might keep a private pool supplied with young trout. She had known, but chosen not to know.

Much was to arise from this repression. It was just this secret knowledge, this resentful sense of the way she had been so long manipulated, that made Melanie feel she now saw Buddy especially plain. In these last few days, with Jack constantly nearby, it was as if Buddy's spell had, if not broken utterly, at least weakened; because he *was* spellbinding. Jacobson, a nondescript man in nondescript clothes, was compelling. It's no accident that the single name most often used to convey the effect of his dark, intent eyes, his insinuating talk, is that of Charles Manson. And if Melanie had spent the best part of five years in the grip of this modern Machiavelli, well, he had also enthralled innumerable other nubile young hopefuls. To say nothing of a bunch of seasoned horsemen, prosaic businessmen, doting parents, and some of the most adamant cynics in journalism. This was the man Melanie now saw with a cold eye.

Too cold an eye, really. It caused its own sort of blindness, and later Melanie was to blame herself for this. Because there was another side of Buddy. Alongside his contemptuous sense that he was smarter than anybody in the whole world, indeed an absolute part of this sense, was a tremendous capacity for fantasy. Buddy had large dreams, and because Buddy felt invulnerable, he knew the dreams would become reality. The dreams might be delayed, but they were immune from lasting reverses.

Buddy wanted to be king of the mountain, and he had become king of the mountain, several times, doing it always his way. He told his few confidants that he could con the world, adding that the first person you needed to con was yourself. "Buddy always said that if you lie, and want people to believe it, you have to believe it first," says Melanie.

The horrid irony of Melanie's new-found cynicism was that she was again blinkered, but in a different way: she positively refused to believe that she played a part in Buddy's fantasy; Buddy's World. This last two weeks of his freakish behavior had inspired her sometimes with pity, more often with irritation or fatigue, and very occasionally with twinges of alarm, but she had entirely failed to comprehend what a heady brew might now be cooking up in the heart and head of Buddy Jacobson.

Even so, Melanie had been startled by Buddy's shouting as she slammed the door. Overt anger. It was so unlike him. Could something *really* have happened to Cheryl Corey? Melanie recrossed the hall, looking idly around. She still saw nobody, hadn't seen anybody for days. Buddy came to the door of his apartment at once, but he was sour and cold.

"Forget it," he said. "I don't want to talk about it."

"Come on," Melanie said. She was placating. "Is it true or isn't it?" She was standing a few feet inside the apartment.

Buddy said that Cheryl's roommates, two models on the fourth floor, had just called him. The police had told them that Cheryl Corey had died in a fall from a terrace. She had been with a man.

Melanie believed Buddy now. He seemed so confused. The thought of the death of this shy kid she had taken with her on a cable TV interview only a couple of weeks earlier unnerved her horribly. *Death.* "We didn't know whether it was she was on drugs, or whether it was suicide, or whether it was murder," Melanie said later. "We didn't know *anything.*"

One thing Buddy did know was that he had no intention of talking to the girl's parents. "I'm not going to call them. You do it. You're better with parents," he said.

Melanie agreed, saying she would stop in at the police precinct house after the signing of the lease and find out the details. Then she would call the girl's parents. It was becoming plain to her, though, that Buddy's perturbation had nothing to do with the dead girl herself, but was centered on the damage that the publicity might do to the agency. "Suppose she had been with a photographer or somebody in the business?" he fretted.

Melanie was angered. She didn't know that Buddy had been putting Cheryl Corey through his usual hoops (as recently as Friday he had sent her to show her little collection of modeling photographs to a man who passed himself off as a big advertiser). But *something* had been going on between Buddy and Cheryl. Self-blinkered she might be, but Melanie knew that.

"If anybody has to worry, Buddy, you do," she said. "*You* were the one that had dinner with Cheryl the other night."

Buddy grew tight. "Don't you tell anybody that," he spat. Melanie stalked out and went down to the fourth floor to talk with Cheryl's roommates. They said they would go down to the precinct house themselves. Accordingly, Melanie left to sign her lease. It was twenty past ten. Jack Tupper had about an hour to live.

Cheryl Corey's roommates were Kelly Lougee and Beth McKay. Kelly came from North Carolina and was nineteen. Beth came from South Carolina and was a little older. Both had been signed up by My Fair Lady after meeting Melanie at modeling conventions—Beth had met her at a convention at the Waldorf, and Kelly at a convention cocktail party in

Rockefeller Center—and neither had been in town longer than a few months.

And now this. It was everything that their parents, friends, and their own private selves feared about New York. The night before, Kelly had been working with a photographer and had returned to an empty apartment at about two in the morning. Cheryl was still out on a date, and Beth, she knew, was staying at the beach.

The telephone had rung at four. Kelly had ignored it. Some dumb photographer, she thought. It rang again at about a quarter to ten. Kelly answered. It was Cheryl Corey's father.

"Is Cheryl there?" he asked.

She said no.

He said abruptly, "She's dead," and hung up. He had been told by the police, and had telephoned in the desperate hope they might be wrong. Beth McKay got back from Southampton about a quarter of an hour later, and found Kelly still hysterical.

Both girls were calmer by the time Melanie came downstairs. Beth hadn't seen Melanie in a while, but it hadn't escaped her that Buddy had been behaving oddly of late. "He was calling all the time," Beth said. "He would say Kelly and I had to come down and meet him at dinner." They would eat at Nicola's or, once in a while, at the Sign of the Dove, and when Beth asked about Melanie, he would refuse to answer. Beth, a bubbly blonde and short for a model at five seven and a bit, found the situation awkward.

After Melanie left Kelly and Beth to sign the lease, the girls talked about the death with Ernie Baumgartner and Joe Pellicane, who lived next door. Ernie said he would go with them to the precinct house. Then Bill Haworth came down from the fifth floor, and he volunteered to go too. So they set off on their fact-finding mission in a tight little band. It was warm outside, but thick with impending rain, so Beth clutched her umbrella.

The 19th Precinct station house is down on East 67th Street. The twenty minutes that they spent there were uninformative, so they took the subway to East 86th and walked a couple of blocks to the place where the girls' roommate had met her death. It was now raining steadily.

At the building, a pale gray apartment tower on First Avenue and 85th Street, they spoke with some tenants and a couple of reporters. Cheryl had been in the seventeenth-floor apartment of a boyfriend, Scott Shepard. At about two-thirty in the morning they had been leaning against the railing of the balcony. It had given. They had gone right through the false roof of an A&P supermarket, crumpling onto the real roof below. Cheryl had been killed instantly, but Shepard, who evidently had landed on top of her, had survived with internal damage and broken legs.

The group walked the few blocks home. Outside the building they saw a yellow van. It was parked partly on the sidewalk, and it was being loaded. Kelly assumed the van had come for Cheryl's things. Both she and Beth broke into a run when they saw it, leaving the young men in their wake holding the one absurd umbrella.

They saw a couple of men then unknown to them. One of the men was short, wearing pants and a white T-shirt. Kelly was later to identify him as Salvatore Prainito.

"Stop!" she shouted. "Wait a minute!"

But Prainito ignored them totally. He jumped into the driver's seat and took off with his partner at a fast lick.

New York manners. They went back into the building, found that the elevator was stuck, and climbed the stairs. Beth called her mother with the miserable news and then went to a movie with Kelly and Billy Haworth. It was *Foul Play* with Goldie Hawn, playing up on 86th Street. They all felt they could use a few laughs.

There is always shadowy terrain in the working out of a story such as this. Events are observed—or created—by different characters, and these characters may have histories, motives, drives that they do not necessarily even comprehend themselves.

One can hear two versions of an event, or two descriptions of a person, or one can hear three, four, six, twelve. They may differ subtly, or they may differ greatly. Some may be outright lies, but they may be easier to deal with than those versions of the truth that are devoutly held, but distorted by anger or by grief. It is most difficult of all to deal with a character like Buddy Jacobson, for whom the truth seems to have no objective existence at all.

Occasionally something will come out one hundred percent, like a puzzle solved, a map correctly read. But almost always there are fragments that make no sense. Paths that started out promisingly dribble slowly into the scrub or end abruptly, like abandoned motorways.

Melanie's real estate agent, Georgiana Ioli, worked out of an office down on East 52nd Street; at first she wanted Melanie to wait until noon.

"I don't want to wait," Melanie said, hurriedly.

All right, Ioli said with resignation, and busied herself with the lease, which was to be for a year. So visibly nervous was Melanie that Ioli couldn't stop herself from asking why. Melanie told her about Cheryl Corey, and it turned out that Ioli knew about the death. She had heard a news report on the radio. The report had said that the death was an accident.

An accident. Melanie was relieved. At least, she thought, it wasn't suicide. Or murder.

The lease taken care of, Melanie left the agent's office, and decided she should call Buddy right away. He would be worried, and there were details to be discussed. She thought, for instance, that it would be proper to send flowers. She popped into a phone booth on the corner and dialed 861-1700.

This was the number of Buddy's apartment; it connected to the My Fair Lady office and to his most recent acquisition, the building on East 83rd Street that he and his workforce of Italians were converting into an expensive co-op.

Melanie finished dialing. It was warmer. The air was fetid, heavy as the breath of a large animal. The rain was streaming from the saffron sky. The telephone rang.

Seventeen days later I was talking with Buddy Jacobson. We were in the Bronx House of Detention. His manner was at once sharp and clouded. He was being allusive, hinting at intricate plots, and only now and then did one catch a glint of something solid, like a fish deep in dark waters.

Such as now. He was asked if, as the tabloids were suggesting, there was any connection between the deaths of Cheryl Corey and Jack Tupper.

Buddy: "The only connection there may be is that . . . I heard about Cheryl's death, learned about it, that morning. And I've been a guy that . . . I don't think I've ever seen a dead body in my life . . . this poor girl . . . I've never been close to death before.

"And I don't think that, hearing about Cheryl, coupled with

the events that were to take place during that day, I was in the best frame of mind to make decisions."

The events that were to take place during that day. . . .

Melanie let the telephone ring three times, and came within fractions of a second of hanging up. "Buddy is a phonoholic," she says. "He always answers on the first ring. Either the first or the second. You know if it's after the second ring you can hang up, because he's not home. Because he's always right near a phone. *Always.*"

She was so surprised that she sort of gasped—"Ohh!"— when she heard the phone picked up.

"Yeah?" said a voice.

The speaker sounded short of breath, and she wondered if she had the right number.

"Who is this? Is this the Jacobson residence?"

"Yeah? *Yeah?*"

The voice was high, panicky.

"Douglas?" asked Melanie. Douglas, Buddy Jacobson's younger son, was then seventeen. "Douglas? What's the matter?"

"This isn't Douglas. This is Buddy."

His voice was a strangled whinny. Melanie was taken aback, but carried on.

"I want to tell you what happened to Cheryl—"

"I can't talk to you, I can't talk to you. I've got to go."

Melanie was outraged. Here was Buddy so keen on finding out what had happened, so desperately keen for the past couple of weeks to talk to her, and now he was trying to get her off the line. She didn't want to have to talk to him again face to face. She wanted to tell him what she knew right now.

"What are you *talking* about?" she demanded.

"I'm on the other line," Buddy barked, and hung up.

Melanie was still simmering as she took a cab up Third Avenue, got off at the corner, and ran toward the building through the rain. On the way, she saw Douglas. He was running in her direction and had a plastic garbage bag over his shoulder. He was passing W. & J. Sloane, the furniture clearance place. She assumed that he was going to put the bag into the green dumpster outside SPB 84. This was something Buddy often did, and SPB 84, an outlet of the art auction dowager Sotheby Parke Bernet, seemed indifferent. Melanie smiled and waved as she passed Buddy's younger son. She had no quarrel with Douglas. She walked into the building and pressed the elevator button.

The elevator wouldn't come. The light showed it was stuck on the seventh floor, her floor, so she climbed the stairs. There are two sets of fire stairs leading from the sixth to the seventh floor. The first stairway she tried was blocked, the heavy steel upstairs door being firmly shut. "Boy!" she thought to herself. "That's a real fire hazard."

She tried the second stairway, and what she found upstairs was even odder. Two boxes of bricks were jammed against the door, the small window was covered with a piece of cloth, and a two-by-four was propped underneath the doorknob. This was the first moment that Melanie felt, like something crawling on the skin, small prickles of doubt. Somebody wanted to keep somebody out. Or in. She moved the bricks, dislodged the two-by-four, and let herself into the hall.

Buddy's doorway was immediately on the left. She had planned to avoid him, but what with Buddy's behavior on the telephone, and now this business with the doors, Melanie was worried; though precisely why, she could not tell. She pounded on the door of 7D.

He didn't answer, which was even more peculiar than his slowness in answering the phone. "Buddy is incredible," Melanie says. "He always answers the door." She put her ear to the door. People were whispering. She knocked and knocked. More whispering, and then a different noise, a creaky shuffling, as though something were being dragged across the floor. Furniture, perhaps, Melanie decided.

"Buddy!" Melanie began to shout. "Buddy! Open the door. I know you're in there. Open the door. I'm leaving, and I have to tell you what happened to Cheryl Corey."

Even the whispering now stopped, and Melanie heard somebody running up the apartment's indoor stairs, as though headed for the bathroom, and now Melanie had a theory as to what was going on. Buddy was with a girl. That would account for the shortness of breath. It was all some sort of game. She smelled something, a familiar aroma, hanging around the doorway, and didn't bother to think about *that*. But a thought quivered, trembling just out of reach.

She left the door, and just then she saw one of the foreign workmen that Buddy had doing construction on the Park East. He was a short young man with black hair, wearing work clothes and heavy-duty gloves. Melanie did not wonder right then what he was doing so accoutered on a Sunday, nor, for that matter, what he was doing at East 84th Street. She believed his name was Tony—she later found it to be Salvatore Prainito—but she knew his grasp of English was less than total. She tried talking to him all the same.

"Are you going into Buddy's?"

Prainito just looked at her.

"You knock on the door," Melanie said. "Maybe he'll answer it for you. Because I have to tell him something."

Prainito approached the door, gave Melanie a long look, retreated, and sped down the stairs: Just like the white rabbit in *Alice in Wonderland*. Melanie walked past the elevator—now working, she noticed—and let herself into 7C.

The place was quiet. It was about noon. Melanie called upstairs, but there was no answer. She decided to let Jack sleep, made herself a cup of coffee, dawdled a few minutes, then went downstairs to face Kelly and Beth on the fourth floor. They called up Cheryl's mother, and then they talked to each other. They talked for quite a while.

"It was strange," Melanie said later, "I'm going 'Yeah . . . yeah . . . It's funny, you never know when you're going to die.' And here am I saying that, you know, and I've never experienced death before. I've never known anyone to die."

Melanie left 4C and ran into another My Fair Lady model, Gail Moore—petite, with brown hair and a heart-shaped face, the daughter of a stockbroker in Clearwater, Florida. She liked Melanie, without knowing her that well—the people she was most friendly with in the building were her boyfriend, Breck Dana Anderson, and Breck's buddy Joe Margarite, who had an apartment up on the seventh floor, alongside Buddy and Jack Tupper.

Gail happened to be in the building on this sultry weekend because she was putting up some shelves. She had started the job on Saturday, and today she had a malaise, a tugging feeling behind the eyes. Flu, she had thought, but then decided it was probably the fumes of the shellac, so she was content to stop. She invited Melanie in, and they talked about Cheryl. Soon Melanie was telling Gail that she was leaving 155 East 84th Street.

Buddy had been threatening her, she said. He was getting troublesome. She was worried, and couldn't wait to get out of the building. She also told Gail that she was marrying Jack Tupper. Gail wondered a bit at the speed of it all, but said that she was very happy for Melanie. Which she was. Gail Moore was no fan of Buddy Jacobson's.

Melanie left Gail's apartment and rang for the elevator. It was now about a quarter to one. The elevator doors opened, and there was Douglas Jacobson, with an armful of garbage bags. Melanie stamped in. She was furious.

"Where's your father? I've been looking all over for him."

"He's upstairs, I guess," said Douglas.

He was flustered and scuttled out of the elevator on the fifth floor.

Melanie went on up, and the elevator doors opened onto a surprising scene. The hallway rug was splotched and smeared with white paint. And Buddy was on his hands and knees right in front of her, apparently trying to clean up the mess. Also, he was nervous. Buddy was more nervous than Melanie had ever seen him.

But though Melanie saw the scene, she somehow wasn't taking it in. Cheryl Corey's death blotted it out. "Buddy, you heartless bastard!" she screamed, following him as he hopped around on that ugly plaid rug, a rug that Melanie had long disliked. Again she asked why he hadn't answered the door.

"What?" Buddy said. "What are you talking about? I wasn't in the apartment. I was over at the hospital."

"I talked to you on the phone, Buddy. You said you were on the other line. You don't *have* two lines over at the hospital."

Buddy veered off the subject. "Somebody spilled paint on my rug," he said. He made it sound accusing.

"Well, Buddy, I sure didn't do it. I don't play your childish games. One of your workers was up here before."

"*What?* There's no workers up here today," Buddy said. He was vehement.

Melanie felt another flicker of puzzlement. Buddy stood up and walked toward his apartment. Melanie followed him and began to see that the seventh floor, so innocent of activity an hour before, was looking very active. Apartment 7E, for instance. This was a small apartment, next door to Buddy's. Melanie had lived in it herself, an age ago it now seemed. The present tenant was Leslie Hammond, a brisk blond stockbroker. Now she saw a man in there, standing on a chair, and apparently working on the ceiling with a tool of some sort. The door to 7D was open, and Melanie followed Buddy right in.

The place was a bigger mess than the hall. The mirror beside the door was broken, and Douglas was sweeping up the pieces. The diminutive Italian she had seen earlier was standing next to the fire, which, despite this gaspingly hot day, was roaring. The cushions that had been on the sofa when Buddy had told her not to worry about the hot water were tumbled on the floor. And the rug—a piece which Buddy had, typically, sheared from the same roll that embellished the hall—was nowhere to be seen.

Melanie stood slowly taking in the picture while she yammered away. Buddy had begun vacuuming, as if trying to vacuum her out of his mind, but he came suddenly alive as Melanie crossed the room, intending to sort out any mail that might be waiting for her on the butcher-block table. He scurried over and yanked at her arm.

"Get out of here!" he yelled. "Get out!"

He was pulling her toward the door, and Melanie was struck by the oddity of it all—that Buddy, who had spent weeks trying to lure her back into the apartment, should now be tossing her out. "What's going on here?" she asked. "What is this, Buddy? Spring cleaning?"

Buddy shoved Melanie out of the door, snarling, "I don't want you to come into this apartment ever again. *Ever.*"

Seventeen days later, Buddy Jacobson, sitting in the Bronx House of Detention, was concerned to suggest that Melanie Cain's observations had been incorrect. His difficulty was that all he knew of her observations was what had been printed in the New York tabloids, and this was not precisely on the mark. According to the *Post*, for instance, Melanie claimed to have seen bloodstains in his apartment, which was not the case.

He explained things to me thus:

"Melanie knows damn well that my apartment is *always* in disarray."

Question: "Yeah. But she said things were turned over and there were traces of blood—"

Buddy cut in firmly. "There was never anything turned over, and Melanie never came in the door of the apartment at any moment. I wouldn't *let* her in the apartment."

Question: "But you are saying she didn't go into your apartment at all? You didn't open the door?"

Buddy: "Well, I did open the door, yes. And if you say that

she said there were couches"—almost coaxingly spoken, this
—"if anything was turned over, it had to be the two couches,
because there was nothing else in there. There was *nothing
at any time* turned over in that apartment. Till the time I
left."

Question: "But she's quoted as saying that everything was
turned over—"

Buddy, firmly: "Till the time I left."

Question (continuing): "—and there's blood on the rug."

Buddy paused, seemed to be considering.

Buddy: "If she's talking about . . . she could not see blood
on anything. I could have had a pile of white paint spilled on
the rug, this is the way my apartment is."

Ah, yes. White paint. He borrowed a sheet of paper and a
pencil and began to scribble a diagram. The apartment. His
mind was palpably clicking away.

"This is the room . . . and this is the front door . . . right
here is a long couch . . . here is the fireplace . . . here's
another couch . . .

"Now Melanie came in here. The only rug I have is here.
You can't see the rug from there. And it's a *red rug.*"

A red rug. Red as blood.

"It's a red rug," Buddy repeated triumphantly. "She
couldn't *see.*"

Actually, the rug is a brown-and-orange plaid.

Ten minutes to one. Melanie walked into 7C and went
straight upstairs to the bedroom, wanting to tell Jack everything. A problem. Jack Tupper wasn't there.

This was already a bit jarring. The morning jaunt downtown had been their first time apart in a couple of weeks. Jack
wasn't fearful for himself, but he was too wary to allow
Buddy easy access to Melanie. Might he have gone outside to
telephone? There was no phone in Jack Tupper's apartment.
Melanie looked around. Jack's diary was there, and his pale-
brown leatherette address book, secured by a rubber band, lay
alongside his gold Mark Cross pen and a pile of change. The
possibility that he was telephoning dimmed. In the kitchen she
found a coffee cup, still containing coffee, and an English
muffin; so he had started breakfast, at least. Could he have
gone to buy the papers?

A natural explanation came to her. Jack was jogging. If

something had happened—if, for instance, an accident had befallen Paul, the son he adored—he would surely have left some sort of note. It made sense. Relieved, Melanie switched on the TV and sat down, realizing she felt deathly tired. A senator from South Dakota was talking to a blond newscaster, a journalist from *Time,* and a slightly balding reporter from the *New York Times*. The program was *Meet the Press,* and they were talking about the deregulation of gas. Melanie fell asleep.

It was a quarter to two when she awoke, and Jack was still not home. And it was now that she began to feel concerned. Outside it was pouring. Rain fell in brown and blinding sheets. It was cooler, true, but Jack wouldn't still be *jogging*. She trotted back upstairs. Sure enough, there were his sneakers, next to his zip-up boots. She looked around. Everything was in place. His razor was out in the bathroom, alongside his rubbing alcohol, his toothpaste, and his preferred after-shave, Eau Sauvage.

The obscure thought which had nudged at her earlier came suddenly into sharp focus: the smell she had noticed in Buddy's doorway.

It was Eau Sauvage.

Buddy never used aftershave.

She thrust the thought aside and grappled with the basics. "He just wasn't there. So it was weird," she said later. "I just couldn't think where he was . . . where he could have gone."

Could he be out making telephone calls after all? She again ran into Douglas, by the elevator.

"Have you seen Jack?" she asked.

"I haven't seen him all day."

She waited downstairs, irresolute, until Buddy also came downstairs. He too denied seeing Jack, so Melanie walked out into the rain. Across the street, Nicola's, Buddy's favorite restaurant, was locked up and lifeless. Nobody was at the telephone booth on the corner, so she crossed Lexington to the G&M Luncheonette, where there was a pay telephone Jack sometimes used, and peered through the moisture that was steaming the windows. Jack Tupper wasn't there.

It was now two o'clock, and Melanie's obscure doubts were ripening. "My mind was—there's been a fight," Melanie was to say later. "Buddy and Jack had a fight, and that's why Buddy wouldn't answer the door. Buddy's beaten him up! But then I thought that sounds so silly. Buddy was such a chicken. If anyone talked physical, Jack talked it more than Buddy. So big, brave me—I go knocking right on the door."

Within the Jacobson apartment she heard a mechanical thrum, the kind of purr a floor sander makes. For all her pounding and shouting, nobody came to the door, so she walked back into her apartment and waited restlessly until another sound, closer at hand, pulled her to the door. She opened it, warily. Buddy and Douglas Jacobson were tearing up the paint-spattered carpeting in the hall.

Buddy suddenly crossed to 7F, which was Joe Margarite's apartment, and knocked, calling, "Joe! Joe!" There was no answer. He worked the combinations (all doors in 155 East 84th had combination locks, the sort that open when you punch out the correct code), walked in, then came out with what seemed, from where she peered, cautious as a gazelle in the bush, to be handfuls of paper towels. Melanie continued to watch sometimes from the peephole and sometimes from the door, which was opened wide enough to permit a few inches of vision, and what she saw was Buddy and Douglas demolishing the rug in front of her eyes. "Hurry up, Douglas!" Buddy was muttering. "Hurry up, Douglas!" as they cut it into fragments and tossed them into garbage bags. Buddy was always a fast worker, compulsively, sloppily fast, but this was unreal, like an animated cartoon. Douglas scurried out of the apartment with other, bloated garbage bags, and father and son went down in the elevator at last.

Melanie crept out of her apartment. Feeling a bit absurd, like somebody in a Sherlock Holmes movie, she examined the pale undercarpeting. Just where the thickest of the pools of white paint had been were two large stains. To her eye, they seemed reddish, and they were still moist. There were red speckles at the bottom of a fire door, some hastily spattered over with white paint. Six inches from the brass runner on the bottom was a tuft of what looked like hair: *her* color hair, which was *Jack's* color hair. A dark and smeary palm print was on the elevator door.

Melanie preferred to leave her fears unformulated. "I felt that . . . I'm exhausted, my mind is running away with me," she said later. "Jack's out, he's going to come back. I just want to get out of 155 East 84th Street and never come back there again."

She returned downstairs, vaguely thinking she might telephone somebody. In doorways, people were hiding out from the downpour. Melanie's eye fell on the dumpster outside Sotheby Parke Bernet, a metal oblong, painted military green, but scrawled with initials and the names of rock bands. This was the container that Douglas had been approaching earlier. She had waved at him and smiled.

Melanie walked toward it, through the rain; forbidden thoughts were churning. Jack had been in a fight, was dead, cut up. But she looked up before she had walked far, and there was Buddy, hanging over the seventh-story balcony of 155 East 84th Street, staring at her. She didn't dare go look; they'd get her when she walked back into the building. She decided to call her best friend, Mel Harris. Cool, rational Mel. It was 2:15 P.M.

Melanie went back up to the seventh floor to collect her change. It took a while to find, several minutes. Then she knocked on Buddy's door once again, but she expected no reaction, and got none, so she returned downstairs.

The green dumpster was gone.

Melanie looked around. Nobody was watching from the terrace, but doubt was hardening into suspicion. She walked to the phone booth on the corner and called Mel Harris, then returned to her vigil outside the building. It was shortly before three.

It was here that Gail Moore, who was on her way to Gimbels, saw Melanie for the last time that day. "She was sitting on the stoop, wearing a green raincoat," Gail says. "She seemed to be waiting for somebody." The brisk brunette was struck by the fact that Melanie, so full of vim earlier, seemed anxious and forlorn.

It was here, too, that Melanie had what was to be her last more-or-less-normal conversation with Buddy Jacobson, and its normality was less rather than more. Buddy walked out of the building, nervous and shaking. He saw Melanie, stopped, and jumped back.

Melanie was mad. "Where's Jack? Where is he, Buddy? If you did anything you're going to be in *so much trouble.*"

Even at the time, she sensed a hollowness to her threats. She felt as if she were scolding a delinquent child.

"What?" Buddy said. "Are you kidding? I don't know, baby. I haven't seen him all morning. I avoid Jack like the fucking plague."

In one hand Buddy was carrying some kind of power tool

with protruding blades, and in the other he had a bunch of keys, and he had his hands knotted so tight that the veins were like telephone cords, and he was shaking, shaking. Despite the rain he was coatless, and Melanie noticed he had changed his beige pants and blue workshirt for bluejeans and a striped shirt, which was striking, because Buddy never changed during the day.

"Where's Jack?" she insisted. "I know you know where he is. What have you done?"

"I haven't seen him all day," said Buddy. "I'm afraid of Jack. He's a big guy." He added intently, "Well, it's three o'clock, and now I'm going over to the building."

The building was, of course, the Park East, a block and a half away, on 83rd, between Lexington and Park avenues. This was the defunct private hospital, which Buddy had bought for $850,000 and change in June, and which he was converting into co-ops. Buddy's remark was uncharacteristic. Normally he wouldn't volunteer information about his plans. And what was he doing working at the Park East on a Sunday? Buddy never worked Sundays.

"I don't care where you're going," she said. "I don't *care*."

"I'll talk to you in three days. Don't forget that you have that commercial on Tuesday." That shampoo commercial! It was almost normal Buddy talk.

Melanie's temper snapped. *"Where's Jack?"* she screamed.

"Melanie, I don't know what you're talking about. Are you crazy?"

Was she crazy? Melanie was in the throes of an internal struggle. She came within inches of blurting out her terrible thoughts—"Did you kill Jack, Buddy? I'm going to the police right now"—but just suppose it was an immense delusion? Neurosis, sickness. And it was now that Buddy grabbed Melanie by the arm.

"Come on," he said. "I've got to talk to you. I've got to tell you something. Let's go out for coffee."

Another strange remark. Buddy despised coffee drinkers. Melanie tried to pull away, and there was Buddy pulling at her arm; this was more like the old Buddy, harassing her, wearing her away. In this brief but critical moment Buddy Jacobson failed to bend Melanie Cain to his powerful will, let go, shrugged, walked to the corner, and was gone. And that was the last Melanie saw of him that day.

Mel arrived in front of 155 East 84th Street a few minutes

later. Mel Harris was born in Pennsylvania and grew up in New Jersey. She came to New York and, like so many aspiring models, moved into Buddy Jacobson's building. She had shared with three girls on the sixth floor for a year, then moved and shared with two girls in 7F. After a while Mel had crossed the hall and moved into 7C with David Silbergeld, the man she was going to marry. Later still, she and Silbergeld had moved out of the building, and Jack Tupper had taken over what remained of their lease.

Melanie and Mel had become close soon after Mel moved to 155 East 84th Street, and they would have been closer except for the fact that Buddy—in a way which Melanie had only recently begun to understand—had skillfully kept her dependent, as distant as possible from friends. Even so, Mel was the first person, that Sunday, whom Melanie thought to call.

Mel Harris had dark hair and was handsome rather than pretty. She is, it so happens, about a year younger than Melanie, but she is so much the sort of young woman who is described as "sensible" that she is resigned to being taken as the older of the two. Her attitude is one of briskness, no nonsense, and she had plans for the afternoon: a rehearsal with a couple of actors over on the West Side. They had a scene to work up for a Lee Strasberg class, but she found Melanie's call so disturbing that she had said she would be over right away.

She arrived to find Melanie sitting on the stoop. The macadam was viscous and streaming, and as they hurried into the 84th Street building, Mel was struck by the fact that the lobby was freshly washed. Why would anybody, even anybody as determined to do things his way as Buddy Jacobson, wash down a lobby on a rainy day?

They got into the elevator. "Well," said Mel, practical as always, "what do you want to talk about?" Melanie shushed her. Like Mel, like all the girls in the building, she knew the rumors that Buddy had the whole place bugged. Was even the elevator secure?

Pale undermatting confronted them on the seventh floor. "Oh, terrific!" said Mel. "Deluxe carpeting." But Melanie didn't respond. Instead, she recounted the various strangenesses of the day. Mel examined the stains. She looked at the handprint inside the elevator door; she looked at the speckles on the fire door.

"Oh, Mel . . . isn't that blood?" Melanie asked.

Mel was quiet. She was not, as Melanie had hoped, laughing off her fears, but she wasn't willing to assume the worst either. Her conversation was upbeat. She asked about Jack, and about wedding plans. One way or another about three-quarters of an hour went by and still Jack Tupper had not returned. Mel's acting exercises were due to start at four, but she felt uneasy about leaving Melanie. "Uh-huh," she agreed reluctantly. "It is *weird*, Melanie."

They went to Buddy's door once more, again fruitlessly, and Mel suggested they go and look in the All-Ireland. The All-Ireland was on 81st and Third Avenue, and until some three weeks back, Jack Tupper had owned it fifty-fifty with a partner, Brian Monaghan. It was a grimly serious drinking place, with a long bar of coal-black oak, a harp of stained-glass, and a photograph of John and Jacqueline Kennedy faded to the hue of pale ale. It was one of the last such bars in the neighborhood, the others having metamorphosed into Upper East Side watering holes.

A similar end was intended for the All-Ireland by Jack Tupper and Brian Monaghan. But both men were strong-willed, and differences soon made their partnership impossible. They held a private auction, which was won by Brian Monaghan. He bid $43,000, of which $30,000 was paid in ready money—a normal transaction in the bar business but which was somewhat later to lend itself to sinister interpretations.

But if Jack Tupper's business rupture with Brian Monaghan hadn't been that cordial, it hadn't been that acrimonious either, and Jack still spent time there. He wasn't there now though. A young woman behind the bar said he hadn't been there all day. It was frustrating. They went into a Daitch Shopwell, where Mel bought some steaks and the makings of a salad—she had promised to prepare dinner for the actors after their session. Then they trudged back to East 84th.

It was just past four. Mel was already late, but she was now apprehensive. They decided to call any of Jack's friends who might have some idea of his whereabouts. Melanie did remember that Jack had been expecting to talk business somewhere that afternoon, but, it now came to her, she hadn't the least idea with whom he was going to have his discussion, or where, or, come to that, just what the talk was to be about.

Melanie Cain is not inquisitive, by nature. It is just one more irony that Buddy Jacobson and Jack Tupper, in most respects so unlike, were, in this respect, similar: they shared a love of secrecy, and the taking of private paths, even when the public road would do as well, or better.

Melanie looked through Jack's telephone book. A couple of names suggested themselves: Al Seifert, whom Jack considered his closest friend, and Ivor Shaw. Shaw, she believed, lived nearby. Both men told her she ought to wait before calling the police. Mel Harris, reassured that help was on hand, left for the West Side, a bit late, and rehearsed a scene from *Barefoot in the Park*.

While Melanie was making her telephone calls, Louis Carattini was driving his wife, Estella, and their three children through the Northeast Bronx. With a practiced hand—Carattini pilots a bus through New York City—he came off the New England Thruway at the Bartow Avenue exit and pointed his car toward home, which is to say, Co-op City.

The landscape which confronts the traveler here is, even for the Bronx, this most dilapidated of New York boroughs, not one to make the heart sing. The blunt, dun-colored towers of Co-op City, which, like so many urban planners' dreams of a rosier future, have the air of being surprised in a dingy present, rise from a large waste terrain, scarred with ruins and pimpled with illegal garbage dumps. The scene might have been assembled by some malicious surrealist, a notion that is reinforced upon learning that this was, very briefly, the site of Freedomland, that fantasy of the bankrupted property billionaire William Zeckendorff. It was there, standing on the edge of an empty lot beside the stop sign at the end of the ramp, that the Carattinis spotted what looked like a couple of perfectly good tricycles.

Two men were standing close by. One was about twenty feet from the Carattinis, beside the tricycles, and the other was about thirty-five feet from their car. He was bending over, wiping his hands on some leaves, and he was staring at the Carattinis. Nobody else was in sight.

Carattini turned left on Baychester and slowed down. Mrs. Carattini was now quite close to the man who was standing beside the tricycles. He was fondling them as though he was contemplating taking them, but he had turned around as soon as their car approached, and now she saw only his back and Bermuda-shorted rump. This struck the Carattinis as peculiar.

The other man was now about eighteen feet away. He was still staring at her. It was because of that fixed, compelling stare that she was later able to identify him as Buddy Jacobson. The Carattinis dawdled a few seconds, but it seemed they weren't getting the tricycles, so they drove on toward the traffic light which stands where Bartow meets Baychester Avenue. A yellow Cadillac was parked on Baychester.

The children were complaining loudly in the back seat about the abandoned playthings, and Estella Carattini turned around. The two men were running toward the Cadillac, and Buddy Jacobson, as she later found him to be, got into the driver's seat. The Cadillac stopped behind them at the light. The other man ducked, but Buddy remained clearly visible.

The Cadillac drew alongside. The second man was folded over, his head invisible. But Buddy Jacobson still looked fixedly at Estella Carattini, as if staring her out.

Carattini waited there alongside the Mobil gas station, while the Caddy glided by. When it was about fifty feet in front, the Carattinis saw a third head bob up in the back seat and as quickly disappear. Their misgivings firmed up. Something abnormal was afoot. Louis Carattini, struck by the coincidence that the Cadillac's number, 777–GHF, so closely resembled his own, 781-GHF, scribbled it onto a route map.

The tricycles obviously weren't in the yellow car, so Carattini turned around. A plume of greasy black smoke was weaving itself into the drizzly texture of the sullen sky as he got out. The source of the smoke, he now saw, was a box lying there in the wasteland. A man-sized box. Oh-oh. Abandoning the tricycles, he got back in the car and drove his family to what he knew to be the closest firehouse to the burning box and to Co-op City, namely, the Asch Loop Station.

After talking to the firemen, Louis Carattini drove back to the Mobil station and parked, to see what would transpire, and did not take the tricycles, for all the children's complaining.

At nine-thirty that morning, when Melanie Cain was still waiting for the hot water and Jack Tupper was still asleep, Dennis Smith had walked past 155 East 84th Street. Dennis Smith, who lives on 84th between Park and Lexington avenues, is a writer. Two of his books—*Report from Engine Company 82* and *Glitter and Ash*—have earned places on the best-seller lists. Dennis Smith is also a fireman. He was on his way to the bus stop at Third and 86th Street, where he was catching the Co-op Express to work; Smith was currently assigned to the station at Asch Loop.

"A civilian came in and reported a rubbish fire a couple of blocks away," Smith says. It was four twenty-five. "Civilian" is what firemen and cops call anyone who is neither a cop nor a fireman. Smith was one of the ten firemen who took off in a couple of firetrucks under the command of Lieutenant Ray Cosenza. It sounded like just one more of the hundreds of reported rubbish conflagrations: "What we call a nothing fire," Smith says.

The firemen clambered onto the mound beside the road. The smoke was gushing from a wooden crate, which lay in a gully, down in the trash-laden landscape, garlanded with bottles, cans, and rags, stained newspapers, and rubber tires. The garbage smell, that thick sickliness, was almost liquid in their nostrils: that, and the stink of burning.

A routine job, Cosenza thought. He ordered up the smallest hose on the truck, the booster line, and they played it on the burning heap. He walked over and quickly signaled that the water be shut off. From the crate's burned-out bottom protruded a blackened leg.

The nothing was a something after all. Cosenza walked across to the Carattinis' car. Louis Carattini told him about the yellow Caddy and the shifty doings, and handed him the piece of paper with the license number. And now his dearest wish was to get out of the area, and out of everything. Hardly. "Remember," Cosenza told him, "we've got *your* license number." The Carattinis finally left.

The cops were called. Cosenza began to look for whatever it was that had been used to fuel the blaze—the "accelerant" is what firemen call it—since a match just won't do, not on a wet day. Quickly he came up with a couple of wine jars—gallon jugs. One of them was labeled Fior di California Chablis Bianco, the other had formerly held Gallo California Port; both were now empty and reeked of gasoline. And they were just lying there. Careless.

The police arrived, which is to say police officers Maxwell and Pinero. They got there at a quarter to five. The sight that awaited them was ugly. The box was padlocked, but the firemen forced the two hasps. "The head was all matted," Dennis Smith says. "You couldn't tell what color he was, white, or black, or Puerto Rican."

"Oh, gee!" one fireman said. "It looks like a Mafia hit."

Another scoffed.

"No way," he said. "What's the point of burning the body? That's dumb."

The corpse was hunkered up, squatting in what Dennis Smith describes as "the Hindu position." The head was lowered, and something was glittering around the scorched flesh of the neck. Winfred Maxwell, who was in his fourth year with the department, removed the body from the charred timbers which supported it. Both crate and body had to be carried onto the morgue wagon.

Nobody, until that moment, had seen the face. This proved to have been nobody's loss. The features were beaten in, and more than just beaten in: They were mutilated. Maxwell was to describe the face as wearing "an expression of pain." As for that glittering thing, it turned out to be a slender gold chain. From the chain was hanging a Capricorn medal, which the killer, or killers, had not bothered to remove.

The killing had been savage, and it had also been botched.

It was now getting near five o'clock.

Al Seifert had not been overly concerned when Melanie first called him. Seifert is a large man, with a placid manner, pale skin, and dark hair styled rather like Napoleon's. He was a few years older than Jack Tupper, whom he had always called John. Just last Wednesday Jack had taken Melanie to Seifert's place in upstate New York, and they had stayed the night. And on Friday—"just hours before it happened," Seifert says—Jack had called him, bouncing with high spirits, and had asked him to be best man.

Seifert had been momentarily reluctant. After all, he and Buddy Jacobson went back a goodish way too. They had even done business together. But Seifert had emerged from those businesses somewhat bruised. The expensive thoroughbred of which Seifert had acquired a share had a leg like boiled spaghetti, and never raced. The two movie houses into which he was thinking of buying—well, that deal had sunk in a swamp of mistrust. Al had known Buddy a long while. He viewed him with much admiration, more bafflement, but no real liking at all, so he eventually said he would be Jack Tupper's best man, and with pleasure.

Seifert was at home in Queens when Melanie telephoned. Wait, he had advised. Al had known Jack fifteen years, after all. He knew much that Melanie didn't—Jack's enormous secretiveness, his disinclination to let his right hand know what his left hand was up to, what his own family called his "James Bond side."

But Melanie continued to call, and Al, bit by bit, began to share her alarm. "She says his keys are there," he told me. "His wallet's there. It's getting to sound more serious. Who leaves their apartment without their keys, their wallet and everything? And she kept stressing, even from the first phone call, right from the beginning: *I think Buddy did something to Jack.*"

Al Seifert knew Buddy's number, and called. He got Douglas Jacobson on the phone.

"Did you see John Tupper around?" he asked.

"No," said Douglas.

"Have you been there long?"

"I've been here all day long," Douglas said.

This eased Seifert's mind; but, though unpersuaded that anything had occurred, he was a prudent man and agreed that Melanie should call Ivor Shaw.

Under certain circumstances it is difficult to know what is the prudent thing to do.

The southbound traffic through the Bronx was the usual fractious mix of commercial stuff and weekenders, hoping to steal a march by returning early Sunday evening. The fitful flow down the Bruckner Expressway was further impeded by a breakdown, smack in the middle of the side bound for Manhattan, and police officer Michael Boylan was steering the flow around the wounded vehicle when the call came. He scribbled down the plate number of the wanted car, and looked at his watch. It was five past five.

It was just then that he saw a yellow Cadillac barreling toward him. The message had one letter wrong, but he quickly found it was the wanted car—the good cop's prayer. Boylan called Central, watched the car glide by, followed it down the Bruckner, and, somewhere around the 138th Street exit, lost it.

*   *   *

Melanie knew Ivor Shaw better than she knew most of Jack's friends. They had dined together as recently as Friday. Shaw has sleek, dark hair, pale eyes, and bland features. His conversation is winning, always teetering on the edge of special confidences, and brimful of rare information. Shaw, indeed, seems the perfect clubman—affable, and dressed, according to the time of year, as though en route to the Hamptons, Palm Beach, Europe, or the Caribbean.

And, if Ivor Shaw's Upper East Side couth represented something to which Jack Tupper had begun to aspire, his knowingness was also useful. At that last dinner, which had been at the Parma on Third Avenue and 83rd Street, they had discussed prep schools, since Jack was pondering sending his son to a private school. Also restaurants. The All-Ireland was behind Jack Tupper, but there were plenty of possible places roundabout, and Ivor Shaw knew them all. He and Jack had been looking at a number of prospects. But where Jack was right now he had no idea.

And he was politely dismissive of Melanie's fears. "He's probably gone out," he said. "Don't worry."

But Melanie was not appeased. "Where would he go?" she demanded. She returned to the idea that he might have rushed off to see his son, Paul. If anything had been wrong with the boy he would have run off stark naked, but she had no number for Ellen, Jack's former wife; indeed, she didn't know Ellen's surname, which is Gannon, her second husband, John, then being with the Narcotics Division of the New York Police Department. But of all this Melanie knew nothing. What she did know was that whatever might have happened, by now Jack Tupper should have telephoned.

Ivor Shaw pondered. He knew things about Jack Tupper unguessed by Melanie Cain. But even with *his* romantic imagination, he found it unlikely that anything untoward should have happened to a man so eminently capable of taking care of himself. There was also the fact that Shaw was watching on TV a golf tournament of extraordinary interest. It was the PGA championship, at the Oakmont Country Club in Pennsylvania, and three players were running abreast. Shaw was stuck to the screen.

"Wait awhile," he had advised when she first telephoned. But doubts began to stir in him as Melanie called again. And when Melanie called a final time—now with unashamed anxiety—shortly after five, Shaw told her that he would be there within half an hour.

Ivor Shaw had not the tiniest presentiment of how much he would come to regret having been in Manhattan on that particular Sunday afternoon. "I was clean," he told me much later. "Suddenly I was tied into two cases. Taking that telephone call was the worst thing that happened to me in my life."

It was another unexpected stroke of luck, like the traffic breakdown on the Bruckner Expressway. At any rate, it so happened that Hector Feliciano's patrol car was only half a dozen blocks away from the expressway when the alarm came through. Feliciano, who was driving, was at the 138th Street exit just before ten past five and immediately saw the wanted car. It was waiting, in a law-abiding fashion, at a red light. Ahead of it lay the Willis Avenue Bridge, and Manhattan. But Hector Feliciano made the siren bray, spun the light on his roof, leaped into a U-turn, and motioned the flashy automobile over to the shoulder of the road.

Buddy was out of the car first, and started walking over. Feliciano met him, leaving Dennis Fitzpatrick, his backup, sitting in the patrol car.

"Officer, what's wrong?" Buddy asked. "What did I do wrong?"

Feliciano still had no idea why he had been asked to stop the car. He took a look at Buddy, who was wearing boots, a pale, stripy shirt, and dark-blue jeans. He looked damp, disheveled; his hair was wild, and his boots, which were zip-up, were half unzipped. A mess.

"You haven't done anything wrong," Feliciano said, carefully polite. "Can I see your license and registration?"

Buddy said he didn't have any papers with him. Who was the car's owner? It was somebody who did construction work for him, Buddy said. He didn't know the name, not offhand. But the man was waiting for him at East 84th Street. Buddy's speech was calm.

"Put out a 1015 call," Feliciano told Fitzpatrick. "Find out if the car is stolen." There were, he now saw, dark stains on Buddy Jacobson's trousers, just below the knees. They were darker than the darkness of the jeans. The rain had washed the stains, but without washing them away. It was sort of a spatter effect. The color was reddish.

Officer Feliciano has a step-by-step approach to things. He rolled up Buddy Jacobson's trouser legs, one at a time, to see if he had hurt himself. No. Feliciano sent Buddy around to speak with his partner while he turned his attention to the Cadillac, and to Buddy's passenger, who turned out to be a Sicilian, with scant English, by the name of Salvatore Giamo.

Fitzpatrick, in his turn, asked who owned the car. Buddy, with the air of one wringing his memory, said that it was something like Salvatore Painito? Peraino? The problem was resolved by Hector Feliciano, who discovered a bill of sale to one Salvatore Prainito in the glove compartment. There was something else in the car. Incongruous in the back sat two large watermelons. The police radio sputtered to life. The occupants of the yellow Cadillac might be tied in with a homicide, Central warned. Proceed with caution.

Buddy Jacobson overheard. "Who? Me?" he demanded, as he was frisked and handcuffed.

The two men were driven to the 40th Precinct. The journey passed in relative silence, neither officer choosing to ask their guests one intriguing question: Just why had Buddy elected to come off at this exit? Things were moving slowly on the Bruckner, thanks to the breakdown, but other reasons were later suggested. One of the assistant DAs on the ensuing prosecution insists that Buddy, succumbing to one of his fits of penny-pinching, was only trying to avoid paying the toll on the Triboro Bridge. It seems more probable, though, that he had made a short detour to drop off his third passenger (Salvatore Giamo was not wearing Bermuda shorts at the time of his arrest). And nobody understands the watermelons to this day.

Jerry Pate, Tom Watson, and John Mahaffey had finished dead level, with 276 strokes apiece: The PGA was fought out for one more hole and taken by Mahaffey. Ivor Shaw turned off the television and looked out speculatively at the weather. He was wearing a tweed jacket with tiny checks, khaki pants from Norm Thompson of Portland, Oregon ("The L.L. Bean of the West Coast," in his words), and a polo shirt—proper attire for a country weekend, apart from a new pair of loafers. The loafers were Italian, with tassels, and made of thin, fine leather. They had set him back two hundred and fifty bucks. But the rain didn't seem imminent, so, concerned about Melanie's calls, he set off for East 84th Street as he was.

Melanie, meanwhile, had found the situation more and more mysterious. There was, for one thing, something going on in the ground-floor office of My Fair Lady. Melanie spotted Douglas Jacobson in there and knocked on the door, but he wouldn't answer. She started really pounding on it. Douglas finally opened the door and Melanie shouted, "You'd better tell me what's going on right now. Where's your father? If Buddy did anything to Jack, you are in a *whole lot of trouble!*"

"I don't know anything," Douglas said, or rather babbled. "I didn't do anything. It's all my father's fault! It was my father." He slammed the door.

Ivor Shaw arrived at East 84th Street shortly thereafter, at about ten to six, and Melanie told him some of the goings-on. They went upstairs. He looked at the spots on the undermatting. They were still moist, and they certainly looked like blood. He tried to look judicious, allaying Melanie's fears, and examined the tuft of hair. He looked around Melanie and Jack's apartment. Ivor Shaw didn't like the situation at all.

This was not lost on Melanie. "He didn't want to make too much effort to find out where Buddy was," she told me later, with something like a laugh. Shaw concurs. "By now, I was quite sure something awful had happened," he says. "I got quite nervous about staying in the building."

Outside, he and Melanie hovered a moment. "We should go to the police," Shaw said.

"All right," Melanie agreed. "C'mon. Let's go."

"We-e-ell, I don't know, y'know," Shaw vacillated. "Jack's still only a missing person. If we report it now they're not going to do anything. You have to wait twenty-four hours."

They decided that Shaw should call Al Seifert, just to let him know that he had arrived on the scene. He crossed the street and walked to the phone booth at 84th and Lexington. And it was while Ivor Shaw was telling Al Seifert about the spots of blood that Melanie saw Joe Margarite walking out of the building.

That was odd. Melanie had earlier (that indelible tableau—the rending of the plaid matting, Rorschach splatterings of white paint) seen Buddy knocking on Joe Margarite's 7F apartment door, but Joe Margarite himself she hadn't seen for weeks. Margarite was mysterious anyway. A tall and gangly figure in his mid-thirties, with longish hair but balding on top, Joe Margarite was ostensibly in the music business, but, according to Buddy, was quite obviously in drugs.

Certainly he was always proffering Melanie a joint, which she would just as often refuse. "Joe was always stoned," she told me. "Always spaced out." He was forever traveling, and she just couldn't work out how he kept his life together. "Joe's the type that'll be going on a trip, and leave his suitcase in the elevator, and get in the cab. 'Joe! Your bag's in the elevator.' 'Oh, yeah? Right . . .' "

Melanie walked up to him, and the look in her face must have been plain to read, because Joe Margarite said, "What's the matter, Melanie? Is there some kind of trouble?"

"Joe, I don't know," Melanie said. "Have you been home all day?"

"Yeah, I've been home. All day."

"Well, did you hear anything? Fighting, or anything like that? Did you hear any loud noise?"

"No," Margarite said. "Why? Is there any trouble?"

"No," Melanie said, still unwilling to articulate her fears. "Well, there *could* be. Have you seen Buddy?"

Yes, Margarite said. "I saw Buddy at around one o'clock, cleaning in the hallway. What's going on?"

"I don't know," Melanie said, confused.

"Well," Margarite said, "he seemed really nervous and really uptight."

The conversation impressed Melanie strangely. Buddy had, she knew, had certain dealings with Joe Margarite, but they concerned, she believed, his two fiefdoms—horses and the property market—and as for herself, she scarcely knew him. This, in fact, had been the most conversation she had had with Joe Margarite in his two years in the building.

There was something else, even more striking. This was not the Joe Margarite to whom she had grown accustomed—the space cadet. This Joe was alert, quick with his answers. *Aware.*

"Is Buddy upstairs now?" Melanie asked.

"No. He's not."

Joe sounded so certain that Melanie was nettled.

"How do you *know* he's not?" she asked.

Margarite rapidly allowed that perhaps he had been out of the building awhile. Perhaps, even, between eleven and one. So Melanie kept her growing fears to herself, and Joe Margarite, who actually was (as Buddy had indicated) a dope trafficker, in fact, a multi-ton hashish dealer, walked away from 155 East 84th Street.

Ivor Shaw was still on the telephone. He had more calls than the one to Al Seifert on his agenda. Shaw's reluctance to scoot down to the precinct house wasn't wholly to do with official procedures regarding missing persons. Shaw, the congenial conservative whom nobody took too seriously, the affable man-about-town with a harmless appetite for the demimonde, was, in fact, a man in good standing with the Drug Enforcement Administration. It wasn't of Shaw's own choosing, exactly—there had been a peccadillo concerning cocaine—but Ivor Shaw was a government agent.

He was working, in point of fact, with the DEA. For several years now, with the rapt attention of a hobbyist constructing a cathedral from matchsticks, the DEA had been building cases against a wild and colorful group. The group had all sorts of connections—elsewhere in the United States, in Europe, Central and South America, the Far and Middle East—but the turbulent inner core was located in the New York borough of Queens.

The group had a specialty. They abhorred heroin. They were not Mob. They were Irish or Anglo-Irish, usually with a cop lodged somewhere close in the family tree, and a crowd of others and what they specialized in was smuggling gigantic quantities of marijuana and hashish. It was almost like the old days, when certain distinguished American families got their start running whiskey across the Canadian border.

In the past few years, the preferred route for the dope had been through JFK Airport. They ran JFK the way a conductor runs a symphony orchestra, except for the times they ran it the way the Marx Brothers did in *A Night at the Opera*. The Feds, scrambling in their tracks, had until recently been trying to put together one case at a time. Now they were trying to prove one single conspiracy. This they chose to call the "Donald Brown Organization" and, with that schoolkid penchant for the exotic they share with the CIA, they had code-named it after one of the group's dummy corporations: The Astro-Electric Affair.

And the past couple of days had furnished information of the most gripping interest to those closely involved. Those lumbering, long-awaited indictments were coming down at last. Within the smugglers' group the existence of a leak had been suspected for quite a while; just too many shipments had been going wrong. Now, perhaps, the identity of that leak would be unmasked. Also, and seemingly right from the core of one of the government agencies, the Airport Gang had gotten hold of the actual list of the people under investigation: They knew the *names*.

Sixteen people were to be indicted before the end, including Al Seifert, who was named, along with Donald Brown, as a leader. Five dozen others were named as "unindicted co-conspirators." This was the list upon which Jack Tupper's name was eventually to appear.

Ivor Shaw dialed an assistant U.S. attorney's home number. Jack Tupper was a stand-up guy, Shaw's buddy, and a man with an eager ear for his advice, but also, Shaw had him under surveillance. This seemed no incongruity in the rococo world Shaw's imagination inhabited.

The Fed answered. Shaw told him of Tupper's disappearance and his suspicions, and rejoined Melanie, beneath the awning of Nicola's, which stands just opposite 155 East 84th Street. The rain was beginning to fall again. Shaw's tweed jacket felt damp; there was a spatter pattern on his fine Italian shoes.

There is a routine to police matters. Back at the 40th Precinct in the Bronx, the two suspects, Jacobson and Giamo, were taken into the dayroom, and their handcuffs were removed. They were asked for their valuables. Buddy Jacobson was carrying $933.41, and this was vouchered by Officer Fitzpatrick.

More cops arrived. It was about 6:00 P.M. Ronald Marsenison, a detective with a tan, a natty suit, and a resonant voice, informed Buddy that he was under arrest, and that the charge was murder. He read him all the Miranda warnings, and asked if he understood his rights.

Buddy Jacobson said yes, and that he did want an attorney, but first he would have to call his accountant. A Cadillac, nearly a thousand in cash, and now an accountant—it was clear that this caper wasn't just one more Bronx dump job.

Marsenison asked Jacobson and Giamo to give up their clothes. They did so, and there was a sort of silence. Buddy Jacobson wore no underwear. He had no undershirt, no underpants. Beneath those unzippered boots, he wasn't even wearing socks. He stood there in the station house entirely naked, pale and scrawny, a mute appeal for sympathy, until somebody got hold of a regulation-issue blanket. It was grayish-green, and prickly, but Buddy pulled it around himself in silence.

Marsenison, meanwhile, had separated the clothes into two piles. He felt and smelled them, finding them pungent with sweat, and smoke, and gasoline fumes. Both sets of clothing were stained and spotted with what Marsenison assumed to be blood.

Soon Detective Sullivan arrived. Bill Sullivan is a veteran, with a meaty face and an expression of permanently weary knowingness. His manner is phlegmatic. Sullivan, who had come to take charge of the Jacobson investigation, signed vouchers for the two piles of clothing. At a quarter of seven, Buddy Jacobson was walked out to a patrol car. The skies had opened, and there was a steady downpour. The air was cooler. The drive to the nearby 43rd Precinct customarily takes about ten minutes. Buddy, who was sitting in the car wrapped in his blanket, suddenly, and rather unexpectedly, spoke.

"Can anybody tell me what is going on?" he asked.

"Suppose you tell us?" suggested a cop.

Carefully, Buddy Jacobson explained. An employee had come to his apartment, not once, but often, suggesting that Buddy buy his car. Buddy hadn't wanted to, but the guy had insisted.

Jacobson had amiably agreed that he would take the Cadillac out for a test drive, at the least. Giamo just happened to have been sitting there, a passenger; Buddy didn't even know his name. So he had taken the yellow Cadillac, and the car had felt pretty good, so he had driven on, and on.

In the Bronx he had lost himself on a parkway. He had stopped once, and gotten out for a leak, then continued on his way. Which had taken him to the 138th Street exit, off the Bruckner Expressway.

And now this. His voice was soft, compelling, wondrously plausible.

They reached the 43rd Precinct at about seven o'clock. Buddy Jacobson was put into the detention cell, on the ground floor just behind the duty officer's desk. He sat on the narrow bench in the cell, still wrapped in his dingy blanket, and was silent. The banana-colored two-door Cadillac was also there, parked in the station-house garage. The Eighth Homicide unit, with which Detective Sullivan served and which was lodged in the 43rd Precinct, was as yet unaware that these were the beginnings of what was to be its biggest case.

It was at just about that time Sunday night that I noticed Ivor Shaw. Shaw, whom I had known casually for some years, was standing on the corner of 84th Street, telephoning in the rain. I was on my way into Nicola's, where I was seated not at the big front table, behind which hangs a photograph of former horse trainer Buddy Jacobson with one of his last Belmont winners, but at the small table to the left, behind which hangs a photograph of Melanie, a *Cosmopolitan* magazine cover.

Outside the restaurant the rain was slackening, but still slanting down. The sulphurous sky was turning purplish-brown, like a rotten eggplant. Melanie and Ivor Shaw sat in the G&M Luncheonette, their options dwindling.

Intermittently, they continued to telephone. The G&M commanded a good view of the 84th Street building. The luncheonette was marvelously seedy, its seediness the greater for its aspirations to class. The mirrors on the back wall were gold-flecked, like a Beverly Hills bedroom, and here and there stood magnolia-petal pearlized lamps. Scuffed plastic domes on the counter displayed glazed doughnuts and powdered buns. The taped music was bouzouki.

The owners, a surly couple from the island of Chios, watched without expression as Melanie and Ivor Shaw occupied a table, neither eating nor drinking, but incurring, nonetheless, the dollar minimum. Shaw was working his way through Jack Tupper's telephone book. He tried to call Jack's brother-in-law Tom Myers, the FBI agent, and a man Jack much admired, but it was a faint hope, and he couldn't get through anyway. He called Jack's answering service again, but again there was nothing. And he called his friends at Manhattan's 19th Precinct—Shaw has many friends—but they were out, or unavailable. Jack Tupper hadn't returned, nor had Buddy, and the darkness of night sat on the seventh floor of the building like a huge black hat.

At seven-thirty Melanie asked if they shouldn't go down to the precinct. Shaw managed to talk her out of it. "I didn't want that," he told me later. "If Jack came back and found the police in his place, he'd skin me alive." One hour later, he had come around to Melanie's point of view. "I called Al, and said I was going to the cops. He said okay. . . ."

So Melanie and Ivor Shaw took a cab down to the 19th Precinct. Both were reluctant. For their different reasons.

That evening, Detective Sullivan called Salvatore Prainito at home, since his name had cropped up on the papers found in the Cadillac. Actually, for several hours it had been assumed that Prainito was the corpse in the Bronx. But Sullivan was careful on the telephone. He is a careful man.

Which was not true of everybody at the 43rd Precinct. As Louis Carattini had feared, he and his family were now involved, and had been brought along to the station house. They told what they had seen, then a couple of police officers were asked to see them home. Accordingly, they took the stairway down from Eighth Homicide and walked past the duty officer's desk toward the front door. The police officers taking them home were Hector Feliciano and Dennis Fitzpatrick, and, or so they were resolutely to maintain, they hadn't the remotest idea who the Carattinis were.

It was Estella Carattini's brother-in-law who pointed toward the cell behind the duty officer's desk. Estella Carattini, a conscientious woman, found herself looking into that face, those eyes; hypnotic, bleak, dark, unmistakable. She whispered something to her brother-in-law—but she didn't mention it to Fitzpatrick or Feliciano. Which was just as well. Estella Carattini's identification of Buddy Jacobson was vital, and that instant of contact down at the precinct was just the first of the egregious blunders that almost demolished this simplest of cases, and let Buddy walk free.

The 19th Precinct, which polices, or attempts to police, Manhattan's East Side, is on 67th Street. Melanie and Ivor Shaw got there at about a quarter to nine, and Melanie was, by now, lapped by contrary waves of doubt. "I think I'm going to tell the guys the whole story," she said. "And they're just going to look at me and say you're *crazy*."

They spoke with a detective, a tall man of somber mien. He did no such thing. "Why didn't you come sooner?" he asked pointedly.

Melanie looked at Shaw, meaning: Why didn't we? Shaw blustered about missing persons. The detective, a seventeen-year veteran named Charlie Lienau, stolidly pointed out that this was a possible homicide. Melanie stood there, stiff as a puppet, as light began to play on a shadowy place: murder. Lienau collected another detective, a shorter and somewhat jollier man named Giagrande, and the four went uptown to 84th Street. Shaw was masking a certain inner disquiet, and Melanie, among all her tangled thoughts, felt a twinge of relief that the two policemen were in civilian clothes.

On the seventh floor, the two detectives went about their task. It was plain to Lienau that whoever had been living, or was living, in apartment 7C was either moving in or moving out, what with the piles of cardboard boxes and the family photographs stacked together on the sofa. There seemed to be no signs of any sort of fracas in there, but out in the hall things were otherwise.

Melanie and Ivor Shaw pointed out the smear on the outside of the elevator door—it would become known as the "bloody palm print." They pointed out the pinkish stains on the undercarpeting and the speckles of white paint. Low down on one of the fire doors, Ivor Shaw indicated the tuft of hair, bristling out of what was now crusted blood.

The detectives knocked on the other doors on the seventh floor, without success. 7D, Jacobson's door, was shut, locked. They left it so. They spoke little to Melanie or Ivor Shaw, and Shaw realized that his presence was only tolerated within certain limits. "They would go outside and talk in the hall," he says. "Then they would go and call from the street." He understood. He was, at least theoretically, a potential suspect.

Melanie took her decline into insignificance with less calm. Her head now felt clear as a crystal globe and utterly shatterproof. That muzzy ache which had been her familiar for the last three weeks, since she had tried to extract herself from Buddy's World, that feeling of moving swimmily through an out-of-focus world, had passed away. Now Melanie felt she was treading a fresh landscape, clear-cut, and gaily colored, like an illustration in a children's book. It seemed to her imperative that she be listened to, that she exert some influence on the flow of events. But, no, they rushed on by, leaving her, unregarded, on a shore.

Charlie Lienau, who recognized strain when he saw it, plodded on. It was quite apparent that whatever had happened on the seventh floor, there was more to this than just a missing-persons report. He called in to the Fourth Homicide unit; then he and Giagrande got to their knees and began to examine surfaces. They were dismembering the undercarpet and carefully sawing off the bloodied section of metal runner beside the door when Mel Harris arrived with her husband, David Silbergeld. Silbergeld had a red setter, quivering at a leash, and he was in the combat uniform of a Green Beret.

David Silbergeld, a computer specialist now in his early forties, had spent several years in the military, though not in the Green Berets but in another unit of the Special Forces, the underwater-demolitions arm, which goes by the acronym SEAL. Silbergeld much enjoys the business of war, from the plainest logistics to the swashbuckling heroics. He sports dog tags even when wearing civvies, and will, with some prompting, speak, with a mysterious air and carefully doled-out smidgens of security-cleared fact, about missions in the core of the Vietnam jungle, and an HQ in the vicinity of Can Tho. When Silbergeld left the service, he joined the reserves, as a matter of course, and thereafter spent merry weekends with a command, and the rank of major.

This weekend had been one of his reserve obligations. "I was guarding a naval air station in South Jersey. A lot of fog had set in," he recalls. "We were using naval aircraft to jump. They have a big drop zone there, where the old blimp base used to be. For paratroopers it's ideal."

Silbergeld had duly gotten in the jumps prescribed then had driven back home in his sporty red Mercedes. Home was now a duplex in a brownstone on East 75th, done up by Silbergeld himself with a built-in stereo and artful lighting. Bookshelves in an upstairs gallery hold a military library, chockablock with recently declassified pamphlets, which have such resonant titles as *Special Forces Operational Techniques.*

Mel, now back from her *Barefoot in the Park* rehearsal, was on the telephone with Melanie in the living room when David returned. The telephone is next to an old ammunition chest that has been pressed into service as a coffee table. Stenciled on the chest is a record of its former contents: 100 SIMULATOR PROJECTILE GROUND BURST. Mel came off the telephone as David walked in. She hid her alarm with crispness. Melanie was in some sort of trouble, she said. They had to see what was afoot.

It had been a difficult drive back from Jersey, slow business in the rain, and Silbergeld had driven unchanged—that is, he was still wearing his mottled-green camouflage uniform. A notched knife was strapped to his leg. "I had a knife belt on because I always wear it when I jump, like the British commandos," he explained later. "And I had a shoulder holster, because it's easier. A pistol holster you can't get at when you're in a parachute." The holster at least was empty.

He was tired and hungry. "Okay," he said. "But first I want to get something to eat." He crossed to the refrigerator and helped himself to some stuffed cabbage.

But Mel was antsy, all pins and needles.

"Forget eating," she announced. "I'm leaving right now. With you or without you."

Her husband complied. They agreed they might as well use the trip to take Mulligan, their red setter, for his evening walk.

It was about nine-thirty when they reached Buddy Jacobson's building, and such was Mel's perturbation, and so used was David Silbergeld to roaming the Upper East Side as though it were a Viet Cong-riddled terrain, that neither of them seemed to realize for a moment or so what a figure they cut when the seventh-floor elevator doors opened and they—one Green Beret, one *haute couture* model, and one hairy red hound—came under the scrutiny of a couple of kneeling policemen.

Mel made no smart remarks about the undercarpeting—not this time. Melanie was standing there, with Ivor Shaw, whom David knew only slightly.

"Are you all right, Melanie?" he asked.

Lienau looked at him, allowing no expression to settle on his face. (Stick around the East Side beat long enough, and you get to see everything.)

"Do you have business here?" he inquired formally.

"I'm a friend of Melanie's," Silbergeld said, bristling.

Melanie walked up. "I'm okay," she told the Silbergelds dispassionately. It was apparent that she wasn't, but Mel and David said they would wait in the lobby. They were downstairs when a further contingent of police arrived from a different borough—the Bronx.

An odd business. Mel and David sat on the stoop. The afternoon coolness had dissipated long since. It was again stifling. They waited for half an hour, but the police did not call them. Melanie was safe. They walked home through the damp.

Major David Silbergeld had then no inkling, of course, what Buddy Jacobson and the reverberations of the Jacobson case were to make of his life—his private life, his professional career, and even his military career.

He would, because of Buddy Jacobson, become what he most loathed. A victim.

Buddy Jacobson gave me his account of events seventeen days later, sitting in the Bronx Detention Center. Even at the time, this description, at once fluid and awkward, sounded like a shooting script for some eccentric thriller.

"Now, you have two possibilities when you are arrested," he told me. "One, to say, 'Hey! Here's everything that happened! Listen to me!'"

He altered the timbre of his voice. It had been as open as an open window, as true as a fingernail flicking a sound wineglass. The voice now became hoarse, confidential, a Reliable Source explaining some glitch in a program. He was mesmeric, self-absorbed, blanking out our unpleasing surroundings—the locks and bars, the dingy institutional paintwork on the walls.

"And, two, you say nothing. Now why did I pick the say-nothing routine? Because, simply because, when I was arrested, first of all, it was quite a shock. I've never been arrested before, and I had twelve police cars—maybe I'm exaggerating—I don't think I was—surround me.

"I didn't run. I wasn't speeding." He sounded almost self-righteous at this point—plaintive, puzzled. "Get up against the wall! Take your shoes off! Handcuffs behind my back! I mean just like you see in the movies."

He gave a little snort of a laugh.

"It was really something. So they take me down to an old, dinky police station. Right in the middle of the open police station they take all my clothes off, before I'm allowed to say anything. And I sat there for hours, naked, with my hands behind my back.

"It was *funny*. It's a comedy thing."

Was he told why he had been arrested?

"No. They just . . . different patrolmen—not even detectives, *patrolmen*—would walk in. All right! Did you do this? Or what *did* you do? I'm not going to answer those kind of people.

"This went on for hours. Now, finally, two detectives came, and they got a blanket to put around me. No shoes on. And I walked out in the rain, through puddles. I didn't care. It's summertime, and it's no big deal. But it's so *unusual,* you know.

"And all the time I asked for a glass of water. I was *so thirsty.*" Again, that laugh. "Well, for fourteen hours I had nothing in my mouth. *Fourteen hours.* In a cell right behind the sergeant's desk."

He looked around, as if for the first time cognizant of his surroundings.

"A little cage. Where everybody who walked by was glaring at me. You have never—nobody has ever—felt this if they've never been in it. If you feel that you're going to open your heart out, or tell people everything you know, at this point you have second thoughts about it." He looked at me. I could sense the brain humming away, elastic and resilient, navigating through possibility, as a squid will zigzag, in clouds, through a tricky area in the sea. "All this stuff is shocking," he said. "Unless you're used to it. I'm not." His black eyes held mine briefly for a moment, then looked restlessly away.

Jack Tupper, Sr., and his wife, Marie, Jack's parents, had gone out to Shelter Island for the day, with their younger son, Kevin, and his wife, Kathy. Jack Tupper, Sr., is a quiet man, of dignity and humor. Now retired, he was a tool and die cutter by trade who had achieved office in the union; and the most dramatic moment of his career, the turning down of a six-figure bribe, is something of which I learned from others. It's an attractive place, Shelter Island, a short ferry ride off the Long Island shore, but wooded and tranquil compared with the high summer bustle and frantic partying-chic that afflict the neighboring Hamptons. It had been a pleasant day, the sea having dispelled the worst of the sultriness. The Tuppers dined on the island, took the ferry, and drove to Kevin's house—his parents were staying with him—at Port Jefferson, Long Island. They got there at about ten-thirty.

Their time had been agreeable, but it hadn't been merry. There was much grief in the family. Jerry Tupper, the younger brother of Jack, Dorothy, and Kevin Tupper, an athlete and a popular youth, everybody's favorite, had a few months before been cut down by leukemia. The disease had progressed with horrible speed. His brothers and sister had given blood, but the youth had died in April, more or less in the arms of his oldest brother, Jack. Soon afterward, Kathy Tupper had miscarried.

Back in the house, Marie chatted briefly with Kathy.

"I couldn't take anything else right now," Marie had said.

"Neither could I," Kathy agreed.

It seemed only moments later that the telephone shrilled. A late call. Kevin took it upstairs in the bedroom. It was Al Seifert, and Kevin went instantly on the alert. "It was the first time that I talked to him in about four years," he said. Kevin is his father's son, a moralist, with an upward drive. For a living he devises Armageddon games, computer programs for the military. Kevin Tupper was wary of Jack's friend Al Seifert.

"Now, don't worry," Al told Kevin. "But do you know where Jack is?"

Kevin's alertness sharpened. Right away he knew it was something bad.

"No," he said. "What's the matter? What's up?"

"Nothing," Al Seifert said, as lullingly as he could. "We don't know where Jack is, but there's nothing to worry about. Gee! I shouldn't even have called you."

"Then why did you call me?" Kevin demanded.

Very reluctantly, Al Seifert told Kevin about the traces of what might be blood. They probably didn't mean a thing, he said. Jack might be heard from at any moment.

Kevin was not lulled, but he decided not to speak to his parents—not yet—and the elder Tuppers went up to bed. (Their sleep was to be restless. There was an extension to the telephone in their bedroom, and the telephone was to be much in use all through the night.) Downstairs again, Kevin and Kathy busied themselves with chores. Marie Tupper had left her spectacles in her own house, nearby, and the young couple killed some time by driving over to pick them up.

Still, Kevin and Kathy heard nothing about the missing Jack. Kathy Tupper is a sensible young woman, formerly a nurse, with blue eyes and a blond pageboy. She tried to be sunny, even managing to dismiss Seifert's mention of blood. "Maybe Jack had a nosebleed," she suggested.

But Kevin, who seems stolid at first, is filled with an emotional intensity which is this English-Irish family's dominant trait, and his mood was darkening quickly. "You know how you get a bad gut feeling?" he was to explain.

Then Kathy had a thought. She had a sense of her brother-in-law, the unpredictable nature of Jack Tupper's comings and goings. She knew of his well-developed sense of mystery. And she did *not* know about Melanie Cain. "Knowing Jackie," she said, "it wouldn't be so unlike him to fly to Puerto Rico. On the spur of the moment."

Certainly Jack had never bothered to keep his family informed of his whereabouts. Kevin and Kathy called Dorothy and Tom Myers in San Juan, prepared for disappointment, since the lines were often down. But tonight the phones were working. Dorothy answered. She had been writing a letter.

Kathy spoke. "I was just thinking of you," she said, affecting the cheeriest of tones.

They chatted of this and that for a while. Dorothy didn't mention Jack, and Kathy, not knowing how to frame a sufficiently casual question, felt at a loss.

"Oh," she said, in the end, brightly, "by the way, have you seen Jackie?"

Dorothy felt an inward surge. She was the family member closest to Jack. He and Melanie had stayed with the Myerses two weeks before, and Melanie had told her stories about Buddy's strangeness. Indeed, she had telephoned Jack at the All-Ireland several times, just to put her mind at rest, her last call being just four days before. Now, when she finally heard that he was missing, her thoughts became as black as the night landscape. When she heard about the bloodstains, she became hysterical.

Everything was suddenly as clear to her as if that nocturnal landscape had been illuminated by a lightning bolt. "I knew Jackie was dead," Dorothy told me later.

Her brother was dead, and Buddy Jacobson had killed him.

It was now, as Dorothy Myers remembers vividly, just eleven o'clock.

Al Seifert remembers this time with equal precision. He also was using the telephone. He had been trying to find Douglas, Buddy Jacobson's seventeen-year-old son, for a couple of hours, and it was now that he got the boy on the line.

Douglas was in his mother's apartment, down the street from Buddy's old duplex in Silver Towers, Queens.

Seifert did not yet know that Buddy had been arrested, but his conversations with Melanie and Ivor Shaw and their description of the state of the hallway had disposed him to fear the worst. "I thought there was a fifty-fifty chance that John Tupper was dead," he told me. "You see, I knew this with Buddy—there was no half measures. He wouldn't just give John a beating. He might send him to the hospital, but Buddy knows that when John gets out of the hospital, *he's* going to get twice the beating. So, if the fight took place, it was to the finish. That was my feeling."

So Seifert launched himself into a savage bluff.

"The police know everything already," he told the boy. "What happened? Tell me everything that happened. The police know it *all*."

Douglas crumbled. "I didn't do it," he said. "It was my father! It was my father!"

The quickness of the collapse took Al rather aback. "Stay right where you are," he told Douglas. "The police know all about it. If you run away, the police are going to think it's worse—what you did. They understand that your father made you do it."

His wording was wily. He still did not, after all, know precisely what it was that Buddy Jacobson had done. "I didn't want to pin Douglas down," Seifert explained later, "because he's trying to blame his father and take himself out of it, and I didn't want him to get too panicky. I didn't know. I just wanted him to stay there till the police got there."

But he couldn't resist one more probing question: *"Why* did your father do this?" Seifert asked.

The words came tumbling out. His father had done it because he had money problems, and because Melanie had left him, Douglas said. He barely knew his father, who had left him when he was little, and had only recently reentered his life.

"I don't really know my father," he said desperately. "I never knew he was like this."

The conversation went on for about ten minutes. "Oh," Douglas wailed at the end, swept by new terrors. "I know Jack was your friend. Don't come over here and hurt me!"

"I'm not going to hurt you, Douglas," Al Seifert said.

"Your father made you do it. Just stay there. The police will be there in ten minutes."

Seifert now spent a while calling various police numbers, finally deciding to call the East 84th Street building direct.

There was a longish wait, and then a detective came on the line. Seifert repeated exactly what Douglas had told him, word for word, and gave him the exact address where Douglas could be picked up. "He's waiting for you," Al Seifert said, with some satisfaction. "Go over there now. He's going to confess."

And that, he assumed, grimly vengeful, would be that. For all his quirkish brilliance, his manipulative subtlety, Buddy Jacobson was as good as tried, convicted, and jailed.

That, at any rate, is what Al Seifert thought.

Well, hardly. Lienau was still there, conducting his missing-persons inquiry, and there was a team from Manhattan Fourth Homicide, and now the team from the Bronx Eighth Homicide—Bill Sullivan and his partner, a fellow named Porteus—and there were search teams, and police photographers, and there was a potential tug-of-war between Manhattan, where the murder had presumably been committed, and the Bronx, where a body had indubitably been found, so that, what with one thing and another, all the proceedings required were words by Gilbert and music by Sullivan.

"It seemed there were a good twenty detectives there," Melanie says. "I mean, it was really a nuthouse. You know, they were looking around, and they were finding things. They were on the roof, and they had found a rug that had been in Buddy's apartment. They went through My Fair Lady. They went everywhere."

Melanie just stood amid the turmoil with Ivor Shaw, the detectives navigating around them, and occasionally one or another of the law officers would put Melanie to use. At about eleven, Jeremiah McCarthy, a detective with Fourth Homicide, asked whether Melanie could get into Jacobson's apartment.

Melanie jiggled at the combination awhile—Buddy had changed it since she had moved out of his flat, but it wasn't a complex code—and at last got the door open. She walked inside a few paces, but McCarthy, recollecting that he had neglected the tiresome formality of getting a search warrant, called her back. The door was relocked, and the Jacobson case again just narrowly missed being blown to bits.

The detectives now left Melanie and Shaw pretty much alone. It seemed to her that they treated her brusquely—"Go and sit down. Be quiet"—and they asked no questions, which nettled her. "They would just push me out of the way," she said later, adding, with a sardonic bite, "They *know* what's going on. They don't need my help."

Ivor Shaw also felt a sense of inutility, but, not being in Melanie's state, which might be described as a sort of bright false practicality, found the entire experience merely draining. For lack of anything more forceful to do, Ivor said that he was going to park Jack's car. "They tow in the morning," he explained to the police. The red sedan (which had been borrowed from Jack Tupper, Sr.) was unlocked. Shaw picked it up, drove it around to the Ardor Garage next door to Buddy Jacobson's building, and returned to the seventh floor.

Melanie was standing there, now white as a glass of milk. Her eyes were huge, and she looked as if she would never blink again. The cops were still noting scraps of this and that, and now and again they would whisper to each other confidentially. Which is to say that the whispers were supposed to be confidential, and Melanie was doing her best to ignore them, but that was proving impossible.

We've got the car, went one whisper. Another was *We've got Buddy Jacobson.* But the most ear-catching of all, for Melanie, had been something about *We've got the box.* The box, whatever it was, had been *burned.* And the box, whatever it contained, was *in the Bronx.* It was as if the very attempt at confidentiality, this clumsy groping for secrecy, had pushed up the volume control, so that in Melanie's overcharged brain the whispers were aimed at her, directly. It was like being surrounded by the whirring wings of startled birds.

The cops were now wrapping up, unmistakably so. They were returning to their various precincts. But Melanie now had a precise sense of what it was that she must do. "I'm going up to the Bronx, whether you want it or not," she told the police flatly.

It was close to midnight. Ivor Shaw asked Melanie politely, if without too much enthusiasm, whether she would like his company. Melanie said thanks, but no.

"That's okay," she told him. "I can handle this myself."

And that was just the way she felt. A wondrous simplicity; the pure logic of a dream.

"My attitude was that I was alone," she remembers, "and I was going to take care of this *myself*.

"I felt everything was *so slow*. My attitude was, well, we have Buddy. Let's kill him."

She laughed, but at herself.

"Instantly! Buddy did it. That's *it! Put him in jail. Then send him to the electric chair."

So Melanie went to the Bronx, and Ivor Shaw crossed the street and went into Nicola's, Buddy's favorite place. Nicola is a Genovese, a small man with knowing eyes. Once headwaiter at Elaine's, the favored meetingplace of celebrated writers and celebrated written-abouts, Nicola had gathered his own clientele, which was fast money—the raffish heirs of American fortunes, the refugee rich from Europe and Latin America. His was a place where Buddy Jacobson, dining almost nightly with his bevy of dangerously young beauties, had become a fixture; famous for the things that money cannot necessarily buy.

Shaw seated himself at the long bar and ordered a double Jack Daniel's on the rocks. Nicola came over. He had been looking down his long nose at the activity across the way, and he was agitated, Shaw says.

"What has happened?" he asked.

"It looks like Buddy just killed Jack Tupper," Shaw replied.

Nicola was incredulous. He disliked Tupper. Indeed, some time before the murder he had gone out of his way to warn this writer that Tupper's friends were "killers." Nicola liked Buddy Jacobson.

"Buddy would never do that," Nicola said.

Ivor Shaw shrugged glumly. He realized that he had left his apartment with no money, and borrowed twenty dollars from Nicola. Then he drained his Jack Daniel's, ordered another, and looked around. He wouldn't have minded talking the whole thing out with somebody, but chic restaurants have a melancholy air on summer weekend evenings; their regulars are still at the beach, or exhausted by the rigors of their return.

Shaw, who takes much pride in the hardness of his head, knocked down four doubles. When he left Nicola's, he stared up at Buddy's building. It was dark at last, silent. What with its unconvincing classiness—that trim facade of rough red

brick, those balustrades of white and twirly wrought iron—
the building looked a bit like an opera set after the last aria
has been sung, or so it seemed to Shaw, his imagination freed
by bourbon. Appropriately, even the outdoor carpet on the
sidewalk outside the My Fair Lady office had been taken
up.

This seemed entirely satisfactory to Ivor Shaw, lending a
finality to the Sunday's awful events. Buddy Jacobson had
killed Jack Tupper, and Jack Tupper was Ivor's friend, even if
he was, in an abstruse way, part of the game that he, Ivor
Shaw, was playing. Now the game was ended. "If anything
else comes up," he told himself, "I'll take a Pasadena."

Meaning a pass. Thankful the night was growing cooler,
Ivor Shaw walked the ten blocks home.

Neither Kevin Tupper nor Dorothy Myers had been getting
far. Dorothy had called Brian Monaghan and babbled about
blood. Kevin, no less overwrought, worked through a process
of elimination. He telephoned everybody and anybody. Repeatedly, he called his brother's answering service. He faced
the more somber possibilities squarely. "If he was hurt, where
would he go?" reasoned Kevin. "I called all the hospitals, and
asked if any John Does had come in. DOA, or whatever. No
luck."

By two in the morning they were running out of options.
Kathy Tupper, sunny no longer, came to a decision. "I'm
going to talk to Al Seifert," she told Kevin. "He's going to tell
us what he knows."

Al was still at his home. Kevin listened as they spoke.
"Listen," Kathy said. "If you know something, you have to
tell us. We are Jack's family. I have his mother and father
asleep in the house."

With much reluctance, Al Seifert told Kathy about his conversation with Douglas. Also, that a body had been found in
the Bronx, and that it was being handled by the 19th Precinct.

Further calls crisscrossed the night. Tom Myers now called
Seifert from Puerto Rico. "Is Buddy Jacobson capable of
murder?" Myers asked.

His manner was quiet, reasonable. Myers is a handsome,
square-cut man, in the purest FBI tradition; a rock where
Dorothy can be a storm. He hoped, perhaps, for reassuring
words, but Seifert thought briefly, and said, "Yes."

Kevin, meanwhile, was calling the 19th Precinct. The duty

officers wouldn't tell him a thing. He managed to get a number of an apartment in Buddy's building from the telephone operator, and he called it. But no policeman was forthcoming.

Defeated, he called Al Seifert again. Al told Kevin just what the cops were up to, which inflamed him. "He knew where the police were, blow by blow," Kevin said, later. "Which I thought was quite strange, because he was in Queens."

Kevin was anguished, of course, and frantic, but there is still something remarkable about the speed with which his suspicion budded and flowered. Buddy Jacobson was to prove he had a green thumb in seeding and tending a proliferating jungle of intrigue and treachery, but there was fertile soil from the start.

Melanie's journey to the Bronx took her no closer to reality. "I'll never forget some of the talk," she said. What seemed unreal to her was that she was sitting in the police car with the detectives and they were making jokes, wisecracking about people they had picked up. "I mean, they're joking about *murders*," she said. "They were acting like murders were *funny*."

Melanie understood that in their blunt way, the cops were trying to be nice to her, but she refused to respond. That fierce sense of certitude she had felt in the apartment had faded, and now she found herself unwilling wholly to accept either Jack's death or Buddy's guilt. So she sat in the car, nervous and dazed, until the cops, to her bemusement, decided to stop for a bite.

"They say, 'Let's stop at McDonald's.' So we stop at this drive-in. We're there for *twenty years,* and all I could think is, this is so *stupid.* How can anyone think of eating and drinking at a time like this? It was incredible to me that they make such a big deal about their apple turnover."

Except that it was then that Melanie realized she had neither eaten nor drunk anything since her morning cup of tea for that entire day. Hunger was still beyond her, but she began to feel an acute thirst. So when one of the cops asked if she wanted anything, she said she would like a Seven-Up. He came back with a packed carton, and they all then drove on to the 43rd Precinct station house.

Melanie marched straight in. She looked around impersonally: the lobby, with the Coke machines; the groups of chairs, where a few people were slumped; and a couple of men in uniform, standing behind a desk. The desk must be where they book the prisoners, she thought. And just to the right of the desk, she saw a small window. The window, perhaps eighteen inches wide by two feet high, is guarded by both bars and a grille, and it looks into a small green-gray cell, which bears the sign 110 BOOKING ROOM, but which is known to cognoscenti as the cage. A man was staring out at her, through the bars and the grillwork. It was Buddy.

"There's Buddy, with no clothes," Melanie said, later. "His bones were sticking out . . . he's got this old blanket, just thrown over his shoulders, an old gray wool blanket . . . his hair's a mess, and he's got like two days' worth of beard."

Buddy Jacobson, this most controlled of men, someone who scorned emotion in himself or others, was gripping the bars so tightly you could see his knuckles gleaming like polished marble. "And he's going, 'I didn't do it! I didn't do it!' " Melanie said. "He's just shaking his head, looking at me, saying, 'I didn't do it!' "

All of Melanie's pent-up emotions exploded. She made for the cell like a wild thing, screaming, "You creep! I hate you! I'm going to kill you!" and much else besides. She was, by her own admission, both loud and rude, and what her intentions were she now cannot quite fathom—"I probably thought I could stick my wrists through the bars." A couple of startled cops grabbed her, quieted her down, and led her away, with Buddy still looking after her, shaking his head from side to side, as though he could hammer her with his will, as though the recent past could be undone, as if it had never been.

Melanie was now in a state which was, at one and the same time, trancelike and oversensitized. "Hallucinatory" is perhaps the best word for it. The cops walked her into an escalator, which went up to the first floor, and then steered her down a corridor, which seemed extremely narrow and extremely blue.

"I hate that blue," she says. "I just think it is the most putrid color. And they have it in so many places, that blue. It's so tacky, a blah color." She spoke with striking vehemence, but this same vivid shade of blue is to crop up again in this story. And now, swimming in front of her, she saw a door. There were big, black letters on the door, reading HOMICIDE.

For Melanie, the sight was like a brutal slap to the side of the head. "This was it," Melanie told me. "Like the movies. You know . . . *murder*."

The office of Eighth Homicide was a large, open room, though there were five small cubicles partitioned off along the edges. It was institutional, with huge banks of metal filing cabinets, grimy green Olivettis on the desks, and vinyl flooring the color of oyster shells. The room's more specific function was indicated by a wallful of mug shots and large black index books, inscribed *Victims* and *Perps* (Perpetrators). The room and its occupants disappointed Melanie. "It was just the grossest place," she remembers. "With all kinds of desks, and papers scattered all over the desks. There were some plainclothes police, some uniform police. A lot of big, fat detectives."

She giggled at the surreal memory. "I was just amazed how fat they were. I thought it was awful." Her mind began to wander. "I began thinking of the reputation of the New York City Police Department. I just thought they should all be on a diet. A nutrition program or something. You know, you go to the movies, and you see thin detectives. I mean, if they ever had to chase somebody, forget it!"

Melanie suddenly realized how hot she was. She took off her coat, but it didn't help. She watched, and she saw that the McDonald's box was being emptied in a twinkling. "And now," she says, "I was *parched*." She walked up to one of the cops. Quite without thought or design, she heard herself speaking in a little-girl voice.

"Where's my soda?" she asked.

He looked at the box and saw the empty containers lying around among the crumpled wrappings.

"Somebody must have drank it, honey," he noted. "It's all gone."

Melanie, childlike, was devastated. "Well, can I have a drink of water? Because I am really thirsty."

The cop was all comfort. "Yeah," he said. "We'll get you one."

And they did. "They bring me this cup of water that obviously coffee had been sitting in all night, and they had dumped it out," she said. She took the water from him, feeling the dryness in her mouth, and looking at this cupful of warmish water, a smear of dried lipstick at the brim, and the slimy ring of brown, which was the mark where the coffee had once reached, and hesitated.

She sipped the water at last, and coughed. There were ashtrays everywhere. "People were just smoking up a storm," she said. "It was disgusting. Everything was disgusting about the place." The cops were joking, and Melanie didn't understand what made them laugh, because to her there seemed to be no humor in their jests. Melanie had now lost any sense that she could control events, or even hold on to them. Without thinking, she asked a passing detective for a cigarette. He offered a Marlboro and left her the pack. She lit up and sat there nonchalantly puffing at the cigarette and sipping the lukewarm water. This was the first cigarette that Melanie had ever smoked in her life.

One of the cops walked up to her.

"Uh," she said, "do you smoke?" She thought it was a strange inquiry. Didn't she have a cigarette in her mouth?

"Yes."

"Well, do you have any cigarettes with you?"

"Yes."

"Uh," he said, "can I have one?"

Melanie gave him a cigarette, though she wondered why he couldn't have come straight out with the question. But soon she realized that this circuitous line of questioning seemed to be part of the job: detective talk.

So far these were the only sort of questions she was getting. Melanie was beginning to be baffled by the incuriosity with which she was being treated. "They didn't want to know *anything* about me," she says, not realizing that at this early phase of the investigation nobody had quite figured out where Melanie fitted into the case.

This just wasn't the way that Melanie had imagined policemen to be. When she had been in the eighth grade in Texas (which was where her father, a salesman, was then employed), and every other girl had wanted to be a movie star or a model, Melanie had wanted to go to the law-enforcement school at Houston State and become a police officer. "I used to watch all the TV detective shows," she says, "and I was always reading the Alfred Hitchcock mysteries. I used to have daydreams—being the only lady cop in the office, going out in patrol cars, shooting at people. You know, cracking all the tough cases. But never getting in any danger, of course."

Now Melanie became pressingly aware of another gap between illusion and reality. People were swirling around her, and there was a crackle of activity, with telephones ringing, cops walking in, cops walking out, and a persistent stream of accusers and accused. Mostly black people, it seemed to Melanie, and mostly they had been involved in assaults, killings, sudden deaths. "The police were bringing them in and out real fast," she said. It was as if a movie were being unspooled in front of her in fast motion. But she, the viewer, seemed glued in some slowed-down world, thirsty, and puffing smoke into the airless room through chapped lips, as the moments limped past.

Because they had Jacobson, the possible killer, and Prainito, the possible victim, on their minds, the police gave a lower priority to Jack Tupper who thus far had only disappeared. This was frustrating for Melanie, because she heard them puzzling over the motive for the disappearance. "I'm telling them that I could *give* them the motive, but they don't know me. They don't know why they should *talk* to me."

And when the cops did start paying attention to Melanie, it wasn't the sort that she wanted. Originally when Melanie had been asked who she was, she had just told the police her name—Melanie Cain. Simple as that. "I never said I was a model," she says. "I didn't think that had to do with anything." The cops seemed to think otherwise. One of the detectives had picked up one of Melanie's composites in the Manhattan apartment and had brought it to the Bronx precinct house.

Composites are as basic a part of a model's credentials as her book of photographs. They are the leaflets given to photographers, art directors, and clients. A composite carries the model's name, the relevant physical information, and, most important, some photographs. The photos include a head shot, to show her facial structure and her hair, and other shots showing the photogenic qualities she perceives to be her modeling strengths. Melanie was a top model working in the mainstream. Her composite included a full face, a couple of magazine covers, and a swimsuit shot, used in *Vogue*. From the way the cops began to crowd around it, or so it seemed to Melanie, it might have been the latest *Playboy* centerfold.

"Suddenly they were saying, 'Oh, are you a model?' And I was repulsed," she says. "I just thought they were sitting there, looking at my pictures—'Oh, let's look at the measurements!'—making a joke out of me. I just, ugh, I just hated it."

Yes, she was a model. Yes, she had worked for *Cos-*

mopolitan. Yes, she had done television commercials. Melanie answered their questions politely, but tightly. The detectives, Melanie now decided, were giving her sneaky little looks. Thinking about her *measurements*, no doubt. Melanie picked up her coat and self-consciously slipped it back on, disregarding her chronic thirst and the heat.

Melanie's status—a "cover girl"—did awaken the detectives' interest. Perhaps she might have some answers after all. Perhaps it might be Jack Tupper, not Salvatore Prainito, in the morgue. Melanie went through her whole story. How she had lived with Buddy for five years, and how she had broken up with him. How she had gone to live with Jack Tupper, and how Buddy had tried to get her back.

The detectives were not shy about their incredulity.

"Show us what the motive was," one detective said. "He couldn't have loved you that much that he'd *murder* for you." Melanie found this doubt a reasonable one. "Okay," she said. "It wasn't just that with Buddy."

Melanie tried to explain their unhappy My Fair Lady partnership, Buddy's perilous property-mortgage pyramid, Buddy's need to dominate. She knew the police were trying to establish the motive, and she tried hard to help, but she could hear how muddled her story sounded. She found herself being asked to repeat it over and over again.

"Some of the detectives were nice, some weren't so nice." One was a big fellow—a "good-looking man, but what a mouth he had on him!"—who lost little time in telling her that he had been written up in *The New York Times* as one of the detectives who broke the Son of Sam case. She looked at him open-mouthed for a moment, not in admiration, but because the detective's boasting had awakened a memory. Buddy had never believed that Son of Sam was a madman. He had always said that Berkowitz had some game plan, was thinking of doing a best-seller, or a movie story. Buddy thought Son of Sam wasn't crazy, but smart: that was the way Buddy's mind worked.

But now the big detective was scolding her.

"If I was your father," he told Melanie, "I wouldn't have left you in New York. I would have taken you straight home. I would have made you take up a new bunch of friends."

Melanie was incensed by the criticism. "The one person who was straightforward with me," she says, "was this Detective Sullivan."

Known as Billy or Sully, Detective Sullivan was laconic. The questions that he asked Melanie were sensible questions. Nuts-and-bolts stuff. It was Sullivan who finally showed Melanie the jewelry. Though to Melanie the time seemed to have been endless, she had, in fact, been in the homicide office only two hours. She was now in the cubicle customarily used by Eighth Homicide's captain. Besides table and chairs, its decor consisted of a small Hitachi TV and an agate desk set; a chart showing current homicide statistics was pinned to the wall. It was at least relatively soundproof and shut off from inquisitive eyes. The jewelry that Sullivan showed Melanie consisted of a watch, a key ring with a Capricorn emblem, and the chain with the same emblem. The chain was burned.

Melanie was never able to identify the watch, and wasn't entirely sure about the key ring, but she had no doubts about the chain. Jack had been wearing it when she had last seen him some nineteen hours before.

Melanie wept.

She was told she would not be asked to identify the body, a formality that must be done by a relative. Nonetheless, the last of Melanie's faint hopes that Jack might still be alive were gone. She now *knew*. "Jack's dead, and Buddy did it," she said.

Melanie began to realize that she was all alone—none of her friends and none of Jack's friends or relatives were with her. "I couldn't understand," she remembers. *"Why isn't anybody here?"*

The cops sympathized. "Call somebody," they said. "Call a friend."

Melanie didn't want to worry her family. It was almost four in the morning. Call a friend? Something became very clear to Melanie at that moment. Buddy had choked off all her friendships.

"Who would I call in a case like this?" Melanie wondered. *"I would call Buddy."*

A chill thought. Melanie sat and waited for the district attorney.

Word spread.

Brian Monaghan was woken by Dorothy Myers, calling from Puerto Rico, at about half past three. "Jackie was murdered by Buddy Jacobson," she said.

Monaghan, a trim six-footer, is no stranger to violence as a concept. He holds an Irish passport, and there is nothing covert about his Republican sympathies. But Buddy Jacobson a murderer?

Brian Monaghan despised Buddy. The charge seemed ridiculous.

The cops called Al Seifert back at four in the morning. Apparently they had finally come around to considering Douglas.

"What's the address of that Queens building where the Jacobson kid lives?" a detective asked. "Nobody is answering the phone."

Seifert gave the address, without comment.

Kevin and Kathy Tupper had slept no more than Tom and Dorothy Myers. Now there was something that had to be done.

Kevin went upstairs and woke his parents.

"Is it six already?" his father asked, mildly surprised, seeing that outside it was still dark. It was, in fact, only four.

Kevin told his parents what he knew.

Tom Myers called John Gannon and his wife, Ellen, at four-thirty. Ellen Gannon was Jack Tupper's former wife and still his confidante. John took the call, listened with growing dismay, spoke briefly, and replaced the receiver. Fearing further calls, he turned down the sound. Ellen was half awake. It seemed like a fragment of a dream.

It seemed only minutes before the same detective called Al Seifert yet again.

"How do you get to that address in Queens?" he asked Seifert. "There's still nobody answering that phone." Al decided that the question showed a lack of investigative brilliance, and the first misgivings assailed him. It had seemed so simple. "Douglas was going to spill it," he says. "But nobody bothers going over to Queens and picking him up." He gave the detective the necessary directions, all the while feeling any interrogation of Douglas Jacobson was now too late. Douglas might have gone into hiding, or at least composed himself, within minutes of that first phone call. "All I know is the police didn't try to call Douglas back until four hours had passed," he added.

Before he hung up, the detective asked Seifert if he would come later that morning to the precinct house. The police needed a statement so that they could get a search warrant for the Jacobson apartment.

Seifert agreed, and seized a few hours of sleep.

Mary-Beth Abbate, who happened to be the Bronx assistant district attorney on duty while Melanie waited in the Homicide office, normally worked with the family courts. She was a young woman, with pale skin and straight brown hair, and when she had taken this particular tour—which stretches from nine on Sunday morning till nine on Monday—she had believed it would be a time of relative peace.

This proved not to be the case. Apart from the matter of the corpse in the burning box, Eighth Homicide found themselves dealing with the following problems during Mary-Beth's time-slot:

- A woman was stabbed to the heart in her apartment. And Manuel Vasquez, her common-law husband, was indicted for Murder Two.
- Charles Johnson, a black, was shot dead in front of his house after returning from a visit to a girlfriend. His wife, Irene, was indicted, also for Murder Two.
- A male, unidentified but presumed to be Hispanic, was found dead with four .32 slugs in his body on the road to Orchard Beach.
- Finally, Jorge Hernandez, sixty-three years old, was discovered with a slit throat in the stairwell of a housing project. It was believed he had been robbed.

It was about this later killing that Mary-Beth Abbate had telephoned Eighth Homicide from her Grand Concourse office. Abbate's office is deep in the great pale-gray chunk of modernismus at 215 East 161st, a building which houses various of the district attorneys and some of the courts, though it houses neither the Bronx district attorney himself, Mario Merola, nor, for that matter, the courtroom in which Buddy Jacobson's trial, the longest and the most expensive in the borough's history, was to take place.

Mary-Beth Abbate was given the data on the Hernandez case. "What else is going on?" she asked, by way of routine. She now heard for the first time of the corpse found in the burning box and the arrest of Buddy Jacobson, and she decided she might as well pay the Eighth Homicide a visit.

Abbate, seeing that Melanie was still upset after identifying Jack Tupper's chain and Capricorn medal, tried to be gentle. She warned Melanie that she might have to repeat her story a number of times, and she tried to explain about testimony, grand juries, and the legal system.

Melanie listened dutifully. Then she talked. And talked. Abbate scarcely found it necessary to put the questions.

Afterward, Melanie wandered around the Homicide office. Her changes of mood were still violent. One moment she would be feeling drained and almost placid, and the next her brain would be flashing with images of Jack and Buddy, and she would be trembling and in tears. Suddenly a way of release occurred to her. It was so simple.

"Can you take me down to Buddy's cell?" she asked a couple of cops.

They asked why. "So I can kick him in the face," Melanie said.

She tried to explain her ingenuousness later. "It was because I had my Frye boots on. I figured the cops could hold him down, and I could give him one swift kick in the face and . . . I don't know, give him a cut lip."

The cops just laughed. One of them said kindly, "You can't do that. You'll jeopardize the whole case."

Melanie persisted.

"What do you *mean* I can't?" she complained. "I mean, he's *killed* somebody. The least I can do is kick him in the face. I'm not going to *say* anything. And you can hold him down."

All the detectives in the office were laughing by now and saying, "No, no, no!" And Melanie was saying, like a spoiled child, "I want to! I want to!"

Now Melanie learned that Buddy was being brought upstairs to be interviewed by Mary-Beth Abbate. She was contemptuous.

"I don't know why you even bother," she told the police. "Because he's not going to talk."

"We'll see," the detective said—it was Bill Sullivan—and he told Melanie that she could stay in the room only if she promised not to make a scene.

"All right," Melanie said. "I promise."

She was lying like a schoolgirl who has both hands stuck behind her back, fingers crossed.

It was 5:45 A.M. when Buddy was brought into the room. Still wrapped in the cheap gray blanket, he looked terrible. His hair was wild, his feet were bare. Melanie launched herself at him in a frenzy.

"I was going to tear the blanket off him," she says, "and throw it across the room—to humiliate him." Then, while Buddy was standing naked, Melanie planned to kick him, this time in the shins.

Later, Melanie came to know that the confrontation had been set up with a purpose. The assistant district attorney, she says, had wanted to see how Buddy reacted to Melanie's presence. The answer was: hardly at all. "He was *passive*," Melanie says. "He just walked in, all slumped over, stone-faced. He stood there, he wouldn't look at me. And then he does look at me, like he was surprised I was there, and it was because of me he was arrested. And he shakes his head."

Buddy walked into a private cubicle and spoke briefly with Mary-Beth Abbate. Mary-Beth was taken aback. "He was cool, calm, collected," she says.

Buddy asked to make a telephone call. He phoned his sister, Rita Costello, who lives in Great Neck. "He said he'd been charged with murder, as if he were stating the time of day," Mary-Beth Abbate remembers. "It was *amazing*." She was the first official to realize that Buddy Jacobson was no ordinary defendant.

By the time Al Seifert arrived it was 7:00 A.M. Salvatore Giamo, who Buddy continued to insist was "a hitchhiker," had been released and Buddy was back in the cage, "his head hanging out between the bars," as Seifert put it. Al spoke with Melanie and with a couple of detectives—Bill Sullivan and Charley Moreno—and then with Mary-Beth Abbate, and he repeated his phone conversation with Douglas Jacobson of just eight hours before.

This was taken down by a stenographer. Then Seifert, together with Melanie, Moreno, and Mary-Beth Abbate, went to the courthouse—the big Bronx courthouse where Buddy was ultimately to be tried—and waited for about an hour.

Seifert was acting as any citizen should—especially a citizen who has had a close friend butchered. But only Al Seifert knew what he risked by coming forward. It had been as recently as a few days before that he had been warning Tupper about Jacobson's talent for deviousness, his taste for revenge. "He's got a history of viciousness," he had said.

Now Seifert had a presentiment that he should have taken his own advice. He knew that an indictment was winging toward him as one of the two bosses of the Donald Brown Organization. He also knew that Jack Tupper's name had been added to the list of gang members. Seifert did what he could to comfort Melanie, but his inmost thoughts were gloomy. Nonetheless, he gave his testimony, along with Melanie, in front of Judge Goldfluss, who granted the police their search warrant for the Jacobson apartment. It was past eleven.

On her way out of the courthouse, Melanie met Rita Costello, Buddy's older sister. She gave Rita her telephone number, and was talking to her when Abbate and Al Seifert arrived on her heels, and she was urgently motioned away. "She said she wanted to help," Rita Costello says. "I was very fond of Rita," says Melanie, "I was sorry for her." It is a dismal irony that to this day Rita Costello believes that Melanie had been about to tell her of her brother's innocence.

George Cain, Melanie's father, had arrived by the time she got back to the precinct house. He was vehement about his daughter's wellbeing. Melanie found this puzzling. "He was going on as if I was five years old," she says. "But I felt very strong. Placid. I told him: It's okay. . . ."

Everything was going to be all right.

Claire Normandeau was in her office at 10:00 A.M. that Monday, drinking a cup of coffee. Claire has long brown hair and elfin good looks. At age thirty, she looked a decade younger, and was one of the most successful, and decorated, undercover narcotics cops in the city. Her office was in the Manhattan headquarters of the Drug Enforcement Administration at 555 West 57th Street, several blocks west of Carnegie Hall.

Normandeau had already been through the *Daily News*, and had read a tiny item headed MAN FOUND SLAIN IN BRONX INCIDENT without interest. The item had concluded with ten lines about the burning box which held "the charred remains of a man."

A few desks away, she heard Curtis Fillmore talking Fillmore, whose own office was out at Kennedy Airport, is a stocky man with frizzy hair and the face of a cherubic tough.

He is a Mormon out of Utah, who had done his statutory spell as a missionary. Right now he was a DEA agent, and struggling to stem the narcotics flow through Kennedy Airport.

Claire Normandeau knew that Fillmore was on the trail of the Donald Brown Organization. It had been a month since she had first punched the name of Donald Brown into NADDIS, the central computer where information on the narcotics trade is stored. Claire comes from Queens, and she had known the boisterous Brown for years, just as she had known, but had chosen to ignore, as is etiquette when dealing with acquaintances from one's own neighborhood, that Brown's career on the wrong side of the law had been as illustrious as had hers on the right, and that, judging by the gold watches and the handmade silk shirts from London, far more profitable. What Normandeau had not expected was that so many other familiar neighborhood names would figure on Brown's computer printout. She had been especially shocked to see the name of John Tupper.

Jack Tupper was a close friend of Claire's brother Tom, who was also a cop. To her, Jack was like another brother. Both Tom and she had been surprised, and a bit wounded maybe, that Jack had failed to show up for the soon-to-be-married Tom's stag dinner just the previous Friday.

Curtis Fillmore was still talking, but it wasn't about the Brown Organization, Claire realized. He was talking about murder: the body in the burning box.

Then Claire heard Fillmore mention Buddy Jacobson.

Buddy Jacobson, too, was from the neighborhood. Tom had suggested she have nothing to do with him at least ten years before.

Now she heard Fillmore saying that the murdered man was probably Jack Tupper. Ivor Shaw's telephoning had not been without effect.

She couldn't disguise her horror. Fillmore pounced.

"Do you *know* Jack Tupper?" he asked.

Normandeau wanted to hit him. She could not know that the career she treasured was about to be shattered, as irretrievably as if she had dropped her coffee cup and it had splintered into fragments at her feet.

It was 8:00 A.M. when John Gannon was awakened by another call. The caller was Brian Monaghan. Not paying particular attention, Ellen got up and set about her chores. John Gannon was on duty that day, and they would all be driving back to the city.

Finished, she walked outside. The Gannons' house in upstate New York, near a fine ski district, is a pleasant place, mostly built of wood and sitting in a shaggy, undulating landscape. They were converting part of it into a restaurant-bar against the rapidly approaching day when John Gannon would retire from the NYPD. Sunday's muggy, rainy weather had passed. The morning was cool and blue.

Ellen was surprised. She had expected John to be going through the usual Monday-morning rush to get to work on time. She says: "But he's vacuuming the swimming pool. He was looking very vague. This was not like John at all."

What was going on? asked Ellen. Her husband told her that his duty times had been changed. "You can take your time," he said.

He came back in the house, and they sat together for a bit. Ellen's puzzlement remained. "John had a very subdued expression," she remembers. "Very wistful."

At last they set off on the long drive to Manhattan. Just the three of them: John, Ellen, and Paul, her son by her marriage to Jack Tupper.

Ellen remembers that Paul began talking again about going to live with his father in the city, and that John was gentle. "Your place is here," he said quietly. "With your mother and me."

They reached Manhattan and drove to 81st Street. Ellen had left her own car, a Fiat, parked close to the All-Ireland. Paul pleaded with his stepfather: Couldn't they drive by the building on East 84th Street? Just so he could run up and see his father?

"No," said John Gannon. He was firm.

Ellen and Paul got out at 81st, and John said he was going to follow them back to their apartment in Queens. Ellen was surprised. "I *do* know the way," she said. John Gannon muttered something. Ellen marked it up as just one more oddity in an odd day. She and Paul climbed into the Fiat and drove home.

Ellen's mother was in the apartment when they arrived, and her expression was stern and sad. But all she said was: "Let me take Paul out for an ice cream." "We've only just got back," Ellen thought to herself, but assented all the same.

After Paul was led away by his grandmother, John Gannon sat his wife down.

"I have something very bad to tell you," he said gently.

When Ellen's mother returned, John was still talking, and Ellen was still refusing to accept the news of Jack Tupper's death.

"You don't understand," she said, in her most reasonable voice. "It must be a mistake. John's calling me today."

Then she broke.

As a garden will exhale scents in the night, so the press room in the Bronx court building throws off a cheery daytime cynicism. It is a smallish room on the ground floor, with grungy linoleum on the floor and walls painted green, except the green is scaling away from the naked plaster in huge, sick flakes. Telephones, overflowing ashtrays, and sheets of fibrous gray copy paper marked with ballpoint squiggles and coffee rings cover the large metal desks.

A street map of the Bronx is tacked to one wall, alongside a ribaldly captioned photograph of Bronx district attorney Mario Merola, and a poor attempt at drawing Charlie Brown and Snoopy. Charlie Brown is saying: "Doing a good job around here is like wetting your pants in a dark suit—it gives you a warm feeling but nobody notices." Against a second wall are armchairs and a sofa, for those stale stretches when the robberies, rapes, and sudden deaths for which the borough has such a deservedly high reputation have been replaced by temporary calm.

Al Soschten was sitting in this press room when he got the tip. It was a few minutes before nine. Soschten is a veteran reporter. He had been on the *New York Post* for forty-six years, and had been in the Bronx press room for about a year. He has a long face, an imperturbable manner, corrugated hair, and a penchant for wearing dark glasses indoors. He had, of course, read the *News* item—a mere forty words—but hadn't seen anything that suggested the body-in-the-burning-box item was worthy of a follow-up.

The tip was from a friendly cop. Soschten was told that Howard "Buddy" Jacobson had been arrested. For good measure the reporter was given the names of the two Italians, Salvatore Prainito and Salvatore Giamo.

Soschten confirmed it with Edwin Dreher, the Bronx chief

of detectives and called Ed McCarthy, a former wire-service reporter—a framed photograph in his office depicts him, press card in hat, scribbling in the wake of Marilyn Monroe—who handles press relations for the Bronx DA's office. "What the hell are you bothering us for?" McCarthy said breezily. "Why are you telling me all this?"

Soschten explains, in retrospect, "They didn't know who he was. The goddam cops didn't know who Buddy Jacobson *was*." But Al Soschten goes to the track. "I knew," he says gleefully. "As a gambler, I *knew*."

Pete McLaughlin of the *Daily News* came in. McLaughlin, a burly man, born in Queens, had been with the *News* for twenty-odd years and working out of the Bronx press room for the last couple of them. Now and again, a case might turn up with the right elements, and there would be a mild flurry, with reporters coming in from the wire services, and perhaps some important byliners, hungry for a column. But mostly, Soschten, McLaughlin, and another *News* man, Dan O'Grady, had the press room to themselves. *The New York Times*, for instance, did not feel it needed to maintain a reporter permanently at the Bronx courthouse, and this forbearance from the newspaper of record was to have a marked effect on the reporting of the Jacobson case.

Al told Pete what he had learned, which is correct etiquette with one's press-room colleagues, and they plotted a strategy. Should they stay in the courthouse or go down to Eighth Homicide? They went to Eighth, which was a disastrous choice.

Buddy was in the cage. A shock.

"He didn't look like the guy I'd seen leading horses in the paddock," Soschten says.

"He looked scurvy," McLaughlin agrees. "He had a three-day growth of beard. He didn't look like any well-to-do horse trainer. Al couldn't make a visual ID." To check it out, they asked one of the cops to go into the cage.

"Are you Buddy Jacobson, the horse trainer?" the cop asked, formally.

"Yes," Buddy said. His eyes were dead in his head.

Al and Pete knew they had their story. Now they saw Melanie Cain, and they were both impressed by Melanie's fire. "I loved him," she said when they asked her about Jack Tupper. "I'd like to get right in there"—she gestured toward Buddy in the cage— "and *kick* the little creep."

Soschten and McLaughlin had it entirely to themselves. "Television didn't know about it," Al says. "The wire services didn't either." But Ed Dreher was uneasy. He implored Al to cool the news, just for a bit. "We're keeping this under wraps," he said. That sort of request is part of the compact with the police, the give-and-take, and without helpful sources, life for reporters in the Bronx press room could prove impossibly bleak. Al and Pete sat on their story.

Meanwhile, the telephones had been ringing for the two reporters nonstop in the empty press room. "By eleven-thirty we had enough to go on," Ed McCarthy says, speaking for the DA's office. Though Melanie and Al Seifert had both testified, the police had still not perceived the real dimensions of the case, but obviously it was not run-of-the-mill. "It was a class murder. And we don't get many class murders in the Bronx," McCarthy exulted. Headlines danced in his head.

"I was aware of the story's importance," Soschten says. He briefed the *Post*'s metropolitan editor and phoned in his story at half past one. "It should have been the Monday front page," he mourns. "It was the biggest one in twenty years." Deadlines squelched him.

Meantime, Al and Pete had company. The story had sprung a leak. A senior detective had tipped off Heather Bernard at New York's WNBC-TV's Newscenter 4. She arrived in the press room about 3:00 P.M., and what with her customary look of combat elegance—Heather Bernard favors Saint-Laurent safari jackets—she seemed a presence from some shinier media universe.

Heather Bernard, who was the first of the media stars to wing into the Bronx but not the last, did a little horse trading with Al Soschten. Al Soschten gave her some background on Buddy, and Heather gave Soschten a fashion magazine that contained a spread with pictures of Melanie. But it was Heather who scooped the cream. She talked with Melanie, and put the story on the six-o'clock news. "She fell into it," Al Soschten says, without ill humor.

By now, the metropolitan editor of the *Post* had put another six people on the story. One of them, George Carpozi, Jr., was briefed on the facts when he arrived at three, and began working away with a vim. The genre of journalism practiced by Carpozi was to achieve some sort of apotheosis in the Jacobson case.

Carpozi is a veteran. He is a slight man whose seamed face and grizzled crewcut attest to his fifty-nine years, but he has a spry figure that belies his age. He is a top rewrite man, which is to say that his skill lies in turning the research of reporters working in the field into the brash tabloid style. The *Post* occasionally likes to describe Carpozi as an "award-winning journalist," and in this it is correct. Some front-page Carpozi stories dealing with George Metesky, a notable figure of the 1950s otherwise known as the Mad Bomber, elicited some personal replies from his subject. The Bomber's letters to Carpozi had some giveaway details that enabled the Feds to capture him. Carpozi got to capture some awards.

Since those palmy days, George Carpozi, a snappy set of fingers at the typewriter, has written at least forty-five paperback books. Indeed, at the time the Jacobson story broke, he was contemplating reissuing three early works—"*Red Spies in Washington, Red Spies in the U.S., Red Spies in the U.N.* . . . We might do them as a trilogy"—and had two new books at different stages of gestation: another work on the amorous Washington typist Elizabeth Ray, and a biography of Frank Sinatra, entitled *Is This Man Mafia?* Carpozi saw the possibilities inherent in the Jacobson material right away.

"George calls me with the theory that the model agency was the cover for a prostitution ring," Soschten says. "Which was complete bullshit. Also, he says there's a connection with this girl Cheryl Corey, when we knew there was no connection. I said, 'Knock that *out.*'" But Al Soschten did so with a presentiment that those angles probably would not be knocked out, and in this he was absolutely right.

The magnitude of the case was still not apparent to the cops as late as two o'clock on Monday afternoon, which was when the autopsy was conducted on Jack Tupper's body. But not by Michael Baden, New York's chief medical examiner and never one to shun the limelight. "Don't you think he would have been licking his lips if he'd known?" asks a Bronx ADA.

The body might have been found in the Bronx, but the murder, it seemed safe to assume, had been committed in Manhattan. Theoretically, either borough could have claimed the case as its own. But the Bronx asked for jurisdiction first, and Manhattan chose not to argue.

"I'm not one of those who believes in fighting over cases,"

Robert Morgenthau, Manhattan district attorney, told me judiciously. "I might have thought that we could do it better. But if another borough wants a case, let them have it. I've never tried to muscle in."

The Bronx chortles a bit at this.

"We had everything," Mary-Beth Abbate says. "We had the body. We had the evidence. Everything."

Peter Grishman was more direct.

"The bottom line," he said, "is that Eighth Homicide threatened Fourth Homicide."

The Bronx is the favorite dumping-off place for corpses from all over New York City, and the other boroughs seldom prove helpful in reclaiming the human debris.

"You want to take this dump job?" the Bronx told Manhattan. "We've got another sixty-seven. Take 'em all!"

The Bronx was allowed to keep the Jacobson case, but there were to be occasions when they doubted the wisdom of their greediness.

The Jacobs family, which is to say Buddy's uncles and his cousin Patrice, who is married to the contentious millionaire Lou Wolfson, are an important presence in thoroughbred racing. That Monday they were in Saratoga, where the grandees of racing gather every August.

One of Buddy's uncles is the trainer Gene Jacobs, who was then the occupant of the position that Buddy had himself formerly held—the presidency of the Horseman's Protective and Benevolent Association. Joe Finnegan, a white-haired and canny horseman, was at a desk in the HPBA office that morning when David Jacobson, Buddy's elder son and a trainer himself, came by, and asked if he knew when Jacobs was coming in. Finnegan didn't, but was interested.

"I look at David, and I *know* something's wrong," he said.

David finally reached Jacobs on the telephone. Gene Jacobs is an amiable, rounded man, with gingerish hair and a soft, high voice. His brother, Hirsch, now dead, was arguably the greatest trainer in American history. His sister, Florence, is Buddy' s mother.

David told him of Buddy's arrest. Gene Jacobs was no more well disposed toward Buddy than the rest of his family but the news was horrendous.

"It was a shock," Gene said later, in characteristic understatement. "Buddy's mother was with us. She's no chickadee. I had the pleasure of telling her."

Later in the day, Joe Finnegan was in conference with a crony of his, a professional handicapper. Finnegan, by then, knew about Buddy. The handicapper was looking through the card.

"I love this race," he told Finnegan. "I *love* this race."

He was working out an exacta, meaning that he needed to pick a first and a second in the same race. Finnegan looked at the handicapper's selections and saw that one of the horses was David Jacobson's.

"That horse isn't going to make it," he said.

"What do you mean?" asked the handicapper. "It's a good 'un."

"I'll tell you later," Finnegan said, working on a different selection.

He explained his rationale to me thus: "David has to go to the paddock to get the horse, and he has to be nervous, worried. He'll transmit the nervousness to the horse."

How did Finnegan's hunch work out?

"We had a good exacta," he said merrily.

So the news of the Tupper murder and the Jacobson arrest came out—a trickle, and then a rush. Family heard soonest, and then close friends, and then acquaintances, and then word of the affair spread around the nation's racetracks, and the modeling world, and the Upper East Side, and certain picturesque, if more secretive, worlds.

- Bill Levin, at Saratoga like the Jacobs family, was staying at the Gideon-Putnam. Levin, a textile magnate and a force in the state's Democratic party, was the last major thoroughbred owner Buddy trained mounts for, before his banning from the track. Levin heard about the killing from his chauffeur, who caught it on TV. Levin's response was simple, and direct. "I don't believe it," he said. "This guy never felt enough emotion about any woman to kill for her."
- Sarah Hall, the blond sometime model from Alabama, certainly Buddy's most glamorous thoroughbred owner, was at Hialeah in Florida. "They were saying that a trainer had been arrested for murder. I know thousands

of trainers. Then somebody told me it was Buddy, and it had something to do with drugs. I didn't believe that."

- Rose Marie Taylor, who supplied My Fair Lady with such items as tote bags and model books, remembers, not without a twinge of shame, that her immediate reaction was that Buddy owed her for a bill submitted to him only a few days earlier: a sizable $1437.75.
- Donald Brown was telephoned the news by a friend, Billy Sharrocks, at his house in Los Angeles, which is what a local realtor describes as "the former Raquel Welch home," and situated where West Hollywood meets Beverly Hills. He grieved for his friend Tupper, who was never part of the Donald Brown Organization, he insists, whatever the Feds may say, and he marveled at the plight of Buddy Jacobson, whom he had known for eighteen years.

Donald Brown did not then know that he and Billy Sharrocks would soon be finding themselves on different sides of the same multimillion-dollar federal narcotics case, with Sharrocks a defendant and Donald Brown cooperating with the prosecution. But the killing of Jack Tupper seemed so brutally straightforward that not even Brown, a man light on his feet, could imagine the agility with which Buddy would exploit his split with Sharrocks. And it would have seemed preposterous that Buddy Jacobson would escape from the high-security Brooklyn House of Detention some twenty months later, and be recaptured in Los Angeles, saying he was there to track down Tupper's "real killer." Who was, he said, Donald Brown.

But there was fertile ground in the Jacobson case for fantasy. Other men and women were to come into the affair from even farther afield. Breck Dana Anderson was a venturesome young pilot from Anchorage, Alaska. He moved into 155 East 84th Street because of his crony Joe Margarite. Anderson, as it happens, wasn't even in New York at the time of the murder. This did not prevent him from becoming a suspect in the case the following June when he was careless enough to crash a DC-6—by overshooting the strip at Kanawha, West Virginia, thereby incinerating his cargo. The DC-6 was loaded with ten tons of Colombian marijuana, valued at $8 million.

By the time of the Anderson caper, though, the Jacobson case was so complicated that the crash was just one more knot in a maddening tangle. Everything had seemed so simple at the start; transparent. Jack Tupper was the victim; Buddy Jacobson, mute and defeated, was the murderer; and Melanie Cain, all hard flame, was the woman they both loved. "It's an open-and-shut case," Detective Sullivan told Jimmy Wood, for many years Jacobson's confidant. "Forget it."

Wood was not disposed to do so. "You haven't seen the last of Buddy," he told Sullivan. "He's a genius. And he's fighting for his life."

- II -

Buddy's Tale

*I*n later times Buddy Jacobson would be nicknamed for the borough of his birth: the Brooklyn Cowboy. And what started, perhaps, as a sleek Jockey Club joke would be turned around by an admiring press into a term of pride. It was ironic, however you looked at it. Buddy Jacobson visited Brooklyn as seldom as he could after his youth. And when he talked about Brooklyn, it was of the dark, fantastic city of the old gangsters, and he would tell curious anecdotes; for instance, the manner in which Abe Rellis, key witness against Murder Incorporated, found himself while supposedly under police guard taking an unscheduled flight from a high window in Coney Island's Half Moon Hotel. Of the streets in which he grew up, Buddy spoke seldom.

He was born on December 10, 1930. His mother, Florence, and his father, whose correct name was Joseph, but who was always called Sam, were living in the Steeples apartment house on Ocean Avenue and Avenue K. He was the second in the family—his sister, Rita, is a few years older—and he was to be the last.

The young Howard Jacobson, then known as Howie, went to Midwood High School (some sense, possibly distorted, of this Brooklyn school can be gained from semiautobiographical moments in the work of a later Midwood student, Woody Allen). If Buddy was remarkable, it was in only one thing: the fierceness and tenacity of his competitive streak. "There was no television in those days. Everybody lived on the street," says one of his confidants. "Buddy was the yo-yo champ. He was the handball champ. He was the Ping-Pong champ."

Sam Jacobson was a not particularly successful salesman in the hat business and a small-time gambler. He had all of a salesman's affable manner, and most people who knew both father and son have found the difference a striking one. "Sam Jacobson was different from Buddy," says trainer Frank X.

Pagano. "Sam was an outgoing, regular kind of guy. Bet two dollars on a horse, kid around, have a drink. Buddy was very reserved."

Other acquaintances take a steelier view. "Sam was outgoing, yeah, about as warm as this table," says the textile magnate Bill Levin. Backing up this insight is the coldness and abruptness with which Sam left his wife and took up with a mistress. Buddy's mother was left to support the two kids, while the boy's father and his girlfriend moved just a few doors away. Buddy was then about ten.

In years to come, Buddy would sometimes take a few liberties with the truth where his background was concerned. He would reveal to nubile girls that he was, in fact, not Jewish but Italian, and that the Jacobsons had adopted him. A variation was that he was half Italian and half Indian, an Algonquin from upstate New York. One story, certain to elicit sympathy, had Buddy growing up in an orphanage. In another, his mother had done time in prison. And in yet another, his gangster father had perished, shouting defiance, in a gory shootout with the law.

It was only with a few intimates, and usually a bellyful of wine, that Buddy would hint at the truth: the bitterness he felt about his father's desertion of the family. The experience certainly marked him cruelly.

From an early age, Buddy was in a hurry and he knew just where he would begin. His mother was born Florence Jacobs. She was one of ten children of an immigrant tailor. Three of her brothers—Hirsch, Sidney, and Eugene—trained racehorses. And, in terms of winners saddled, Hirsch Jacobs is the greatest trainer in the history of the U.S. turf. For Buddy the family connection with his uncle Hirsch wasn't quite the same as being born to the purple—that color remains secure on the shoulders of the Jockey Club—but training horses pointed toward a better life than selling hats.

Hirsch Jacobs, an extraordinarily successful man, played an interesting role in what Buddy was to become. His nephew admired and disliked him, copied and contradicted him. And, in the end, it was Buddy who seized his uncle's dominant position in the world of the track.

Hirsch, who was famously genial and not famously imaginative, except where horseflesh was concerned, was born in

1904. His parents had arrived as children from England, where both had lived in Liverpool, a traditional departure point for the New World. Hirsch's birthplace was a house at East 62nd Street and Second Avenue, in what was then one of the slummier sections of Manhattan. Jack Jacobs, who was Hirsch's father and Buddy's grandfather, was a tailor. Hirsch left school at thirteen and became a steam fitter's apprentice. For a hobby, he went into pigeon racing, a popular sport in those days. When Hirsch was sixteen, the older brother of his boss suggested they go into business together: The older man would buy the pigeons, Hirsch would train them. From the beginning, the partnership flourished, the two men consistently winning more than their share of pigeon races. In the winter of 1924, he and his partner took a vacation trip to Havana, where they found themselves frequenting the racetrack at Oriental Park.

Here the older man made a sizable score—some $1,500—and decided to put the money into horseflesh. He claimed a mount called Demijohn, and told Hirsch to train it. At first Hirsch demurred. What did he know about horses? He knew *pigeons*. And as a matter of fact, years later, when Hirsch was known around the track as the Pigeon Man, trainers and owners who had grown up with horses derived no satisfaction from knowing that the number-one trainer in the United States hadn't *looked* at a thoroughbred until he was twenty. "I could identify a hundred pigeons by sight while they were flying," Hirsch would say, explaining how his earlier passion had developed the keenness of his judgment. "It's just having an eye for it. It's been the same way with me with horses."

So Hirsch began to train Demijohn, and by the fall of 1925, he was handling a small stable. A year later, he had his first winner. By the winter of 1927, back in Cuba, Hirsch ran into a turf personality named Colonel Isidore Bieber, better known as B.B. A sometime Broadway ticket scalper, B.B. had become a "sportsman", and big bettor at the track. Using Hirsch's tips, B.B. made himself a bundle at Oriental Park. In due course the Colonel and Hirsch teamed up: B.B. Stables was born.

What ensured Hirsch's rapid rise in the racing world of the 1930s was his discovery that the "claimers"—the so-called claiming races—could be used to spot valuable horseflesh and to buy the horses for reasonable money. What Hirsch was doing, so to speak, was going into thoroughbred racing on the cheap. This was a departure from custom. The best trainers and the best bloodstock had always been in the hands of the well-off racing families—Phippses, Whitneys, Vanderbilts. These families poured vast sums of money into racing, almost always at a substantial loss to themselves. They did this, to use a formula polished with much use, for the improvement of the breed.

Inspired by that noble motive and perhaps the tiniest bit egged on by pride, the energies of the great stables had always been directed toward the famous stakes races. The claiming races interested the rich little. It could safely be said of the older stables that they would rather have had a single winner of the Belmont or the Preakness or the Kentucky Derby than a season full of winners of the lesser races.

But the claimers offer the not-so-rich considerable opportunity. Consider a $40,000 claimer. Any owner who enters a mount in such a race is taking a shot at a winner's purse of, say, $10,000 and risks forcibly selling his horse. Any other owner has the right to "claim" his horse, meaning to buy it for the $40,000 fee. Knowing where to run a cheap horse is a critical part of a trainer's expertise; spotting another man's valuable horse in a cheap race is another.

Claiming races don't get much publicity, and, individually, not even the top $100,000 claimers will generate anything like the betting action that simmers around the stakes races. But it is in these lesser races that most racetrack activity lies. And though Hirsch Jacobs may not have been the first trainer to spot the potential of claimers, he was the first to take full advantage.

"In the 1930s, Hirsch invented a whole new way of training horses," veteran track writer Heywood Hale Broun told me. "He treated cheap horses like expensive ones." Hirsch let his horses eat *grass*. "Hirsch treated cheapsters like champions. He thought nothing of buying a horse for fifteen hundred dollars, taking it to his farm, and spending five thousand dollars on caring for and feeding the horse before running it."

The official statistics for the leading trainers in New York start in 1935. That year Hirsch Jacobs came first, with 104 winners. Between 1935 and 1961 he was numero uno no fewer than twenty-two times. In the five other years, he was second three times and third once. This record is unrivaled.

The other great trainers of the time—Max Hirsch, say, and James "Sunny Jim" Fitzsimmons—come nowhere near it. And all this was at a time when there was no significant competition from California or Florida. Being number one in New York meant being number one. Period.

Of course, the statistics don't tell the entire tale. How exactly could one compare Hirsch Jacobs, who could win a huge number of races with cheap horses, against a trainer for one of the rich stables, who trained fewer horses for the well-publicized stakes races? "It's apples and oranges," says E. Barry Ryan, maverick grandee of the Jockey Club. "Hirsch didn't have Nijinsky. He had horses named Ashtray, Lampshade, and so forth." Ryan himself much admired the red-haired, squeaky-voiced little Hirsch, but many others found galling the fact that he had built his stable from their rejects, that his successes were their lost opportunities. Stymie, for instance. In the summer of '43, Hirsch watched Stymie in three starts. The first two starts he came in last, and in the third next to last. Hirsch claimed him for $1,500. "There's something about him I like," he said. By the end of Stymie's career, the animal had been raced 131 times and had become the world's top money winner, with accumulated purses of $918,485.

In 1948, Hirsch and B.B. did something unprecedented for runners of cheap horses, however successful. They went into direct competition with the old-line horse people, buying a 283-acre spread in Maryland and establishing a breeding farm. They called the place Stymie Manor. Eighteen years later, it was the top breeding operation in the country, with earnings of $1.3 million.

Another famous move came in 1955. Searching was a three-year-old of distinguished ancestry but foot-draggingly slow. Hirsch bought her for $15,000 from Ogden Phipps, then chairman of the Jockey Club. "She was a real delicate filly," Hirsch explained. "The wall of her foot was very thin, and she was afraid that if she ran too hard, the nail of the shoe would go through the wall." Her new owner gave Searching different shoes, and she won him $327,000 before producing more winners as a brood mare.

Yet the red-haired Hirsch was never admitted into the inner ring of the racing world, for all his unbroken success. The Jockey Club never asked Hirsch to be a member. Nor were the reasons too difficult to worry out. There was the fact that

B.B. was so well acquainted with the likes of Arnold Rothstein, who was shot dead while playing high-stakes poker. "The Colonel was in some fairly spectacular coups," Heywood Hale Broun says. "The Jockey Club thought he was a crook."

If Isidore Bieber wasn't exactly one of your Kentucky colonels, neither did Hirsch conform to the niceties expected in what was approvingly known as a "hardboot trainer." His clothing, for instance. "He didn't wear the cowboy attire favored by the other trainers," Broun says. "Hirsch would wear a blue serge suit. He looked like any other Jewish businessman from Brooklyn."

Hirsch Jacobs seemed not to care. Of his six brothers, all but one followed him to the track, and they all began their careers by working for him. Even his father, retired from tailoring, was working at B.B. Stables as a night watchman and walking horses in the early morning when he was well into his eighties. Indeed, almost the only family member Hirsch never put on his payroll was the man who was to supplant him: Jack's grandson and his own nephew, Buddy Jacobson.

It was Gene Jacobs—he had by then set up on his own—who was to give Buddy his start. Gene Jacobs is in his brother's mold. The same rounded look, reddish hair, and nonhorsy wardrobe. On our first meeting, which was at Belmont, his suit was the same piercing blue as his eyes. "I *created* Buddy," he said simply, his voice betraying neither pleasure nor regret.

Buddy had already worked at Gene's stalls when he was eleven years old, walking "hots"—horses that have been exercised—and doing the usual earthy chores. A few years later he decided school was a waste of time, and Buddy Jacobson was always to abhor wasting time. He left Midwood High without staying long enough for a diploma, and took a job with Gene in Florida.

Gene Jacobs gave Buddy the job because he was family, but found no cause to regret his decision. "I put him on when I didn't need him," he told me. "And he just *made* himself needed. He was a very hard worker, very devoted to his job. He did whatever had to be done."

In certain other respects, Buddy seemed unusual. The Jacobs clan is family-family. Not Buddy. "He was inward,"

Gene Jacobs says. "He never really opened up." Certainly Gene Jacobs had no idea of the intensity of Buddy's ambition. As stableboy, Buddy had been earning a starting wage of $25 a week. With unusual speed, he became foreman of the stables and an assistant trainer. And with almost equal rapidity, or so it seems to Gene Jacobs, he left the security of his family and started out on his own.

Buddy got his assistant trainer's license in November 1952. The first horses that he trained were owned by his sister, who was married and called Rita Costello. His first win was in New York with a horse called Teddy Powell, after a popular band leader of the period. Then Buddy decided to try his luck down in Florida. He took his horse down to Tropical Park, where, as chance had it, Teddy Powell was stabled next to a mount called Elixir.

When Elixir's trainer fell ill, Buddy began to handle the horse. "I put Elixir in a couple of races—always got a piece of the purse—and then won the Robert E. Lee Handicap with him at better than twenty to one," Buddy said, much later. "That did it. I was in the training business to stay." Work hours are grueling at the track, with stablehands required to begin their day at five in the morning. Buddy was there with them. "He worked real hard," a trainer told me. "You'd see him there all hours, tubbing horses, doing the most menial jobs. When a stablehand becomes a trainer, sometimes they shy away from that sort of work. Buddy just did it."

In the mid-1950s, Buddy married Joan Miller, an attractive girl with dark hair whose father owned a boardinghouse. Their first child was David. Buddy had settled down. People who knew him during this period vividly remember the domesticity of the scene: Buddy eating his supper with his family; Buddy watching television; Buddy early to bed.

Buddy Jacobson, the 1950s paterfamilias. Admirable, except that the fires were there—banked, maybe, but burning out of sight. One acquaintance of Buddy's in his days of bourgeois bliss, Jack Hershey by name, remembers playing table tennis with him. Ping-Pong champion of the Brooklyn streets though Buddy might have been, Hershey could still beat him.

"And he *hated* to lose," Hershey recalls gleefully. "Every time I beat him he would almost go crazy. He wanted to be the best. The best of everything."

Bill Frankel was the first owner who seems to have picked

up on Buddy's zeal. Frankel was a Wall Street operator, and a hot one; an over-the-counter stock trader. In 1958 he happened to be looking for a trainer for the horses he and his wife, Marion, were buying. And so Buddy acquired not only his first thumpingly rich owner, but a man who had learned from the market that there are times to be patient. "When I started with the Frankels, I won only one race in the first eight months," Buddy was to say. "They never complained. You don't find good sports like them every day."

Frankel obviously sensed that there was a certain toughness in this quiet-spoken young man. He was a savvy owner who enjoyed the idea of building up a trainer. "Buddy learned a great deal from Frankel," says Bill Levin, the Wall Street man's partner in various ventures. "Not training, but how to *place* horses in races. How to *run* them."

Bill Frankel conceived a great affection for Buddy and Joan Jacobson. Some horsemen say that he made the young trainer. Whatever, Buddy was soon making a mark, and in 1960 he finally entered the record book when the New York Racing Association list of leading trainers ranked him second, with forty-eight winners. Hirsch Jacobs was number one, with a convincing eighty-six wins.

In 1962, Buddy came in second again. This time he had sixty-four winners, beating Hirsch, who had sixty-three, into third place. The media began to pay Buddy attention. WINNERS CIRCLE LIKE HOME TO JACOBSON, announced the *New York Post* after seven successful days for the Frankels at Aqueduct. And Buddy began to give the media just what they wanted, a touch of iconoclasm. "Any trainer can win," he said cockily. "The only trick to winning more is more horses."

What, a reporter asked, had Buddy learned from his uncles Hirsch, Gene, and Sidney?

"They've taught me nothing," Buddy said. "They don't come near me at the track. I'm out to beat them, and they know it."

Frank X. Pagano, who met him at about this time, and who was soon to become his assistant and confidant, was impressed by this braggadocio. "Buddy had a consuming desire to be top trainer," he says. "He wanted to be the best at whatever he did." The Jacobs clan would agree.

"Buddy *emulated* Hirsch," explains Frank Pagano. "Hirsh ate an apple a day. So did Buddy." Hirsch didn't smoke, and wouldn't allow smoking in his barn. Nor would Buddy.

Hirsch, once something of a punter, didn't gamble. Buddy not only wouldn't gamble, but refused even to give tips on the races, or let anybody who worked for him read the *Morning Telegraph*.

The next year, 1963, was Buddy's best yet. One of his mounts was Palenque 3rd, which he had bought for $5,000 the previous year. Palenque won twelve of fourteen races, bringing home $29,780. Then there was Bupers, a two-year-old owned by Ogden Phipps. "I got that old feeling that this might be a distance runner," Buddy told a journalist. He bought Bupers at Saratoga Springs for $16,500. That September, Bupers, the horse that Phipps had sold off, waltzed away with the Futurity at Belmont. The purse was $146,000. And Buddy Jacobson, maestro of the cheap claimers, had won a classic stakes race.

Buddy Jacobson was the nation's top trainer in 1963. He had almost twice as many winners as Hirsch Jacobs, who ran second to him in New York. Hirsch was never to occupy first place again.

Buddy moved. The building in which he and Joan Jacobson took up residence was the Silver Towers, which lies a handy few minutes from Aqueduct. It was the grandest building in Queens at that time. Gene and Sidney Jacobs live there still. Buddy bought a couple of apartments and knocked them together. When he was done, the place boasted a tiled hallway, a conservatory, and a large balcony. David and Douglas had their own rooms. Buddy had two German shepherds, named Goniff and Shamus, and a live-in maid from Sweden. Pure class.

He wore a suit and tie to the track in those days. His hair was trim, his mustache ungrown. Buddy worked hard and would go straight home. The quiet life. He had, before his marriage, never dated much. And here he was—breadwinner. "He'd be home at nine o'clock every night," Frank Pagano says, "put his pajamas on, and watch TV. And never go out. *Never* go out."

Joan Jacobson worked hard, too. Not only did she keep house, but she kept Buddy's books. "Well, what happened was she wanted to go out once in a while," says Pagano. "Just to a movie—nothing fancy. But Buddy didn't care to. He only loved the horses."

Buddy apparently had found his niche. He now bought himself a place in the country, the Old Westbury Horse Farm, a long low building sitting on some twenty acres of pasture, just a few miles from Mineola, New York.

Several people whose names are illustrious in the world of the thoroughbred horse have spreads roundabout. Ogden Phipps and Winston Guest, for instance, but Buddy didn't give a damn about that. The $125,000 he paid for the farm was $20,000 or so more than it was then worth, but Buddy didn't give a damn about that either. If Buddy Jacobson wanted something enough, the cost didn't matter.

Bill Frankel used to come out to the farm on Sundays. He and Buddy would look over the horses, and then feast on bagels, lox, and cream cheese. Sometimes Frankel brought along packages of prime beefsteak, and this impressed Buddy, because the steak would be a present from some Las Vegas casino. "They would send Frankel a box of dice," Frank Pagano says. "And they would send him meat and stuff. And Buddy would say, 'Gee! This guy's a high roller.'"

Buddy Jacobson was still withdrawn, still a driven man, in his early thirties, but now he was getting a sense of other possibilities, and the sense was the stronger for the length of the delay. Buddy had never allowed himself an adolescence; now it was as if a picture were forming: Buddy Jacobson's Vision of the Good Life.

For instance. Because of his increasing success with the Frankels' horses, Buddy had been acquiring some additional owners. One of his patrons was Dave Shaer, an owner who would naturally gravitate toward this successful, unpolished trainer. Shaer was a self-made man in his sixties, a shoe manufacturer from Brockton, Massachusetts. "He was a fat, crude guy with a pockmarked face," says track writer Jack Mann. "But Buddy saw his opportunity with Shaer." Bill Frankel was mostly interested in the claimers. With Shaer, Buddy could move into the stakes races.

Dave Shaer "bought horses like he bought broads," Jack Mann says. At the beginning of 1964, Mann ran into the shoe manufacturer and Buddy down in Florida, at the time of the sale of two-year-olds at Hialeah. Shaer's fingers were dangerous with diamond rings, and a diamond stud the size of a cocktail onion winked on his tie.

"Are you looking for horses?" Mann asked.

"If I am," Shaer said, "no son of a bitch is going to outbid me."

Sometimes Jack Mann would go with Shaer and his party, Buddy included, to nightclubs in Miami Beach. One night, the hot ticket was for Jimmy Durante, who was playing the Doral.

"It was just impossible to get those tickets," Jack Mann says. "And, naturally, Shaer had a ringside table for twenty-two. He had this big broad there, a six-foot showgirl type, called Bonnie. There was a bottle of Scotch every eighteen inches. George Raft was one of the entourage. The whole number.

"Durante comes out and does his thing. Suddenly he wants George Raft to do a soft-shoe with him."

Jack Mann was sitting close to Raft. Buddy Jacobson was on the other side. It was Mann and Buddy who lifted George Raft onto the stage. Mann looked across at Buddy as Jimmy Durante and Raft slid into some venerable Broadway routine, and he was startled. Buddy's face was alive. He was studying everything—the club, the merriment, the glossy available girls —as though it were a menu, and he a hungry man about to eat.

"I'm sure of one thing," says Jack Mann. "This was the moment Buddy decided the way he was going to live. It was a logical decision. I've known guys who drifted into fucking around—Buddy's the first guy I've ever seen who made a conscious, intellectual choice."

About this time, Buddy decided to take a Dale Carnegie course. Now, the technologies of the will that Carnegie deploys in *How to Make Friends and Influence People* are fairly basic stuff. But Werner Erhard of est is just one person who has admitted his debt to Carnegie. Buddy did no less.

"He said the Carnegie course changed his way of dealing with everything," says Frank Pagano. "Positive power . . . *the power of positive thinking*. Buddy spoke about it quite a number of times, saying how important it was. He became very *dynamic*. Even some of the owners were afraid to talk to him. They were kind of mesmerized. He created the illusion that he was a special kind of person. You didn't want to argue with him."

Bob Wood, who was to know him better even than his brother Jimmy, thinks there was more to it than pop psych. "It was a combination of things," he says. "It was success. All of a sudden something happened to his head."

* * *

Buddy Jacobson's dominance at the track was to last seven years. In that period, he was the leading trainer in the nation three times and the winner in New York five times (twice he came in second). In the eyes of many of the old order, both owners and trainers, Buddy's emergence was emblematic of a new way of doing things at the track—and not a way they found appealing.

No son of a bitch had outbid Dave Shaer, for instance, at that Hialeah two-year-olds sale in February of 1964. He had raised those diamond-encrusted fingers and spent $70,000 on a well-bred chestnut filly called Treasure Chest.

The morning after the sale, Jack Mann had gone down to the stables. It was early. Buddy was outside his stalls with one of his grooms, who was hosing down two horses. One was Treasure Chest. The other was a seven-year-old gelding—by nothing out of nothing, as Mann puts it—that Buddy had claimed for $3,500.

"The gelding was real dark—almost black," Mann says. "The sun was just coming up, and you could see the sunlight bouncing off the chestnut filly. Beautiful."

Mann made some remark about how curious it was to see two animals of such dissimilar breeding getting the same treatment.

"We're very democratic here," Buddy told him. "We treat them all equally, regardless of their background."

Mann pressed him. After all those claimers, wasn't it fairly exciting to be training what might be a classic horse?

Buddy was contemptuous. "Bullshit!" he said. "They're all the same. They're machines . . . numbers . . . goods.

"A horse can be useful—can win you some money—for one period of maybe three months, six at the most, in his life. The trick is to use him for that period and then get rid of him."

Machines, numbers, goods.

Buddy's effrontery was calculated, of course. It was a slap both at Hirsch—"This is livestock, not machines," Hirsch had said—and at all the traditions of the track. Buddy operated his stables like a small factory. "He was successful because he had a platoon system," says Tommy Trotter, who was NYRA's racing secretary at the time. "He stabled close to forty horses. He would run a string, and there were always fifteen or twenty backups on his farm."

Pat O'Brien, an old Jacobson adversary, once in charge of allocating stalls, was more negative. "He claimed an inordinate number of horses," he says. "It was like a hot-bed hotel.

"He had a theory. It was using the horse as a piece of merchandise, and turning the merchandise over as quickly as possible. You didn't know what horses even were in his barn. Five would go out, and six would come back, and four would go out, and seven would go to Jersey. It was a merry-go-round."

There is, moreover, an etiquette to claiming. When Buddy started, there were some twenty top trainers, the sort of men who had trained for the same owners for decades. There were gentlemen's agreements. You weren't supposed to claim on the first day or the last day of a meeting—that sort of thing.

Buddy enjoyed making it plain that he was no gentleman. "We're here to make money," he used to announce. One of his specialties was claiming horses from people who were getting them in shape for one particular race. "He'd let the other guy do all the work," a writer says. "And then he'd go in, and—wham!"

Often, increasingly often as time went by, Buddy wouldn't bother to look at the mounts he was claiming. He was never in the Hirsch Jacobs class as a judge of horses' legs. "The PP is enough for me," he would say. PP stands for past performance. Meaning go by the records. "And Buddy would claim from anybody," a friend says. "He would claim from people who only owned one horse. He wouldn't care."

It began to seem, in fact, that he did not care about much. Buddy's uncaring was like his charm—both a character trait and a manipulative technique. His casualness worked splendidly on owners. He let it be known that he was picky. "I don't want to handle your horses," he told one owner publicly. "I don't like your operation."

The indifference seemed remarkable. Bob Wood remembers another, better-known owner asking Buddy to handle his horses.

"I've got enough horses," Buddy said. "I'm not interested."

You might call this the reverse whammy. The owner was sucked in, and grew insistent.

"Okay," Buddy agreed. "I'll take your horses. But only if I can do things my way." He wanted only one thing.

Control.

Buddy would *get* the control. Everything would be fine, as long as he kept on winning. His admirers and detractors agree his success was based on two talents: knowing in which race to place a horse, and a keen interest in veterinary medicine. They agree on little else.

Buddy Jacobson, detractors say, was a "drop-down" man. This means that he would buy a $20,000 horse and run it in a $10,000 race. That way he might get a win, but risked the horse. "He was successful for Buddy Jacobson," says another trainer. "But he wasn't successful for the owners. He didn't care for the owners' pocketbook at all."

Others don't agree. Sure, Buddy would claim a horse at $7,000, and race it at $3,000 and win. But a lot of trainers would try that, and *wouldn't* win. And sometimes Buddy would claim a horse for $10,000 and run it for $15,000, and win that, too.

Buddy was also a willing innovator, and sometimes there was a touch of fantasy to his innovations. One assistant remembers Buddy X-raying a horse's leg, not for a microsecond, but for hours, just to see what would happen: as though flesh were something he could master. The assistant never saw the animal again. Brochures from the Department of Agriculture explaining new wrinkles in medication, articles in medical journals—all the material that the hard-boot trainers would pointedly ignore—Buddy would *read*. "Anything that's new, I'll try," he said.

Buddy was pumping cortisone into a horse's joints before almost anybody. Anything to give him an edge. And Buddy Jacobson, like Hirsch Jacobs, was his own vet. He would decide which horse was to get vitamins.

"I want ten percent iron," he might say. "And two percent calcium."

The vet might disagree, suggesting some brew of his own.

"No," Buddy would say. "Give him what I tell you."

It was always a matter of doing things Buddy's way.

Buddy was inventive in all respects. Breeding is an antiseptic sort of business. Clinical. But it once entered Buddy's mind to wonder whether it might not be more, well, primitive. One day he had a mare running in both the first and eighth races. At the end of the first, he and Pagano hustled the steaming animal into a van, and they raced out to the farm. "I held the mare," Pagano remembers, "and he brought the stallion out." They were back in time for the eighth race, in which the mare was *not* a winner.

Frank Pagano was Buddy's only confidant for many years. Most trainers, Pagano explains, need a confidant, somebody to tell them they claimed the right horse, ran the right race. But Buddy especially needed a confidant. "When Buddy got somebody close to him, he wanted them around *always*. He didn't want to go any place alone."

Pagano found Buddy impressive, but bewildering. It was as if his disdain for established procedures was growing with every success. There are protocols on the track. It's a place where the bitterest of foes will exchange polite nods. And Buddy wouldn't. Sometimes this self-possession seemed barely normal. For instance, every trainer will talk to his jockey after a race. If he has won, he will wish to pose with his jockey for the photograph. If he has lost, he will want to find out why.

Not so Buddy Jacobson. "I can see what happened," he would say. He would just walk away, with his quick peculiar gait, hands stuck into his pockets, head tilted down, black eyes unseeing. A picture of Buddy, standing next to the owner, the jockey, and the winner? Forget it. But what many found extraordinary was Buddy's total disdain for jockeys. "A monkey could ride as good a race as a top jockey," he would say. "I don't congratulate the pilot of a plane for getting me to New York."

"If he lost, he wouldn't go up to the owner and say, 'Boy! Did you *see* what that jock did to our horse?' " Pagano says. "You know what he would say? 'I didn't have him trained enough.' " Pagano recalls, "So then it was his responsibility. He had complete control of the situation. He would never blame, and he would never praise. Never!"

Even Buddy's owners could find him intimidating. "Does he like my horse?" they would ask. Pagano explains, "All Buddy would tell them was: 'Every time my horse is running, he's *running*. Don't ask me if I like him today. If I didn't I wouldn't have him in the race. Every time I run a horse, my ego is on the line. I want to win.' " Forget the sport. "The only sport in this business is getting the money," he once said. "You don't have to be bright in this business, you just have to pay attention."

The press ate up Buddy's disrespect, and it was now he began to learn how to handle the press. Actually, he wasn't too subtle. Say something sufficiently pointed and a paper would print it. "Buddy wasn't scared of the press," Jack Mann says. "He was confident that he was smarter than the press. He could use them. If he wanted to give somebody the shaft, he could use the press to do it."

Worst of all, Buddy claimed to despise the animals from which he made a living. "You can't have an attachment to a horse," he said. One morning, Buddy was out at the backstretch. There were some other trainers around, dressed as some trainers like to dress—in spurs, chaps, and five-gallon hats—and sitting atop ponies that gleamed like silk cushions.

"Buddy," asked a reporter, "when are you going to get yourself a cowboy suit and ride around like that?"

Buddy snorted. "What? Me get up on one of those big, clumsy animals? Are you out of your mind?"

Buddy enjoyed such baiting and boasted to sportswriter Pete Axthelm of Ogden Phipps' displeasure when he learned Buddy had bought one of his foals. "I'm thinking of calling it Ogden Flips," he said. Except, of course, that Buddy was famous for never remembering a horse's name. Horses were just numbers: machines, numbers, goods.

This indifference was only partial truth. "That was a game, you know," says Frank Pagano. "Buddy knew every horse, and everything about him. But he didn't want people to know that. Buddy wanted to create an image, an illusion."

This he had done. On August 15, 1964, an organization of track writers gave a dinner in his honor and elected him Trainer of the Year. In April of the following year, he was chosen to represent trainers on the David Susskind show, then called *Open End*. Buddy had achieved success. Now he wanted something else: power.

His opportunity came in 1967. Up for grabs was the presidency of the New York division of the Horseman's Protective and Benevolent Association. The HPBA, the guild to which almost all trainers and backstretch employees belong, was designed to represent their interests in negotiations with owners, New York State, and other interested parties. Actually, the HPBA was a tame pony trotting alongside the New York Racing Association, which was itself controlled by the membership of the Jockey Club. But Buddy Jacobson had plans to give the HPBA teeth.

The election went along ethnic lines. The grand old racing families, with their English and Irish trainers, had previously controlled the organization. But it was gambling that produced the state revenue, and most of the gambling was on the cheap horses. Here Jewish and Italian names were predominant. Buddy Jacobson was promoted as the plucky Brooklyn David taking on the WASP Goliath. He ran for the HPBA presidency challenging a nephew of one of the titans of the Jockey Club, George D. Widener, and he won. Buddy had reached another peak, and it seemed he could only go higher.

But Buddy Jacobson's hurry was as great as ever. He was making some $100,000 a year, but the idea that this might improve his life did not occur to him. "He was a very intricate man," remarks someone who sold him feed. "I had to speak with him every month, because he never wanted to pay his bills. He always had a story. He was always working on a big deal. That was Buddy—always cash-poor."

All that Frank Pagano can remember Buddy's buying for himself was a hi-fi unit. "Buddy, when he had the most money he had, he never had money," he says. "If he had some money, he would buy a tractor for the farm. He would overextend himself." It was as if Buddy was deliberately creating greater and greater pressure on himself. What he wanted was one thing: *more.*

As far as manipulation went, Buddy approached genius. The manner he had of cutting certain other trainers dead and not talking to his help at the track was not, as some charitably assumed, a rudeness bred from shyness. It was naked strategy. "I don't want to know these guys," Buddy explained to a crony. "This way I have an *aura.*"

This process of severing ordinary human ties was to continue. Buddy's little fling with domesticity, the Silver Towers idyll, was doomed. Suddenly he was aware that he was a well-known name in a glamor industry. A celebrity. People wanted to shake his hand in restaurants. The withdrawn youth who had seldom dated was coursing with Positive Energies, and looking around with an avid eye.

A cheerful hustler from the track—sometimes a jock's agent, sometimes a horse broker—fixed Buddy Jacobson up with his first extramarital adventure, an airline stewardess. "She went to bed with him the first night," says the hustler. "He couldn't believe it. Here he was in the hay with this gorgeous eighteen-year-old girl. It turned his head."

Buddy Jacobson's head was so turned around, in fact, that

he paid the rent for the stewardess's apartment for a while; indeed, until he discovered that this particular young woman was not morally abnormal, and that there were plenty of others just as uninhibited. It was as if he had opened a door with an enchanted key. And then he met Rhonda Rieger, a stewardess with Eastern. He invited her out to the track to look at his horses. Rhonda came, they talked, and went out on a date. Buddy Jacobson could, he was finding, be seductive. Rhonda left the airline and went to live and work with Buddy Jacobson.

She was attractive, a slightly built blonde with a turned-up nose. Quiet. Outspokenness in a woman was never something that Buddy cherished. Also, she was a dogged worker, getting up in the raw early-morning light to do the books out at the stables. Nor did she shy away from physical work. Horsemen would see her scrubbing, on her hands and knees. It was not the lure of material things that drew Rhonda Rieger to Buddy.

Joan Jacobson soon discovered the affair. It became a problem of choice. And Buddy simply walked away from the Silver Towers just as he had from Midwood High. It was as if he had taken a pair of shears to a chapter in his life. (After the Tupper murder, I asked Buddy if he had been getting any moral support from his wife, Joan. "I haven't seen her for ten, fifteen years," he said, unconcernedly.) Buddy and Rhonda took an apartment in the Stevens House, an apartment building in Queens.

Nor was this affair the only new terrain that Buddy was exploring. His racing success was breeding a sense of invulnerability. He had the feeling he could do anything, and it was now that his fancy was caught by discothèques. This craze was just hitting Manhattan the first time around. It was the epoch of Le Club and Arthur, Cheetah and the Hippopotamus. One day Buddy took Frank Pagano to visit Sam Lefrak, now one of his more important owners. Lefrak was a builder, a man of abrasive bonhomie, and at this time landlord to a quarter-million New Yorkers. Aside from his string of horses, he had millions in art, more in Texas oil, and an eighty-five-foot yacht. Buddy was trying to talk Lefrak into letting him put a discothèque into one of his buildings.

Lefrak chose to be jocular. Win so-and-so many races for me and you can have the lease, he told Buddy.

"Well," Buddy said, "How much will I have to pay?"

"I'll give it to you for a ham sandwich," Lefrak said.

Buddy was quiet. Later he asked over and over again, "Frank, what do you think he *means?*" It does not seem to have occurred to Buddy that anybody else could be as willfully obscure as himself. Other plans proliferated. Buddy was going to start an advertising agency. He was going to make a racetrack documentary movie. He was going to start, yes, a model agency.

This last project did, in fact, briefly come to fruition. Buddy took an office in the mid-1960s in a pleasant townhouse on Manhattan's East 62nd Street, and printed up business cards indicating that he was operating a secretarial agency and model school. Business was sluggish, so he placed a small ad in *The Village Voice*, requesting "Golden Girls," and promising travel and short hours. The building was soon thronged. "The girls had to be *perfect*," Pagano said. Things didn't work out, though. Buddy, contemptuous as usual of the ordinary, time-wasting procedures, hadn't troubled with the proper licenses. He was forced to close the place down, but not without noting the pleasures that the modeling business afforded.

But Buddy had by no means forgotten about starting up a discothèque. A gaggle of racing folk—they included a trainer, a blacksmith, the writer Pete Axthelm, and Bobby Ussery, the jockey—agreed to go into partnership with him. It was a handshake deal, like most deals on the track. Buddy was to take fifty percent, the others would divvy up the rest.

Looking for premises, Buddy alighted on a place in the prosperous suburb of Great Neck, Long Island. It was called the Bayview Inn, and the owner, who had not been doing well, was keen to sell. This was April 1966. It takes time, naturally, for the State Liquor Authority to satisfy itself on the moral worth of a would-be club owner so that the necessary licenses can be issued, and Buddy agreed that he would move both quietly and sedately, acting as "manager" and without pay, until everything was in order. Frank Pagano, drawing on some experience of his own as a bar owner, underlined this. "Until the liquor license is approved," he told Buddy, "you have to keep a low profile." Buddy kept a low profile by moving into the Bayview Inn, tossing out the owner's furniture, and tearing down various walls. He had not, at this stage, paid the original owner one cent. He then let it be known that he was open for business—by way of a barrage of advertisements, including radio commercials and a banner strung from an airplane. Real low profile stuff.

Even so, there might not have been a problem with the license, but for an incident. Some local dignitary—Pagano believes it was the mayor—came by to check the place out and asked to be introduced to Buddy Jacobson, the celebrity.

But Buddy just didn't want to be bothered with a small-town politician, and played one of his games. "Tell him that guy's Buddy," he said, pointing to a workman putting the finishing touches on the redecorating.

The mayor departed, steaming. The problems of Buddy's Bayview, as it was now called, began that very weekend. It was a pity, because Buddy's hunch had been right, and the discothèque was mobbed from the day it opened.

But he was swiftly charged with selling alcoholic drink to a minor: a criminal charge. Buddy hired a lawyer, Irwin Klein, known as Win, an ebullient figure well known in the sporting world. A barman took the fall on that charge, and Buddy got away scot-free.

But the reprieve was only temporary. The original owner came back into the Bayview and found that Buddy had failed to turn over the proper receipts. He took his license back, put new locks on the doors, and Buddy was out of the discothèque business.

Not for long. Buddy's next place, Chanticleer, was in Brooklyn, under the Verrazano-Narrows Bridge. It could pack in four or five hundred. Buddy had the room painted black, and light machines flipped flickering patterns onto the ceiling and walls. There was a tape deck and live bands, and Buddy, who would never take the floor himself, would stand watching the young girls dance. Buddy was not a dancing man.

It was now that Buddy began to carry fake IDs, papers that cut a decade from his age. All around him was this world he had created, full of sexual promise. Rhonda was still there, doing the books, washing the glassware, sleeping a few hours, then reporting for work in the stables, but the grinding work was beginning to tell. He had to get rid of her, Buddy told Pete Axthelm; "She's losing her looks." Then Buddy came to grief again. Simply, he was trading on the license issued to the previous owner, the Restfair Lounge. "That license was canceled on February 14, 1968," says Commissioner Gedda of the State Liquor Authority. "By the time Jacobson applied, it was too late to renew."

One last note in the discothèque drama: Buddy had also not bothered to pay the legal fees of Win Klein. The lawyer was owed several thousand dollars and got a judgment—a lien on Buddy's horses.

The trainer immediately got into contact with Klein. "Take a horse," he proposed.

"Give me *half* a horse, Buddy," countered the lawyer.

This meant that Buddy would have to stable the animal and feed it, but that Win Klein would pocket half the winnings. The deal was done. The lawyer accepted a horse named Stay Away War.

A vet examined the mount and told Win Klein that he was the proud co-owner of a horse which had the use of three good legs. Stay Away War raced twice, but might as well have stayed in the paddock. What Klein took away from the experience was a considerable respect for Jacobson. "Buddy's a brilliant man," he says.

About this time, a civil suit was brought against Buddy by his once-so-jocular owner Sam Lefrak.

"When Buddy stuck to training, he was super," Lefrak told me. "He won a lot of races. But when he became involved in . . . certain deals, there were infractions of the law. The aggravation just wasn't worth it."

What sort of infractions? In one instance, Buddy, according to Lefrak, had bought a horse called Bleacherite from a horse farm. He had charged Lefrak $30,000, paid the farm $25,000, and pocketed the change. In another instance, Buddy claimed that he had made a sale of four horses to a certain person, whose name was unknown as either an owner or trainer. There was speculation that the name might be a code-name for a Bahamas bank account, and it was commented on that the name much resembled Rhonda's, but reversed. "You'll have to get out of state," Buddy urged, seizing an opportunity. "They may make you testify." Rhonda, who was pregnant with his baby, duly went home for a spell.

The spell was to be a long one.

Apart from this, Buddy treated the Lefrak suit as he was to treat all legal problems—indifferently. His disregard said that he, Buddy, was unassailable, his opponents not worth his contempt, and he was right: Soon the civil suit lapsed.

Buddy Jacobson, prince of the track. In six years he had been the leading New York trainer five times, settling for second place in 1966. He was the vocal president of the New York HPBA, and the more the racing hierarchy detested him, the more he was admired by the proletariat.

Buddy's payroll now ran to twenty, including his mother, whom he paid $50 a week for secretarial services, Joe Porter, a skilled assistant trainer, and Bob Wood, who was inheriting the role of confidant-in-chief from Frank Pagano, and he now had some five dozen horses out in Old Westbury. New York University had even been induced to give diploma credits for a course given at the farm by the New York Counseling Service, an organization composed of Buddy Jacobson and Bob Wood, which offered a course in training. It took place on weekends, lasted two months, and cost $600. Ten hopefuls enrolled at once, and the actual teaching was done by Bob Wood. What the students mostly got to do was muck out the stalls. "But they were happy to pay. They felt they were getting close to the great Buddy Jacobson. . . ."

Wood still sounds incredulous at the memory. Buddy's abilities at getting others to do his dirty work were becoming phenomenal.

Consider those wondrous holiday weekends at Old Westbury. Buddy's young sons might be out there, and a few girls—since Rhonda's departure had left him free to devote more time to this growing appetite—and there would be important people from the track, some of the owners, jockeys' agents, racing officials, and Buddy had his own idea about what made for a holiday weekend: work.

"All right, you guys will do the stalls," a veteran horseman remembers Buddy saying. "And you . . . you can drive the tractor." The track personage who got to drive the tractor was overjoyed. "I can drive the *tractor!*" he crowed.

He was as determinedly controversial as ever. Buddy Jacobson was the first man, naturally, to give a female jockey a ride in New York. The year was 1968, and the jockey was a quiet girl called Barbara Jo Rubin. Buddy announced that he was going to give her a ride at Belmont on a horse called Bravy Galaxy. The race was on a Saturday, when the crowds are largest, and there was a rush of publicity. Predictably, it was favorable. Gallant Buddy.

On the morning of the race, though, Buddy felt uneasy; not about the rider, but the horse. Bravy Galaxy had a funny sort of walk. Buddy thought about scratching the mount, but decided against it, and watched the race from an inconspicuous vantage point beneath the stands. Bravy Galaxy won by three to four lengths, paying $23 and change. Buddy scuttled out and, just for once, was agreeable to having his picture taken.

Robyn Smith was next. Her legend was already brewing. She was supposedly a gamine out in California, tempted by movie contracts, and a prodigy in the saddle. Buddy sent for her: He was going to make her a star. An apartment was readied for her arrival in his building, and he sent Bobby Wood out to pick her up at JFK International.

Wood drove back with her. She had her two pet rats with her. As best he can recall, they were called Pepper and Salt. Buddy took one look, and drew Wood aside. "Get her out of here," he said.

"Buddy, she just got here," Bob Wood said, floundering.

"Get her out of here. Take her to a motel. I never want to see her again."

Wood made Robyn Smith some excuses and booked her into a place behind the Aqueduct racetrack, until Buddy had arranged to have her shipped out to Philadelphia for "more training". The rats went along with her. She never did get to ride for Buddy in New York.

Buddy gave Barbara Jo Rubin a few more rides, and that was that. He had always said that a monkey could do as well as any jockey. So could a woman. "The experiment is over," he said. "I proved my point. It doesn't take any great skill."

This was March 1969, and his remark was typical—affronting at one and the same time male jockeys, female jockeys, and the whole racing community. Buddy Jacobson had begun to radiate contempt.

Buddy now decided that he could do just as well at the track with less effort. He was getting up later, and he would seldom return to his barn for a second visit in the evening. He had stopped reading the latest pamphlets about veterinary medication. Instead of watching the races, he had taken to claiming favorites—going, literally, by the book.

He was hasty. "If a horse broke down, he'd get rid of it,"

says another trainer. "He wouldn't wait and see if it improved. He was *impatient*." Worst of all, he had taken to training by telephone. A fellow trainer recalls being out at Virginia, where he had a few horses running, and Buddy had nineteen. Buddy would telephone him with instructions, making decisions about horses he could not even see.

Bill Frankel, who had been Jacobson's first big-time owner, was becoming increasingly disturbed. His own horses, he felt, were getting short shrift on Buddy's merry-go-round. Moreover, he and his wife had liked and respected Joan Jacobson. Buddy's increasingly frenzied quest of the one-night stand was not to their taste.

The Frankels could have done without the time Buddy brought a model to the paddock at Aqueduct. She was called Lynne, or Sharon, or Sherry, one of those centerfold names. The paddock is a clubby patch of turf where owners admire their horses. Buddy and his model cut through the tweeds, cords, and Dunhill suits with striking effect. Buddy's hair was in its usual yippie tangle and he was wearing his worn blue jeans, and Lynne/Sharon/Sherry was sporting rings on her fingers, an awe-inducing microskirt, and a rose between her teeth. Enough was enough. The Frankels decided to get a new trainer.

The slippage of owners continued. It isn't news when an owner decides to change trainers. Sam Lefrak, as Buddy carefully pointed out, had changed trainers nine times in five years. But first one owner left him, then another, even though Buddy was still winning an enormous number of races.

There was one owner for whom Buddy had been doing particularly well. He was not untypical of Buddy's patrons, a prosperous Pontiac dealer. "A nice, middle-aged guy with a mustache—Italian fellow," says Frank Pagano. "Buddy was claiming horses for him, and winning a lot of races. And the horses were moving up. They weren't being dropped down."

Normally Buddy would never talk racing business nowadays, even to Frank Pagano, but he did say one thing. "I know I'll never lose this guy," he said. "I keep winning races for him." The Pontiac dealer made his farewell the very next day.

"That really shocked Buddy," Frank Pagano says. "But there was a lot of pressure around the track. People were saying that Buddy was against the NYRA. They felt he was a troublemaker."

In short, the pressures upon which Buddy seemed to thrive were building up. That same spring, among the owners out at Aqueduct was the apparel magnate Noel Bernstein. He not only employed Buddy as a trainer, but regarded him, and still regards him, as a close friend. Among Buddy's horses was a stallion: Noel Bernstein owned a share.

One day, Bernstein was out at the track, discussing the studding operation with another fellow in the syndicate.

A man approached the two of them. He was Pat Lynch, then head of press relations for the New York Racing Association, and what he had to say was short but not sweet.

"If you boys want to get along here," he told them, "it would be better if you would disassociate yourself from Buddy Jacobson."

Much later, Noel Bernstein was asked what he had said to Lynch.

"Nothing," he said. "I was in shock."

Buddy had created an image, no doubt about it, but he wasn't bothered. He knew that he was smarter than anybody.

Buddy Jacobson was now sharing an apartment with Bob Wood in the Towne House, a building in Kew Gardens, one of the more prosperous neighborhoods in Queens, with restaurants and lively bars, and brick apartment buildings the color of smoked salmon. The Towne House, with its grandiose name and a touch of marble on the frontage, was one of the better buildings, but Buddy hadn't been drawn there by status. The fact is the Towne House was so packed with airline stewardesses that it was known as the Stew Zoo.

Though he had spent his adolescence on horses, the lateness of Buddy's arrival into the world of sex had given him a blowtorch intensity. His vision of the good life had a weird purity to it: It consisted of an endless sequence of rapid sex acts with the blondest and bluest-eyed and most beautiful young women, none of whom, preferably, was to be a day over nineteen.

"His whole life had changed," says Bob Wood's brother, Jimmy. "He was a star. Everything went into a funnel: *women*. All he wanted was women. It became his full-time occupation."

That Buddy should have begun his womanizing by homing in on air stewardesses seems normal; indeed, banal. This, remember, was before the airlines, becoming uneasily aware of feminist muscle, changed their hiring policies. In the 1950s and 1960s, cuteness was as much a job spec for stewardesses as for Playboy bunnies, and the air stewardess, with her crisp uniform and beauty-pageant smile, was as much a part of male fantasy life as the Playmate, the starlet, the fashion model.

A special kind of stewardess subspecies was to be found in Queens: the beginners. Their more polished colleagues, the ones who had flown longer, had moved to Manhattan. "The girls who live in Queens are brand-new," says one stewardess. "They share four or five to a room—that's all they can afford. They are the youngest girls, the most vulnerable, and the loneliest.

"Stews and nurses are the loneliest jobs there are. You get off a plane, and you have cajoled fifty or a hundred people. You have served the meals, patted the children, and put up with the on-the-make businessmen. You go home. You wash your uniform. You do your nails and your hair. And you have a need to be loved. And the types of guys that hang around stews, they know that."

Nobody pursued these fledglings more assiduously than Buddy Jacobson. Together with one, or both, of the brothers Wood, he would drive out to JFK and cruise. There were bus stops where the girls bound for Manhattan would stand. Buddy would ignore them. Manhattan was still foreign territory. But there the Kew Gardens stews would be standing, and Buddy, or whoever was driving, would pull up and just say: "Hey! We're going to Kew Gardens. Do you want a ride?"

The stewardesses would be tired, and hefting luggage, and few would be in the mood to turn down a lift in a Cadillac Eldorado. They would pile in, and on the way back Buddy would stop off at some restaurant and treat them to a meal.

Buddy and Bob and Jimmy Wood were now, incidentally, passing for brothers. Often they would use assumed names and tell the young things bizarre stories about their families and parentage. Buddy was always to enjoy playing with identities. A favorite name, chosen for its quaint touch of Italianate gobbledygook, was Zippolini, which they would sometimes shorten to Zzzyp. The brothers Zzzyp. Buddy would admit to being the oldest Zippolini, at twenty-six years old. He was at this time, in reality, thirty-eight.

The young stew, or stews, would invite Buddy and Bobby and Jimmy to meet their roommates. It was only common courtesy. Says Jimmy Wood, "One of us would always have the job of walking over to the girls' telephone and memorizing the number."

Downstairs, they would study the mailbox. Usually five or six stews' names would be scrawled there and they would copy down every name. They could then telephone any time, day or night, Jimmy Wood says, repeating a characteristic conversation.

"This is Buddy. Is Mary there?"

"No, Mary's in Chicago on a flight."

"Who's this? *Josephine?* Well, we're having a party tonight. Why don't you girls come over?"

Through one girl, they would meet a half-dozen. "It was incredible," Jimmy rejoices. "The action never stopped."

Many of Buddy's stratagems were more wily. He and his "brothers" had become such familiar figures around the various air terminals that they were free to roam the Crew Only sections without hindrance. Sometimes Buddy would tack "Apartments for Rent" signs to the notice board. He had prevailed on Bob Wood to get a brokerage license, allowing him to rent apartments. "We didn't want to make a profit," Wood explains. "We just wanted to meet girls."

The chances were, of course, that the stewardesses in search of apartments would be the younger ones, and fresh on the scene, which was precisely what Buddy preferred. "He even used to hang around Miami Springs Villas, where the stewardesses train, and pick them up there," Jimmy Wood said. He spoke as a man reformed, but his censorious tone would sometimes fade into wistfulness.

Among the hangers-on whom Buddy would occasionally tolerate was a young man called Roy. He had a nondescript job in a drugstore, close to a building much frequented by stews. The information he could supply was priceless. "When the new girls traveled, they would always take a camera," Jimmy explains. "It was the first time, they wanted photos. So where do you have your photographs developed? At the local drugstore."

Roy was the assistant in charge of that section. He was privy to the names, the addresses, the telephone numbers, even photographic evidence of the quarry's looks. "I mean, what better source of information could we have, right?" Jimmy Wood says. "But whenever Roy didn't produce, Buddy would kick him out. 'Get out! You're not getting me any new girls— get out! I don't want you eating my food and drinking my booze!' " Roy would depart, chastened, but would soon return with fresh material. Says Jimmy, "Buddy used to call it 'a new stable.' "

Life became a party. The entire apartment was set up to that end. There was a rotisserie, for instance, standing close to the front door, which was always left open when Buddy was home. He would sometimes talk, only half in jest, of having it taken off its hinges. The rotisserie would be constantly in use; the inviting smell of roasting beef would steal down the corridors. Occasionally, Buddy and his straight men would bring the elevators to their floor and keep them standing open, just to make certain that the odor of the cooking would permeate the entire building.

It was wonderfully appealing, if you were a young girl, new to the city: a nonstop party that one could slide into as comfortingly as into a warm bath. The apartment was forever stocked with women, as the stews arriving from Atlanta, Seattle, or LA replaced the stews departing for LA, Seattle, or Atlanta in a seamless continuum.

But there was something curiously austere about Buddy Jacobson's passion. Young women were not just an important part of his life; they *were* his life. Toward those other pleasant things that sensualists cherish—silks and cashmeres, claret, well-cooked meals, holidays in the sun—Buddy was indifferent. He bought expensive cars, a new Cadillac every year, but his attitude toward them was purely functional. Anytime a member of the stable wanted a ride, well, the Caddy was in front, key in the ignition. Buddy's car would be borrowed constantly, accumulating parking tickets like so much bureaucratic graffiti. Buddy got rid of the tickets annually—by registering the new Cadillac in Vermont.

Or perhaps an incoming stew might call from the airport and ask him to pick her up. "No problem," Buddy would say. "The automobile's in front of the TWA building. Walk over there and take it."

Jimmy was nostalgically exultant. "This is some little girl from the Middle West, and she's driving a new Cadillac, and she's showing all her friends. You think she's not impressed?"

Where girls were concerned, Buddy's intensity could be bizarre. On one occasion, Jimmy Wood, in the bar on the ground floor of the Silver Towers, met a young stewardess called Linda. Joan Jacobson still lived upstairs in the Silver Towers, with the two boys, so Buddy would reconnoiter it with caution, and this particular evening Jimmy Wood was working the bar alone.

Linda, a handsome girl, agreed to dine. Over the meal, she mentioned that she had met Buddy. He had picked her up at the airport a couple of days earlier.

Meanwhile, Buddy had called the bar. He was told that Jimmy had departed with a girl called Linda. "Linda with the long black hair?" Buddy said. "I've got to get him *quick*."

Buddy could accomplish miracles on the telephone, but Jimmy was taking Linda from place to place, and Buddy kept missing him. Buddy finally caught up with Jimmy only the following morning, and Buddy dispensed with the niceties. "Did you fuck Linda?" he asked.

"Sure. Why?"

Buddy was grumpy. "I wanted her for myself," he said.

As a result of this unhappy incident, Buddy initiated a system: He and his coterie would keep each other apprised of their activities, and before going out in a group they would allocate the girls in advance. "It was kind of like bartering," Jimmy Wood explains.

The hunt was exhilarating. Eventually it became more interesting than the quarry. Buddy would rarely make love to the same young woman more than once. Nor was he interested in Linda after she had spent the night with Jimmy. "He wouldn't make love to somebody if she went with anybody else," Jimmy explains. "He would say it's like digging up somebody's grave."

Buddy Jacobson was persistent, and he had the driven woman-chaser's gift of being unembarrassed by rebuff; female refusals, however brusque or frequent, left him with his enthusiasm unabated. He would employ traditional techniques— the sending of flowers—and he would come up with more rococo ruses such as the delivery of a piano to the address of a young woman who had expressed to him an interest in that instrument. Most effective of all was his ability to listen to hours of the inanest drivel as though it were the most fascinating conversation he had ever heard.

But Buddy was not a kinky person, as that word is normally used, but the straightest of lovers. The word "lover," for that matter, seems singularly inappropriate, since Buddy lacked the human warmth, and the technical proficiency, and, indeed, any of the abilities implied in that multifaceted word. "Love" was not a word that rose to his lips in those days under any circumstances at all.

Bob remembers a conversation. The night before, Buddy's young date had been unusually good-looking. Had they gone to bed? Yes, Buddy said.

"Was she a good fuck?" Bob asked.

Buddy looked at him blankly.

"What do you mean?" he said. "A fuck is a fuck."

It seemed the chase was all, the use of wiles that they called their "Zzzyp Tricks," after that absurd assumed name, Zippolini, but beneath the fun of it all, something other was lurking. Something darker, colder. This was as yet unguessed at by the brothers Wood.

There were young women who, confused by drink, became Buddy Jacobson's less than wholly willing sexual partners. There was LSD dispensed to the unknowing. There was a one-way mirror, looking into the apartment bathroom.

The Woods, though possessed by the lustiness of the young, had limits. Buddy Jacobson, who lacked the excuse of youth, had no limits at all. "He was the East Coast Charles Manson," Jimmy Wood now says. Buddy Jacobson was becoming obsessed with his control over young women.

Buddy Jacobson had become a famous figure in Queens. He was the successful racehorse trainer, the giver of parties, and much to be seen with his few, trusted gofers, expensively wining and dining an inexhaustible supply of nubile, replaceable girls.

Al Seifert first met Buddy about 1967, at a lively spot called the Salty Dog, and he was impressed by Buddy's retinue. Donald Brown remembers that his first meeting with Buddy was at a Chinese restaurant in Kew Gardens. "He was older, and he was a top horse trainer," Brown says. "He had the bucks, and he had the broads. I wanted to get into his circle, and I succeeded. I didn't have a *dollar* then."

Brown was also to live in the Towne House for a while, as, at one time or another, did Tom Normandeau, the cop, and a younger man, Jack Tupper. "Jack was one of the guys from the neighborhood," Jimmy Wood says, "We might meet him in a restaurant. He'd walk over, and say, 'Hi, fellas! How are you doing?' It was like that. You see a guy so many times, you begin to say hello. You become friendly."

Donald Brown was not to remain dollarless for long. Soon he would be journeying to Germany, England, and such points east as Islamabad, Kandahar, and Kabul. He would be taking the first steps toward the creation of one of the most sophisticated multimillion-dollar hashish and marijuana smuggling combos ever.

Brown would get to know John F. Kennedy Airport just as well as Buddy Jacobson, and he was to milk it far more fruitfully. The law-enforcement sky was to fall on Brown just as Buddy faced trial for the Tupper murder. In this, Jacobson was to see hope and Jack Tupper's reputation was to be faced with ruin.

As president of the HPBA, Buddy now found an issue. The backstretch of the New York racetracks employed some three thousand manual workers—grooms, stablehands, and so forth—but provided no pension plan. Buddy thought this deficiency should be remedied.

"The cause was just," observes Tommy Trotter, who was racing secretary at the time. Joseph A. Gimma, a stockbroker who had been appointed head of the State Racing Commission by the then governor, Nelson Rockefeller, agreed that a plan was necessary. Buddy, with the aid of HPBA lawyers, worked out a scheme that called for extra racing days, with some of the state's tax profits on those days going into a pension fund. The HPBA law firm, a senior partner of which was Nixon's secretary of state, William Rogers, said there was nothing in the New York State constitution that would negate the plan.

But Rockefeller brusquely chucked the bill out. It was "ill-conceived and irresponsible," he said, and "of doubtful constitutional validity."

On Thursday, April 24, 1969, the HPBA—whose members ran eighty percent of the horses in the state—held a stormy meeting. Most of them favored using the ultimate weapon: boycott.

The furor wasn't just about pensions for stablehands. Feelings between the HPBA militants, most of whom were public trainers whose surnames were Italian or Jewish, and the NYRA's patrician racing clans had been getting increasingly chilly. One NYRA official had told a group of jockeys' agents, "This game can get along without the cloak-and-suiters"— meaning the Jewish trainers, many of whose co-religionists work in New York's garment district.

Many worthy HPBA people opposed the boycott, but Hirsch Jacobs, who had gone into semiretirement following a stroke, came out in support. Frank Pagano believes that the "cloak-and-suiter" crack was one of the reasons. Hirsch's support was crucial.

Only six horses were entered on the Saturday card at Aqueduct, and racing was canceled. The ten-day-long strike, which was to cost the state some $5 million, had begun.

Different reasons are suggested for Buddy's ardor in the strike, but nobody thinks it had anything to do with his concern for Puerto Rican stablehands. Some saw a profit motive. "In my opinion," observes Bob Wood, "what he really wanted was to get control of that big, fat pension fund." Most discerned a grab for power. The HPBA would be his cudgel. "He wanted to prove he, Buddy Jacobson, could overturn the whole structure," Pete Axthelm says. "Power would pass from the hands of George D. Widener into the hands of Buddy Jacobson."

Frank Pagano, who worked for Buddy throughout the strike, has a special slant. "He was emulating Hirsch, because Hirsch had the best private pension plans," Pagano says. "And he wanted to do something as big as Hirsch had done."

Besides, Pagano adds, "The horsemen pushed him. They said, 'Buddy, if you don't lead this strike, we're going to get a new president.'

"Buddy loved that position. So he led the strike. And when he got into it, he wanted to *win* it."

As the strike progressed, the talk grew tougher. On the third day, Buddy was promising that unless he got his pension plan, there would be no racing for "one day, one month, or one year." The media coverage was considerable. Buddy had been one of the sportswriters' favorite iconoclasts for years, and wasn't he defending the little man against the rapacities of the elite? In fact, the HPBA publicist's main problem was that he wanted Buddy to tone down his rakish image, be the sober union leader. "I said, 'Buddy, enough with the broads!' " He remembers, "He didn't listen. . . ."

But there was growing dissent within the HPBA. "When the pressure was put on," Pagano says, "the same fellows who had pushed him were saying, 'Suppose we made a mistake?'"

"Buddy wouldn't admit that. His attitude was, 'We started it, let's win it.' He wanted to win so *desperately.*"

On day five, disaffected HPBA members attempted to have Buddy voted out. They were crushingly defeated, but the tensions were escalating. On day nine, the NYRA managed to get together a flimsy day's racing card with the help of a few disgruntled HPBA people and the trainers the militants referred to as the "society trainers." Astonishingly, the grooms formed themselves into a makeshift picket, and immobilized the stables for two hours. The police were summoned, and forty of the demonstrators were put under arrest. Horrors. In Jockey Club eyes, Buddy had managed to summon to the turf the spirits of the Black Panthers and the Weather Underground.

The pressure built. The state obtained a restraining injunction, which would have hobbled the HPBA, and that, combined with a Rockefeller announcement that the racing commission would examine the strikers' economic status, did the trick. On the evening of the tenth day, Buddy announced that the HPBA would lift the boycott, and congratulated his members on their glorious victory.

Hardly. It was no victory for the HPBA. Some of the improvements they had demanded would be introduced by the NYRA, which would also control them, and they would come as a favor from management. Nor was it a victory for the NYRA, which had proved incapable of getting a decent day's racing together without those HPBA lowlifes. Least of all was it a victory for Buddy Jacobson.

"It's no use kidding myself," Buddy remarked. "From here on, I'm a marked man." On Friday, May 16, just nine days later, Buddy was at Aqueduct, but most of racing's grandees were in Baltimore, Maryland, where the Preakness was being run the following day. The Preakness is the second race in the Triple Crown, after the Kentucky Derby and before the Belmont, so the sporting media were there in strength. It was now that the Maryland Racing Commission chose to make the announcement that Jacobson was being suspended from the track on three counts, all technical, and to do with the claiming rules. The NYRA cheerfully chimed in that Buddy Jacobson also would be suspended in New York.

Buddy counterattacked. Maryland dropped two of its charges, and a court ruled that the Maryland allegations were none of New York's business. But Maryland fined Buddy an unprecedented $2,500 anyway on the third technicality. It was a pointed warning, but Buddy disregarded it. He waited awhile, and fired off a public telegram to Nelson Rockefeller, nailing him for his tardiness in making concessions. He then reproduced the telegram as a full-page ad in the pro-establishment racing daily the *Morning Telegraph*.

More aggressive than ever, Buddy now tapped into the discontent about stall space. Why should the smaller trainers fight for stalls while the patricians maintained ample, and often empty, barns? "The little guys are racing, not the blue-bloods," he said. "We should break the myth that the trustees and the Jockey Club are the backbone of racing. Their contribution is negligible. The public bets more money on my horses than on theirs."

This charge was far from fair. The best horses that trainers like Buddy were claiming had been raised by the old horse families. The money they had put into the sport was the money that Buddy was taking out. He was being purposefully incendiary. As HPBA president, he soon afterward launched an antitrust suit against the NYRA and the Jockey Club.

Pared down, the suit stated that the establishment was discriminatory, and that all New York racing officials should be unhorsed straight away. It asked, so to speak, for the gelding of the Jockey Club.

"Buddy didn't want to be a loser of *anything*," Frank Pagano says.

Jumping races are very grand affairs, especially at that most decorous of tracks, Saratoga. Even well-regarded trainers for the flat races are usually shy of jumpers. The notion that a trainer with a reputation for running cheap horses should enter a prestige jumping race was outré, which was why Buddy did just that. On August 7, 1969, he entered Lake Delaware, an undistinguished claimer, in the Lovely Nights Hurdle Handicap at Saratoga—and, more outré yet, he won.

Buddy was cock-a-hoop. For the first time in years, he went down to have his photograph taken next to his horse. And in from the stands rolled a thunderous silence.

"I don't think I'll ever make *Town and Country*," Buddy said later; he spoke as though indifferent, but obviously the silence had rankled. He had won a major race, but he was still the pushy Jew from Brooklyn. It was at this climactic time that Buddy found an important owner.

Sarah Hall was in her twenties, ravishingly attractive, and her background, though she was blond and Southern, was no more classically horsy than Buddy's. She had been born into a far from wealthy family in Starkville, Mississippi, a state where, as she says, "really there are only mules."

Sarah left Starkville at seventeen. She was married to a "spoiled-rotten kid gambler," but briefly, and then went to Los Angeles. Where else is a real blonde with delicate features and a quick, droll mind to go? She modeled (and still has some photographs of herself by Marilyn Monroe's photographer, Milton Greene), but was short at five feet five. And she auditioned for a movie director, but "he tried to put the make on me." She rejected the proposition, and decided a motion-picture career didn't appeal. But Sarah had found an enthusiasm: the track. It was at the pleasant San Diego track Del Mar that she met a leading jockey, Dean Hall. He became her second husband.

By the time Sarah came to New York, this second marriage was also over; but she had, by a novel route, acquired a bankroll. "I was one of the biggest female gamblers in America," she says. "I would bet five hundred, a thousand dollars on a race, and fifty thousand dollars on a weekend's football."

One kibitzer is still in awe. "She was in complete control," he says. " '*Put five hundred dollars on this game! I want that spread!*' She bet like a genius."

It was Buddy who talked her into becoming an owner. "Buddy was very good-looking then," Sarah Hall says. "A *charmer*." Buddy appealed to her sense of the outrageous. She admired him for his eccentric slant, his insistence on doing things his own way. Their first sortie was the claiming of three horses for $25,000, Sarah Hall being particularly taken with one called Peedoodle.

This was the summer of 1969. By that fall, there were twenty horses racing under Sarah's name and sporting her colors, blue and gold. She had a backer for her stable, the textile czar Bill Levin, who seems to have trusted much to Sarah Hall's flair and Buddy's expertise, and who didn't let the NYRA's low opinion of Buddy bother him. "The good guys aren't always the ones with the white hats," he told me.

Buddy was exultant. He had lost interest in the prosaic

business of claiming. "Now I've got the right owner," he told Frank Pagano. "I've been waiting all my life for an owner like this."

There was one thing that he needed to crown his career: a big horse. And now this seemed within his reach.

On November 17, Buddy and Sarah Hall went out to Belmont, where there was a dispersal sale; the stable of a recently deceased Jockey Club member, Harry Guggenheim, was being broken up. Buddy laid out $151,000 for five horses, of which a large part, $52,000, went for a bay called Bold Reason. Bold Reason came from a mighty bloodline and should have fetched more. "But he had big knees," Pagano says. "The others shied away from him. Buddy knew better."

Soon Buddy was racing half a million dollars' worth of horseflesh, and he was more flamboyant than he had ever been. As for Sarah Hall, she had become a track phenomenon. Her prettiness was startling, her panache even more so. She had the palest of blond hair, the color of white wine in the sunshine, and she wore it in crisp, puffy swoops, which was the way dolly girls were wearing it at the time. And she wore remarkable skirts with hemlines that swooped up London-style to nine inches above the knee. "I never had the same outfit twice. Never!" she remembers. "I spent ten thousand dollars a month on clothes. You know something terrible? I hardly ever wore the same *mink coat* twice."

The harness on her horses bore her monogram, naturally, and she liked to travel with her personal hairdresser, something which caused a bit of a stir when she paid a triumphal visit back home to Mississippi—"We had to get him out of town before they tarred and feathered him," says Jimmy Wood—and she preferred to arrive at the races by means of a helicopter, which would land in the infield. If Sarah had horses running in more than one meeting, she also would leave by helicopter between races, and a couple of fellows would always be willing to carry her, smiling radiantly, over the plowed turf to the copter. "I had a *following,*" she says. "Some of the tracks, like Liberty Bell, offered me *anything*. They offered to make up races for me."

Buddy never pulled the wool over Sarah Hall's eyes. "He was a manipulator," she says. But she had respect for his abilities, even though, in his new manner of contemptuous disregard for the old, hard-boot methods, he was so much absent from the tack, training by telephone. Sarah felt herself to be equally unconventional, disdaining for instance, the genteel etiquette that governs the claiming of other trainers' horses. "I was famous for having claiming wars," she says. "If somebody claimed one of my horses, we would run him out of business in *a second*." One surprising encounter: Sarah Hall was minding her own business at the bar of the Miami Springs Villas, which is a Florida resort (and happens to be not far from the stewardess training school where Buddy was even then continuing to pursue his quarry), and suddenly there was this man who was entirely unknown to her standing in front of her and screaming.

"Who are *you?*" she asked.

"I owned Peedoodle," the man bawled. "I really *loved* that horse! It was the only horse I ever owned!"

"Well, I loved him too," Sarah replied, nothing nonplussed. "I loved him so much I named my *poodle* after him."

There was more than a tinge of the bizarre about many of Sarah's memories of dealing with Buddy Jacobson. In one case, she watched a race, saw that her entry was going to finish out of the money, and left the track. Later, she telephoned Buddy, mildly curious, to find out where the horse had finished.

"It died in the stretch," Buddy told her, dispassionately.

"I know," Sarah Hall said. "I saw the race. But how did it finish?"

"It died in the stretch," Buddy repeated. His telephone manner was, as always, infinitely reasonable.

"I *know*. But where did it come in?"

"It died in the stretch," Buddy repeated. "Of a heart attack."

There was a similar brutality about the way Buddy's race-track career ended. It was like the closing stages of a fox hunt, in which Jacobson had assumed the role of the fox. Just as he was running for reelection to the HPBA presidency, the New York Racing Commission announced it was opening an investigation into Sam Lefrak's several-year-old charges of misfeasance. Sheer coincidence, naturally. And though Buddy won the election handily, the commission pursued the investigation.

Late in 1969, Buddy was warned that his trainer's license was in peril. It did not affect his deportment. On February 13, 1970, Hirsch Jacobs died. Some feel that the stress of the strike had taken a toll on his already weakened frame, though his family deny this. It was noticed that Buddy Jacobson did not attend his uncle's funeral.

Just four days later, there was an announcement from the racing association: Buddy was to be suspended. And though the suspension was only for forty-five days, it was not to start until March 10, the opening day of the New York racing season. In practice, this meant Buddy would be denied stalls for the whole year, and a trainer with no stalls is a trainer with no horses is no trainer at all.

Jacobson appealed, of course. He seemed oblivious, not even discussing his predicament with cronies. The warning sounds were to him like thunder over the horizon, portending rain, but on someone else.

That winter Buddy's horses had been racing out at Bowie, Maryland. Indeed, on February 18, the day after his notice of suspension in New York, his horse Dowitcher romped in a winner for Sarah Hall. Buddy himself had been absent for most of the week, leaving things in the care of Frank Pagano, but toward the end of the month he showed up. It was time to think of moving the stable back to New York.

Frank Pagano was alive with curiosity. He had heard of the suspension, of course. Buddy was his quiet, convincing self. "The state won't *let* them suspend me for any period of time," he said. "Because I've raised more tax revenue than any four flat trainers put together."

He showed Pagano a statistical survey that he had had made. Buddy was always great on this sort of methodical documentation, and the survey did indeed show that out of the horses he ran, such-and-such a proportion had been favorites, and such-and-such an amount of betting had been generated. "No way they're going to suspend me," he repeated.

Frank Pagano was unconvinced.

"Somebody says we're not gonna get stalls, Buddy," he said.

"Oh, no," Buddy said. "We have stalls."

Bill Levin was also in Maryland. Buddy, he, and Pagano were all staying in the Holiday Inn, and one day in March, Buddy was in Bill Levin's room, saying not only that he had stalls, but exactly *how many* he had. After Buddy left, Levin got a telephone call. The timing was as precise as in a farce.

"Bill, you better get yourself another trainer," the caller told him.

Frank Pagano called the New York track himself. "Don't hurry back," they told him. "You don't have any stalls."

The odd thing was the transparency of Buddy's lie. He seems to have considered it less as a lie than a transformation of the truth, effected by repetition and force of will. "Buddy was a very positive thinker," Bill Levin says dryly.

Back in New York, Buddy confronted reality. The suspension was, he lamented, "the death sentence to my career." His appeal failed in April. Outrage at the heavy-handedness of the Jockey Club was intense. "It was a lynch mob," says Jack Mann. The *Turf and Sport Digest,* not the most fire-breathing sheet, compared the racing commission's hearings to the trial of the Chicago Seven. Pete Axthelm likened the beleaguered Buddy to student militant Mark Rudd. Stirring stuff, when you consider that Buddy's political hero was Richard Nixon.

The whole controversy still seems almost inexpressibly painful for financier Jack Dreyfus, then NYRA chairman. "It was such an unhappy period for me," he says. "The facts are that Buddy was suspended for breaking the claiming rules. And he at the same time did lose a liquor license"—thus did the discothèques come back to haunt him—"but Buddy told his story. And I was roasted by the press."

As to the other trainers, well, there were a few glints of quiet, unholy joy. "When Buddy was ruled off, everybody came up and shook his hand," says Frank Pagano. "But, you know, there were a lot of horses that he wasn't going to be training anymore. They would go to the other trainers. And this is one business where everyone can be very friendly, but there's a tremendous amount of competitiveness. It's unreal." (Sarah Hall and Bill Levin, did, indeed, find other trainers— Bill Levin took on Frank Pagano—and even stalls.)

Buddy Jacobson had taken on the system, and he had lost. He soon initiated a lawsuit against the NYRA, claiming $750,000 in damages, and made the correct noises about fighting to the end, but many doubted his desire to return to the humdrum routines of training. His suspension, after all, was only for New York State. "He could have come back in some other state," says his uncle Gene. "But he had other interests." Perhaps, as Buddy said at the time, his pride wouldn't let him be driven from New York. But certainly his other interests were beginning to consume him.

* * *

One of these, curiously, was skiing. Buddy's interest in skiing had been fired by the fact that Bill Jacobs, Hirsch's son and one of the few family members not to have gone into racing, operated a ski lodge in Colorado. Buddy had taken up skiing a few years back, and as his zeal for training waned, his enthusiasm for the slopes increased.

Buddy did it, of course, in his own fashion, dressed as he normally dressed, which is to say in ratty jeans, and wearing neither socks nor underwear. There was a multiple message to this. In part, Buddy was telling the world that he was not as other men are, but was immune to sickness and cold. And in part it was that Buddy considered dressing a waste of time. Buddy Jacobson was always fearful of wasting time.

Before the start of the 1970 ski season, Buddy began looking for a ski place. After negotiating unsuccessfully for the North Wind in Wilmington, Vermont, he heard of another possibility: the Norway, near Mount Snow. The Norway had been built by John Martin Yunos, master plumber and tax assessor for the town of Dover. Buddy drove over in that year's Cadillac. "He had a couple of airline stewardesses with him," Yunos said. The Norway was unpretty, being built of cinder blocks, with an asphalt roof, and had some twenty rooms. Buddy and Yunos agreed on a price of $135,000.

This presented a certain problem. "Buddy didn't have any money when he left the track," says Jimmy Wood. Buddy was always cash-poor. He took on some junior partners, a bunch of younger men who had lived in the Towne House, and borrowed $5,000 from Donald Brown (whose business, the importing of certain proscribed herbs, was beginning to thrive). He sold his horse van, began selling off his forty or so horses, and looked for a buyer for the Old Westbury Horse Farm. Was it wrenching? "I don't think so," Frank Pagano said. "He needed the money. Buddy never became too attached to anything."

Buddy left the track with hardly a backward glance. He made an initial payment to Yunos and set to work improving the lodge. Much of the work he did himself. He felt he was as good as any contractor. He had made a deal down at the docks and had bought a quantity of lumber: an artfully wormy chestnut, chosen to impart the rustic look. This went on the interior. "Most of the work that he was doing was just wasting money, if you ask me," opines Yunos.

Charlie Maxton, who runs a local ski-reservation outfit with his wife Susan, agreed that Buddy was "overimproving the property," but was otherwise impressed. "He had added an A-frame, and converted every last inch," he says. The capacity was now eighty. "The season opened," Maxton says, "and we started doing business."

It went like a dream at first. "It seemed like Buddy was the only one in the whole state of Vermont who always had room," says Charlie Maxton. "We were calling him ten times a day."

Maxton thought it a bit too good to be true, which it was. At ten o'clock in the evening of December 27, two young women beat on his door. They were in their late twenties, and in floods of tears. The Christmas vacation was not going well for them.

"They had booked a double room for two," Maxton says. "Buddy had stuck them in a bunkroom with twenty teen-age girls. There was a band playing upstairs all night. They couldn't sleep."

The next morning, they had gone to Buddy to ask for their deposits. "You don't like it, you get out," Buddy had told them. "I don't give refunds."

The Maxtons drove over the next day to reconnoiter. On their arrival, they immediately saw that Buddy was packing in about two hundred people. The Norway was lively enough, with a bar and a sauna, but the food was rudimentary. "People were paying top dollar, and sitting on the floor to eat spaghetti," Maxton says. "Buddy's overriding principle was there's a sucker born every minute."

Maxton asked about the deposits, and Buddy confirmed the house rule: no refunds.

"Jesus!" he said to his wife. "We're dealing with a crazy man!"

For that season, and through into the next, the Maxtons continued to do business with Buddy, but they were careful to specify exactly what people would be getting into: "It's a swinging-singles type of place," they would warn.

Where his own diversions were concerned, Buddy had now refined things to a system close to automation. "It was his life," says Jimmy Wood. "He would have one girl, and he would have her driven away. She thinks she's going to the supermarket, and suddenly she's going to New York. The next one is on her way in. The girls would pass each other in toll booths."

This was, of course, the same merry-go-round technique that Buddy had employed so successfully at the racetrack with claimers.

Sarah Hall remained on friendly terms with Buddy. She was, at that time, engaged to a pro footballer, and they would stay at the Norway, which she loved. She waxes nostalgic. "I can see Buddy now," she says, "sitting back in a big beanbag chair, or lying in front of the fireplace, with his latest girls around him.

"What he'd do with these girls, he had a system. He'd make them work like dogs. They were his maids—he never paid them a dime! A *soul!*"

Sometimes Sarah would just relax, watching old movies, NFL footage, and such, but often enough Buddy managed to get *her* working. "I paid through the nose for my room and I'd be cookin' away a storm in my three-hundred-dollar jacket, or one of my cashmere sweaters. One time I was working behind the bar with my full-length chinchilla." She remembers Buddy trying to talk her into another dream. "He wanted me to buy him a mountain," she says.

Not everyone has such roseate memories. The sheets at the Norway were hardly ever changed, for instance—"Buddy's theory was that people never go back to the same ski lodge twice," Bob Wood explains—and he was soon turning over thousands a week in cash, which he would stuff into a ski boot, or an old shoebox. Buddy seemed, in short, well on his way to making good on his theory that he could run a lodge better than people who had been running lodges all their lives. It was then that he had the problem with the nuns.

A group of nuns had asked for a block booking. Buddy took it with his customary equanimity and checked them in. Right opposite them he put a different block booking. It consisted of firemen.

The firemen got themselves pretty drunk and tried to break in on the nuns, who did not appreciate their interest. The nuns left at daybreak.

The other lodge owners ostracized Buddy after what came to be known as the Nun Incident, and barred him from their association. They seem to have thought that he wasn't helping their reputation. Buddy, naturally, just shrugged it off, but, once again, he had gone too far. Over the edge.

* * *

It was the summer of 1971. Buddy and Bob Wood had worn out their welcome at the Towne House, and had left. Since then, they had been living in a sequence of apartments around Kew Gardens. Buddy had found a buyer for the Old Westbury Horse Farm, namely Bill Levin, who was bucked up by the performance of Bold Reason, the horse which Buddy had bought him the year before, and which ran third in both the Kentucky Derby and the Belmont. That August, Bold Reason actually won the Travers in Saratoga, which is the oldest and one of the most important stakes races in the country, so Buddy Jacobson did have his big horse in the end, but it was too late, and he wasn't interested. He had moved on to other schemes. "We're going to buy a building in the city," he told Bob Wood, "and we'll fill it full of broads. Only broads!"

When the inhabitants of New York's other boroughs allude to "the city," what they mean is Manhattan. Nor did Buddy have to explain which part of Manhattan he had in mind. Just as Manhattan regards itself by comparison with, say, Queens, so does the Upper East Side regard itself by comparison with the rest of Manhattan.

As soon as the ski season was over, Buddy began cruising Manhattan with his coterie. He had a double quest: properties and girls. The latter were the more numerous, Their quest for a building was still going nowhere when they espied two young women walking together down the street. The young women were notable not only for their good looks, but for their extreme height. As usual, Buddy left the proposition to his straight men.

Bob Wood popped out of the Caddy and approached them with his usual assumed casualness. "Hi!" he said merrily. "We're having a party tonight, and we'd like you girls to come."

It was the Queens street ploy, and Buddy wasn't really expecting it to work with a couple of nifty Manhattanites, but, yes, they did come. Their names were, let us say, Kay and Coco, and they were young models. They shared an apartment on East 69th Street with three other young women with similar career ambitions. It had been as easy as pie.

Models.

The Fashion model plays as great a part in male fantasy life as the airline stewardess but is a couple of status notches higher. The younger models, moreover, are much like the younger stews, in that they have usually come to the city from the sticks and are vulnerable. Buddy absorbed this fresh information with intense interest.

Now he found his buildings. They were seedy brownstones, 153 and 155 East 84th Street, between Lexington and Third. Buddy first saw them in the late fall of 1971, and he closed a deal in January, buying both buildings for $245,000, with $75,000 as a down payment. The neighborhood in which the buildings stood is Yorkville, a German enclave long sunk in dim grubbiness, but an area whose fortunes were markedly on the rise. That summer of 1972, Buddy and Bob Wood set to work, gutting the buildings to make way for Buddy's future home.

Buddy and the brothers Wood were now taking out three of the would-be models, and they would sometimes stay over at East 69th. But since there were girls doubled up in both of the bedrooms, and the fifth consigned to a fold-out bed in the living room, too often this meant the floor. So they decided to look for an apartment. Buddy had spotted a place on York Avenue that had a familiar feel to it. He grabbed a doorman and asked, "Do a lot of stewardesses live here?" The doorman mumbled an affirmative, and that was that.

But now Buddy was obsessed with his building. He and Bob Wood would get up at seven and go to 84th Street. They had a small group of laborers, including one Salvatore Giamo, a native of Borghetto, a few miles from Palermo, Sicily; and his fellow townsman, a diminutive but muscular young man named Salvatore Prainito. But Buddy and Bob Wood worked harder than any of them.

Buddy hired skilled workmen—plumbers, electricians, and the like—out of the yellow pages. The local German plumber would talk admiringly of the way Buddy worked three shifts, hauling the bricks himself, and not stopping until dark. They labored like that through much of the winter, and the spring.

As soon as the first apartment was ready, they moved in their gear. They then completed the second, moved into that, and rented the first. And so on. There was no problem getting the stews as tenants. They would ask a girl with a little seniority to put up a sign on the Crew Scheduling bulletin board. Or they would offer a fee. "Just like an agent," Jimmy Wood explains. "The girls would go crazy. Two or three hundred dollars!"

They started renting in April 1973, and the whole building was rented by May. There was, as yet, no Certificate of Occupancy, mainly because there was, as yet, no roof. Once the roof was added, Buddy chose one of the seventh-floor penthouses for himself and constructed a rooftop swimming pool. This pool was put together poorly, a fact which was to have severe consequences. He made a few alterations. Unhappy with the tunnel vision peepholes in the doors, he changed them for fish-eyes, snappy numbers with wraparound vision. This, too, was to have consequences.

The 84th Street building was complete. A few of the workmen were unhappy—the admiring plumber became less admiring when he was stiffed for $18,000—but Buddy and the Woods were very happy indeed. "The building had thirty units," Jimmy Wood exults. "I had one, and Buddy had one, and in the other twenty-eight there were two, three, four girls. We used to laugh like crazy guys, and say: 'We have ninety girls here, and *they're all ours.*' It was beautiful. Absolutely beautiful."

There was a friendly feel to the building. The girls tended to talk not about their apartments, but their "rooms," and the doors did not have key locks, but opened by combinations. The girls knew the combinations, and so did Buddy. He wasn't a greedy landlord—the rents were low, and the bills often would pile up, unpaid, for weeks and months. The tradition of parties soon was reestablished, though Buddy was not backward in letting it be known that he didn't care for his tenants' inviting boyfriends. In the same way, the girls were welcome, but the presence of male outsiders discouraged, at the rooftop pool.

Another tradition became formalized. Buddy and the Woods had always enjoyed taking out stews to fancy restaurants. Now every night the three of them, and a few other males, if numbers became topheavy, would take out the prettiest of the girls, and the places they would frequent were those brashly popular Manhattan night spots with which they had grown familiar while living in Queens—places like the Sign of the Dove and Mr. Laffs.

One day the intercom buzzed in Buddy's apartment. A man's voice asked, "Do you have an apartment for rent?"

An absurd question. They didn't rent to men.

"No," Buddy said.

Jimmy Wood, meantime, was peering down from the window. There were, he saw, two bicycles in front of the house, one of them a girl's.

"Hey! Buddy! Wait—it might be a girl," he called.

The man who had buzzed was Marco Ricotta, a contractor in his early thirties, the owner of a fancy midtown restaurant. He was looking for an apartment not for himself, but for the young woman he was accompanying, who happened to be a rangily built fashion model. Call her Eleanor.

Upstairs, there was a certain degree of mutual male recognition. "I sized up the situation," Marco said. "The whole building was a setup."

"He knew he was putting her in the lion's den," agrees Jimmy Wood. And Buddy did indeed give Eleanor an apartment next to his, the apartment which would next be leased by Melanie Cain, but Marco had confidence in Eleanor's ability to handle herself, and in this he was correct.

The building began to metamorphose. "Eleanor's girlfriends started coming around," Jimmy Wood says. "Top models." Such a building could not be kept a secret. "I zeroed in on the building right away," said the Publicist. The Publicist is a sallow semi-young man who talks like a shoal of leaping fish. He does press for preppy parties, but is best known for being an assiduous friend to millionaires like Huntington Hartford, and for ownership of the fullest Rolodex in Manhattan. He got himself an entrée and was impressed: from Stew Zoo it had become a Model Menagerie.

In fact, the Publicist was even impressed by the slapdash way that Buddy ran the place. "He would have gotten three twenty-five a month for a one-bedroom apartment," he computed quickly. "Put in three girls at one fifty each and he's getting four fifty." What if some girls are living free for a while?

Not all the stunners liked life in the Menagerie. Pamela West, a long-legged brown-haired girl from Los Angeles, a beginner at modeling, moved in when she was eighteen. The attractions of Buddy's place were obvious. "Free rent and free dinner. It's difficult to beat," she says. But soon Pamela West became discontented.

"I'm very independent," she says. The clannishness of the building began to disturb her, the sense that her own male friends were unwelcome and that the whole structure was a big cupboard stocked with cookies for what she still calls "the Zippolini brothers." Within six weeks, Pamela left.

She was not difficult to replace. But neither Marco Ricotta nor the Publicist nor Pamela had any idea quite what a fun place the building actually was. Right at the beginning, Buddy had asked an electrician to embed bugs and similar devices in every apartment. The man had refused. Buddy had done the work himself; 155 East 84th was as wired as a diplomat's suite in a Moscow hotel.

The intercom system, for instance. Down at the front door, the buzzer had been so rigged that Buddy or his coterie would know whenever anybody came in or left. If somebody was coming in, a glance at the elevator lights would show the floor at which they were alighting. Additionally, every apartment had a couple of intercoms in the walls, and one of these listening devices was connected directly with a false closet in Buddy Jacobson's apartment. "We would listen to what the girls were saying," Jimmy Wood says. "We knew every move they made. We called them Our Girls."

It became important to sever Our Girls from rivals in the outside world. If flowers were delivered to such-and-such a young woman, for instance, Buddy and the brothers Wood would go down, tip the deliveryman a buck, tear up the card, and give the flowers to whomever they pleased. If a girl was expecting a date, the trickiness became more elaborate. Her intercom would be artfully disconnected, and the ground floor would then be reconnected directly to Buddy Jacobson in 7D. Soon the buzzer would sound.

"Yes?" one of them would say.

"This is Bill. I'm here to pick up Mary."

"She's on a flight. She told us to tell you she had an emergency call from Crew Scheduling. She'll call you in a couple of days."

They would wait awhile, until their tenant downstairs was steaming at being stood up, and then they would take her to dinner themselves.

Perhaps the most important element in the building's electronics network, though, was the telephone tap. This was what they called among themselves the Buck Rogers Setup. Every telephone in the place was gimmicked, wired into a small tape recorder. They had bought the components, which are sold as "security devices," and assembled the system themselves. Their central control was in the boiler room, down in the basement—a part of the building where nobody but themselves had any reason to go.

Telephones always fascinated Buddy. They were his tool, his weapon, almost his medium. The telephone-tap system worked admirably. He and the Woods would listen to the girls discussing the most intimate details of their lives. They would listen, and plot their strategies of seduction accordingly. Every time the girls picked up their phones, the system would be activated, and all the conversations would be taped. And later, hour after hour, Buddy Jacobson would listen to the tapes.

"Total control. It was incredible," says Jimmy Wood. "That was his whole game."

This was the extraordinary building in which Melanie Cain, an aspiring fashion model, came to live. She was cheery. She was naive. She was eighteen years old.

- III -

Melanie
and
Buddy

When Melanie was young, New York was a city stuffed with delights. Her parents were living in Mayport, New Jersey, at the time, and she would be taken into Manhattan by her mother's aunt, her Great-Aunt Evelyn, a tall woman, thin to the point of gauntness and given to conservative skirts and blouses, who had worked for the telephone company and lived in New York for thirty years. They would catch the train at Maplewood, rattle in on the Erie-Lackawanna line, and make a change at Hoboken, a dingy station. But Melanie was always aware of Manhattan lying ahead, its huge and glittery buildings pressing up energetically into the sky.

Christmas was tops. Christmas meant ice cream at Schrafft's and a trip to Radio City Music Hall, where Melanie would see a movie on-screen, and the Rockettes onstage. She and her great-aunt went everywhere by subway. That was the best part. The subway that whooshes through Melanie's memory was perfectly clean, with no grungy stuff on the floor, no graffiti, no scruffy people.

Melanie would sit in the subway and stare at the posters and the billboards. There were enchanting models on the posters. Melanie imagined them to be a superior sort of New Yorker. The models were impossibly tall and lovely, with silk stockings, and furs, and brilliant smiles. New York, Melanie decided, was wonderful.

Years later, journalists trying to get a quick fix on Melanie Cain in the aftermath of a murder would gratefully accept a stereotype: Melanie was the bright-eyed kid from the Midwest, trying to make it in the big, bad metropolis, and this stereotype, like most, was compounded of both truth and falsehood.

Melanie's parents, for instance, are Easterners. Both George Cain and Jane Sharkey, Melanie's father and mother, grew up in New Jersey and spent much time going between

New Jersey and New York. Indeed, her grandfather, Patrick Sharkey, had spent much of his life in the city as a reporter for the *Saturday Evening Post*.

George Cain was of English stock, and Protestant, and Jane's family was Irish Catholic, so the marriage caused the normal commotion of those days. George agreed that the children should be brought up in the Catholic faith and, soon thereafter, became a convert himself. Melanie was the second of six children, and the oldest girl. She was born in Norfolk, Virginia. George Cain was in the navy at that time, but left the service to pursue a sales career, a way of life almost equally nomadic. In Melanie's youth, the family lived successively in Virginia, Washington, D.C., New Jersey, and New York State. Then, when she was thirteen years old, George Cain took another new job. The family moved to Dallas, Texas.

Melanie hated the relocation. So far, with all the moving about, she and her family had stayed in the East. Texas was —different. "It seemed just so slooooow!" Melanie says. At the same time, everything seemed huge and cold. "Big homes, big roads, everything was big—gigantic!" Melanie, who had spent her childhood in funky old three-story houses, now found herself in a sprawling Dallas suburb, and plunked into a junior high with three thousand kids. So miserable was she that the name of the school and even the name of the road on which she lived have been expunged from her memory.

After one year, Melanie's mother had her transferred to the Ursuline Academy, a private girls' school run by nuns. The standards were high—there were only twenty to a class—and Melanie did well. Melanie found herself making friends. But the nuns disturbed her.

They were strict, of course, locking her in the cloakroom if she was "bad." But there was something that went beyond mere strictness. The nuns told Melanie terrible stories. The stories were of sin, and of punishment. She was warned not to repeat them to her parents.

The implications of the stories preyed on her. "I was petrified—*petrified*—when I made my first Holy Communion," Melanie says. "And, sure enough, the Host stuck to the roof of my mouth. Well, I just let it sit there. I didn't dare touch it. I went home, and I couldn't eat. I thought it would be stuck there forever."

Her mother was brisk. "Go on," she said. "Eat your lunch."

"I can't," the panicky girl mumbled.

"What do you mean you can't?"

"Because God's in my mouth," Melanie cried.

So finally Melanie did disburden herself, telling her mother of the hellfire that threatened to devour her. Mrs. Cain was appalled. She took Melanie out of the Ursuline Academy straightaway, fearing for her daughter's faith. Indeed, for several years, Melanie was to feel uneasy at the sight of a nun or a priest or even a crucifix on a wall, and going to church would make her feel headachy.

Meanwhile, Melanie had become passionate about sports. Her gawky frame—she was taller than boys of her age—made her a natural for basketball. And that summer she became a tennis zealot, joining a club and playing tennis eight hours a day. "My dream was to be a Chrissy Evert," she says. "I couldn't tolerate losing, so I was very nasty to play with." Like Buddy, Melanie wanted to win.

It was then that the Cains picked themselves up again and moved to Naperville, Illinois. "Right when we'd started liking a place, we'd move," Melanie says. "We would complain, we would cry. And my mother would say, 'You'll meet new friends.'

"And it was true. Every time we'd move somewhere, we *would* meet new friends." Traveling around so much made Melanie not so much an army brat as an optimist.

If they had been Easterners on arrival in Dallas, the Cain children arrived in Naperville as Southerners. "We had the accent," Melanie says. "We were slow-moving, slow-talking." Melanie was fifteen when the Cains arrived in Naperville, and she was to spend the next three years there, longer than she had thus far lived anywhere.

They were three good years, with A's in class, and a place on the school tennis team. Moreover, her healthy good looks won her the Marilyn Monroe part in a school production of *Bus Stop*. She smoked a little grass, as was conventional for kids in her generation, but didn't take to it. Beer parties were more her style.

The friends she made in Naperville remain among her best friends today, and almost all are girls. "I was too tall, and scared of boys," she says. "I wasn't big on the dating scene." Melanie and her then best friend, a girl named Jane with very straight blond hair, decided to go to college together, and share a room at Western Illinois.

It was now that the Cains again uprooted themselves. George Cain was offered a new and promising job as a salesman with a copper company in Cherry Hill, New Jersey. The senior Cains were delighted at returning to the East, but Melanie, who found herself abruptly transplanted in the middle of her senior year in high school, was not delighted at all. "I was very mad at leaving my friends," she says. "I hated it so much that I had what you'd call an anxiety attack. I stayed home, and sat in my room. I didn't make any friends. And I worked at my schoolwork." She collected straight A's, a scholarship, and a problem.

The problem was this. Melanie's scholarship was not valid for out-of-state schools, but she was quite set on going to an out-of-state school: Western Illinois. It was, she felt, home. Nor could George Cain help. Not only was there the rest of the family to be brought up, but after just six months, new management had taken over his copper company and his job had been phased out. Melanie took part-time work. She parked cars, packed chickens, sold men's shirts at a Cherry Hill shopping mall. But by midsummer she had to face facts: She wasn't making nearly enough money to take her through college.

It was George Cain who suggested that Melanie try modeling. This wasn't something she had ever thought about. But her father had a business friend whose daughter was a model. "He'd heard that models make a lot of money," Melanie explained.

George Cain learned that his daughter would need some photographs to show the agencies, so he and Melanie went to Philadelphia, where a local photographer took some test photographs. He charged a hundred dollars or so, gave Melanie twenty pictures, and waxed enthusiastic: "You have the all-American look. That's just what they want."

Her parents were pleased. And George Cain had some advice. "Don't get in a cab," he warned her. "They're rip-offs. They'll take your money." Getting out a New York subway map, he tried to show her how to get from here to there, and for all the sense it made to Melanie he might have been showing her how to navigate the canals on Mars.

Another caution: "Don't sign anything!" George Cain said. "I don't care what it is. Don't sign it."

Melanie got on the bus to New York the next morning.

"Well," she blithely told her parents. "I'll talk to you later." She was seventeen, with her eighteenth birthday still looming, and she had only enough money for that one day in the city, but both she and her parents were unperturbed. "My mother never batted an eyelash," she says. "I was always very independent, always very sure of myself."

The agency that Melanie first visited, at the suggestion of the Philadelphia photographer, was Stewart Modeling, at 405 Park Avenue. As chance had it, there was nobody interviewing that day, but somebody did hand her an entry form to what was called a Model-of-the-Year contest, explaining that it took place at the end of the summer. The fortunate winner would get a "guaranteed contract."

Melanie eyed the entry form distrustfully and, mindful of her father's warning, didn't sign. Besides, at the end of summer she was going back to school. No way was she going to model for longer than a matter of weeks.

She walked out of Stewart, had no idea what to do with the rest of the day. "I didn't know anything about agencies," Melanie says. "I had never worn makeup or looked at fashion magazines." She opened the yellow pages, where agencies are listed under "Models—Living," and chose an agency toward the beginning of the list, because its name was printed in larger type than most of the others and it was nearby on East 59th Street. She had never heard of the agency, which was Ford Models Inc., and happens to be the world's biggest.

Melanie telephoned, and was asked to come over. She walked into the reception room, a daunting sight, with innumerable cute, willowy young things milling about, smiling bright smiles. They seemed very poised to Melanie, and they were carrying professional-looking model-books. A young woman appeared, examined Melanie's photographs, and led her into a private room.

Here, Melanie was confronted with an older woman. Eileen Ford was looking her over. Ms. Ford is short, and slight, with large eyes. At first impression, she seems fragile; this impression does not long persist. Being looked over by Eileen Ford is rather like being examined by a government food inspector.

Eileen appraised Melanie silently for a few moments, and then said crisply that she needed to lose five pounds, she didn't know how to stand up straight, and she needed a haircut.

"Call us tomorrow morning," Eileen added. "We'll send you to a testing." Melanie walked out of the room. All the pretty girls, she saw, had gone. She was told that they had all been turned down flat. She was puzzled, but had the haircut anyway.

That night her parents were curious. "What happened?" they asked.

"I don't know," was all that Melanie could say.

What had happened was that Melanie had been accepted. The date was July 17, 1973, and the Ford Agency, as promised, sent her off to a photographer for more test shots the next day: She had to concentrate on building up her model book.

Melanie was warned that success would take time. Modeling is often a grind for beginners, involving a couple of years or more crowding into the model's equivalent of casting calls —they are known as "go-sees"—and wearing out shoe leather and tempers on rounds of fashion editors, photographers, and art directors. Melanie listened to the wisdom, and ignored it.

It was late afternoon of her second day, which she had spent as she had the first, testing with photographers, when Ford told her about a go-see at an advertising agency. She now believes that they had suggested she attend just to familiarize her with the business. Melanie walked in jauntily and was introduced to a man. He turned out to be the art director, and he was exhausted. He had, he told Melanie, interviewed something like a hundred girls for this job, which was a "print" ad—meaning a still photograph—for VO5 hair conditioner. Finally, he asked about her experience. Where did she have her pictures?

"Oh," Melanie told him airily, "I'm new in New York. I don't have any pictures yet. I'm just going to model a couple of months, so that I can make enough money to go to school." They chatted awhile longer, and before Melanie left the art director told her that he was worried by the shortness of her hair. That haircut!

The Ford Agency called the next day. "You got the job," they said. "It's with Hiro. And it'll be a national ad."

They were shocked, Melanie says, but she herself was quite unsurprised. "I just thought, well, that's nice! It was no big deal. I mean, I wasn't glowing over it or anything. I just thought, I got the job."

Melanie had never heard of Hiro, who was one of the two or three most important fashion and beauty photographers in America at this time. But she did decide that a visit to his studio—that much she had picked up from the respect given Hiro's name at Ford—deserved some attention to detail. Accordingly, she dressed and prettied herself, the way she fancied a fashion model should look.

"I'll never forget," she says, still gleeful. "I wore this cotton outfit from Sears, and I had these fishnet stockings. Really, the worst. And I set my hair, and I went to Montgomery Ward's to get some makeup. I had never worn makeup in my life. I got that blue Maybelline eyeshadow, and some pink stuff, and I thought I looked *wonderful*."

Hiro's studio was shining white, a place of luxurious austerity. Melanie sat in the models' room and waited until Hiro finished a shoot and the model he had been using joined Melanie in the room. She was Annie Coverly, a striking blonde who was soon to leave the business for Hollywood.

"Hi!" she said cheerfully. "I'm Annie. Who are you?"

"I'm Melanie."

"What's your last name?"

"Melanie Cain. I'm just starting."

Coverly smiled and flopped into a chair. There was a male makeup artist in the room, and a male hairdresser, and they were assembling the tools of their trade and turning their attention to Melanie, while Annie Coverly wriggled contentedly out of her top.

Melanie goggled and grew pink.

Annie Coverly was not wearing a bra.

There was Melanie, immobile, and conscious of her Playtex, her slip, and her other undergarments, and there was Annie Coverly, indifferent to the males and naked as a fish. While the makeup artist determinedly swabbed all the blue powder and pink goo from Melanie's face, all that she could think was, "Is *that* what you have to do to be a model?"

Now it was her turn. The scene to be photographed: Melanie in a bath towel, and dripping wet, suggesting that she had just emerged from a shower. With one hand, she was combing her hair, while with the other, with a stroke of the surreal whimsy ad men love, she was dashing off a letter to VO5, thanking the company for its wonderful hair conditioner.

An assistant put Melanie in place, and she turned gracefully, faced the camera, and straightaway froze. "There are all these *serious men* behind the camera," she says. "They have their arms folded, and they're wearing business suits. I was petrified."

She tried to force a smile. It wouldn't come. "And my lips started quivering," she says.

But Melanie came to, like a motor starting up, and the session began. Hiro, who is Japanese, works with the quiet precision of a surgeon. Rock music pulsed gently through his studio as he shot, and he spoke to Melanie seldom, but, after the awkward beginning, things were soon moving easily, and Melanie was never to have such a cold fit of stage fright again.

Alas, VO5 never did use the pictures. Melanie's hair was too short after all, the art director told her, but he gave her some color transparencies, which went straight into her book. Thereafter, when photographers remarked on the shots, Melanie would just say, "Oh, that was my first job—with Hiro." They would be much impressed.

Melanie continued to work at her tests in the days that followed, and soon collected a fashion assignment. It was to model various fall outfits, and she was working for the first time with a male model. The shoot was not in a studio, but out at Rockaway Beach. And while Melanie thought she was changing fast enough, the photographer did not.

"Hey, you!" he yelled at her. "Move your tushie!"

He was a middle-aged New Yorker. Relaxed charm was not his forte.

Melanie was affronted. "My name is *Melanie*," she told him.

"I don't give a fuck what your name is," he barked. "Move it."

The male model told her that the photographer always talked like that, but Melanie again contemplated the profession with dismay.

Melanie soldiered on. She was still living with her nomadic parents, who had moved from Cherry Hill to Ridgefield, Connecticut, and she would rise at six, driving for thirty minutes to the station at Katonah, New York, where she would catch the seven-fifteen. The train would deposit her at Grand Central around eight forty-five, and she would go straight to work.

Her forebodings about modeling began to dissipate. The photographer who had harried her on the beach booked her several more times, and he turned out to be pleasant enough beneath his surface gruffness. Nor was it necessary, it turned out, for her to pop out her bosoms in public. As for Melanie's darker fears, well, she had suspected that it was necessary to "know someone" to get ahead, or go to bed with people. The rumors were false. "I can hardly think of one time a photographer made a pass at me," she observes. "Or, if they did, I didn't realize it. I would laugh, and kid around."

Nor did they often try to divest her of her clothing for professional reasons. "I was the junior model," Melanie explained. "They wouldn't want me to do lingerie. I was the sneakers, and the jogging shorts, and the smile. Nobody ever really wanted to do a nude of me. I don't know whether to be flattered or insulted."

Melanie began to study the leading models—how they worked with a photographer, how they would alter their look. She studied them as a traveler will study a map, and it paid off rapidly. A Polaroid camera shoot had followed the fashion job, and within days she picked up her first TV commercial. It was for Fayva shoes. "These seventeen- and eighteen-year-olds come and go. You hardly notice them," says Steve Oren, who modeled with Melanie at the beginning. "But Melanie was different. She was a tiger. I knew she was going to go somewhere."

The speed of Melanie's rise was startling. She made money from the start, never less than $300 a week, but spurned the luxury of taxicabs, going to her jobs by subway or by bus. She lunched on sandwiches, returning home as soon as the day was done. She would be exhausted, and she had no social life at all, but by the end of August she had saved almost $2,500. College awaited, or seemed to, but whenever she would talk about it, people were incredulous. "You're doing so *well*," they would say. "You'd be foolish. You can always go to school here in New York. Or you can go back to school later."

Melanie began to waver. She had been a good student, but she was only going to college, she realized, because *everyone* goes to college. It would keep. "I liked the excitement of the city," she says. "And I kept on making more money!"

Her parents were tolerant—telling her to do what she thought right. Melanie traveled back to Illinois and talked with her planned roommate, Jane.

"I know," Jane told her. "You have to see if you can make it in modeling."

Taken aback, Melanie temporized. "I haven't *completely* decided," she said.

"No," Jane said. "You'll never come." There was no re-crimination in her voice.

But if Melanie was on her way to becoming a New Yorker, at least in the eyes of Jane, she still had a goodish distance to go. For all the effect that the fashions she was modeling had on her private taste, she might as well have been photo-graphed in monkey suits. "Some of the outfits I used to wear were really incredible," she says. "I was into colors. *Bright* colors. And dresses, and great big clunky platform shoes, because I wanted to be taller. And the shoes looked just terrible on me, because I had very thin ankles, and they were so awkward. I would walk down the street, and people would just know I was not New York at all."

Nor was Melanie's attitude typical of New York. This spindly girl, with pink cheeks, pale-brown hair and huge, can-did eyes, was never to become a sophisticate, but at least she eventually would acquire some elementary street smarts. Right now, these were sorely lacking.

In Naperville, Illinois, for instance, there is a set of un-spoken rules that governs behavior in the street. "You look at people when you pass them," Melanie says. "You say, 'Good morning! Hello!' " Melanie, ever thrifty, would do a great deal of walking in Manhattan. In the daytime, she would trot from job to job, and afterward, as often as not she would walk to that dismal terminal the Port Authority, where she would board the bus for Connecticut and home. Often enough, she would walk west all the way along 42nd Street, a thorough-fare best known for its pimps and pushers, whores, runaways, winos, madmen, and for neon signs promising live sex acts, topless co-eds, and porno movies, and this was the route that Melanie would take, bubbling over with Good evenings! and Hellos!

"I would just be amazed at these swarms of people," she says. "And rather than just going straight ahead, the way I do now, I would look everyone in the face. Well, as soon as anyone had eye contact with you, they would pick up on it right away. Some of these nuts would talk to me, and I would talk to them. The whole thing."

The street talk and the propositions struck her not as threatening, but only bewildering. One graphic memory. It was four in the afternoon, and Melanie had finished a shooting. She was walking west on 57th Street, making for the Port Authority. She was carrying her model book, and further burdened by a suitcase packed with makeup, shoes, and clothes. Melanie had just passed Bergdorf Goodman when the man approached her. He smiled courteously and offered to carry her impedimenta.

Melanie could see that he was well dressed and, in her view, elderly. "He was in his fifties," she says. "To me he was a grandfather image. I mean, all I know is *boys*. He's not some man trying to make a pass at me. I would never think that. Why would a man want to go out with *me?* Right?"

She was grateful for the considerate New Yorker's attention. "Thank you so much," she told him. "I'm new here. And you're *so nice*."

The man lifted the suitcase and asked where she was going. Melanie said she was going home—she had been on a shoot, she was a new model with Eileen Ford.

"Oh," the man said, in apparent delight. "I know Eileen and Jerry. They're very good friends of mine." This was to prove a fabrication, and now the man, who had introduced himself as Murray, told Melanie that she looked tired. "Why don't you let me buy you a drink?" he asked.

"Well," Melanie said later, "I had come from Illinois, where the drinking age was twenty-one. Beer is what I liked. And here was this elderly man who was going to let me *drink*. I thought, oh boy! This is wonderful."

Murray guided her into a restaurant, and an imperious headwaiter seated them at a small, velvety banquette. The room was red, green, and crystal. Melanie decided that this restaurant—she later found out it was the Russian Tea Room —was the fanciest place she had ever seen. A waiter in a tunic hovered at her elbow. Murray asked her what she wanted to drink.

A quandary. Melanie didn't dare ask for a beer, fearing it wasn't classy. Murray saw her hesitating. "How would you like a screwdriver?" he suggested.

Well. Melanie had drunk beer, and she had drunk Boone's Farm apple wine. A screwdriver was something she hadn't tried, but it sounded like something you drank in a plush restaurant. "Okay, I'll have a screwdriver," she said. She polished it off quickly. Murray ordered her another, and they began to talk.

New York was a great place to work, Melanie said, but she

missed all her friends back home in Illinois. She grew sad at the telling. "I'm going back there one day," she confided.

"*I'll* be your friend," Murray promised Melanie, ordering her a third screwdriver. She was elated. A fifty-year-old man was promising to be her friend!

By now, Melanie was having quite a good time. In fact, she describes herself as "silly drunk." "Why don't you come over to my house?" Murray said. "We'll have dinner."

"Oh, *no*," Melanie said. "I have to catch the bus."

"Call your parents from my apartment," Murray said.

The apartment, which was handily nearby, seemed the picture of chic to Melanie. Murray showed her his stereo system and, walking her into the furry-carpeted bedroom, particularly drew her attention to his round and gigantic bed. He took her into closets the size of small rooms, and showed her his silk shirts, cashmere sweaters, and tailor-made suits. Melanie was puzzled, though, at the photographs of girls everywhere. Murray said they were his "friends," and that mostly they were with Eileen Ford. Melanie simply didn't believe him. "They were *sexy*," she says. "They weren't the All-American type at all." She felt small jangles of alarm.

The clincher came when Murray offered her a joint.

"You smoke *grass?*" she asked, unbelieving.

"Sure," he told her.

Melanie simply didn't believe that anybody over twenty-five smoked grass. Melanie wouldn't touch the joint. She telephoned her mother, who jumped clean down her throat: "Come on home, and right away, Melanie Cain!"

Melanie threw up all over the back of the chauffeur-driven limousine in which Murray sent her home to Connecticut. She never did use the apartment key he gave her—"Drop in and use the shower"—and the messages that came into the Ford Agency from him for weeks were ignored.

Murray's last shot was in the classic tradition. He sent her a rather fine fur coat. She sent it back. Melanie had, she thought, learned her lesson about older men.

Melanie was going on a test shooting when she met the first model she really liked. Tracy had white skin, deep-blue eyes, and a sweet manner. She was just Melanie's age, and they had rapport. After the shoot, Melanie didn't go home directly, but went with Tracy to her apartment for coffee and conversation. The apartment was at 155 East 84th Street.

Tracy had a couple of roommates, who were models too. As their friendship developed, Melanie and Tracy would have lunch, and Melanie frequently would drop by the building. "Half the doors in the place were open," she says. "And everyone I met was very friendly. It wasn't stiff and cold like a lot of places in New York. I felt very comfortable there." Sometimes Tracy and the other girls mentioned their landlord. They just called him Buddy.

But it wasn't through Tracy that Melanie was to meet Buddy Jacobson. A photographer was to do test shots of Melanie and a couple of other models wearing swimsuits and took them to a building with a pool. And Melanie was mildly surprised to find herself once again at 155 East 84th Street. They spent a couple of hours up at Buddy's pool, smiling and going through their poses while the photographer clicked away.

"The sun was out. Melanie was wearing a little pink two-piece," Bob Wood says. "She was all peaches and cream."

"She's mine," Buddy told the Wood brothers. *"I want that one."*

Melanie was in the pool when she first became aware of Jacobson. He was staring at her. "He was so . . . beady-eyed," she remembers. She wondered who this man in the scruffy clothing could be. A caretaker?

But Buddy's demeanor was impassive when they spoke. Indeed, shy. "I just thought he was quiet," she says. "Very nice, very personable, but very quiet."

Buddy soon had Melanie talking about her plans. George Cain had landed a new job, and the Cain family were making another move, this time from Connecticut to Virginia. Melanie's career was going well. It would make sense for her to move to the city, but that was a step she felt fearful about. Buddy was very reassuring. "Move into this building," he suggested. "Share an apartment with some other girls." She thanked him, and forgot it.

Weeks later, Melanie ran into another girl at the Ford Agency. The girl, whose name was Shona, told her that she was moving into an apartment, with another Ford model, Toni, and would Melanie like to make it a threesome? Toni was a black girl who had just arrived from California, and Melanie took to her at once. She promptly agreed.

It was only when George and Jane Cain drove their daughter to her new home, and the 84th Street building, the address of which she had hastily scribbled down, actually hove into view that she realized where she was going, and was glad. "This is where Tracy lives," she told her parents. "A lot of models live here. I met the guy who owns it." The date was October 15, 1973. The apartment Melanie was sharing with Shona and Toni was on the ground floor and looked out onto a garden in the back. It had two rooms, and was sparsely furnished. Melanie had brought an old sofa from home, and her grandmother's orange rug. Buddy lent the girls mattresses, but no luxuries like beds. "For tables we had crates," Melanie says. Crates were almost a design motif at 155 East 84th.

Melanie now had a boyfriend. His name was Bradley, a male model a couple of years older than she, and he had straight-arrow, campus-athlete good looks. But Melanie's work schedule kept her dating to a minimum. She would tell herself that she hadn't come to the city to have a good time. Not all the models at 155 East 84th felt the same. Shona was a bit older, a onetime stewardess, and she would be out dancing night after night. Toni was quieter, but even Toni dated more than Melanie.

Sometimes the girls would tease her, and once Melanie joined them for a night on the town. It was Friday. Melanie got dressed up, which she hated to do, and put on makeup, which she hated more, and a group of models from the building went to one of their favorite haunts, a jazzy singles bar on Second Avenue.

Melanie was dumbfounded. Guys drifted over to talk to the girls without any pretense of an introduction, their shirts open to the third button, and Melanie went into the bluest of funks. "I was so depressed," she says. "I couldn't even sit there." She mumbled something to the other girls and hurriedly left.

What Melanie liked best about the city was the early mornings, when it was fresh, and largely unpeopled. She would get up at six and go for a brisk walk. "I was always ready to start work at eight," she says. "Even if I didn't have any specific assignment. I would make lists, I could court photographers. I was most ambitious." So Melanie plugged away, intent on her career, and Buddy Jacobson's first moves toward her were lazily casual.

Her phone would ring. "Hey!" Buddy would say. "Why don't you girls come upstairs and eat Chinese food with us?"

Melanie would trot up to the seventh floor, but never alone. She would always take Toni, Tracy, or some other girl. Buddy would be there with the Woods, Bob and Jimmy, and it would be the Woods who would crack the jokes and horse around. But it would be Buddy, for all his withdrawn quality, who was in charge. "They said they were brothers, they told us the craziest stories." The familiar Zippolini brothers routine, had Melanie but known.

Next, Buddy took to inviting her to his parties, or to join the bevy of young girls that he and the Woods would take to restaurants. Melanie went to a few parties, and found them noisy, intimidating. And the dinner parties were likely to drag on till two in the morning. "Mostly, I wouldn't go," she says.

Occasionally, on a Friday or a Saturday night, she would accept, and she found the evenings bewildering—the extravagance of it all. Her own family was middle-class Republican, and she had grown up in a climate of sensible economies. "I still don't buy designer clothes," she says. Even when she was earning better than $80,000 a year, she was doing supermarket comparison shopping, but here was Buddy Jacobson, running up sizable restaurant checks nightly, and barely glancing at the total, let alone carefully adding it up the way her father might. Nor would he pay in the normal manner, which is to say with plastic. "He would reach into his pocket, and he would pay *cash*. He would flash hundred-dollar bills.

"My first reaction was: He must be in the Mafia. Who else walks around with hundred-dollar bills?"

Melanie was impressed not so much by the money, but by the sheer indifference of Buddy's manner. He just didn't care!

She was interested in him, but not that interested. "I would never go to his apartment," she says. "I would always shake his hand at the elevator door." Buddy's next tactical maneuver, accordingly, was another mixture of the obvious and the subtle. "Every night when I would come home from work," she says, "I would find flowers at the door. A dozen long-stemmed roses. It was great!"

What was more unsettling was that she would sometimes find the donor outside the door as well. "He would be just curled up there, sleeping," says Melanie.

Bradley knew Buddy Jacobson's reputation. Most people in the fashion world did by this time. He grew alarmed and, finally, irritated. "I saw what was coming," he says. "I warned her. I said, 'He isn't for you. *You'll find out!*'"

Melanie was scornful, though. By now she quite liked Buddy. Buddy wasn't pushy. He was quiet. As for the determined way he was romancing her, Melanie just couldn't take him seriously. "I thought he was very funny," she says. "His sense of humor was weird."

Melanie concentrated on her work, which went better and better, and soon she was earning more than $750 a week. This created prickles of tension. Toni accepted Melanie's greater success placidly enough, but Shona did not. She moved out of the building, and, for all Melanie knows, out of the business.

Melanie and Toni found a new roommate, a green-eyed blonde called Erica, who had already lived at 155 East 84th Street for a couple of years. They moved up to the seventh floor, Buddy's floor, where a bigger apartment was available. Buddy charged them the reasonable rent of $500 monthly.

The apartment was 7C. This was where Melanie was to stay with Jack Tupper.

It was now November. *Seventeen* booked Melanie for some bikini layouts, and sent her for two weeks to Bermuda.

Another sequence of events was now developing. It involved a young man named Dermot, a close friend of Bradley's and like Bradley a male model. Dermot had been introduced to Buddy's parties soon after arriving in New York. He was callow, and Buddy, who eyed male competition sourly, made a show of friendship toward him. Dermot was struck by the fact that Jacobson was always asking him close and detailed questions about the modeling business.

"Sure, I knew he was pumping me," Dermot says. "But here's this guy . . . his jeans are torn, and he's wearing old shoes . . . and he's got this mustache and long, straggly hair, streaky with plaster . . . he's pumping me, but what's he gonna do? He isn't going to become a model, he isn't going to take my *jobs*."

Jacobson pretty much allowed Dermot (who was living elsewhere) free run of the 84th Street building, and that suited him just admirably. "I could drop in anytime," he says. "At night, there would be terrific parties. The hot photographers would be there. All the new girls in town, too. You know, the ingenues, kids on the fast lane without a learning curve."

It was a Manhattan fantasy. Throbbing music, limitless stuff to eat and drink, predatory millionaires, suave men-about-Wall Street, the occasional Hollywood type, and slide carousels would be flashing photographs of the models onto the walls.

"The guys would be shouting, 'Hey! Run that one by us again,'" Dermot remembers. "For a red-blooded American boy, it was the Big Rock Candy Mountain!"

He fell off the mountain thus. In the third week of November, Buddy approached Dermot with an offer. "Go up to Mount Snow in Vermont," he suggested. "I've got a ski lodge there. See what needs doing . . . if the wood needs cutting, that sort of thing. Take a broad if you like. You'll be doing me a favor."

Dermot needed no persuasion, and Buddy handed him the keys. There was one model whom Dermot had been admiring for weeks. He would see her at Buddy's parties; lovely, silent, and apparently alone.

The model, as it happened, was Melanie's friend Tracy. "Hey, Trace!" Dermot proposed. "Come up to Buddy's lodge for Thanksgiving. We'll have a blast!"

Tracy accepted, and he promptly roped in another couple to make it a foursome. Next day, they rented a car from Hertz, loaded it with beer and groceries, and got off in the middle of the early-evening Friday rush hour. They arrived at the Vermont ski lodge around midnight, at the end of a long drive, and collapsed into their respective beds.

Saturday was sunny, mild, and clear. They checked the sauna, which worked, and the saw, which, happily, did not. So much for the firewood. The two couples set to work on the beer.

Evening came, and an autumnal chill. They built up a blazing fire and drank a great deal more beer. The other couple went up to bed, but Dermot and Tracy stayed downstairs, talking and laughing in front of the tremendous red blaze. In time, they made love in front of the now-subsiding fire. About three in the morning, they fell into a deep sleep.

The telephone rang at eight, and Dermot, who took the call, didn't recognize the voice at first, so strangled and harsh did it sound. He was shocked when he realized the voice was Buddy's.

"What's the matter, Buddy?" he asked.

Jacobson gave him a graphic description of Dermot's love-making a few hours before. "I want to speak to Tracy!" he finished. His voice was a guttural hiss.

Dermot looked at Tracy. Always pale, she was now like paper. He gave her the receiver with foreboding.

Tracy listened, then handed the phone back wordlessly.

"I want you two back right away," Buddy snarled at Dermot.

Tracy now admitted that she had been seeing Buddy, and had wanted to break the affair off, but had been nervous. The weekend had been, in effect, her dash for the wire. Dermot is sure someone had been outside the lodge window that night, an informer. At any rate, his alarm soon subsided in the sun. "Fuck it!" he said. "It's a beautiful day. Let's enjoy it." The four drove back in their own time, and it was evening when Dermot reached East 84th Street and helped Tracy upstairs with her things.

Tracy's apartment was on the seventh floor, alongside Buddy's. Dermot happened to be in the hallway when Buddy appeared. "He walked straight by me without a word," Dermot says. "He walked straight into her apartment."

Dermot was still standing there, feeling a bit foolish, when Buddy reappeared and backed the younger, taller man into a corner by the fire door.

What happened then was so unexpected that it left Dermot feeling not so much afraid as astonished.

"Jacobson had a thirty-eight," he says. "He was pointing it right at me." The gun was pressed disagreeably hard just above his belt, and Buddy again was hissing. "I *own* Tracy," he said. "She's my *property*." He prodded harder with the gun barrel. "I don't want to see you here again. *Ever*."

The contretemps didn't end there. Tracy and Dermot were in love, and, early in the next week, Tracy surreptitiously moved a few of her things into his East 89th Street apartment. That Wednesday, a couple of men called on Dermot with some advice—don't contact Tracy again. Their manner, he says, was "menacing." Eventually, the storm blew over. Tracy moved in with Dermot, and that was that. "But I didn't dare walk down East 84th Street for a year afterward," the male model, now turned businessman, admits.

In Bermuda, Melanie was coming to the realization that her feeling for Buddy now went beyond mere liking. It had developed into a crush. She regretted her primness, the playing hard to get.

She sat down and wrote him a postcard. Melanie liked to

write, and she took to sending Buddy a chatty postcard every day or so. On her return to New York, therefore, it was with some anticipation that she walked back into the building. She was just moving her luggage out of the elevator on the seventh floor when Buddy's apartment door opened, and he walked out. He was holding hands with a teenage model from the Stewart agency.

Melanie's smile congealed on her face.

"Hi, Melanie!" Buddy said, imperturbable as ever. "How was your trip?"

"Well!" was all that Melanie could say. In her apartment, she began to rage, considerably to the surprise of Toni and Erica. "But you don't even *like* him," Erica said. "You *hate* him."

Not any longer. Melanie now had one passion, and this was to supplant the young woman from the Stewart agency. And she quickly accomplished this.

Melanie's romance with Buddy began early that December.

From the beginning, it was more than an affair. It was as if Melanie had decided to offer herself to Buddy, giving him the opportunity to take possession of her—body and mind. Her other interests, other friendships, were to be discarded. In only one outside direction did Buddy encourage her to press forward: her career in modeling.

And in modeling, it soon became plain, she was headed for the heights. *Seventeen*, a mass-circulation fashion magazine, at this point decided to make a teenage model the subject of a cover story. "We decided to take somebody just on the edge," says Annette Grant, who was then at the magazine and is now employed by *The New York Times*.

Melanie was one of four candidates. The requirements were that the girl should not previously have appeared on a magazine cover, but should already be a proven money-earner. Melanie was chosen. "We all liked her very much. She was easy to work with," says Annette. "We knew that putting Melanie on the cover would push her to the top."

The *Seventeen* cover shows Melanie wearing a hat and a scarf, and her smile is huge and slightly diffident. She looks delectable—All-American-Girl Delectable. It hardly seems an accident that her outfit is red, white, and blue. "Meet Melanie Cain," the cover line says invitingly. Inside, she appears in fashion shots, a photographic diary depicting a model's day, and a fairly lengthy profile. The headline on the profile promises that "Cover girl Melanie Cain talks about her past, present and future," and finishes with a quote from a French photographer, who rhapsodizes that "Everything about Melanie is refreshing—she's the image of everything wholesome, like Kellogg's cornflakes."

Melanie's career was now set: a rising Ford Agency star. When Eileen Ford heard of the liaison with Buddy—and she heard about it right away—she was concerned. True, successful models often have boyfriends who have dubious backgrounds, but Buddy, the creepiest of the professional model chasers, seemed no bargain even by the most unexacting of standards.

At this stage, Eileen Ford approached Melanie, offering to take her to an international model contest in Capri, Italy. All expenses would be paid and it would be good experience. Melanie stayed in Capri a couple of weeks, and enjoyed herself hugely. She found the other girls good, if sometimes incomprehensible, company, and giggling groups of them would trot around the island in little carriages and oooh and aah on boat trips through the Blue Grotto. At night they would go to trattorias in the Marina Piccola or the Marina Grande, and stuff themselves with voluptuously buttery pasta. Chaperones with eyes like cobblers' awls kept off the local menfolk, and the odd Latin who broke through the *cordon sanitaire* was likely to get short shrift. "Half of them didn't speak English," Melanie says, "or they had corny little lines."

The contest itself came at the end of the stay. Melanie, who felt nervous at the idea of parading in a swimsuit, Miss America fashion, was not looking forward to it. She got together with three or four like-minded girls, and they prepared themselves by drinking beer. "Because we thought the contest was ridiculous," she says. "And the only way to get through it was to be totally bombed."

In a nicely woozy state, they put on their swimsuits and their designated numbers, and the obligatory cocktail-party spiked heels to show off their legs. A stage had been set up in the town square, and six judges were seated there, as the girls walked out and stood, smiling beatifically to either side.

The principal judge began a speech. Melanie, who spoke not a word of Italian, soon found her attention drifting. Suddenly, she heard a whisper: "Say! Aren't you Melanie Cain from Naperville?"

She looked down from the stage. The whisperer was an old schoolmate in Italy on an exchange program. They talked in low tones for a while, and Melanie simply didn't hear her number being called. She had won second prize. Somebody pushed her toward the judge, and she fell in a heap. "I fell in front of hundreds of people, and I was laughing, and they were taking pictures and throwing flowers. I was in the papers like that. Sitting on the stage."

Eileen Ford now suggested that Melanie go on to Paris. "You could do very well in Europe," she said. Eileen Ford's real motive, Melanie suspected even then, was to sever her from Buddy. Grudgingly, she assented.

But everything went awry in Paris. She got lost perpetually. She fell ill. She found the male Parisians conceited, the women affected. Miserably homesick, she phoned Buddy every day. Much of this was Buddy's conditioning: He had persuaded her, and continued to persuade her, that any place other than Manhattan, and in his company, had to be terrible. "I never even took a camera with me," says Melanie.

Eagerly, she returned to East 84th Street.

Melanie found Buddy in a state of flux, looking for a new focus for his restless energies. The ski lodge near Mount Snow wouldn't do: his broken promises to individual guests and tour groups had made the lodge a problem. When a new owner acquired Mount Snow itself, Buddy tried to forge an alliance. The new owner, Mark Fleischman, a curly-headed wheeler-dealer, made his money on the ski lifts and the concessions. Initially, he didn't even want to meet the lodge people. But Buddy sent him a calculated message. "Tell him I'm the only Jewish lodge owner," Buddy instructed an emissary. "Tell him all the other owners are out to get me."

Fleischman saw Buddy and heard him out. But he found that his unhinged operation—the lockless doors and unchanged sheets—was the problem, not a flare-up of anti-Semitism in the Vermont hills.

But Buddy kept trying to make him an ally. "I had a certain degree of power," Fleischman says. "I owned a mountain that had five thousand people skiing on it every day. Buddy was always hanging around me. He would sit at the bar in the base lodge, the expensive bar, and he would always have half a dozen girls and a couple of flunkies with him."

Fleischman took a fancy to one of these young women. She

was called Merrilee. One weekend Buddy telephoned. "I've brought Merrilee up for you," he said.

They dined, and Fleischman found the experience unsettling. "The vibrations felt bad," he said. "It was just a manipulative thing. She didn't really like me."

Buddy's relations with his partners in the lodge were also deteriorating. One, in particular, had taken to making a fuss about money, often in front of the guests. Donald Brown, who was staying at the lodge at the time, told Buddy not to put up with it. "Do something," he urged. "This is embarrassing."

But Brown did not believe that his remarks would have any effect. Few had ever heard Buddy raise his voice in anger. The notion that he was capable of a violent act seemed absurd.

What happened next was remarkable. That very night, Buddy exploded. Within moments, his disputatious partner was on the floor, and Buddy was kicking him. He kicked him and kicked him, like a machine that couldn't be turned off. In later years he would recount this episode with both surprise at himself and pride.

Buddy and his lodge partners were soon in litigation, to the astonishment of none.

But by now Buddy was taken with a different scheme. He was going to open a restaurant on the ground floor of the 84th Street building. He would call it Surprise. Forthwith, he applied for a liquor license, using his own name. This was careless. The State Liquor Authority had not forgotten his antics with the discothèques, and turned him down flat.

Buddy was, as usual, undaunted, and simply applied again, this time under the names of Bob and Jimmy Wood. He confidently printed up a number of yellow T-shirts with the Surprise in blue, and talked Melanie and some of the other girls into wearing them as they walked around the neighborhood.

At this point, Jacobson tried to bring Fleischman, who had just sold Mount Snow, into the new enterprise. Fleischman had already been to one of Buddy's 84th Street parties. Indeed, he had even asked one model out. But when he telephoned to confirm the date, he found it had fallen through. "Buddy told me I have to do something else," the girl told Fleischman.

"It was like he was *controlling* her," he says. Fleischman attended no more Jacobson parties, but later, when Buddy sounded him out on the restaurant proposition, he was somewhat interested. "It was a good concept," he says. "All the girls would be around the place."

But Fleischman, though intrigued, walked away from the deal. His reasons did not deal with fact, but instinct. "Normally, I don't become afraid of people," he says. "I've done business with people in jail. But I did become afraid of Buddy. He was *strange*." There would be no Surprise restaurant anyway. The State Liquor Authority saw through Buddy's use of the Woods as a cover right away, and the second license application was disapproved on February 27, 1974. Surprise was stillborn.

When Buddy's uncle, Gene Jacobs, succeeded him as president of the Horseman's Protective and Benevolent Association, it was cause and effect. Gene Jacobs was pressed to run for the job by Lou Wolfson, the millionaire breeder, who had married Hirsch Jacobs' daughter Patrice.

"Lou wanted me to . . . to repair the damage that had been done," Jacobs said, a weight of family hurt in his voice.

As for Buddy, for the benefit of the press, he would portray himself as a horseman ill treated; he would tell *The New York Times* he considered himself "an exile." In fact, he showed no interest in racing until he became involved in the opening of a new track. This was to be in Connecticut, where it was looking probable that a state prohibition might be lifted. Two schemes were quickly launched. They were nicknamed the Republican track and the Democratic track. Buddy's interest was in the former.

The track was to occupy 437 acres and was to sit in the Zoar Berkshire countryside, close to the town of Newtown. It was to cost $30 million, and the nifty prospectus promised "a total annual wagering of $186 million." The president was Noel Bernstein, Buddy's former owner. Jacobson's controversial name did not appear on the list of sponsors, but Bob Wood's did; he was in for five percent, and was described as "the vice-president of New York Counseling Services, a real estate development firm." This company was named for that long-gone credit course in stablecraft conducted on Buddy's farm in Old Westbury.

Bernstein is emphatic that Buddy had no direct financial participation in the track. "But the fact that I would talk to him on a day-to-day basis, the fact that we would talk about the construction and what people wanted at a racetrack, the fact that he had some very unique and different ideas—that's something else," Bernstein says. "In that sense he *was* my partner."

Buddy seems not to have seen his role in this altruistic light. He was within striking distance of big money and, what was more important, of *power*. "Buddy would draw up designs for the stalls area on a napkin," Bob says. "We would have control. We would say who's going to get the stalls. We would say who's going to get the hot-dog concession." At a referendum, the Connecticut citizenry came out resoundingly in favor of the track. All seemed set. It was then that the Bernstein group ran into a muscular lobby.

Environmentalists.

Various groups said they were disturbed by the impact that a racetrack was likely to have on a sparsely populated area. The fight promised to be long and sticky, and there was no alternative but to wait as the matter plodded through the courts.

Another legal process was holding Buddy's attention more closely at this time. In June 1974, his $6 million suit against the New York Racing Association was finally tried in front of a state supreme court judge. The venue was an unimpressive courtroom in the town of Mineola.

"It was like the big boys used their influence to get the smallest courtroom in the state," says Joe Finnegan of the HPBA. He arrived to see the small cluster of Jockey Club heavyweights whose presence had been deemed necessary sitting on one side of the courtroom, while Buddy's scruffier partisans sat on the other. "It was like a wedding," he said. "The bride's friends were on one side, the groom's on the other."

One group conspicuous by their absence were Buddy's former fellow trainers. "There wasn't a trainer there," Finnegan says. "None of them dared go near it. Afterward, they gathered around me, wanting to know what was happening."

In Finnegan's view, it didn't look good for Jacobson. "If I had been Buddy's lawyer," he said, "I would have tidied him up. His appearance was practically contempt of court in itself. I would have given him a shave and a haircut. I didn't know whether he was Sacco or Vanzetti."

Buddy entertained no such doubts about the outcome. He felt that the New York Racing Association had been unfair in refusing to allocate him stalls, and he was certain he would win his suit.

"We have a great many more people who want stalls than we have stalls to give," Alfred Gwynne Vanderbilt told Buddy's lawyer, Jerry Moss. "So there are always people that are going to be refused stalls. When you get yourself in a position at the track where your record is not good, and you have shown that your character is under suspicion to some extent, [the persons] giving out stalls tend to take those people who are above reproach."

Moss: "And discard the ones who are not above reproach?"

Vanderbilt: "Well, at least slide them down toward the bottom of the list."

Moss pointed out the anomaly: many track figures who had committed offenses at least as dastardly as Buddy's had been punished far less stringently. He listed a number of famous horsemen and their misdeeds, even having the temerity to drag in Lou Wolfson, Buddy's cousin by marriage, The low points of Wolfson's dynamic life were, of course, the Abe Fortas payment which resulted in the resignation of Judge Fortas from the Supreme Court and the Florida jail term Wolfson incurred for selling $2.5 million of unregistered stock. Yet Wolfson was again established at the track.

No matter. Buddy's case was found to be "without merit." He was astounded.

Melanie's love for Buddy was, in these early stages, exhilarating. It sent her on her modeling rounds each morning willing to assert herself. And now she was coming into conflict with the Ford Agency. She was doing well with the wholesome look, and wholesome was the way Ford wished her to stay. "They said I'd be a junior model for seven years, *then* I'd do high fashion. Well, I wanted to do high fashion right away. They wanted to put me in a *category*. I wanted to do *everything* right away—commercials, TV, catalogues, print."

So it was without Eileen Ford's blessing that Melanie started banging on the doors of the high-fashion photographers and the more sophisticated magazines. Results were rapid. She worked for everybody from *Vogue* to *Cosmopolitan*.

"Melanie quickly became a great crossover model," says Suzanne Flynn, an editor who used her frequently. "She could be a high-fashion model, a professional woman, a college girl." Buddy took to calling her the Girl with a Thousand Faces. His knack for publicity had not deserted him, and the phrase was duly used in a laudatory piece on Melanie by fashion journalist Eugenia Sheppard.

But her success brought its own problems. Melanie began to feel she was always expected to be *on*. One evening she went to a dinner party in the Fords' townhouse, a sizable place in the East 60s. She made conversation with the other guests, a few Scandinavian blondes, and some well-groomed men with successful smiles, and left as soon as she decently could. It had seemed an alien world.

Melanie would pour out her frustrations to Buddy.

"Why don't you start your own agency?" he suggested casually one day.

"Oh! I can't do that."

"*Sure* you can," Buddy said.

Melanie thought he was kidding. She mentioned the suggestion to Erica and Toni, and they giggled about it. Soon model was chattering about it to model, and the thought might as well have gone out as a press release.

Melanie Cain was starting her own agency.

It happened to have been another model-agent who called the Ford Agency with the news. Eileen and Jerry Ford were in Rome. Their office reached them there and passed the rumor on.

It was now July 17, 1974. Melanie was doing an ad for Bonwit Teller. She was actually on the set, wearing a nurse's uniform, when the agency telephoned. It was one of the executives, Joey Hunter.

"Hi, Joey," she said.

Melanie will never forget what Hunter said.

"Melanie," he told her calmly, "I'm afraid we have to drop you from the agency."

"What?" Melanie yelped. A dozen reasons washed around her head. Had she gained weight? Had she grown ugly? Was it that they suddenly disliked her? "Why?" she asked.

"We understand that you are going to start your own agency," said Hunter.

By the time Melanie finished the booking, she had become less upset than furious that, without questioning her, Ford had assumed the worst. Until that moment, Melanie would have been quite happy to discuss anything with the agency, even to sign a binding contract. Not now. "I was angry, angry, angry," she says.

Curiously, it was Buddy who was alarmed. Did Melanie want him to try to explain things to Eileen Ford? Did she want to talk to the other leading agents? Wilhelmina maybe, or Zoli.

But indignation made Melanie adamant. Buddy could have learned a lesson here.

"My attitude was, well, if that's what they think I'm doing, then maybe that's just what I'm going to do," Melanie says.

She called the agency after her favorite musical—*My Fair Lady*. When Melanie was younger, she had dreamed of being an actress or, especially, a dancer. Modeling had intervened, but My Fair Lady, the agency, now embodied a different dream. Melanie already had success. Now she wanted control. Not, like Buddy, control of others, but control of herself.

It was Buddy, though, who took care of all the legal matters: setting up the company, appointing directors, issuing stock. He had magical fingers when it came to issuing stock. Supposedly there were one hundred shares. Melanie believed she and Buddy each owned fifty. Bob Wood was under the impression he owned twenty-five shares, and Buddy handed smaller clumps of stock to people he felt might add luster to the enterprise. Noel Bernstein, for instance, got a few shares, as did the jaunty horseman-financier Jerome Castle, chairman and chief executive of the multimillion-dollar corporation, Penn-Dixie.

Buddy had handled the details. Now Melanie got the agency going. An office was handily available, the ground-floor space which was to have housed the Surprise restaurant. Melanie needed a booker, which is to say somebody to handle telephone calls and keep track of upcoming jobs. She called Josephine, who had been working at the Ford agency, and offered her more money. "She came over with the go-see lists," Melanie says. "She knew the clients."

There was only one model at the My Fair Lady agency for the first few months, Melanie. She found her career quite undamaged by her departure from Ford's. "If anything, it helped," she says. "I sold *myself*."

But it was not Buddy's plan that Melanie be his only talent. He telephoned Peter Glenn and said he wanted to be a judge at a modeling convention. Glenn is the publisher of the *Madison Avenue Handbook* and, together with an associate, Rose Marie Taylor, runs Model's Mart. An influence. Cautiously, Glenn said he would see what he could do.

That wasn't good enough. "I want to be on the same panel as Wilhelmina and Eileen Ford," said Buddy.

Glenn was taken aback, until Buddy added that his agency's star was "the top model, Melanie Cain." Nor was this all. "You're a publisher," Buddy said. "I'd like to talk to you about a book I'm putting together." The book was to be about the track. Buddy had always wanted to be in a book.

Glenn, who used to go to the track, suddenly realized which Buddy Jacobson he was talking to. The two men met, and Glenn was surprised. He had been expecting some urbane, sophisticated type, and here was somebody who looked, as he puts it, "like a cross between Hitler and Groucho Marx."

They had dinner a couple of times, and Glenn became convinced that everything was "on the up-and-up." "So I got him involved in all the associations. I even sent him to a tailor."

In March 1975, Buddy and Melanie were both judges at the shindig the World Modeling Association gave at the Waldorf. Thus they met the owners of all the modeling schools. These are the schools which, all over the South and Midwest, have replaced the finishing schools of yore, except that they offer not merely social poise but dreams of commercial glory.

Buddy's arrival proved opportune all around. "We were having a feud with Eileen Ford," says Margo George of the International Models Association. "She had been attacking the modeling schools." My Fair Lady might be an embryo agency, but Melanie Cain was a top New York model. Buddy and the schools *needed* each other.

It was, after all, like calling to like, according to the Publicist. "The conventions are a great scam," he says. "Registration is a hundred bucks per girl. Maybe a hundred and fifty. And Buddy was terrific. He would send Melanie over to the girls, and he would romance the women who ran the schools. A brilliant maneuver."

Certainly Buddy proved tremendously artful at dealing with the school owners. Millie Lewis, for instance, runs four modeling schools in South Carolina, a state which takes beauty very, very seriously, and she first met Buddy at Peter Glenn's. She was distinctly unimpressed. Those worn jeans, those tacky shirts. "He looked like he should be out cleaning the streets," she says.

But Buddy talked to her, and he proved uniquely pleasant-spoken in a modeling world that is fiercely vituperative. "He never had a bad word to say about Eileen or Willy," she says. Buddy would wine and dine her, and send her fruit and flowers. He didn't seem like a New York person at all. "He was so *mild*," she says, still fondly. "He looked like a little shaggy dog."

Buddy drew up some contracts, and set off with Melanie for talent hunts in the heartland. "He told me he would just throw a dart at the map, and go where it landed," says a strawberry blonde from Minnesota. The blonde was offered what most likely prospects were offered—a contract, a ticket, and a free apartment, which just happened to be at 155 East 84th Street. She accepted. But once Buddy had worked out the mechanics of the operation, he found his enthusiasm for that part of the United States which lies outside Manhattan waning.

"When he was out of New York, he just wasn't Buddy," says Melanie. "He was nobody. He was streetwise in New York, but anywhere else he just wasn't sure of himself."

Soon Buddy began to dispatch Melanie to find prospects on her own. She would go on weekends. "God forbid I should lose a day of work," she now says. "I would fly out on Friday evening after a whole day of modeling in the city, and come back Sunday night. And I would work Monday morning."

She felt the control of her life slipping away. She was in love with Buddy, but an abhorrence of what she was doing began to build in her. "I mean, he would put me on a plane, and I was nineteen years old, and I would go to these modeling conventions and talk to the schoolowners." Buddy would press Melanie to sign up young girls—the younger the better. "I was supposed to say, 'Why do you have to finish school? Start early, you're sixteen. New York is marvelous.' "

But here, for the first time, she rebelled against Buddy. College was still something she felt herself cheated of. Melanie was not going to scoop kids out of high school and plunk them down in Buddy's building. Blinkered by love though she might be, she was growing suspicious of her paramour's motives.

Occasionally all that she would bring back to Manhattan

was a portfolio of photographs. The pictures would show some fresh-faced cuties from the Corn Belt, the Sun Belt, the Bible Belt. Buddy would study the photos and ask, with some nonchalance, when the girls were getting to town.

Melanie would tell him that the girls were only sixteen. They couldn't come for a couple of years.

And Buddy would be outraged. "*What?* You should tell them not to waste their time," he would tell Melanie. "Bring them to New York *right away.*"

"But there were some things not even Buddy could make me do," Melanie says.

Melanie Cain met Dolly Robertson when they were modeling party dresses for *Seventeen*. They took to each other instantly, though it was a curious friendship in certain ways. Dolly, the older of the two by a couple of years, was beautiful and loving, but wracked by insecurities. She walked through life with a sort of erratic briskness, as somebody treads who is trying to wish demons away.

Dolly was head over heels in love with Jimmy Wood, and that was potential trouble. It was always to Melanie that she would go with her woes. And if Melanie suggested a course of action, Dolly would hang on every word. "She was so naive," Melanie says. "It was like I was her big sister."

They were, indeed, often taken for sisters, so alike did they look when they went around town together, traipsing from studio to go-see, from go-see to studio, swinging their model books. And Melanie realized that she had something of importance: a true friend.

Buddy's reaction was utterly in character. He decided that he needed another successful head on the My Fair Lady model sheet and put Jimmy Wood under continuous pressure to sign up Dolly, even offering to forgo the agency commission. Jimmy was not enthusiastic about the scheme, but Dolly walked out of the Ford Agency, and came over to My Fair Lady.

Melanie was sinking more and more deeply into Buddy's private world. Where Dolly was concerned, he simply bided his time, in the meanwhile working the girl like a willing pony. But under Buddy's influence, Melanie found herself losing touch with most other people she knew. Later, she was to find this was no accident. Betsy Fitzgibbon, a model with whom she had become friendly, often telephoned, asking her to play tennis. Buddy would say that Melanie was "away." Finally, Betsy stopped calling.

He didn't even approve of the tennis in itself: The game, after all, requires partners. "*I'll* play with you," he told Melanie. "But Buddy," Melanie said, "you can't play tennis." Buddy felt that he could do anything, and took out membership in the Park East, a nearby tennis club. He and Melanie walked out onto the court, and Buddy lifted his racket.

"You don't hold it like that," Melanie said.

"I'll hold it my own way," he answered.

Melanie played as badly as she could, but she could not avoid giving Buddy a whipping. He threw his racket away in a rage and stalked off, denouncing the game as childish. From then on, Melanie played tennis less and less.

Her parents knew by now of her relationship with Jacobson. They looked forward to seeing Melanie married, of course, but at least Buddy was hard-working and, as far as they knew, clean-living. They hungered for details about her boyfriend, but she could tell them little. Unquestioningly, she had accepted Buddy's fast shuffle with bogus driving licenses and fake IDs, and believed that he was in his late twenties. She had accepted that he was mostly of Italian extraction, though with a smidgen of Indian thrown in, and he would often speak disparagingly of "typical New York Jewish schmucks."

Buddy's immediate family seemed invisible. Melanie had been told that he had a brother, David, and the two "brothers" would telephone each other. His father, she knew, was dead. Jimmy Wood had told her that so great was Buddy's dislike for his father that he had bitterly resented the single visit he had paid, at his mother's entreaty, to the dying man. But Wood did say that Buddy, while driving away from the hospital, had shown a rare flicker of compassion. "You feel frustrated," he had said to Wood. "It's like part of *you* is dying. And there's nothing you can do."

Mostly, though, Buddy would talk about his dead father in the bleakest terms, as a "creep" and a "failure" whose mistress wore furs while Buddy's mother, Florence, struggled to raise the family on her own meager resources. He would always speak of his mother warmly, though he made it plain that he now paid her bills.

Florence would telephone at least once a week. Sometimes Melanie and she would have a chat. Florence would reminisce about the young Buddy helping her paint the apartment, that sort of thing. Quite clearly, she adored her son. But Buddy would always be brusque when talking to his mother. Once Melanie asked if she could meet Florence. "You'll meet her when we get married," Buddy said.

Melanie grew more puzzled. His mother lived only a few miles away in Queens. "Why don't you ever go to see her?" she asked.

Buddy looked at her blankly. "Why?" he said. "What do I have in common with an old lady?"

Melanie, who never was to meet Florence Jacobson face to face, was troubled by this attitude, but accepted it. This was part of Buddy's absolutism. Affection was a weakness. Old age was worse—a disease. Such was the stark landscape of Buddy's World.

But now Buddy's World was undergoing a few modifications. Some of Melanie's friends had moved on. Tracy went to work in Europe, and Erica was trying her luck in Los Angeles. But Dolly was there, and Melanie had also become friendly with two other tenants: Mel Harris, a dark-haired girl from Pennsylvania and Ingrid, a placid girl with black hair who had both recently joined My Fair Lady.

The females-only policy in the building had been maintained with considerable success. Buddy had made an exception for Marilyn Chambers, protagonist of such porn classics as *Behind the Green Door*, who was permitted to rent with her husband/manager, Chuck Traynor. But this was because Buddy had been excited by her notoriety. He had reacted differently when Betsy Fitzgibbon, Melanie's occasional tennis partner, had asked for an apartment. When Buddy discovered that Betsy was engaged to be married, and to a pro footballer at that, the apartment he had promised suddenly became "unavailable."

But the airline cutbacks of the mid-seventies, which resulted in the layoff of a great number of stewardesses, introduced a new element. Those fired were usually the girls most recently hired—just the nubile creatures with whom Buddy had been stocking the East 84th Street building.

The girls went forlornly home, and Buddy was forced to open the place up to tenants and habitués previously unwelcome: single men. Among them were Donald Brown and David Silbergeld. Donald Brown, Buddy's ebullient acquaintance from Queens, had now set up his international hashish operation and had gravitated to Manhattan. It was Brown who introduced friends like Carlo Carrara, a huge and amiable man from Long Island, the owner of a construction company, who never formally rented an apartment at 155 East 84th, but became a familiar figure there. David Silbergeld, the military zealot, came into Buddy's World by accident. He had been intending to look at the building next door.

Buddy's style was not noticeably cramped by the invasion of males. With the passage of time, as his savoir faire had increased, he had abandoned those gaudy night spots frequented by out-of-towners, and his favorite venue was now Elaine's, on Second Avenue at the foot of 88th Street.

Elaine's is famous. It has a darkly cozy interior, the food can be described, perhaps, as nourishing, and Elaine herself is not a hostess of the bubbly sort, but the place has had an astonishing longevity as a home away from home for writers, actors, and movers and smoothies. It was to Elaine's that Buddy would go with the Wood brothers, perhaps, or some other temporarily in favor male acolytes, and Melanie, and five, six, seven, eight goggle-eyed young girls, in the biggest rented limo they had seen in their entire lives.

Jimmy Wood still speaks of this period with nostalgia. "Woody Allen would be sitting there with a famous movie star," he says, "and nobody would be looking at Woody Allen. They would be looking at *our* table." Well, maybe, but it's a blasé crowd at Elaine's, one not short of lovely women. Elaine herself says merely that Buddy would come in with "no jacket, shirt hanging out of his trousers," and that the young things "used to drink crap drinks. You know, sugar drinks. Kahlua! *Kid* drinks." And when her bartender, Frank, a former cop, spotted that one of the Woods—Elaine still calls them "Buddy's brothers"—was carrying a gun, Elaine Kaufman, not caring that, as a dealer in precious metals, he was licensed to do so, began regarding the high-paying table with an increasingly glum eye.

Not so Nicola Spagnolo. Nicky, Elaine's headwaiter, had recently become her partner: a small, determined man, with eyes as black as beetle wings, he saw much to admire in

Buddy and his ornamental retinue. The two men took a liking to each other. Buddy had questioned him while he was still planning his ill-fated restaurant, Surprise, and Nicky confided that his relationship with Elaine was worsening. He, too, was set on opening a place of his own. Buddy said he would keep his eyes open. He was dreaming of becoming a real estate magnate, and was scouting around for property anyway.

Donald Brown found the actual premises. It was an eating house called the Old Foresters, located on East 84th Street, directly across from Buddy's building. The Old Foresters was a mint-condition relic of those days when Yorktown was a purely German neighborhood. It had an antlered deer's head and glazed beer steins surmounting the bar, a glassed-in alcove filled with carved pipe bowls and kitsch figurines, and a look of timbered folksiness. Donald Brown, who would eat there from time to time with such cronies as Carlo Carrara, heard that the elderly woman who owned it would be happy to sell, asking only that one house specialty be left on the menu for her regulars' sake. The news traveled from Brown to Buddy to Nicola, and the deal was done.

There was, indeed, a specialty on the menu when Nicola's opened—wiener schnitzel—and the decor was little changed, but the restaurant soon showed it didn't have to depend on former regulars. It was successful from the start, and the celebrated faces who haunted Elaine's trekked secretively over to Nicola's to inspect it, daring Elaine's wrath. To and fro, to and fro: *New York* magazine called it the Saloon War. Soon Nicola's walls were blossoming with framed book jackets signed with compliments from such authors as Peter Maas, Mario Puzo, Gay Talese.

Other pictures were also hung there. Melanie's face was prominent, with a remote look and a sensual glimmer, adorning a cover of *Cosmopolitan.* "To Nicky," she had scrawled across the bosom. "Best Joint in Town." On the wall beside the bar hung a photograph of David Silbergeld. He was in his Green Beret uniform, holding a submachine gun in a sternly martial pose. The picture was signed "The Major." And here and there were photographs of some of the winsome girls from Buddy's building, Mel Harris being one, wearing little but T-shirts, inscribed NICOLA's.

This idea was, of course, borrowed from Buddy. His further participation in Nicola's had been discussed, but in the end it was limited to the installation of a cigarette machine and a juke box, which he brought from his embattled ski lodge near Mount Snow. It was in Nicola's that Buddy began to dine almost nightly: the pasha of East 84th Street.

Buddy had a small problem, though: he was again running out of money. This, as a matter of fact, had always been his way. It was as if he required tension in order to thrive. "He was *always* in trouble," says a trainer. "He *looked* for trouble. If things were going well, he wasn't happy. He'd go out and buy another building, and then there wouldn't be enough money." He was under pressure now, with all his money embedded in the 84th Street building and more constantly required. His checks to the My Fair Lady models began to bounce. Buddy, in peril, turned back to something he knew: the racetrack. He went to see financier Jerome Castle. "He said he was broke," Castle says, "and could I get him back into racing."

When Castle's own father had gone broke, Buddy's uncle lent him over $5,000: A debt. "I went to see Jack Dreyfus," Castle says. "Jack said that Buddy was a charlatan and a thief." But others spoke up in Jacobson's favor, including his formidable cousin by marriage, Lou Wolfson. In the end, as Gene Jacobs puts it, "Jack Dreyfus relented." Buddy was given fifteen stalls—a stingy allotment, compared with former days, but he was back in business.

This was the summer of 1975. Buddy promised Jerome Castle that he would lead a proper trainer's life. Down to the stables at six-thirty, and no hanky-panky. They came to terms, agreeing to go fifty-fifty on losses and wins.

Jerome Castle's friends were skeptical, none more so than the man responsible for Buddy's eminence in the first place. "Bill Frankel told me it was a mistake," Castle says. "He said Buddy would never change."

In some ways, Buddy proved the truth of this skepticism right away. As iconoclastic as ever, he promptly told the *New York Post* that he couldn't care less about the sport of kings. "I never was a racing fan," he explained. Quickly he began to claim $20,000 horses, just like old times. And it was a source of much gleeful wit around the track when one of the first unhappy owners from whom he claimed was Lou Wolfson, one of the men who had just helped him back to the track.

Buddy soon picked up another owner, and an important

one. Jim Edwards came from Berryville, Virginia, and had been in racing since 1931. "But seldom at a profit," he observes. "It was an avocation." His spread was called Audley Farm. "At that time," he says, "I had four hundred horses, including brood mares . . . yearlings . . . weanlings . . . sucklings."

Of these, perhaps a hundred and fifty were more or less ready for the track, and Edwards had just lost his longtime trainer. It seemed the answer to a prayer when he heard that former champion Buddy Jacobson had been reinstated by the New York Racing Association. "I felt that, being reinstated, he would make every effort," Edwards says.

Between Castle's and Edwards' mounts, Buddy now had half a million dollars' worth of horseflesh under his control, and at first things went quite well. He made good on his promise to Castle, rising early and putting in time at the stables. Almost at once, he prospered. The gallery of photographs at Nicola's was augmented by a picture of Buddy standing alongside De Lite Jr., a winner for Jerome Castle at Belmont. He stands there, looking at the camera, in what appears to be an army-surplus jacket, his mustache and hair full and straggly.

But Buddy's reformation did not last. With success and cash flow, his interest slackened. Soon he was yet again training by telephone. About six o'clock one morning, a sportswriter arrived at the track to prepare a piece about Buddy's triumphal comeback. He was stopped by a security man from Pinkerton's.

"What do you want?" asked the Pinkerton.

"I'm interviewing Mr. Jacobson."

"I'll take you to him."

They arrived at the barn, and Mr. Jacobson was there: David Jacobson. The sportswriter drove into Manhattan and went to see Buddy at East 84th Street instead. Buddy revealed his plan: He wanted his older son to be number-one trainer in the country the first year he had his license. This would be his, Buddy's, masterstroke.

"Okay," the sportswriter said, "I'll write it."

Buddy grew panicky. "You can't do that," he said. "You can't write that I've got a kid who's eighteen years old. How the hell are all the broads going to believe I'm thirty-three? It's gonna screw my whole act."

The sportswriter fudged the story. Buddy always did have a winning way with the press.

Melanie, meanwhile, remained ignorant of Buddy's act. Her life was programmed to the exclusion of almost everything. On summer weekends, there were afternoons on the building's roof, sitting beside the pool, with a barbecue and beer. The usual bevy of girls would be around, and a few permitted men.

Carlo Carrara, sometimes, and David Silbergeld, who was now engaged to Melanie's sensible friend Mel Harris, and living in 7C, which was to be Jack Tupper's apartment. Not Donald Brown, who by this time had left for Los Angeles and, he said, retirement. (The Drug Enforcement Agency would, in due course, take issue with that claim.)

Very occasionally, Buddy and Melanie would leave Manhattan. Once they went to stay for the weekend with Jerome Castle at his country estate. This was not a success. "Lucia hated him," Castle says. Lucia is the financier's wife. "He had dirty fingernails. He was rude to women over twenty-one."

Buddy, he says, did not enjoy the weekend either. "He was bored out of his kazoo," Castle says. "He told me he never wanted to live outside a five-mile radius of New York."

In this one respect, Buddy and Melanie were similar: Both were tireless workers. Melanie pounded on toward a goal that shimmered tantalizingly ahead, but that she couldn't quite recognize. It wasn't money. It wasn't power. Was it freedom? All she knew was that she was working harder than ever. My Fair Lady now had reached a size it was to maintain, between a dozen and twenty working models, all female, in which it differed from its mightier competitors, Ford, Wilhelmina, Zoli, and Stewart, which did valuable business in male modeling. And many of the girls were going nowhere. This is true at all agencies, but it was truer at My Fair Lady. Dolly was doing well, and Ingrid was showing promise—she had just collared a prestige booking, a Newport cigarette campaign— but, mostly, My Fair Lady was Melanie Cain.

"Buddy was running things, and I have to say he was energetic," Melanie says. "You know, the bigger agencies, they'll say, no, she's not available at those hours. They won't try and work the booking out. They won't call up the first client, and rearrange both times, so I get both bookings.

"But Buddy was great at maneuvering. He got every little booking in there. Sometimes I would have fifteen minutes to get across town. I wasn't only working eight hours a day, I was working twelve, or fifteen!" Ingrid did not enjoy the pressure, and Dolly was growing plaintive under the regimen, but Melanie throve on it.

It was not in Buddy's nature to socialize with the fashion world any more than he had done with track personalities, but when he chose to do so it was with quiet relentlessness. "Whenever he would see me, he would send over a Sambuca or a bottle of champagne," says fashion editor Suzanne Flynn, and on one occasion, she says, Buddy called a group of editors and offered them a free weekend at his ski lodge.

The notion seemed horrendous to Flynn, even without knowing of the lodge's reputation. She pictured herself blizzard-bound, forced to make small talk with seventeen-year-olds from Idaho. She telephoned her colleagues, out of curiosity, and found that few, if any, were planning to take up the offer. "But I respected Buddy," she says. "He had this insane style."

His style was apparent at the various modeling conventions. The attempts by Peter Glenn of the *Madison Avenue Handbook* to turn Buddy into a simulacrum if Eileen Ford's well-groomed husband, Jerry, by sending him off to a tailor were not a success. "He arrived at the Hilton with tags on his suit," says Rose Marie Taylor. "I had to snip them off." But as long as Eileen Ford and the other nabobs of the Manhattan modeling business withheld their blessing from the conventions, Jacobson did them a valuable service.

And, of course, vice versa. Sometimes Buddy seemed to be allowed a free hand by the conventions. He and Melanie became judges. Then Dolly became a judge. As Buddy's grip tightened, David Silbergeld became a judge, Jimmy Wood became a judge, a couple of young Upper East Side old-money types who had impressed Buddy in Nicola's became judges. On one characteristic occasion, a convention program reproduced single-page letters of welcome from Mayor Beame and Governor Carey; a double-page advertisement for My Fair Lady (the only model agency mentioned in this way); and a smiling photograph of actor Peter Lawford, with the caption: "In from California just to be with us on Saturday and Sunday. Will serve on our Celebrity Panel, and will give out the awards at the Awards Banquet." Lawford, who had been introduced to Buddy by Donald Brown, never did show up, but Buddy just shrugged off his absence.

Melanie, who was skeptical about the schools and their "training," felt equally unkeen about the conventions. Maybe one girl out of a hundred actually becomes a model, she says, and as often as not, it's somebody who only recently started. "You'd rather take her like that anyway, and make her into a real model yourself," she says. But she went along with what Buddy wanted. Jimmy Wood remembers one convention well. He was standing with Buddy in a hotel ballroom. Both men wore expressions of studied calm as they watched scores and scores of adorable dolls with their pretty party dresses and bright, fearful smiles.

"Buddy! Look!" Jimmy Wood said, sotto voce. "How about *her?*"

Buddy studied the young woman in question: She was exquisite.

"She's the best," Buddy agreed.

He and Wood leafed through the program. Conventions are judged in various "categories," beauty-contest style. The judges at this stage of the proceedings included three Jacobson nominees, including two of the old-money types. Melanie was not sitting on this particular panel.

Jimmy Wood strolled briskly across to the line of contestants. Again in beauty-pageant style, they bore identifying signs, and were about to mount the runway and face the audience and the judges. Wood beckoned the young woman in question aside and handed her a My Fair Lady card. "Mr. Jacobson—this gentleman here—would like you to join the agency," he told her. "And I would like to take a Polaroid."

The Polaroid gambit was a gem. While the picture developed, Jimmy would casually cross-examine the girl, asking her name, the school she had come from, her address, and, just in case something came up, her telephone number. This particular creature was a seventeen-year-old with limpid green eyes, a honey blonde from the Deep South.

"Okay," Wood told her. "Get back in line. You've won."

She shied like a pony. "Whaaaat?" she said.

"You've won the contest. Just don't tell anybody."

Wood walked quickly through the crowd and up to the judges. He had an official pass, he had a camera; nobody bothered him. Leaning over, he whispered the Southern girl's name in the ear of one of the rich sprigs. "That's the winner," Wood said. "Make sure these guys vote for her. You understand?"

"I understand," he said, but added, "What about that girl over there? She's good too."

"Will you please *stop?*" said Wood. "You don't know what a pretty girl is. This is the girl you've gotta vote for. I'll be back to tell you who's gonna be number two."

Magnanimously, Wood added that the judges might choose number three themselves.

Two days later came the official announcement: The Southern belle was, indeed, a winner. She joined the My Fair Lady roster and came to New York to try her luck. Jimmy Wood does know that she never had a serious degree of modeling success, but beyond that he doesn't have the remotest idea what happened to her. New York, apparently, just swallowed her up.

Buddy was skillful with a prospective model's parents. To them he would appear the image of propriety. David Silbergeld talks of lending Buddy the appropriate wardrobe—a clean shirt, a dark suit, a subdued tie—and Buddy would take some cozy little out-of-town group—father, mother, and daughter—across the road, and they would dine in Nicola's. This restaurant, incidentally, had now found its character. Elaine's, by and large, maintained its dominion over the writers, the actors, and the gilded intelligentsia. Nicola's had become a focal point for a new class: a bit raffish, very preppy, and with a strong admixture of the émigré European rich, fleeing socialist depredations at home.

The more knowing habitués of Nicola's would watch Buddy's performance for the parents-from-Kansas entranced: the confident mastery of his demeanor, his level tones as he expounded his plans for the beloved daughter, the whispered explanations that such-and-such a person over there was the heir to a fortune and that so-and-so, smiling at the corner table, was an influential ad man.

One evening David Silbergeld and Mel, entered the place to dine, and Buddy, unnaturally effusive, invited them to join his table. He was with a couple of out-of-town parents. Silbergeld, cannier at this time than either Melanie or his wife, saw what was going on right away. He and Mel were the Young

Married Couple, the lovely model respectably married to the successful businessman: a reassuring image. "I felt uncomfortable," Silbergeld says. "I left as soon as we decently could."

There had always been talk about the My Fair Lady agency, but now the rumors began to take an ugly turn. "We were hearing that Buddy was a pimp," a magazine editor says. This talk was insubstantial, but wholly characteristic of an industry where the most active bodily organ is the bitchy tongue. Model agencies deal with lovely young faces, well-proportioned young bodies, and even lovelier mountains of dollars, francs, lire, pounds, Deutschmarks, and yen. Certain model agents, moreover, take a proprietarial attitude toward their young charges, giving small parties at which the girls can meet the "right sort" of person. Private lives and private "arrangements"—the line can be very thin. And Buddy Jacobson *was* certainly wont to decorate his table with beautiful women when sitting down to a business chat. But Buddy's dirty little secret was more devious: This was the period that saw the rococo blossoming of what he and the two Woods, the Zippolini brothers of yore, called their Zzzyp Tricks.

It was Buddy's Zzzyp Tricks that were to bedevil the Tupper murder trial in the closing-in future. His feelings for Melanie, which were already singular and were to reach such a curious intensity, were unadmitted to others. Perhaps at this stage, which one might call the first half of his affair with Melanie, he wouldn't have admitted them to himself. Buddy was in control. Melanie, it seemed to the outside world, was a piece of little-cared-for property. And who kills for a piece of property? Certainly Buddy was as sexually unfaithful as it is possible to be, untiring and mechanical—a robot of ruttishness.

The Zzzyp Tricks had been legitimized back in 1962, when Buddy took the last entry in the Manhattan telephone directory under the name Budd Zzzyp. In time to come, George Carpozi of the *New York Post* would find that this "secret" number was proof positive that My Fair Lady was a cover for a call-girl operation. But the reasoning here was muddy, since Budd Zzzyp's telephone number was the same as that given for the agency, and for Buddy himself, and would be answered the same way: "My Fair Lady . . ."

In fact, of course, the Zzzyp number was a ploy. You meet

a pretty girl somewhere—on the street, at a party—and tell her to call you: last number in the book. What could be simpler? The Zzzyp Tricks had grown more sophisticated since the fun and games in Kew Gardens but the objectives remained the same. Zzzyp Tricks were a means to sexual power, conquest, display.

But Buddy now had developed rules. It was important, for instance, to act as if money were utterly irrelevant. Once a crony fell into error by totting up a dinner check. Later, Buddy waxed wroth.

"What were you doing?" he demanded. "The girls saw you looking at the check. It was *embarrassing*."

"The check came to three hundred dollars. I just wanted to see what we were buying."

Buddy was finality itself. "If you don't want to play by the rules," he said, "don't play the game."

Some of the rules trespassed on neurosis. Buddy and his male cohorts would decree which man was getting which girl, with Buddy, naturally, getting first pick. Dana, an elfin doll from Minneapolis, who had been used to joshing around with all the males in the East 84th Street building, suddenly found that they were giving her a cold shoulder.

Mystified, she asked why. "You're for Buddy," they told her.

Dana, who had just joined My Fair Lady, was flattered. That night Buddy took her to dinner at the Sign of the Dove, followed by a carriage ride through Central Park, a nightcap at P.J. Clark's, and then to bed. "I had stars in my eyes," Dana says. "He made me feel like a queen."

Other techniques were less classic. There was, for one, the wineglass trick. Buddy would hand the wineglass to the object of his attentions and fill it to the brim. The young woman would probably be unused to wine, so she would take a polite sip or so and try to put down the glass. *Try.* Because it would be now that she found that this particular wineglass had a piece missing from the base, and if she relinquished hold, it would tip over, which would be very gauche, and not the behavior expected of a glamorous new model.

She would finish off the wine. And Buddy would quickly refill the glass.

Games for the dinner table had a parallel aim, which is to say getting the nymphs from the heartland utterly bombed.

There was always a birthday, for instance. It would be Buddy's birthday. It would be Jimmy's birthday. It would be *anybody's* birthday. Buddy would propose a toast. Then Jimmy would propose a toast. Toast would follow toast.

There would be trivia games. Buddy had a masterful memory for trivia. "It would go around the table," a former acolyte says. "Buddy would say everybody had to give a song title with the word 'blue' in it or chugalug a drink. Something like that. And if a girl didn't give a title, or got one wrong— bottom's up! Soon they're getting"—and here he mimed wooziness—"and that's when Buddy took them home."

There were more advanced games, with accomplices. Here Buddy's study of psychology was brought into play. A new My Fair Lady model would be sent trundling off to an office. The man in the office would be a crony, masquerading as a potential client. "I would look at the model books," the crony says, "but I wouldn't know what the hell I was looking at." Yet the routine was polished.

"Very good," he would say. "Where are you from? Ford?"

"No. My Fair Lady."

"Oh, yes! That's run by Mr. . . . Jacobson? He was talking to me about you. He *really* likes you. He thinks you're going to be a *star*."

So the young model is sitting there, eyes pinwheeling, and the crony would remember, casually, that he was having dinner with Buddy. Why didn't she come along? "She would think—wow! It wouldn't matter if she was having dinner with her fiancé, she would cancel it."

Then there was the photographer's studio. This was a rented space on the second floor of a building on the corner of 84th Street and Third Avenue. It had a crisp, professional look to it. The studio itself was equipped with a white "infinity screen," and lights, and an umbrella to bounce the light, and a camera: a Nikon on a tripod.

It was here that Buddy would bring prospective models for "test shots." What the studio lacked, though, was a photographer. This part might be taken by Jimmy Wood. "I would be an Italian or somebody with an unpronounceable name," Wood says. "Buddy would say that I had done four covers for French *Vogue*." Buddy would do the talking, and Wood would ape being the photographer. The would-be model would never get to see her test shots. There was no film in the camera.

This particular scenario seldom resulted in sex. That wasn't the point. "The game was worth more than the candle," explains Jimmy Wood. It came into Buddy's mind to do a book about his girl-chasing. He and the Woods would sit around and tape-record material. Buddy, the embryo author, would draw a great deal on his track experience.

"It's like claiming races," he would say.

Spotting models and good horses was much the same—you went by the legs. Buddy then went into the psychology of the relationship, explaining, "You've got to be nice to them—girls or horses. You've got to be their friends."

The book, of course, remained unwritten. But among Buddy's small coterie of intimates, his sexual extremism was legendary. One evening a fire broke out in his apartment. A crony happened to know where Buddy was dining, and called him.

Jacobson was abrupt. "I can't be bothered with that now," he said. "I think I'm going to fuck this girl."

Buddy's own fire was not one of pure lust. Until his relationship with Melanie deepened, in fact, he was the brusquest of lovers: Dana, the Minnesotan, remembers that they made love on the sofa rather than the bed "because Buddy had to get down to the stables," and that he never went near her again. Such was his urgency, in fact, that some girls took to calling him, unflatteringly, the Minute Man. Buddy performed the act of love the way he did everything—cutting his own hair in the bath with a rusty pair of scissors, omitting to put on socks or underwear, throwing away the caps from toothpaste tubes—to save time.

No wonder Buddy's acquaintances, even his handful of intimates, perceived Melanie as his chattel, sometimes useful, sometimes an encumbrance. This was an idea actively encouraged by Buddy himself. He would say that he didn't love Melanie and never had. She was necessary, for the agency's sake. "There was nothing he wanted to do more than send Melanie off to Bermuda or Mexico so he could be with the teenyboppers," Jerome Castle says. "He couldn't wait for her to get tired in Nicola's, and leave."

Talk was Buddy's forte. Here he was a virtuoso. Fixing his dark eyes on Melanie or whomever, his tones would be level and low, and what he said would have deep within it the serpentine flicker of his strange sense of humor. His talk would be plausibility itself, hypnotically rational. The only thing he could never do was relax. "He never let down his defenses," Melanie says. "He never talked to you in a casual way. He did not talk *with* you, he talked *at* you."

But for a long while Melanie found Buddy both convincing and fascinating. Others were less kindly disposed toward him. David Silbergeld remarks that Buddy was constantly rummaging through his military library. "He read all my psy-ops books," he said. "They explain how you can manipulate people's minds—using a fraction of the truth." Silbergeld was not amused by the way that Buddy used psy-ops on Melanie, his wife being one of her closer friends, but he felt powerless. "Jacobson controlled her life," he says.

Claudia Baker, who lived awhile on the building's seventh floor, describes Buddy as easily the most extraordinary liar she ever met. "He would say one thing one moment, and the next moment the complete opposite; butter wouldn't melt in his mouth. He would be absolutely convinced of his new line." Gail Moore, a young model, had dinner with Buddy on various occasions. They would be having what seemed to be a heart-to-heart talk, but if she grasped for a solid handful of information, it would sift through her fingers. "Buddy would always talk in circles," she says. "You could never get a straight answer out of him. He delighted in pulling the wool over people's eyes."

Bill Levin is even stonier. "He was totally amoral," he says. "If he told you something at three-thirty on a Monday, all it meant was that he had told you something at three-thirty on a Monday." Jacobson would lie quite purposelessly, Levin says, and for the sheer pleasure of it. "He would overwhelm you with his insincerity."

Melanie now knew of Buddy's compulsive deviousness. She had not known at the beginning, and there were certain surreal sides to his twisting and turning which she would never fully comprehend.

"I just wanted him to be straight with me. I would say, 'Come on! Cut the baloney! What are you really thinking?'"

Melanie grew aware that Buddy's group, coached by Buddy himself, perceived her as little more than a convenience. "I was a showpiece. But there's always two sides."

Buddy had set himself to molding her. "Never grow up, Melanie," he advised her. "I don't want you to turn into a *woman*." He spoke the word almost with fear, and the Wood brothers gleefully hammered the point home. "Once you turn nineteen—forget it!" they told her. "It's downhill all the way. Once you're twenty-four, you're old, you're a hag!"

Others would age; time would not touch Buddy. "When you guys are married and old," he told the Woods, "I'll be here with two seventeen-year-old girls." "He lived in a bizarre world," Melanie says. "You know, he wanted to be eighty years old, and still have that agency, and all the girls around him." Always single-minded, Buddy discouraged Melanie from reading anything but health books. They would prolong her usefulness.

But time did pass, Melanie was nineteen, twenty, twenty-one, twenty-two, and still Buddy had not put her out to pasture. "The guy grew to love me very much," she says. They would spend lengthy periods alone together. Mostly, of course, they would spend the time Buddy's way.

They might go to the movies. Or they might go to Catch a Rising Star, a cabaret where would-be comics try out their material. Sometimes they would stay home and watch movies on TV. Buddy abhorred mainstream television, but he enjoyed old movies, especially love stories with the grand old stars, and he watched programs of the more relentlessly informative sort—news analyses, talk shows, almost anything on public broadcasting—with the greedy appetite of the self-taught.

Buddy did have heroes. They were men who (it seemed to Buddy) owed little to others. That apart, it was a rum pantheon, including Woody Allen, Truman Capote, Norman Mailer, Henry Kissinger, of whose wiliness Buddy stood in awe, and Richard M. Nixon. "Buddy idolized Nixon," Melanie says. "He thought Nixon was incredibly wonderful that he could get away with the things he got away with. And on TV in front of all these millions of people."

Sometimes they would listen to music and drink wine. The music would be Buddy's favorite music, which tended to the smokily sentimental. "He loved forties music," Melanie says. "The Ink Spots . . . 'If I Didn't Care' . . . 'As Time Goes By' . . . he knew every musician, every song.

"He would drink wine. And that's when sometimes he would open up a little.

"I would say, 'Buddy, what are you really thinking about? Do you have a problem?' "

"No," he would always say. "What are you talking about?"

Buddy would never admit that he would be troubled by a problem. Just as he would never admit to being afflicted by anything so commonplace as a hangover, a sickness, an emotion.

Melanie says that toward the end, Buddy had "softened," but admits that in four years she had never heard him use the word "love." But sometimes, tentatively and usually late at night, he would unburden himself to her.

"You know me better than anybody," he would say. "You're my only friend."

Closer than, say, Jimmy and Bob Wood?

"Totally. I have no other friends."

Even now, Melanie finds Buddy absorbing: "He really was on the borderline."

Melanie was growing up. Her will was beginning to assert itself, and she was trying to take over a set of controls that she had temporarily abdicated, and she staged a number of minor revolts over the nights at Nicola's. "Buddy just loved Nicola's," she says. "He was really impressed by those people. But I would rather be home reading a mystery novel."

So Melanie would get up and go.

Buddy would return later, professing himself bewildered. "I don't understand you!" he would say. "Don't you know what kind of place that is across the street?" Nicola's was a place of fame, riches, and power—but Melanie was firm.

"They're all fake to me, Buddy," she said. "I'm not going to spend the rest of my life over at Nicky's."

In her mind she could see a frightening tableau. There she was, sitting at Nicola's front table, and she was *old*. Buddy was at her side. And sitting all around their table was a lively group of young lovelies, perpetually replenished, always fresh. Melanie would shiver, and she would plug away at her modeling and—most especially—at her dance with more determination than ever.

But Buddy, lost in his dreams and schemes, was failing to concentrate on the ventures in which he was already engaged, like his racing comeback. "Soon he's not there early anymore," Jerome Castle says. "He's screwing all the broads, and claiming by telephone." But the owner, seduced by the dazzle of Buddy's former statistics, went along with him for another eighteen months, at the end of which Buddy had "trained" twenty-five of Castle's horses, and lost him something in the neighborhood of $200,000. Nor, of course, did he pay his agreed-upon fifty percent of the loss.

The relationship broke up over an insignificant race: a $10,000 claimer. Castle had a horse running, as did a friendly rival, Frank Martin. He and Buddy examined Martin's horse, which they agreed not to claim. Castle bet his own horse and watched the race. He was a winner, and Frank Martin's horse finished out of the money. "I was happy!" he says. "I'd won a few thousand for a change."

That night he had a celebration in his house. Buddy was not there, but Frank Martin's son, Jose, was present.

"Why did you claim my father's horse?" Jose asked.

Castle was aghast.

"I was with Buddy just ten minutes before claiming time," he said. "He *couldn't* have done that!"

He had, of course.

Castle got away from Buddy clean and easy, compared with Jim Edwards, the squire of Audley Farm, who was not around, as Castle had been, to keep an eye on things.

Soon Buddy was getting money from Edwards to claim a horse, selling the horse or running it in a cheaper claimer, and then losing it. He turned Audley Farm into another Zzzyp Trick. It all meant some wonderful cash flow for Buddy. But there was one difficulty: He wasn't winning any races.

The disagreeable truth dawned on Jim Edwards: Buddy's early successes had been with stock developed by his previous trainer. He called Buddy's apartment one evening and asked him how the training was going.

"Great," said Buddy. *"Great!"*

Well, Edwards asked, how about the horses he had been buying? *They* didn't seem to be doing too splendidly. Buddy had paid $15,000 for this one, $25,000 for that one—did he really believe these horses were worth that kind of money?

Buddy was stung. "Sure they're worth the money," he said. "I wouldn't have bought them if they weren't."

Well, then, Edwards went on, Buddy wouldn't have any objections to buying them back, would he?

Buddy paused. They were, after all, talking about $250,000 worth of horseflesh. "I don't have that kind of money right now," he said.

"I'll take your notes," Edwards assured him.

Buddy was in a corner, but there was Jim Edwards on the line, and Jimmy Wood looking at him. His ego stiffened like a bicep.

"Sure, I'll buy them," he told the owner. "They're worth every penny I paid, if not more."

In Nicola's, Buddy was in an unaccustomed mood, a mixture of excitement and dismay. "Jesus Christ!" he said. "I've just bought two hundred and fifty thousand dollars' worth of horses!" The deal, he said, demanded monthly payments of $30,000.

His mood darkened suddenly. "I don't have any money," he said. "I don't know what to do."

Payments here, payments there. The ski lodge was the first to go. Buddy sold it for $200,000 plus monthly payments of $2,500 which he would get for ten years. The purchaser was a former barman at Nicola's, a pudgy, sallow man with shaggy black hair—called Anthony De Rosa. We shall encounter De Rosa again.

There were also problems at 155 East 84th Street, some arising from the impatient rush with which Buddy had put the building up in the first place—the lopsided fixtures and indiscreetly thin walls, the roof which had taken to leaking dolefully all over the seventh floor whenever it rained—but others from the erratic way the building was run.

Buddy, for instance, was obsessed with cleanliness, and would himself hose out the sidewalk and the lobby three times a week. As everybody knew, Buddy acted as his own janitor; and there was the darker side. The building was alive with ugly rumors. The telephones would emit insectile clicks. One young woman stumbled on a tape machine in the basement, flicked on the switch, and listened to her own voice talking with a friend. She left that same week.

At the same time, the extreme rent differentials—with transient young lovelies paying little or nothing—continued to cause some surly speculation. But it was Buddy's behavior with essential services, such as the Consolidated Edison electricity bills, that was most characteristic.

Buddy's bamboozling of Con Ed was masterly. Some tenants would pay the bills direct. In such cases, Buddy would rejig his cobweb of wiring and suck their electricity so that they ran the elevator and the hallway lights. Others would pay

Buddy, say, an extra $25 a week, on the assurance that he would handle Con Ed himself.

This, in his fashion, he did, intercepting the bills and tearing them up. Con Ed caught up with a couple of girls, and they went to see Buddy, mystified.

"Con Ed is asking us for three thousand dollars, Buddy," they said.

"So?"

"But you were going to pay for the electricity."

"Yeah? Show me your lease."

There was nothing in the lease, naturally, and the girls had to run for it. Buddy speedily relet the apartment, and took the great Con Ed scam into a different phase: He took an associate down to the basement at midnight, donned welding goggles, and sheared the locks off the meters with a Carborundum drill. Then he readjusted the meters so that they registered only a fraction of the actual electricity consumed.

Con Ed examined their destroyed equipment, and howled. "I don't know anything about it," Buddy said. "It's vandalism."

Jacobson is believed to have taken Con Ed for some quarter of a million dollars. Then, in September 1976, the state penal code changed. Until then, Con Ed had to catch somebody *in the act* of fixing a meter. Now, if Con Ed finds a meter has been fixed, it can be presumed that the person who benefits is the one who did it. And meter-rigging became a Class A misdemeanor, punishable by a fine of not more than $1,000 or not more than one year in jail; moving a dead body, incidentally, is also a Class A misdemeanor and carries the same penalty.

It was at about this time that Buddy's apartment was broken into. The intruder came in from the roof and made off with the television. Buddy, irritated, decided to get a novelty weapon, the Taser, which he had seen used in a John Wayne movie, *McQ*. The Taser is an electric gun that immobilizes instantly, but does not kill. It carries two darts attached to batteries by eighteen-foot wires. A Miami gas-station attendant who was the first victim of a Taser attack describes the effect thus: "I fell on the floor and couldn't move. It was the worst pain I ever felt." The electric guns were soon made illegal in New York, but Buddy had already acquired a couple by mail order. One he kept downstairs in the My Fair Lady office. The other was upstairs in 7D, handy, in a drawer.

* * *

Melanie's professional triumph was now complete. She was one of the handful of top models in the country. My Fair Lady's only other success was her close friend Dolly Robertson. Buddy continued to shoehorn in bookings for them as if every day might be their last. It was the technique he had used with the horses. Race them now. Forget tomorrow.

Melanie was delighted that Dolly was working so hard and so well, but had occasional glimmerings of disquiet. "She used to be happy-go-lucky," Melanie says. "Always smiling." Even at first, Dolly had lacked Melanie's ingenuous self-confidence. Now, three years of increasing success had only made Dolly's insecurity the more mountainous, and she would spend the money she made on expensive presents.

If Melanie returned a present, this would only make things worse. "She would think I didn't like her," Melanie says.

Dolly took to keeping a diary and would show it to Melanie. The diary was rambling, and spoke of malevolent conspiracies out to do Dolly Robertson harm. Melanie grew truly alarmed.

She had always kept an apartment of her own, and had done so since the beginning of her relationship with Buddy. This one was just next door to Buddy's on the seventh floor. It was six in the morning, and she was taking a shower.

Melanie heard the front door slam, and somebody running up the inside staircase of the duplex. Suddenly, whoever it was had come into her bathroom. Melanie remembered *Psycho*, and screamed.

A figure jumped shockingly into the shower. It was Dolly. She was stark naked, and she had bright, mad eyes. "I hate you! I hate you!" she shouted at Melanie, delivering a flurry of hard little punches. "You're not my friend!"

Melanie somehow got Dolly and herself out of the shower and wrapped in towels. Dolly was taken home to Ohio. Her breakdown was total. A few days later, Jimmy went to Ohio and visited Dolly in the insanity wing of an institution. She was in a straitjacket and was mouthing gibberish. Jimmy stayed out there for several harrowing days before returning to Manhattan in a melancholy mood.

"Where were you?" Buddy demanded. "You should have been with us last night. *Hot broads!*"

Jimmy described Dolly and the psychiatric ward.

Buddy was not interested.

"Why are you wasting your time with this girl?" he said. "It's just as well she had a breakdown—now you can get rid of her! *Turn the page!*"

It was what Buddy would have said of a broken-down horse. Jimmy Wood should not have been shocked by the words, but he was, and they had an interesting aftereffect. Wood was now entering his middle thirties, and was seized with a growing discontent. The Dolly Robertson affair afforded him a harsh objective look at the World of Budd Zzzyp.

It gave Melanie something to think about, too. With her, Buddy rationalized his indifference. Breakdowns were an unnecessary absurdity, he said.

"Nobody has to have a crack-up," he insisted. "I have complete control of my feelings."

His words echoed. Where Melanie would once have admired Buddy for his self-mastery, she was now troubled by his coldness. And his other words to Jimmy Wood haunted her.

Now she realized that when she was no longer productive she wasn't going to be sitting with Buddy in Nicola's or anywhere else. *Get rid of her! Turn the page!*

It was because of Dolly Robertson that Melanie now toyed briefly with writing a book. "It was going to be a novel," she says, "about two girls coming to New York to be models." Always the doer, Melanie sat down with a yellow legal pad and wrote a twelve-page outline.

The "Dolly" and "Melanie" figures are strongly differentiated. "Melanie" is strong, practical. "Lives drift apart for so many girls," she writes. "And the years go on and one matures. Friends become few, acquaintances many. Studio gossip is lessened and one is more reserved, self-assured. Work becomes less rewarding and more routine. . . ."

Her other protagonist travels a different road. "Some lives have tragic endings," Melanie writes, and mentions mental problems, man problems, dope problems, that "take girls to the deep end of darkness—with no distant promise of happiness."

Should Melanie pursue her "ambitions . . . for money, fame, recognition" and "keep going to the top"? Or should she settle for "marriage, family, house"?

She would sometimes talk to Buddy about the book, and wonder whether she would ever write it. "I've just got to think of a good ending," she would say. "Maybe I get killed, or something like that."

* * *

A throng of young hopefuls had started out in Jacobson's East 84th Street building. Some had settled into marriage, like lilac-eyed Tracy, who was now the wife of a rock-and-roll producer, and lanky Verena, who was wed to an executive in the instant-foods business. Many—most, perhaps—had left New York and returned to their homes, and jobs in banks, insurance offices, department stores. A few had vanished, gulped into the heady world of dope and discothèques.

The agency itself, though, was not so much succeeding as surviving. Melanie Cain was a star, unquestionably, and there were a handful of other girls who worked regularly, like the lovely, lazy Ingrid, who just hadn't hustled hard enough after her first impact, and soon drifted into the undemanding netherworld of modeling lingerie. "My Fair Lady was a nice small agency," says the established agent Zoli. "It had pretty girls. They did lots of things . . . hands . . . legs. There's always work around."

Melanie enjoyed the business. "I had my cranky days," she says. "But I really liked the girls." She became a bit of a mother hen, and took pleasure in teaching the younger girls how to apply makeup and behave. Buddy was more cavalier. It was now, for instance, that he brought Gail Moore to the agency. Buddy had spotted her, in the spring of 1977, at a convention at the Hilton, and had told her she should try to make it as a model.

One month later Gail telephoned him from her parents' home in Florida. "Fine!" Buddy said. "Come up right away. Bring five hundred dollars."

Gail arrived, and found that the promised free apartment at 155 East 84th Street was not yet available. She checked into the Barbizon Hotel, a then ponderously respectable place on East 63rd, and stayed a month. She was well into her last $100 and close to despair when Buddy put her in apartment 5B, which she shared with two other girls.

Gail Moore, who is both sensible and plucky, persevered through the tedious modeling routines, the testings, the go-sees, and built herself a career. Other girls were simply too vulnerable to last. Robert Brown, a writer who had become intrigued by the phenomenon of these young hopefuls adrift in the big city, interviewed a number of them with a view to writing a piece for *Esquire*. One of the girls he interviewed was with My Fair Lady.

"She was incredibly naive about everything except sex," Brown says. She had described an extraordinarily sophisticated sex life that had begun at thirteen, and then suddenly said haltingly, "Can I ask you something really embarrassing?"

"Sure," said Brown. His socks had just been knocked off by her description of pubescent goings-on in Wichita or wherever, and he wondered what could be coming *next*.

"Is it okay to pour a glass of wine by myself?" the girl whispered. "Do I ask you to pour it? Or what?"

Brown found the question incredibly moving. He asked whether the girl's mother didn't worry about her a bit.

"Worry?" She looked at him blankly.

"About you, so young, coming to New York to be a model."

The blankness turned to surprise. "She thought it was the best thing that could ever happen to me," the girl said. Robert Brown was afforded a nightmare glimpse of the empty landscape from which the nymphet must have come, but he never did write the *Esquire* article.

Melanie did her best for the young models and came to enjoy her role, giving them the benefit of better advice on how to handle New York than she had ever received herself. Their naiveté would wear off soon enough in most cases, but the dispiriting thing was that when one of the My Fair Lady models began to do well, she was likely to desert and head for the better-known agencies: Zoli, Wilhelmina, Ford.

Buddy would take the defections badly. "I'll never take them back," he told Melanie. A couple of times girls did try to come back, and he lived up to his word. Slowly, his ego became involved. For whatever reasons My Fair Lady had been founded—a Zzzyp Trick for Buddy or, as Melanie puts it, a "game-toy" to keep her occupied—he was now seized by a new idea. He would build My Fair Lady into a superagency. He would use his contacts on the track, his smart contacts in Nicola's. This was at a time when the top agencies seemed to have the modeling business firmly in their control. But Buddy's instinct was that the tree was ripe for shaking.

It was now, ironically enough, that a tough fresh contender *did* arrive in the modeling business. His name was Johnny Casablancas, and he came to New York from Paris, where he ran the Elite Agency. Elite would handle many of the top American models when they were in Paris. In turn, American agencies would handle the Europe-based girls when they came to work in New York. Fair exchange, no robbery.

This was the fragile concordat that Johnny Casablancas nonchalantly overturned, and his arrival in Manhattan launched an acrimonious period, with models being lured by promises of better deals from agency to agency, and it was while I was at work on an article concerning this situation, in the early summer of 1977, that I first met Buddy Jacobson and Melanie Cain.

Oddly, it was Eileen Ford who brought them to my attention. I had been interviewing her in her office, and she was in a baddish mood. The office had a pretty-peasant look, with the bluest of blue walls and painted wood chairs. Eileen Ford had been telling me about the iniquities of Johnny Casablancas, but she interrupted her tirade long enough to dictate a telex, and flipped through some magazines. One of them aroused her attention, a copy of *Redbook*. The girl on the cover, Eileen told me, used to be one of her models. "She moved in with the guy who runs My Fair Lady." Judging by her intonation, My Fair Lady might have been a reptile farm.

Eileen Ford continued to study Melanie's photo on the cover, then smiled and said, with infinite sweet pity in her voice, "It's a pity she's so fat."

Shortly after, I fixed a meeting with Buddy and Melanie. I knew them by sight from Nicola's, and I knew of Buddy by reputation, but we had never spoken. Our meeting was up in 7D, on the second floor of his duplex, and I was struck by the minimal way that the place was furnished. This was ten in the morning of June 30, 1977.

The discussion was pleasantly low-key, compared with the thunders and lightnings elsewhere in the modeling wars. Besides Buddy and Melanie, who, despite Eileen Ford, was looking rather slender, I met Bob Wood, who circled around, smiling agreeably but warily, as we talked about the situation.

Yes, My Fair Lady also had lost models to Elite. Three, said Buddy, but only two concerned him. "They're sixteen years old," he said, his voice soft and grave. "Children! But they started going to Studio 54. And then I couldn't control them anymore. . . ."

What happened at Studio 54?

"That's what I would like to know," he said.

Melanie chimed in. "They meet people," she said. "Next

thing, they're being wined and dined. They're not used to it."

Buddy said that he also was planning to sue Elite, as Ford and Wilhelmina were doing. But it was soon apparent that the Casablancas modus operandi held a certain appeal for him. "We took a girl from Ford," he said, with a sort of discreet pride. "Blonde. Twenty-two. She had made thirty-five thousand dollars in twelve months. Here she made fifty-five thousand dollars in six months. We got her Scavullo bookings. We worked her till eight at night." He was talking of Dolly.

"Some people say it's because we worked her so hard that she had a nervous breakdown. She went back home."

At once cocky and soothing, he added, "One day, she'll just walk back in. . . ."

Neither Melanie nor Bob Wood ventured a comment on this story. Buddy finished his remarks by saying jauntily, "Whatever people say, it isn't that difficult a business."

This was, of course, just what he had said in the past about training horses—the problem being that to succeed either on the track or in modeling a close attention to detail is crucial. Buddy was brilliant in conception, but increasingly hurried in execution. His attention span was diminishing in length even as it grew in intensity.

"Buddy loved the agency," Melanie says. "But at the same time, he couldn't be bothered with details. He couldn't be more bored than sitting there making appointments on the phone. He couldn't be bothered with entertaining clients—he hated that."

So, though Buddy's dream of the superagency persisted, it flickered on and off. He watched Johnny Casablancas assault the modeling world's equivalent of the Jockey Club, but he was not yet ready to make his move. At the same time, Buddy became less interested than ever in horse training. He tried to sell the former Jim Edwards stable, purchased for an overblown $250,000, to Bill Levin for $400,000. Levin showed no interest. So Buddy, which now increasingly meant his sons, David and Douglas, began racing the horses, getting them claimed, and selling them off as rapidly as he could. The proceeds of these transactions were not, however, going into the payments that were due Edwards. Rather they were going to go into the latest of the methods by which Jacobson hoped to attain greatness.

He would be a property magnate.

Just before my first meeting with Buddy and Melanie there had been an unfortunate incident. It had taken place early in the morning of Tuesday, June 28, outside the house of a Mr. Harvey Hochlerin, who lives at 57 Soundview Drive, Port Washington, which is a sedate community on Long Island.

What happened was that the Hochlerin family car, a 1974 Peugeot, was blown to bits. This was not just unfortunate in itself: The explosion was, as they say, to have repercussions.

Hochlerin saw a blue van disappearing down the road, and called the Port Washington cops. Hochlerin, incidentally, was described by *Newsday* as "the owner of the Sanitary Hauling Corp. of Brooklyn, a firm once owned by his father, William J. Hockey, whose business partners were Harvey L. Strelzin, now a Brooklyn state assemblyman, and Anthony Ricci, reportedly a onetime partner of mobster Charles (Lucky) Luciano." Be that as it may, the metamorphosis of a perfectly good French automobile into so much shrapnel left Harvey Hochlerin imperturbable. His son described him as a "man of iron."

The blue van was stopped by the police five minutes later. The cops saw that there were two men in the van. One was the driver, the other was slumped in the back, writhing in the grip of what seemed to be intense pain. He was covered with blood and saying: "I can't see, Joe! *I can't see!*"

"Yes?" the driver asked the cop politely. "What's the problem, officer?"

The driver was named Joe Audino and the man in the back was Carlo Carrara—the construction executive who was so popular around East 84th Street. There were two fairly dissimilar theories quickly advanced as to just how Carrara should have wound up in such a sorry situation.

Theory one was advocated by the Carrara lawyers. It went thus. Carlo had been out partying. He had run into this fellow he used to know, Joe, in a bar in Queens. Driving home in the van, they had stopped so that Carlo might relieve himself by the roadside. It was his great ill fortune that the bit of roadside that he chose was opposite an about-to-disintegrate Peugeot.

Theory two was that of the government men. In this version, Carrara had gotten hold of an explosive device, a species of Claymore mine, to be specific. Carrara loaded the mine into the back of the van, dined well in Manhattan, and set off for Port Washington.

At the Hochlerin home, as this version had it, Carrara placed the Claymore beneath the automobile. So far, so good. He armed it and began to pay out a wire. A tricky matter, this, and perhaps best left to the professional military man. At any rate, Carlo was too forceful; the Claymore went up.

Through his lawyer, Carrara derided this scenario. The bomb, they pointed out, blew a hole in the driveway as big as a basketball. Had Carlo been as close to the device as he must necessarily have been, he would have been ground to hamburger, rather than getting away with what he himself describes as an "audio problem."

Mel Roth, the district attorney assigned to the investigation by Nassau County, sonorously ascribed Carrara's relatively good shape to "the nature and durability of the human body." He didn't see it as a tough case to try.

Ivor Shaw found it droll. "If you guys take out a contract on me, I want Carlo to handle it," he told Al Seifert. Buddy read an account of the event in the *Daily News*. Carlo's popularity in the building had irked him. Overjoyed, he called his son David. "Read the paper . . . read the paper," he told him, gleefully. But not even Buddy, of course, foresaw the future usefulness of the Carrara case.

Buddy would buy and sell property in Manhattan. He would build an empire. He began to buy the Sunday *New York Times*, extract the real estate section, and discard the rest. All that summer he pursued his quest. "Every day we'd go out on bicycles," Melanie says. "Up and down, looking for buildings to buy. Every street! Buddy spent twenty-four hours a day at it. He did it in his sleep."

Buddy's success with his own 84th Street building, that dexterous handling of banks, tradesmen, and utilities, was just a prelude. Now he spoke broodingly of the "big score." He focused on the block of East 70th Street that runs from Madison Avenue to the Frick Museum, sitting serenely on the corner of Fifth.

The buildings that interested Buddy were numbers 11 and 15. They weren't quite as grand as the Frick, which is one of the last robber-baronial mansions left, but they were what the property agent, a brisk brunette, describes as "a brace of Stanford Whites." Landmarks, of course.

It hadn't been easy doing business with Buddy. "He was flaky," the agent says. "It was three hundred telephone calls for everything! Three hundred telephone calls! But he just loved the buildings. We had a deal. . . ."

They agreed to finalize the next day. "That night, I had a nightmare," the realtor says. In her dream, she was with Buddy, and she had signed the deal. "And I dreamed that Buddy stood up, and said: 'What do you mean it's a landmark?' "

Next morning found her in an apprehensive mood. "I was looking at a commission of sixty thousand dollars," she says. "And I needed the money." But she realized she had to face the problem.

"You do realize that the buildings have landmark status?" she asked Buddy.

"No," he said. But his mind began whirling at once. He told the agent that he wanted nine months with access to the buildings. What would happen, he wanted to know, if the contractors made some 'mistakes' in remodeling the buildings?

What indeed? There is one fairly commonly known story in the trade about the developer who acquired some pleasant landmark in the East 70s, just because he wanted to own a landmark, you understand, and then some fool backed into it with a bulldozer, and the developer had been forced to put up a high-rise. But *that* building hadn't been just down the street from the Frick.

"Buddy," she said, "you want my opinion? The Frick will make you put it back, stone by stone."

The deal was dead. But a loftier one arose. Juliet I and Juliet II were a couple of moribund movie houses standing on a prime slab of ground just a couple of blocks from Buddy's building, on Third Avenue between 84th and 83rd. It would cost upwards of $400,000 to buy the movie houses as they stood, but the project with which they were to be replaced was worthy of Sam Lefrak.

Plans were drawn up for an eighteen-story tower. The new Jacobson building would be the embodiment of everything to which the old one had aspired. There would be an indoor swimming pool. There would be a superagency. The place would be packed with lovely girls. Only one thing prevented Buddy from vaulting into the upper echelon of realtors: a couple of million dollars' worth of seed money.

Buddy would not concede that this was a problem, but

Melanie was herself entering into a new phase, and seeing things with a sharper vision. Her time with Buddy Jacobson was, she now recognized, finite. Several times in the past, she had tried to break with him, and moved out of the 84th Street building, but he had gotten her back. Thus far.

"He had ways of making me dependent," she says. "In our years together there was not one day that went by—no matter where I was—when I didn't speak with him. Once, twice a day. New York, France, St. Croix." This was the other side of Buddy, the side that nobody else saw. "He always sounded so lonely when I was away," Melanie says. "And when I was with him, if he had a problem, we'd sit down on the couch. He would keep his arms around me. It was like I was a . . . possession."

Now Buddy told her he needed her more than ever. "You're my only source of strength," he would say. "At least stay until I finish the building."

Melanie did stay, but grew increasingly skeptical. She had, after all, been hearing for four years that they would soon be rich. Where was he going to get the money? He didn't even have the $400,000 to acquire the property, let alone the couple of million to get the project under way. Jacobson's financial legerdemain had always been impressive, but unorthodox. Too unorthodox for most financial institutions. He had no credit cards, and as one bank after another soured on his wayward ways with checks, he moved his account from Chemical Bank to Irving Trust to Manufacturers Hanover. His attitude toward the funds of his friends was similarly casual. He had borrowed at least $25,000 from Jimmy Wood, for instance, and he had persuaded David Silbergeld to endorse his checks.

The warmth had gone out of this arrangement when the checks started bouncing. Buddy made them good, but later complained that Silbergeld was cheating him. "I didn't sign those checks," he said.

"Buddy, I *saw* you sign those checks," Silbergeld said. "You signed them on the wall there!"

Now, in these tense months, Buddy approached David Silbergeld again. He owed somebody $50,000, he said. They were going to beat him up. They were going to hurt Melanie.

"I said, okay," Silbergeld says. "I lent him ninety-two hundred bucks."

Buddy returned, asking for more. He first claimed that various of his checks were missing. "What do you mean the checks are missing, Buddy?" Silbergeld said. "Go to the bank. Microfilm. They can reproduce your checks in a minute."

Then Jacobson tried to claim that the signatures on the checks were fraudulent. The subterfuge did not work. David Silbergeld finally did get his money back, but his relationship with Buddy was finished for good.

The financial pressure also took its toll on Buddy's longest-lived friendship, the one with Bob and Jimmy Wood: The Zzzyp brothers, formerly the Zippolinis.

Jimmy, still brooding over the harsh insight that the Dolly Robertson affair had afforded him into Buddy's character, didn't understand how Buddy could survive. "How can he sleep at night?" he wondered. "He owes everybody money."

"What do you tell Melanie when she asks you for money?" Jimmy asked Jacobson.

"I give her a couple of thousand, and that keeps her quiet. She thinks I'm investing it."

Jimmy Wood was awed.

"You must owe her two hundred thousand dollars," he said.

"More," Buddy said.

Jimmy Wood was impressed, despite himself. It wasn't simple fraud, it was as if Buddy had decided that anything that he could get his hands on was his, by right. And that included whatever his cronies possessed. It was at this time that Jimmy, an increasingly successful trader in gold and gems, bought a new car.

"Buddy went out of his mind when he heard that," he says. "*What?* I need to make a mortgage payment, and you've bought a car?"

Jimmy Wood tried to explain: What did the one thing have to do with the other? Buddy wouldn't listen. His sense of ownership was absolute and ferocious. Jimmy now began to assert some degree of independence. He bought a summer house for weekends in the country. He acquired a boat and took up game fishing. Outside interests. "This was against the rules," he says.

The world of the Zzzyp brothers had always depended on a punctilious adherence to the rules, but Buddy at first attempted to brush off Jimmy's independence. "He did his best to get me back into the fold," Jimmy says. "Under his thumb, so to speak. He would be extremely good to me. He would always try to pick up the tab. He would throw girls at me." But Jimmy maintained a distance, and Buddy began to be rankled by this.

Bob Wood now sensed something different in Jacobson—almost a chemical alteration. Buddy had always been ruler of the Zzzyp world, but Bob had felt that he was at least a valued confederate. No longer. One morning a young woman came into the agency. Bob looked through her book of photographs. Buddy was at his elbow.

The pictures were amateurish—typical beginner material. "These aren't any good," Bob told her. Flipping on, he found one truly dire photograph and grimaced. "This is terrible," he said. "You should take this photo out right away."

Buddy, who had been silent, now spoke up. His voice was brusque. "How can you say that?" he said. "These are beautiful pictures. And don't you realize that this is her most important picture?"

He spoke to the girl kindly. "This is the best picture in your book," he said.

The would-be model looked at Bob with scorn, and he realized something with great clarity. "It wasn't enough that Buddy had the ultimate authority," he says. "He was the *only* authority." That July, impelled by a twinge of self-survival, Bob secured the My Fair Lady corporate books and worked his way through them. The company, he found, was not split into a hundred shares, as he had thought, but a thousand.

His own twenty-five shares gave him not a quarter of the agency, but two and a half percent. Buddy, who had always been talking about "zipping" people, had zipped the Zzzyps. It was perfect. Bob had to laugh.

He was still wondering whether to make an issue of the stock watering when he heard Buddy on the telephone. He was talking to his son David. Bob was listening with only half an ear. David, evidently, was talking about some friend of his, and Buddy was sounding incredulous.

"There's no such thing as friends in this world," he said. "There's only people who try and hang onto your coattails."

Buddy began unspooling a list of names. The names were of people who had proved false to him.

"Friendship does not exist," he told David. "There's only people *using* each other. And that's perfectly all right."

His voice was, as always, calm, measured, hypnotic.

"I use *you*," he told his son. "You use *me*."

Bob Wood was riveted, and incredulous. Here was Buddy instructing his son in what he perceived as the ways of the world. "I suddenly decided something," he told me. "This guy is sick." It was not a comfortable thought. The world of the Zzzyp brothers had been Bob's world, and he contemplated leaving it with difficulty. He agonized with his brother. What happened next happened abruptly. Buddy called Jimmy Wood and asked him to bring $600 to the office. Jimmy, who had his apartment rent-free as a result of his loans to Buddy, did not know what Jacobson meant. He went to the office, and Buddy asked him for $600 rent.

They argued for hours, with Buddy accusing Jimmy Wood of "stealing his money." He was obsessive, and stony. "Everybody steals from me," he said, bitterly.

Jimmy Wood was shocked, flustered, indignant, and fished out a paper, detailing his loans. "Throw it in the wastebasket," Buddy advised. "It's in your handwriting."

"What's the bottom line? Do you want me to move out?"

"Yes."

"Our friendship is over? And for a few dollars?"

"That's it. Yes."

They looked at each other. "I think you're going insane," Jimmy said. "You're going to be a very lonely guy."

"Maybe," Buddy said. He required satellites no longer.

Jimmy agreed to leave in November, but this evidently wasn't fast enough for Buddy. Three weeks later, returning from the Labor Day weekend, Jimmy found that a small group of workmen, including "the two Sals," Prainito and Giamo, had demolished most of his exterior wall. Prainito apologetically told him that he had to carry out Buddy's orders. "We're supposed to finish," he said.

Jimmy brought out his .38. "The next man in here gets shot," he remarked. Buddy arrived. He was nervous, but affected noncomprehension. "What are you so upset about?" he asked. Jimmy looked around, speechlessly. "You've got insurance, I've got insurance," Buddy told him, impatiently. Exit the Woods.

This small drama had passed Melanie by. All she knew was that the battle for the movie-houses was absorbing Buddy.

"For months he was by the phone every single night," Melanie says. "He never went *anywhere*. We hardly even went across the street to Nicola's. I cooked, and stayed home, and watched TV. The deal was constantly on his mind. He was always looking through papers, making phone calls, waiting for the deal to come through, waiting for the phone to ring. It drove me crazy."

She remembers the day that Buddy tried to articulate just what it was he was searching for in life. This was the day that Buddy had, at last, managed to put together a paper mountain, worth $400,000, and had signed the contract for the Juliet movie-houses. The Big Score had floated deliciously close. "You work for something, and you make it," Buddy explained in a rare moment of self exposure. "And it doesn't mean a thing. It's on to the next. . . .

"You make money. And that doesn't mean anything either, except that money gives you one thing. *Freedom!*"

Melanie was impressed by the urgency, the nerve—"Buddy always took chances"—but she was increasingly aware of his beleaguered state. Con Ed watching. Mortgages falling due. The feed merchant, demanding fifty thousand bucks for horse feed. Jim Edwards, making increasingly ominous noises. Buddy quickly put his properties in the name of his son, David, and worked the telephone. 'His equity was like sand," Bob Wood says. "But Buddy could always keep going, just so long as he had the telephone: *What do you want to do? Do you want to break me and get nothing? Or do you want to wait?*

"You listen to Buddy on the telephone, you're listening to a maestro."

Melanie, though, was beginning to realize just how much Buddy lied. She began to rebel. "You know that's not true," she would tell him after hearing him talk to some creditor or other. "Why are you saying that?"

Although she and Buddy were living with a togetherness of which she used to dream, her unhappiness was growing. True, to Melanie's relief, the Woods were gone: They had been too actively a part of that shadowy other life of Buddy's —the jokes, the tricks, the furtive dates. But it was now, oddly, that she was forced to confront the reality she had avoided. Casually walking into Buddy's apartment, she found him with another girl. *In flagrante.* She left, sobbing.

What made the treachery hurt all the more was that the other girl was Melanie's friend, Ingrid. Later Buddy sought out Melanie. His approach was one of his favorites, an exercise in reverse-psychology.

"I've decided to forgive you," he announced.

Melanie looked at him, dumbfounded.

Buddy elaborated. But for her uncaring attitude, he explained, he wouldn't have been driven into Ingrid's arms. It was her fault, her fault.

This time, the stratagem was a failure. Melanie said she was leaving, and not just to another apartment. She was returning to Europe. They quarrelled. Buddy became very drunk, and they had their first real fight. "He took me by my hair, and flung me across the room," Melanie says. "I packed my baggage that night, and sat down in the agency all night, bug-eyed. When he came in, I was going to hit him with a broom."

That squall passed, but soon there was an ocean between them.

Mel and David Silbergeld had been holidaying in the South of France, but Mel had grown itchy and gone to Paris, looking for work. She and David found an apartment. A poky but pleasant place, with a single bedroom, and an antiquated bath, like a moored boat, in the kitchen. The place cost $800 a month, and Melanie moved in with Mel, while David returned to New York.

The apartment was well located, being on the Champs Elysées close to the Rond Point and within easy walking distance of both the Métro and Melanie's Paris agency, Glamour. "There were no other women in the building," Melanie says. "The tenants were all wealthy Arabs. They were always trying to pick us up in the elevator."

Melanie applied herself to modeling with her usual vigor, and, the French being as besotted as ever with wholesome American looks, she was soon working steadily. First she did a TV commercial, then a picture spread for *L'Officiel,* that most conservative of French fashion magazines.

For the most part, though, she simply rebuilt herself. She loved the city, and, away from Buddy, she began to bloom. In a social sense, Paris didn't exist for her. There were many American models there, and she would chat with them, and they would talk about so-and-so, who was rich, and such-and-such a place, which was currently fashionable. But the gossip did not engage her interest. Occasionally some well-dressed man might suggest dinner. Melanie would politely put him off. She set herself two tasks: adding to her modeling portfolio, which occupied the daylight hours, and learning French, which took up almost all her evenings.

Weeks turned to months. Mel returned to the United States, leaving Melanie alone in Paris. Her tranquillity was complete. Even the Arabs in the elevator now smiled politely and let her be. She had not felt so buoyant in years. Manhattan was dark light-years away.

Buddy phoned every day, naturally. Melanie was not unaffected by the aching loneliness she sensed in his voice, but she was resolved. His grip on her had loosened. Her will, so long dormant, would not again be stifled.

It was now December. Christmas was approaching, and Melanie realized it was time to be going home. The day before she left Paris, she was saying her goodbyes to a group of models, and they bewailed the fact she was leaving without ever going to the smart disco they so loved.

"Okay," Melanie said. "I'll go with you."

It was, after all, her last night. The discothèque, which was Le Privé, turned out to be no great distance from her front door, and it was more or less as she had expected. The hectic clangor, the smell of money, the restless smiles only brought home that her respite was over. The following day she would be in Manhattan.

The thought did not disturb Melanie. "I felt I had this great inner strength," she said. She did not yet realize that she had gained her fresh purchase on life by her distance from Buddy Jacobson.

Buddy picked Melanie up at the airport, immediately enveloping her in his concerns. She was bubbling with her Parisian experiences during the past months, but, from Buddy's lack of reaction, she could have been opening and closing her mouth like a goldfish in a bowl. "He didn't want to know about Paris," she says. "He didn't want to know about my work at all."

Melanie was back, Buddy seemed to be saying. She had never been away. Life would go on as before.

Not quite as before. Buddy now began demanding that Melanie move in with him. This was novel. Melanie had always had a place of her own. Indeed, before leaving for Paris, and as part of her attempt to pry herself free, she had not even been living in the 84th Street building, but had kept a small apartment at 77th Street and First Avenue.

"No, Buddy! No."

"You can't *afford* the apartment right now. We'll make money with the movie houses. And then you can do whatever you want to do."

It made a sort of sense. Buddy had Melanie's money, as he had all available money, tied up in the big score. But she was obstinate.

"I don't want to, Buddy," she said.

He pleaded.

"Come on—we'll sell the agency and everything will be all right," he said. "We'll get married!"

Melanie did, at last, move in with Buddy, but quickly found that his faithfulness was wanting. In particular, she suspected that he was bedding a blonde from the Corn Belt. In this she was quite correct. She and Buddy began to bicker. After one dreary bout, she decided again to move out. Buddy was away, doing one of his deals. By eleven in the morning, when he returned, Melanie was in the street with her last piece of luggage.

"You can't move out!" he yelled.

"I'm moving," she said.

He pulled at her, and she tugged herself away, and they moved so, back and forth, for what seemed like ages, tussling absurdly, in the street.

"It's over with!" Melanie said.

"Oh, Mel!" pleaded Buddy. "Let's *talk*."

His accents were familiar; caressing, wheedling, reasonable. Her resolve faltered. They went back upstairs. Buddy talked and talked, and Melanie wept. The tiny struggle in the street showed that Buddy could still talk Melanie into acquiescence. He always had in the past, surely always would in the future. "I promise everything will work out," he told her.

Melanie's newfound will asserted itself.

"Okay," she told him. "It's easy to work out. The girls go, or I go."

Buddy agreed. The girls went. Indeed, the young woman from the Corn Belt was given twenty-four hours to leave the premises, and remains puzzled to this day.

Melanie made an effort. She moved her clothes into the closets and did her best to temper the austerity of Buddy's apartment. Couldn't they have some carpet? she asked.

Buddy agreed. Characteristically, he cut a square of carpeting from the same unattractive material that he had used in the hallways, a plaid, with oblongs of sepia and orange. But the relationship didn't improve. Melanie now found her victory meaningless. "I threw all the girls out," she says. "And then I didn't care. All of a sudden, it didn't make a difference. . . ."

As her Paris-won vitality waned, modeling ceased to fascinate her. She challenged Buddy again. "Okay," she said. "I'll stay with you—but I don't want to work all the time."

Work now bored her, she said. If Buddy was proposing to support her, then that was fine. "If I'm going to work," she added, "I'm going to work at something I like to do." She did cut down on her modeling schedule, and returned to an early ambition: dance.

Melanie had, in fact, been dancing off and on for a couple of years, but she was now possessed of a special enthusiasm. It was, simply, a world where she could be free of Jacobson. Buddy, realizing this, was bitterly opposed. Dance was worse than tennis, an environment over which he could exercise no control. "You're too old," he told Melanie. "How do you want to end up? As a hoofer in Vegas?"

Melanie ignored him and enrolled in a dance school. She celebrated by buying a diary. Melanie always liked confiding her emotions to paper. In her diary, she planned to describe what she called "the dream world of Broadway dancing." February 9 finds her opening thus: "My first serious day of dance. My body is in rotten shape—which makes for a very sloppy dancer."

It was a tough regimen. Part of the day, Melanie would be modeling or running My Fair Lady. The rest of the day and evening would be dance classes. "I was constantly doing something," she says. And it was now, in this flush of tentative freedom, that Melanie Cain, for the first time in more than four years, became interested in another man.

He was her dance instructor. Melanie would stay after class, often till quite late. They would drink coffee, and have long talks. But Melanie never dreamed of going out with him. He was, she says, a married man. The infatuation was kid stuff. Just a crush.

She told her mother about her dance instructor on the telephone. Melanie now knows that Buddy taped the call. In confronting her, his method was, as usual, indirect.

"I think you should go to a better dance school," he said. "Why don't you go to Martha Graham? The place you're going is second-class."

"All right," she said. "That sounds like a good idea." But, she added, she was still going to attend her present school.

"No, you're not!" Buddy said, with a gruff hiss.

"Why not?" asked Melanie.

Buddy, angrily abandoned his reverse psychology and accused her of having an affair. She had seldom seen him so enraged, and Melanie was, for once, wary. "I didn't admit that I had a crush on the guy," she says. "But I didn't lie. I just said, 'No, I haven't gone out with him.' "

Buddy was aflame, and Melanie realized that she couldn't tell whether he was more angry with her over the suspected affair or with himself for his display of jealousy. An emotion, a weakness.

He went cold, dead. "Forget it!" he told her. "What do I even care?"

Melanie did go to other dance schools. But, ignoring Buddy's strictures, she also returned to her first school, where her crush lasted but a few more weeks.

Melanie's determination was not misplaced. One of the West Side dance schools offered her a job, teaching two nights a week. She was ecstatic. "I'm going to teach dance class for two hundred and ten dollars a week," she told Buddy. "That's all I need to get by on." This, too, was framed as a challenge. "Are you still going to want me to stay with you?" she asked. Her curiosity was genuine.

Buddy was unnerved. "What are you? Crazy?" he asked. *"You're a star."*

Realizing he had no choice, though, he tried to take over. "You know what he started doing?" she says. "He started making phone calls." Buddy called up people involved with Broadway shows. He called up producers and directors in California. He believed, as always, that with the telephone he could accomplish anything.

"You want to dance, you can dance on TV," he told Melanie. "Do you want to be in a Broadway show? A movie? I can get you in a movie."

Melanie tried to argue. "No," she said. "I don't want you

putting me in a show. I want to get in a show because I earned it myself."

Buddy did not want to hear. Power over Melanie was something he had to have. It was now, also, that he grew irked that so many of her dance classes took place on the West Side, a place so foreign it might as well have been the Mato Grosso. "Wait till we build the new building," he told Melanie. "We'll have a dance studio all our own."

The dance studio would, naturally, be the most splendid in New York, and Melanie would be its queen. And it is now possible to detect a new element in Buddy Jacobson's fantasy world. The dance studio was not to be a game, like the photo studio with the empty camera. Where Melanie was concerned, Buddy had gone beyond games. He sensed their growing apartness, and the thought that Melanie might leave him was intolerable. The dance studio, indeed, in all its not-yet-existent glory, was only one of the phantasmal enterprises with which he planned to keep Melanie bound to him.

He was going to build My Fair Lady into a superagency. "It'll be *yours*," he insisted. "I wouldn't go near the girls. I wouldn't even know their names."

Besides, he stressed, Melanie was twenty-three. "Buddy said that I was getting old. I needed something to fall back on. I should become the next Eileen Ford."

When Melanie pooh-poohed the scheme, Buddy would do a 180-degree turn. "I'll do all the work. *I'll* run the agency," he said. "You won't have to do anything."

Melanie was recalcitrant. "Something's awfully wrong, Buddy," she said. "Face up to it. Don't you owe *everybody* money? Besides, don't you see? I don't love you anymore."

He would act as if he hadn't heard, or as if she were a little girl being naughty. Melanie had always been impressed by Buddy's entrepreneurial quirkiness, his driven quality, his capacity for sheer hard work, the way that every evening he continued to bicycle through the Manhattan streets, looking for buildings. "He was going to buy them," Melanie says. "He was going to renovate. He was planning on becoming the biggest contractor in New York."

But now Buddy's schemes were taking on a touch of the unreal, a troubling shimmer. Melanie had only to express interest in some business and he would seize on the subject. He was going to start an advertising agency. Or they would be casually discussing magazines, and Buddy would say, "Do you want your own magazine, Melanie?" Or: "What do you want? Your own radio show?" Right. She would *have* her own radio show.

Melanie was impervious. The schemes were jerry-built, the promises hollow. She had tasted success on the Upper East Side, and much of it had been sweet, but now it was bitter. She had a covert dream. "I was going to save my money and start my own little dance studio, somewhere up in the mountains." She saw herself in a clean, fresh place: a world of her own.

Buddy now decreed that it would be *he* who would take Melanie away from Manhattan. All right, he told her, they would marry. He would close down the modeling agency. They would have children. They would settle down. He began to talk confidently of buying a horse farm or a country house. The routine began in April, and was to persist through May, June, and the beginning of July. On weekends, just as on weekdays he bicycled through the city, Buddy would drive Melanie up and down the highways and byways of New York State.

Every now and again they would spy a prospect, some tremendous mansion, say, or a horse farm with rolling fields and woodland, and he would find the local realtor and get into one of those interminable discussions that he so enjoyed. Melanie would listen and nod, but she was suffering an increasing sense of moving through a limbo. Her will was watery, but skepticism had gripped her like a hard, bright frost. "I would go with him," she says. "I would look at the places, and I would suddenly realize how out of his element Buddy was.

"I don't think he will ever come out here," she told herself. "It's all a joke!" And then they did find a place. It was emphatically real. It was a mountain.

This mountain, which might perhaps be better described as an enormous rock, stands overlooking the Hudson. It is only an hour from New York, but the region is thickly wooded, and comparatively unpeopled. The closest town is Garrison.

It appealed to Melanie immensely: its remoteness, its grandeur.

Buddy started talking money. The place would cost $100,000, and the land swept down to the water's edge. Melanie allowed herself to hope.

Now Buddy behaved characteristically. His mind churned away. He would do a deal with the scouts, and the Army Corps of Engineers would help him build. On the hilltop he would build a house. That's where they would live. "And down by the water I'll build a gambling casino," he said.

Rich pleasure-seekers would stream out from Manhattan. Melanie could help. "You'll need something to do," he said, again harping on a familiar theme. "Soon you'll be too old to model." Her hope withered: Buddy's mountain was just another money-making scam.

Suspicions began to sprout. Melanie would be stuck in the house while Buddy would be up to his old tricks down at the casino, which would be a riverside Nicola's. Or worse, even. "He'll put me away in the country, and do all his philandering around Manhattan. I don't think Buddy will ever come out here!" Melanie told herself. She would be his property for good, immured on his mountain even more securely than she had been at 84th Street.

Buddy's dream mountain died. He never alluded to it again. Now he found something less speculative on his hands. The Park East, a small private hospital on 83rd Street between Lexington Avenue and Park, had expired and been bought by a Manhattan realtor. Buddy decided it would make a profitable co-op. It was now mid-June.

The preliminary details were all worked out in the realtor's office on Park Avenue, which has the discreet comfort of a library, with oak walls, Chinese vases, and a naval portrait by Gilbert Stuart. The realtor, a soft-spoken, sober-suited man, remembers Buddy's visit well.

"I was surprised," he says. "His clothes were dirty, he had dirty shoes. He was unshaven. Yet significant money was involved. Just under seven figures.

"But I was very impressed. His clothes weren't *dirty* dirty. They were honestly dirty. He had paint specks on his trousers. His appearance didn't faze me."

Buddy bought the Park East for roughly $850,000. He immediately set the Italians who had worked on East 84th Street to ripping the former hospital apart. But, as the costs mounted, so did the pressures. He moved the My Fair Lady office upstairs to his own quarters, and would talk airily about the "convenience" of operating in his own apartment, saying that the downstairs office was "a cell."

Melanie, who didn't welcome the turning of their apartment into a quasi-public place, wasn't fooled. The move had been made to confuse the IRS, another of the creditors after Buddy. She would periodically find official-looking envelopes downstairs in the abandoned office, and would show them to Buddy. He would tell her to leave them there, as if they had not been received.

His problems were becoming widely known. Al Menziuso, another realtor, began to look at the Park East with an acquisitive eye, and mentioned it to a group of investors from Buenos Aires. They liked the speculation.

"He's in a lot of trouble," Menziuso told them. "I think he's going bust."

He, too, went to see Buddy, and made a substantial offer for the Park East. Buddy just wasn't interested. "Why should I sell?" he said, poker-faced.

Also, he was growing noticeably quirkier. A French model agent visited Buddy at 155 East 84th Street and discussed one of his models, a girl they were thinking of taking to Paris. He found the bare, semifurnished Jacobson apartment distinctly odd, and Buddy himself even more so. The talk was inconclusive.

He was back at their hotel that evening when the telephone rang. It was Buddy, insisting that they go through with the deal. He was vehement, to the point of incoherence.

The Parisian concluded the call by slamming down the receiver.

Mel Harris, who still lived in 7C, knew that Buddy and her husband, David Silbergeld, had quarreled about bad debts. But she had been prepared to tolerate him until he threatened to throw her pet kitten off the terrace. His manner was not that of someone joking. He mumbled something about Melanie's being allergic to cats.

Now, in mid-June of 1978, the Rackets Bureau in the Nassau County district attorney's office received an anonymous telephone call. The caller, who was male, said he had some information relevant to the Carrara case, which was expected to go in front of the jury before the end of the year.

Mel Roth of the Rackets Bureau found that the husky-voiced caller had something interesting to tell them. The explosive device which had been used to demolish the Peugeot had been given to Carrara by David Silbergeld, he claimed. The caller added that Carrara had also acquired machine guns from Silbergeld, and hung up.

The unknown caller was Buddy Jacobson, of course, seizing the opportunity to revenge himself on Silbergeld. Smart. Except for one thing. The Rackets Bureau was now in possession of a tape recording of the entire conversation.

The Wood brothers would bump into Jacobson at the usual places—Nicola's, Elaine's, the Sign of the Dove. They would nod at each other, but not converse. Jimmy Wood, though, sensed that Buddy was trying to reach out.

"I could see it in his eyes," he says. "He was trying to say, 'I'm sorry: Come back—let's be friends again.'" But the Woods felt the time for reconciliation was past.

As Buddy would so often tell Melanie, she was his only friend. It was, unfortunately, a concept that he would repeat rather than examine. The physical side of their relationship had diminished: Indeed, they hadn't made love for months. In time to come, Buddy would emphasize this again and again, suggesting that abstinence was incompatible with murderous jealousy. In point of fact, Buddy Jacobson was never a sensual man. The act of love was less his forte than the rite of conquest.

"We'd still have laughs sometimes," Melanie says. "But it was like a brother-sister relationship. Or father-daughter. I was growing up. And he was insensitive to the changes I was growing through."

Melanie's blinkers were almost completely off. Buddy's marvelous fabric of fantasy and lies was beginning to unravel, and she now cocked an ear toward the whispers which she had ignored for so long. How old was Buddy really?

A couple of models told her they had read some article about his racing career, and that he was older than he admitted. Much older. Melanie had never seen any such articles— "He would always steal them out of the paper,"—but, curiosity aroused, she paid a visit to the New York Public Library and studied their files.

Buddy was nearly fifty years old. He was an *old man!*

After all this time, the discovery was horribly disorienting. It was as if she had slipped out of focus and a shutter had clicked, fixing her in a blurry picture. "I was miserable," she says. "I was distraught. I didn't even want to get out of bed."

One day, Buddy, an obsessive fan of the Mets, was watching baseball on TV. Melanie sat there, conspicuously moping. During the commercials, he asked what was wrong.

"I'm going to leave you, Buddy," she said.

His reaction was a mixture of complacency and irritation. "Babe, are you crazy?" he demanded, and returned to the game.

Toward the end of June, Melanie was sitting in Rose Marie Taylor's office on East 48th Street between Madison Avenue and Fifth. It is a tiny office on the sixth floor, and it is from there that Rose Marie runs Model's Mart. Melanie was ordering some materials for My Fair Lady, tote bags for the models to heft around the city, and modeling books to display their photographs.

Melanie discussed the details and called Buddy from the office. "She didn't do anything without his approval," says Rose Marie. Buddy did approve, and Melanie ordered twenty-five of the books and the same number of bags. The books were royal blue and contained a thousand sheets of transparent plastic to hold the photographs. "My Fair Lady" was inscribed on the cover in white. Underneath was written 861-0700, the telephone number which served both the agency and Buddy's apartment (and, indeed, all of Buddy's enterprises, including the line to the Park East hospital, where the Italians were now hard at work, and the last number in the telephone book, attributed to the soon to be infamous Budd Zzzyp). The tote bags had the same color scheme, but reversed, blue script on white.

Rose Marie decided she would have a heart-to-heart talk with her visitor.

"Melanie," she said, "what about all these rumors about the agency?"

The rumors to which she was alluding ranged from the vague to the detailed. Rose Marie had heard of a young woman, a My Fair Lady model, who had returned to her Arizona hometown in great distress, telling dire tales of Buddy's grabbiness, and a similar story from Alabama had reached the ears of Peter Glenn, who publishes the *Madison Avenue Handbook*. A predecessor of Rose Marie Taylor's at Model's Mart, who joined My Fair Lady as a recruiter, had quit in unease and alarm. "People had gotten very leery of

Jacobson," Peter Glenn says. Buddy's predilection for the youngest of the girls at the conventions was now much on their minds, and Glenn had been disturbed to hear that they were lodged—free—in Buddy's building. "There's always a time when you pay the piper," he had said.

But, Rose Marie thought, it was difficult to take such gossip seriously with Melanie actually sitting opposite her. "Melanie was always nice," she says. "She was a delight."

Nonetheless, she put her questions forthrightly enough. Melanie was startled, but her answers were candid.

She explained that she would always tell new models how to comport themselves, the mother-hen warnings. "I tell them that if they are asked to do back shots, they don't have to work nude," she offered as an example. "I always carry a scarf."

Rose Marie was assuaged and saw Melanie later at a cocktail party that Peter Glenn was giving for the out-of-town agents, who were attending the International Fashion Fantasy. This was the snappy name for yet another modeling convention. The convention itself was at the Waldorf Astoria, but Glenn's cocktail party was at an Indian restaurant, the Tandoor. It was Saturday, June 24.

Rose Marie was surprised to see that Melanie was alone.

"Where's Buddy?" she asked.

"He's building," Melanie said. "He's doing it just about by himself. The pressure has gotten to him. I'm trying to keep him in bed."

Rose Marie said she was sorry. Melanie began to do her stuff, chatting with the women who ran the schools, talent-spotting, and making the usual small talk, while her jaws grew quite sore with smiling.

She telephoned Buddy. He was not quite as sick as she had indicated, but certainly he seemed much out of sorts. He was watching football on TV, and refused to budge. Aimlessly, she telephoned her cousin Lindsay, an artist, who had taken a temporary job tending bar at the All-Ireland, close to the 84th Street building. The party was winding down, Melanie's duties were done, and reluctant to go back to the apartment and Buddy, she took a cab to the bar.

The All-Ireland stood on Third Avenue between 81st and 80th streets. It was for old-fashioned drinkers, and unprettified, typical of the Irish bars that used to line Third. Some claim to feel nostalgia for the days when the El clattered overhead, and habitués were tossing back boilermakers—beer and a shot—at eight in the morning. But the actual owners of the bars were happy to sell and see them transformed into fancifully named eating houses. The All-Ireland was one of the last survivors.

The bar's unprettified days were numbered. It had been bought by two young men: Brian Monaghan, a strapping fellow who already owned a bar in Queens, and Jack Tupper. Coincidence occurs so frequently in the chronicling of these events that it comes as no surprise to learn that the Mrs. Kennedy from whom Monaghan and Tupper bought the bar is the mother of Suzanne Flynn, the fashion editor who helped give Melanie her start. Suzanne Flynn remembers the bar as "a P. J. Clarke's for the doormen at the Carlyle."

The All-Ireland was still unaltered this day when Melanie walked in. The light was murky. Lindsay was there, and a handful of other people. They included Jack Tupper.

Melanie knew Jack slightly, and she knew that Buddy had known him in his former days in Queens. Tupper had been brought to see Buddy early in the year by Jacobson's Queens friend the boisterous Donald Brown. Shortly afterward he had moved into the 84th Street building, taking 5A, a three-room apartment that rented for $500 monthly. At one point, in Melanie's presence, Buddy affably remarked, "We have to get a girlfriend for Jack." Such talk made her uncomfortable, and she had been pleased when Tupper seemed uninterested in Buddy's largesse.

Jack Tupper was a powerfully built young man, just over six foot. He was casually dressed, his pale-brown hair was already thinning, and his face was strong rather than handsome. His eyes were dark and lively.

What Melanie did not remember was her first chance meeting with Tupper back in 1975. Donald Brown had taken Jack to Buddy's apartment, and she had been present. The meeting had been brief, but the impression she had made on Tupper was profound. She had happened to be on the cover of *Cosmopolitan* that month. Bob Kronenberg, a longtime friend of Tupper's, says, "He could talk of nothing else but Melanie for months."

Just that June, Tupper had changed apartments. David Silbergeld and Mel Harris were buying a condominium. There were two years left on Silbergeld's lease, and he had the right to sublet. His well-appointed 7C duplex cost only $20 a month more than Tupper's 5A apartment, so Tupper had moved to the seventh floor. There he lived next to Buddy and Melanie in 7D, and Joe Margarite, who had also moved up from the fifth floor, to apartment 7F.

Despite his proximity, Melanie had seen little of Tupper, who had been preoccupied in renovating the All-Ireland. In a sense, this was their first real meeting. They sat in the poolroom at the back of the bar and had a quiet drink, while Paul, Tupper's son from his now-dissolved marriage, attempted to master the pinball machines in the front.

After a while, Melanie telephoned the apartment and told Buddy where she was. "Sure, babe," Buddy said.

She and Jack chatted of this and that. He talked about his son a good deal, and that impressed her. She called Buddy a couple of times more, at intervals, but he didn't seem bothered by her absence, so she ordered another drink and lingered on.

She stayed most of the evening, in fact, sitting in the murky bar of the All-Ireland. She talked nonstop and laughed, and when she finally left, she knew two things: She liked Jack Tupper immensely, and she had been having a thoroughly good time.

Such respites had been getting rarer and rarer. The more that Melanie's reason told her she had to leave Buddy, the feebler her willpower seemed. She felt embedded, like a trophy in Lucite, in what she had taken to calling "Buddy's World." "He was so *weird* in those last weeks," she says. "You know, I was in a state of shock *before* the murder."

At six o'clock the evening of July 12, Melanie and five of her My Fair Lady models were sitting in Marco's, then a lavish night-spot in East 45th Street, owned by Marco Ricotta, an occasional guest at Buddy's parties ever since turning up at the building five years before. This evening, Marco's was the venue of a cable TV talk show. The guests were Melanie and the other models, including a young girl new to the agency, Cheryl Corey.

Melanie spoke the most. She was briskly informative about the modeling business, and smiled freely, showing none of the strain she felt: a pro. The taping lasted half an hour. Afterward, Melanie sat alone with Marco Ricotta at the rear of the restaurant. Behind them, an artificial waterfall ran down a wall of rock. "I like Melanie," Marco says. "I like her, like a sister. We talked. She stayed till one in the morning."

The core of her conversation was a dreadful contradiction: Melanie loved Buddy, but she wanted to leave him.

At the same time, she didn't love Buddy, but she couldn't leave him.

A despondent mood overwhelmed her. She sat beside the waterfall, over a glass of wine, and wept. There was little Marco could do or say, so he settled for a pep talk. "Stand on your own two feet," he told her. "Get in control of your life. Then look for somebody else." But he was one of the few people who knew Buddy that realized there was another dimension to the problem. "Buddy loved Melanie," he told me. "No matter what he says, Buddy loved that girl."

Melanie's Journal: Monday, July 17

Well, this book is getting filled with a lot of thoughts that are exploding through my head.

Buddy, Buddy, Buddy . . . It is over and we both know it. Why do we keep playing such foolish games?

Is it pride, insecurity, ego, or are we just plain SCARED—the both of us—leaving one another to be alone or maybe WITH ANOTHER.

You get to know a person, they actually become such a part of you. But Buddy you are no longer part of me—that certain feeling has disappeared—God it saddens me—but nothing lasts forever I've heard so often.

Goodbye my darling Buddy—what an extraordinary man you really are. . . .

The following day, Jack Tupper was standing with Ivor Shaw where 84th Street crosses Lexington Avenue. It was four-thirty in the afternoon and the sunlight was rich as marmalade. They were talking desultorily about the All-Ireland when Tupper's eye was caught by one of the furnishings being disposed of in a nearby store. It was an impressive length of wood, and might serve as a bartop, he noted. He and Shaw walked into the store and found somebody else foraging among the sale items. Melanie.

She looked bewitching, Shaw remembers, even in her shapeless jogging clothes. They chatted briefly, and then Melanie asked Tupper if he wanted to go jogging. He was at once startled and flattered. "Just give me a few minutes to change," he said.

So Jack Tupper jogged with Melanie around the reservoir in Central Park. That was how it began.

Jack called Ivor Shaw that evening. "She's a very stand-up broad," he told Shaw. "She has never cheated on Buddy in five years."

The next morning, Jack and Melanie went jogging again. And Melanie now realized something. "I've got a crush on Jack," she told herself. The time for her long-postponed break with Buddy had arrived at last.

Melanie's Journal: Wednesday, July 19

Well, another 2 days have passed and my feelings for leaving are stronger and stronger.

Buddy knows we can't talk anymore.

Business we're coping with pretty well but—us—forget it. I don't want to lie in the bed at night. We don't sleep—either of us. Our backs are turned to one another.

Buddy is glad, I'm sure, Douglas is around to avoid . . . conversation of any kind. I guess Douglas is my excuse too—for not pushing Buddy to a final talk. We both are ignoring the situation, at least till the weekend.

God, I'm tired, and drained—please let me go, Buddy—and don't hate me soooo when I do leave.

God, I feel so guilty too. What I'm trying to say is I'm so sure of myself now—and I do have deep feelings for a man named Jack. In 4½ years I never had such feelings for anyone. Jack is not my excuse for leaving Buddy. I have to make that clear. Yet, I'm really falling in love like I never did before—not even with Buddy.

Jack is an individual who so understands others' thoughts, ambitions, frustrations—could he have been through so much himself that he learned from past experiences? He is so real though—nothing like Buddy at all. He respects me as an individual, something Buddy has never done. Last week he even tried to mend my relationship with Buddy. I guess he felt if I had coped with Buddy for 4½ years I must really love him. And yet Jack is the man I'm so impressed with—so special a human being he is to have thoughts for other people's relationships. I wonder why—maybe he likes me—I think he does but he couldn't let me know because, after all, I'm still living with another man. Oh Melanie—don't be silly—he's just being a friend.

Anyway, whatever thoughts are running through his head, I know what my thoughts say—and I'm falling in love with Jack Tupper. Buddy has been gone from my thoughts for so long—yet I'm scared to tell him. . . . Will he understand? . . . that it's gone, but maybe we'll still be friends. Friends—sounds so funny after 4½ years. If only Buddy could have known the real me . . . I think he did inside but he possessed me so. He never respected me enough to let me be me.

I'm tired—tomorrow I go and never shall I return. "Once lovers, never friends."

Seems so sad and endless.

I'll be okay, because I'm Melanie.

This was the last entry Melanie was to make in her journal for three full weeks.

The next day—Thursday—she told Buddy that she was leaving him. She did not mention Tupper, nor indeed had anything sexual occurred between them which would have given her reason to. Buddy took the news calmly. This was the seventh time, at least, that Melanie had tried to leave him, and each time he had drawn her back to him.

In the middle of the afternoon, Melanie was walking down Third when she met Jack Tupper, coming out of the All-Ireland. She told him that she was leaving Buddy and looking for a place to live, and he volunteered to help her with her search.

They found nothing, though they looked until dark. Jack took her to dinner. This was one of her few dinners alone with any man other than Buddy in almost five years, and she was nervous, so Jack took her to the West Side. They ate at the Red Baron, which is a Frenchified place on Columbus Avenue. Both realized they had found what they were looking for. It seemed to Melanie that a grim chapter in her life had finally ended. But a new one was already beginning.

- IV -

Jack's Tale

When those people who knew Jack Tupper best attempt to define the man they knew, a wholeness emerges. He was, for one thing, likable. "He was very engaging," observes Tom Myers, who is married to Jack's sister, Dorothy. "He always had a quip. Lots of New York savvy. That'll take you anywhere."

He was also something of a loner. "Jack was a very private person," says Marie, his mother, and Ellen, his former wife, described him in identical words. There was something else sensed by those who came anywhere close to him: a powerful romantic streak. This is what Dorothy, the member of his family to whom he was always closest, calls his "James Bond–Walter Mitty side." Jack Tupper, from the beginning, was an optimist.

This attitude had, in part, been instilled in him by his parents. Jack Tupper, Sr., whose own father was of English stock and whose mother was born in County Kildare, Ireland, grew up in New York, and in poverty. In his teens he took a job on Wall Street, clerking, but he had a mother and four sisters to support, so he forsook the desk and joined the longshoremen's union. For three years he worked on the waterfront, where he was known as the Professor as he studied to keep up with his contemporaries in school. Then, offended by the corruption, he took a job at a Brooklyn factory that made inner tubes and valves.

In 1940, the elder Tupper, now married to Marie, was drafted into the 343rd Engineers. He was stationed in London during the Blitz, was sent to North Africa, and played his part in the invasion of Italy. His first child, Jack, was born while he was at war, and he was not to see him till he was eighteen months old, an encounter lovingly recorded in an album of photographs.

After the war, Jack Tupper, Sr., duly returned to his job.

His experience on the docks had made him strongly anti-union, but he found that the factory local was Communist-controlled and deeply involved in sweetheart deals. Tupper, who describes himself as a moderate Republican—"I was in the Taft Club"—disapproved on both counts, and became involved in union politics: in due course, rising to the presidency of his local, in which job he was famously immune from payoffs.

His son Jack was the first of four children, followed by Dorothy, Kevin, and Jerry. All the children went to Catholic grammar schools, and the elder Tuppers were content with cramped quarters and stinted on small luxuries so that the children might have opportunities they themselves had missed. Jack and Marie did not, though, believe solely in book learning. The elder Tupper had been an athlete in his youth. Indeed, he had skated so well as a boy that, but for his need for wages, he would have entered the Silver Skates Competition, and he had boxed in the army, ending up as heavyweight champion of his division. "I always kept the boys sports-minded," he says. "My wife and I spent a lot of time on our kids."

Young Jack—his family were always to call him Jackie—was an agreeable, unassertive child. In parochial school, his parents made certain that his hair was the proper length, his uniform clean. He applied himself to his books and soon distinguished himself at athletics. His sister Dorothy, called Dee, who was his junior by eighteen months, talks of Jackie's working out with weights in his early teens. After high school, Jackie entered St. John's College in Queens.

If there is something very Victorian about the determination of the Tuppers, both parents and children, to do both honorably and well in the world, there is another strain which runs alongside this doggedness: a deep emotionalism. It is certain that Jackie Tupper, as the firstborn, felt the pressures the most. At the age of seventeen, he told his family that he was leaving home.

They were shocked. "Jackie, when younger, was never a leader," his father says. "He always wanted to be considered one of the boys." His demand for independence was more than they could bring themselves to accept. "We said, if you leave home, we aren't going to pay for college," Marie Tupper recalls.

Young Jack left anyway, and worked his way through college—mostly in construction and demolition. A powerful young man, he was soon among the leading basketball players at St. John's. He was a popular student, with his sandy hair, dark eyes, and what a friend describes as "that slight grin he always wore." His breach with his family soon healed. "Children do leave home," Marie Tupper says. His parents feel, in retrospect, that they had been too stern with their oldest boy, too inflexible.

Oddly, few of the young man's close friends were people with whom he was going to college. Mostly they were from his own neighborhood, like Eugene Leonard, with whom he had gone to parochial school, and Eugene's older brother, Jimmy. Through Jimmy Leonard, an energetic fair-haired youth, he met Billy Sharrocks, a sturdy and handsome young man whose forefathers came from Burnley, Lancashire. Jack Tupper was to share an apartment with both Billy Sharrocks and Jimmy Leonard, and it was through them that he was to meet two men who were a few years older than he, but to whom he was to become very close, Al Seifert and Donald Brown.

Al was a brawny man, and taciturn. Both his parents had been journalists, his father as a weatherman with the *Daily News* and his mother in the woman's department of that same newspaper as a writer on the "Doris Blake" column, a now-defunct rival to "Dear Abby." Al Seifert, like Jack Tupper, was a graduate of St. John's.

Donald Brown was quite different from Seifert. Brown has auburn hair, pale-blue eyes in a broad face, and a permanent onstage manner, as if his adrenaline were several degrees higher than the norm. He dropped out of school at seventeen, not so much from incapacity as from sheer impatience. His early life was colorful. "I took the back roads," he told me. "Not the highways, the back roads." His forte was the scam: dashing piracy was his style, and he had the panache and the mouth to achieve it.

Jack Tupper thus became part of a fairly close-knit group. Indeed, Donald Brown—or, D.B.—celebrated Jack's graduation from St. John's in 1966 in characteristic fashion. He borrowed Tupper's car, an elderly gray Cadillac with a busted transmission and a scrap-metal engine, and drove it into a repair shop with false plates. "Two weeks later, I stole it back," he told me. "I changed the plates back, and gave it to Jack as a graduation present."

Jack admired Donald Brown and appreciated the appeal of the back roads, but felt that for himself the highways beckoned. In the meantime, though, he took the customary short-term jobs, and it was while he was tending bar at a Queens hangout called the Step-Inn, that he met Ellen Lanzillo. He knew her brother. Ellen, the daughter of a dance instructress, had walked in to get out of the rain. She was seventeen and a beauty. She was also uncommonly bright, a top student at Jamaica High School, but was resisting pressure to apply to a good college. She poured out her confusion to Jack and found him reassuring, solid. "He was always a romantic where women were concerned," she says. "He liked a *cause.*"

Ellen grew to love Jack, but was determined to cure him of what she perceived as a certain indolence. He was sharing an apartment and enjoying himself. Late at night, in the Step-Inn, he would talk grandiloquently of working for himself, "wheeling and dealing," making a pile in stocks, but he seemed to regard the preliminary steps as a matter of small urgency.

Ellen was more determined. "You're in a rut," she told him. She would read the *Times* and circle the desirable openings. Management traineeships, jobs in sales, that sort of thing. But Jack—Ellen herself called him John—would demur, saying that he wasn't a "nine-to-five man." He had not moved out of his father's house merely to embed himself in some larger structure. He would be an entrepreneur.

Ellen was a believer in programs, not dreams. There was an abstract painting hanging on the wall of Jack's apartment, a splashy canvas, a present from a former girlfriend. One day Ellen, in a particularly exasperated mood, scrawled a message in lipstick across this artwork.

The message read: "Write your résumé."

They married in April 1967. Jack was twenty-four and Ellen not yet eighteen. Donald Brown was to have been best man, but some trifling problem with the law in Puerto Rico intervened, and he was replaced by Jimmy Leonard. A few weeks later, Jack did indeed get that serious job. It was with a life insurance company, Connecticut General.

The man who hired Jack was Joe Casale. A former marine and FBI agent, and chairman of the New York Athletic

Club's Judo and Karate Committee, he was well pleased by his recruit. "I liked him a lot," Casale says. "He was one hundred percent honest. You couldn't buy him a drink—he'd want to do his round."

He tells how somebody once approached Jack Tupper asking for insurance. It was individual insurance, however, and this wasn't Tupper's line; he specialized in selling group insurance. "But he had a license," Casale says. "He *could* have sold it. He didn't. He said, 'I'll send you to a pro.'"

The man Jack sent the customer to was Casale himself, and Jack Tupper refused to take the finder's fee, which he could have done with complete legality. This commission was $600, which, for a young agent starting out, was not negligible.

Jack liked to make his own hours, but the company found nothing wrong with that. One laudatory letter to his supervisor from a Manhattan firm concluded: "I feel you should know how much we value Mr. Tupper and what a credit he is, not only to your Group Department, but also to the image of Connecticut General."

Sometimes Joe Casale would invite Jack up to the judo room in the Athletic Club to work out. "He was only a brown belt, or a green belt, something like that," Casale says. "But he was one tough piece of work." This, coming from a black belt of the third dan, built on the lines of a GE refrigerator, is not idle talk. A couple of years later, when Casale left Connecticut General for a Phoenix-based agency, he asked Jack to go with him.

Tupper refused. Donald Brown had offered him a partnership in something which appealed to the racy side of him far more than the world of insurance could ever do: the bar business. The year was 1970 and the place was on Lefferts Boulevard, a major Queens thoroughfare. A bakery had stood there, and a dry cleaner's, but they had been bought by the food chain Bohack's, which had planned to build a supermarket there but had changed its mind. The bar took nine months to build, and much of the time the partners were only a few dollars from disaster. At one stage, Bohack's went so far as to foreclose.

"I went to the president," Brown says. "I bypassed everybody. I showed him my arm." He rolls up his sleeve, disclosing a long scar, the mark of some long-ago road accident. "I said I had bone cancer, and didn't have long to live. It was my last wish on earth to finish this bar.

"I had him *crying*. He got on the telephone, and told his people to reinstate the lease."

Throughout the construction, Donald Brown and Jack (who was simultaneously struggling to keep his insurance job going) were on the site whenever possible. Jack's parents felt ambivalent about the venture, after his promising beginnings in the corporate world, but his kid brothers set to with zeal. "We did the schlep work," Kevin says. "We helped the brick-layers, the carpenters, the electricians."

A friend of Donald Brown's also helped out—Carlo Carrara's construction firm did some work on the doorway and the bar. And it is Donald Brown who takes credit for the way the place eventually looked, which is to say rustic, with dim, sherry-colored lighting, oval barrels protuberant from one wall, and a pattern of crazy paving behind the bar.

All that was necessary was a name. The partners wanted an English one to go with the English look. "We thought of a million names," D.B. says. "Sergeant Pepper . . . nothing was right."

Finally, they took the name off a brand of wrought-iron lantern; the place became the Sherwood.

Everything from the booze up was purchased on credit, and the Sherwood Inn was already in debt the day it was launched. It never truly recovered, and, as is the way in such matters, the reasons for the decline of the Sherwood Inn vary, depending on the teller. There was soon much dissension between the partners.

Certainly business management was not the Sherwood Inn's strong point. "Jack would call me and say, 'Are you coming tonight?' " remarks the attorney Bob Kronenberg. " 'Will you stop at the liquor store? We're out of Scotch.' Not that the Chivas Regal had run out, and they were having to fill it up from the Teacher's bottle. They're out of *Scotch*. Or he says, 'Can I borrow the car? I have to go to the store. We've run out of meat.' "

Tupper's family believe that it was only Jack's own hard work that kept the Sherwood Inn out of Chapter XII for the time it did manage to struggle by. Donald Brown ascribes what little success the place had to his gregarious performance as host. Perhaps the most balanced view comes from Jack's younger brother Kevin. "I think they all thought they could be playboys rather than businessmen," he says. "They made a lot of poor business decisions."

It was a time for learning. Jack now had a son, Paul, to whom he was devoted, but his marriage had come to an amicable end. "The fact that we were separated didn't mean we weren't close," Ellen says. "We were best friends."

Jack Tupper, in due course, began to go out with another girl. She was Eurasian, and possessed of a feline beauty. Her name was Yolanda, and she met Jack through Anne, who was to be the wife of Bob Kronenberg. Yolanda and Anne flew together as air stewardesses on Pan American. "He was crazy about her," his sister Dorothy says. "He fell very much in love."

He had moved to the Towne House, where Donald Brown also had an apartment. It was at a moving-in party that he first met the building's best-known tenant, Buddy Jacobson. Jacobson seems to have cottoned onto the young man. Jack Tupper, though, was too independent a figure to fit comfortably into Buddy's world, so, like Donald Brown, he would show up occasionally at those famous parties, but grew no closer than that.

At the Sherwood Inn, though, the deficits kept mounting. The bar just wasn't gelling into the sort of place the partners had in mind, a joint which would attract a clientele with bonhomie and class. What happened was that the inn soon attracted the chilling attentions of some of the most famous heist artists in Queens. Among them were the craftsmen who were to pull off the $10 million Lufthansa Airlines holdup, a grim caper that was to leave at least nine participants dead in its wake.

"They would come in and just put their guns on top of the bar," says Al Seifert. One evening Jack had thrown out a member of the gang. "John stood up to him," says Seifert, who always called Tupper "John," "John made him leave." True, but according to Brown, there was a hairy sequel. "Fifteen of them came in," he says. "They were going to blow Jack away." It was late. The only people left in the Sherwood Inn were Tupper, Brown, the barman, and Tom Normandeau, a cop who had become friendly with Jack. And they were petrified.

"I went over," Brown says, "I talked them out of it. That's

straight." The leader of the group chucked a couple of hundred dollars on the bar, asked for drinks all round, and everybody relaxed. "I like this place," he told Brown, looking around with evident appreciation, "I'd walk over nine dead bodies to own a place like this." This particular fellow was known for a tendency to literalness, but, on this occasion at least, he was evidently joking. But the patronage of the heist artists did not make for a relaxing ambiance, and trade slackened dramatically.

Jack had now quit his job, although he had been doing well until the end, and in the years to come would sometimes talk about his time as a comer in the insurance world with a tinge of regret. Nor did he have the bar to fall back on. They were looking for a buyer.

It was now that Yolanda walked out on Jack, leaving him for a married man, an Englishman. Jack swung between rage and grief. "She's the only girl I have ever loved," he told his family. In differing moods, he would send lovelorn notes or utter dark threats. "Jack behaved just like Buddy," Bob Kronenberg says, remarking though on one critical difference: The Englishman is still alive.

It was Jack Tupper's nadir. Friends saw that he was on the fault line of a breakdown. One who set out to help him was Tom Normandeau, a cop who had grown to know Jack at the Sherwood Inn. Tom's sister, Claire, was also drawn to Jack. She was a slight girl, with something of her French lineage showing in her waiflike prettiness. Claire Normandeau was twenty-two, but looked sixteen. She felt a closeness other than love, finding in him the strange combination that existed in herself: a straightness, and a love for the shadows. Claire Normandeau was already working undercover as a narcotics cop for the New York City police department.

Later, the Tupper-Normandeau connection was to have harrowing effects. Right now, Jack—broke, aimless, and in the bleakest of spirits—began to share an apartment with Tom Normandeau.

He knew he would have to start all over again from the beginning.

Jack Tupper's friends, meanwhile, were pursuing their own careers—and the route they had chosen was a touch hazardous. Here was Jimmy Leonard, Jack's former roommate, who had never gone to college and had, indeed, been driving a city bus. Suddenly he seemed very prosperous.

"Jack told us Jimmy had bought a gold-plating business," the elder Tupper said.

Or consider Donald Brown, who hadn't troubled even to finish high school, but despite the failure of the Sherwood Inn now walked around looking as if he had stepped straight out of *Gentleman's Quarterly*. The Tupper parents, who were fond of Brown, were curious.

"What's with Donald?" Marie asked her son. "Why's he so rich all of a sudden?"

"Does Macy's tell Gimbels?" Jack said.

Jimmy Leonard himself was a bit more to the point when I spoke with him some years later in Chequers, the bar that Jack Tupper had bought on the Upper East Side. I asked him what he did for a living.

"I smuggle," Jimmy told me genially.

He added, "I used to drive a bus. My favorite route was away from the airport."

The DEA was to call Tupper's friends the Donald Brown Organization, and the case it tried to put together against them was code-named the Astro-Electric Affair after the dummy company name the organization used to front one of its more brazen capers. The group, which smuggled drugs through Kennedy airport, included Brown, the Leonard brothers, Billy Sharrocks, and Al Seifert. When the DEA did finally manage to piece a case together and hauled the group into court, the trial took place in Brooklyn at the same time as Buddy Jacobson's trial in the Bronx for Jack Tupper's murder. Tupper was also named, posthumously, as an "unindicted co-conspirator" in the case, and Jacobson was to weave a splendidly intricate web suggesting that Tupper's murder arose from some upheaval in the Brown organization. The real story of Tupper's relations with his neighborhood friends in their often brilliant, sometimes wildly improbable drug-smuggling capers is far more interesting.

The Donald Brown Organization had its genesis in 1969, when a GI from Queens who was stationed in Germany wrote a letter to Al Seifert's brother, Robby. The GI was a member of a smuggling operation that wanted to move hashish through Kennedy airport. Robby Seifert flew to Europe and met the GI, whose name was Julius Negron, and an assortment of characters that included a couple of Greeks, an American named Doug Carty, and a Puerto Rican named Rudy Dehesa. The thought was that the hashish could be secreted in stereo speakers. Robby Seifert flew home and sounded out Donald Brown on the scheme.

This was a smart move. Brown's wandering on the back roads of life had been productive; he had made friends everywhere, and one of the places where he enjoyed a strong coterie of admirers was Kennedy airport. He had, in fact, been toying with the idea of getting into gold smuggling, but was easily convinced of the superior merits of the hashish business. Brown derided the idea of shipping the stuff in hi-fi speakers and came up with a better plan. A footlocker marked "Personal Effects" duly arrived at Kennedy by Alitalia, and was taken from the terminal for customs inspection in Building 80. By the time it arrived there, someone had lightened it by twenty-two pounds of Lebanese hash. Street price: circa $20,000.

Consider the situation. Hashish and marijuana were illegal, but their use was ubiquitous and met with a high degree of social approbation. Trafficking in hash and grass wasn't the same thing as dealing heroin or amphetamines. It was like bootlegging during Prohibition. Okay, it was against the law. But it wasn't . . . *evil*.

Even the government accepted this, it seemed. The smuggling of heroin or cocaine brought lengthy sentences, while the penalty for smuggling in the herb was a maximum five years, irrespective of the quantity. The Mafia and other lethal groups showed little interest in hash and grass, since in terms of weight the profits, compared with heroin, were too puny. But Donald Brown saw something very clearly: It was a matter of *weight*. If one could move the stuff in bulk through Kennedy, the risk would be small, the profits exhilarating. Again, like booze during Prohibition.

He set to building a network. In August 1970, at age thirty, he left the United States for the first time ever. He went to Kabul with Doug Carty and stayed at the Intercontinental, moving on to Islamabad, Karachi, and Kandahar. "I stayed at Deane's Hotel," he says. "Rudyard Kipling stayed there. It's *history*." The trip was supposed to set up a connection, and it almost ended in disaster. "It was a setup," he says. "My perceptions were very good." D.B. returned rapidly, and empty-handed.

That October, Brown went to Europe, specifically, to Frankfurt, which can lay claim to being air terminal to the world. Soon he was making some new acquaintances, among whom was an Australian artist named Robert "Rinky" Dancke. Through Dancke, Brown met the experts who could create a "library"—fake passport, fake birth certificate, fake everything—for just $5,000.

Brown's next stop was London, where he lay low, Donald Brown style, which is to say he purchased a number of suits at Harrods, and then went on to Carnaby Street to make sure he had a sufficiency of shirts and ties. He was ebulliently noticeable at such high-profile venues as San Lorenzo, a restaurant in Beauchamp Place that is seldom out of the glossy magazines, and Tramp, the intensely fashionable discothèque. When he would hint, broadly, that he was interested in "horticultural" imports and exports, his circle of useful acquaintances became enlarged further.

Things moved briskly when he returned to New York. First came the suitcases—two suitcases, one in each hand. Whoever was carrying the suitcases would take a flight on an approved airline—D.B., at one stage or another, knew friendly fellows who were baggage handlers at such estimable airlines as Alitalia, Braniff, Japanese Airlines, and Pan Am. The suitcases would be distinguished by a decal or whatever, and would never go through the disagreeable routine of customs. Simplicity itself.

This easy rhythm was interrupted when Dancke was arrested in Germany with a cohort named Frank Natiello, another Queens man, who had lost a leg in Vietnam. They were actually carrying the suitcases onto the plane when apprehended. Dancke and Natiello got six months apiece, and since neither Brown nor Seifert could guess how the modus operandi had been discovered, they abandoned the suitcase game forthwith.

The ploy had, anyway, been primitive. D.B. now went back to Germany. It was 1971. By his own account, he sweet-talked Rinky Dancke out of jail and recovered his passport. Whereupon a gratified Dancke arranged for Brown to meet his supplier, an Arab whom he knew as Malek, in Munich.

Malek dealt quantity. But how, he asked, did Donald propose to get the hash into the United States? This required research. The schemes that Donald Brown now began to devise were grounded on one dazzling aperçu. The air freight that came into Kennedy and is stored there temporarily while waiting to be flown elsewhere does not normally get searched by customs —that happens at the final destination.

It was an extension of the suitcase method. All that was necessary was for a few friendly souls to remove the hashish while the crates were in Kennedy, then send the freight on its way, purified. D.B. consulted with a lanky redheaded cargo handler at Braniff, called Peter Splain: it was go.

But there was a complication. Malek the Arab promised to send two hundred pounds of hash as a first shipment. Only forty arrived. Malek was to have been paid after the sale, but, what with payoffs, Donald Brown found he was losing money on the deal, and was enraged. So he told Malek that the shipment had been seized. Profit: minus.

Malek hurried over, telephoned Jimmy Leonard at his gold-plating establishment, and asked about the shipment. "It was fine," Leonard said. Malek went looking for Brown, with three of his compatriots. "They had guns and knives," Brown says. He talked himself out of it—just. Brown was to claim that "Jimmy Leonard had tried to set me up." Jimmy Leonard insists with parallel fervor, that D.B. simply hadn't told him the facts. A coolness grew between them.

Now, Donald Brown was broke. His airport schemes were not yet in full working order. The deals were small-time, unremunerative. Indeed, Donald was *worse* than broke. The Sherwood Inn was consuming dollars. Depressed, he went on a gambling binge, and ended up owing the bookies about $18,000.

This was 1973. Donald Brown went to see Buddy Jacobson. He had, after all, helped out Buddy Jacobson when he had needed cash for his ski lodge. D.B.'s own need was now more dire. Buddy offered him $500. "I never even bothered to cash the check," he says.

Instead, he hastily left for Florida in a Hertz van. There he brooded, and regretted his precipitate departure. Returning, he faced his creditors. "I did the manly thing," he says. "Of course, they smacked me, and abused me." His voice was low.

It was not a pleasing memory. But he and the bookies came to terms, and Brown promised to repay his debt.

Better times were coming. Brown, whose wife was an air stewardess, set off on further travels. They took him, for instance, to Beirut, Acapulco, Lima, and a segment of Iran not too far from the Soviet border. His network of acquaintances, which included, for instance, a Pakistani general, continued to grow. The DEA was, in the end, to unspool a list of some six dozen names they felt constituted the Donald Brown Organization's American end alone.

But Brown's group was always a loose agglomeration, fissured by feuds, with warm friendships turning to bitter enmities, then sometimes warming up again—or so it seems—within a few weeks. Billy Sharrocks and Jimmy Leonard did not always work in cahoots with Donald Brown, for instance. Nor, come to that, was Brown necessarily the undisputed leader. The mercurial presence, yes, but the cooler organizing head belonged to Al Seifert. Various names that the Feds threw onto the list often were peripheral. And the most notable of these, as we shall see, was that of Jack Tupper.

They were not, of course, the only group smuggling hash. Nor, for that matter, did they always confine themselves to the airport. "By 1974, it was madness," says Jimmy Leonard, and tells a tale of going out to where a boat was being unloaded on Long Island, where, after some confusion with the passwords he found he was talking to a different group of smugglers entirely. He made the sort of apology you give when you find yourself sitting in the wrong seat in the theater.

Kennedy was the main arena, though, and at the airport the operation was beginning to hum like a machine. Between that first regrettable meeting with Malek and the middle of 1974, Donald Brown, using Peter Splain at Braniff, moved something like three thousand pounds of Lebanese hashish, with a street value of something like $4 million, out of the airport.

Brown's organization was wonderfully slick and wonderfully sloppy. There was no attempt to "smuggle," in the sense of concealing the goods in hollow table legs. "All you had to do was open the right crate. It was all just sitting there," a Fed says, with glum admiration. The Feds have always known, of course, that there is monkeying around with in-transit freight, and there is a DEA team at the airport whose job it is to stop this. The assignment is no easy task. D.B.'s baggage handlers made sure that his crates of merchandise were placed in the most unobtrusive and out-of-the-way locations possible. If a shipment did fall under suspicion, the news got back to the Brown group right away.

The operation began to seem almost too easy. The hash would come in, and they would remove it from the crates and then repack the crates with used clothing, which weighs much the same and can be bought by the bale. The shipments would then be flown on to their stated destination. "Do you know where the kids must be really happy? In Quito, Ecuador," one of the group crowed. "They're *never* gonna run out of Mickey Mouse T-shirts in Quito."

Airport documentation—cargo manifests and such—posed no problem. On occasion, records could be removed from the computer, and a cargo actually would wink out of official existence. "It got so that Donald Brown could smuggle a pink elephant through the airport," one of the ring says. "He could have smuggled two pink elephants *in heat.*"

Nonetheless, accidents would happen. One decent-sized dope shipment which was ostensibly coming in as machine parts from Japan, a non-dope-producing exit of which they made much use, was headed for Asuncion or somewhere, and the problem was that zealous cargo controllers all over the world kept on saying, hey, this shipment doesn't have to go through New York. It'll be quicker if we rout it through Rome, or Los Angeles, or wherever. "The shipment was four or five million dollars' worth," Ivor Shaw says. "It was flying around to different cities for weeks. Brown's guys almost had nervous breakdowns. By the time they got the stuff, it was so covered with labels that it looked like Lady Astor's steamer trunk. . . ."

Geopolitics also had to be watched closely. The toppling of a general in Latin America could throw a whole operation out of kilter. The outbreak of war in Lebanon was a business catastrophe: Warehouses were jam-packed with dope, while Brown was going crazy.

There were darker problems. A Mafia grouping got wind of these doings and "invited" Donald Brown to a meeting. "They had sixteen thousand pounds of heroin they wanted moved in," Al Seifert says. Brown listened, masking his emotions, which were horror. People who dealt heroin were animals.

You can be put in a painful position, even knowing such gentry. He mumbled something, and departed.

"And that was the last they saw of him," Seifert says, making a gesture as of a swimmer cleaving a wave. "He got out of the state. That was one of about twelve times Donald got out of the state. . . ."

Curiously, the supposed airport authorities—the cops, the DEA, and so forth—never bothered Brown and his allies too much. They understood cops and, indeed, under other circumstances might well have joined the force themselves. One of Jimmy Leonard's brothers was a cop, as was Billy Sharrocks' brother. Donald Brown's cousin was a cop actually stationed at the airport. "He's so *embarrassed*," Brown says.

As to the DEA, the Brown organization was far less alarmed by the humans than by Smack and Brandy, the dope-sniffing dogs. "Donald was terrified of them. He was talking about having them kidnapped," says Ivor Shaw. Turning away from such desperate measures, the gang built special vacuum-sealed crates to foil the dogs. Occasionally, Shaw says, there was some gleeful inventiveness. "They sprayed the cases with stuff like Right Guard," claims Shaw. "I always knew when a big load of dope was coming through the airport. You couldn't buy underarm deodorant in the whole of New York."

Certainly the greatest bane in the lives of the narcotics squad was Donald Brown. One day he sallied up to the agents keeping him under surveillance. He was looking particularly obtrusive that day, $2,000 in Mayfair goods on the hoof, from the striped shirt with the attached white collar from Turnbull & Asser, to the Wildsmith loafers, to the cashmere jacket, to the Boucheron watch.

Brown examined them critically from head to toe. "Boys!" he announced. "Where do you get your clothes? You look *horrible*."

The narcs did not find this comment amusing, and found what followed even less so. D.B. and Malek had decided to forget their earlier unpleasantness, cash down being a great healer. Accordingly, Brown took a Pan Am flight to Beirut, and booked into the Phoenicia Intercontinental; typically enough, he did so under his own name. Nattily attired in black tie, he won twenty-five thousand Lebanese dollars at the Casino du Libon, dined at the Cedars of Lebanon. Malek then took him to Beka'a, on the Syrian border, and Brown invested

$30,000 in blond hash, which would be worth twenty-five times that in the U.S. He then returned to New York.

The shipment left the Middle East on June 4, 1974. It consisted of two crates lined with foam rubber and holding 367 pounds of hashish slabs in burlap sacks, this merchandise being described on the cargo manifest as "machine parts." The crates were flown out of Damascus, Syria, aboard PIA, the Pakistani airline, and their first stop was to be Heathrow, London.

London! This was irritating. The British are notoriously deft at nosing out smuggled goods. "We avoid London like the fucking *plague*," says Ivor Shaw. Unfortunately, though, a flurry of terrorist goings-on—the PLO, and Baader-Meinhof, even the Dutch Moluccans—had gummed up the airline schedules, and there was no alternative.

The crates duly arrived at the PIA shed in Heathrow's Cargo Village. From here they were to be transferred to a TWA flight for New York. In New York, the crates would be trundled across to Braniff, where they would be in the care of Peter Splain, and their ultimate destination, supposedly, was to be a company called Maquinas de Comercio, of Quito, Ecuador, which happens to be the outlet for the National Cash Register Company.

Unfortunately, the British, possibly wondering just what sort of machine parts Quito would require from Damascus, did peek into the crates. The jig was up. They telephoned the DEA, which was jubilant. The hashish was replaced by rocks, and, since rock theft is not much of a crime, one slab of hash was left in each crate.

Meanwhile, Brown and Seifert were getting twitchy. Freight did get stuck, but seldom as long as this. They went out to the TWA terminal, the International Arrivals building, and called the TWA cargo shed in London. The call just wasn't *right*—the man at the other end was slow, unconvincing. But it was typical of Donald Brown's confidence that he left a callback number—an attorney known to him—even as his nerves crackled like charged wires.

It would, of course, have been folly to abandon a $750,000 load over a mere attack of nerves. Back in Queens, they telephoned TWA, the Kennedy facility, from a spot called Teddy's Diner. The shipment would be coming in later that evening, they were told, so they called Peter Splain and gave him the details. One point: Each crate was crisscrossed by four metal bands in a distinctive fashion. Should the bands seem to have been tampered with, Splain should leave the crates just as they were.

It was time to move. Donald Brown went out to the airport. With him were Al Seifert's brother, Robby, the one-legged Vietnam vet, Frank Natiello, and the Puerto Rican, Rudy Dehesa. It was their job to look out for any signs of surveillance.

There are differing versions as to what happened next. The DEA, embarrassed to this day, claims that the information given by the British was faulty, and that its men were carefully watching a totally innocent shipment. The Donald Brown group suggest that this is not so, and that the cargo, which was in the Braniff shed, was being watched by five agents, parked some distance off in a car.

Brown sauntered over to the quintet of sleuths during their vigil. "I used my personality," he says. "I distracted them." What he did was offer them some cookies. While they were thus bemused, Peter Splain hit the crates with a forklift truck. Within minutes, the two crates were on a Hertz van driven by Lou Prikas, a Brown henchman, and two other crates had been substituted. This passed unobserved by the narcotics men.

"A lot of people got into trouble," attorney Bob Kronenberg observes.

Prikas, meanwhile, had reached his own street in Queens with the Hertz truck. The plan had been that he would store the crates in his garage. This went awry for a characteristic New York reason, which was that so many cars were double-parked in his block that Prikas couldn't get near his house. They drove elsewhere.

The group, which now consisted of the Seiferts, Prikas, the artist Robert Dancke, Natiello, and Brown, carried the crates into the second house's basement. They tore them apart eagerly, but with foreboding, since they had noticed that the four metal bands were already broken. There lay the rocks. On top of the rocks in each crate, like a wedge of Cheddar in a mousetrap, lay a half-pound tongue of hashish.

There was panic. "Mayhem," says D.B. The gang fled in all directions.

Though the Donald Brown Organization was cash-poor for a bit, it was back in business and prospering greatly soon enough. The legacy of the Rocks Job, as it came to be called, was this: The DEA did not forgive nor forget. "They've had a hard-on for Donald ever since," Bob Kronenberg says. A DEA man agrees that it was the Rocks Job that led the agency to keep on the Brown case with particular urgency. "I think," he says, with a slight edge to his voice, "that the people here were somewhat disappointed that the rocks thing didn't figure in the indictment."

It was at this time that Jack Tupper moved to Manhattan, taking an apartment on East 74th Street, just round the corner from the Third Avenue restaurant, J.G. Melons. It was a move he had long contemplated. "He liked the city," Ellen Gannon says, "He was all a-quiver about the city. When I say he was *excited*. . . . He was going to be a millionaire. He had stars in his eyes!"

For the time being, though, he was broke. He tended bar for a while in Churchill's, a joint popular with preppy East Siders, and he sold leather jackets on commission, but these were expedients. "He said the only way to make money is to set up in business on your own," Marie Tupper remembers.

Ellen was not at all surprised that her former husband put the insurance business behind him. "From the first time I met him, he always wanted to be on his own," she says. "He was very ambitious. He was always running after what he wanted."

What that might have been, though, was harder to say, and Ellen believes that this is because there was a degree of confusion in Jack Tupper's own mind. He was an obsessive reader of such magazines as *Fortune* and *Business Week*, and was forever clipping out articles on business openings, technical innovations, and success stories of the most Horatio Algerish nature, and he would file them methodically away as if he knew that among them, somewhere, the correct opportunity lurked. "Scheming was a hobby of my brother's," Kevin Tupper says. "I would say that money was only important to him second to glamor."

In the meantime, though, he was forced to borrow small sums from his family to make ends meet. "I lent him money," his father says, and adds that he hid the fact from his wife by maintaining a small special account for that purpose. Jack also borrowed from his sister, Dorothy, and from his brothers. "Each of us told him not to tell the others," Kevin says.

Jack Tupper's brothers and sister were by now, to one degree or another, settled. Dorothy was a head nurse and would shortly marry Tom Myers, the FBI agent. Kevin was a computer programmer, on Long Island. Jerry, the youngest, was a salesman with the Burroughs Corporation.

They were, in fact, conducting their lives the way their parents wished. But Jack, though he was very close to his family, was somehow different. He was, for one thing, the only Tupper child who was touchy about the lack of money in his background. "Jackie was the only one of us who resented we were lower-middle-class," Dorothy says. "We never lived in a house—we always lived in an apartment, or the upstairs of somebody's house. My parents had a choice between giving us a good education or putting the down payment on a house. And we each had a very good education."

It got so that Jack would joke about the middle-class sedateness of his siblings' lives. When he discovered Kevin's salary, he would groan and say, "Oh my God! It's not worth getting up in the morning for that kind of money." Dorothy remembers that as a head nurse she was earning $16,000 a year. "I paid my rent, I put a little money in the bank," she says. "Jackie would say, 'I could never live like you.'"

"Jackie was *glitter*," she says, her voice full of a harsh love. "If he had four hundred dollars, he would carry it in his wallet. He would spend it, and worry about tomorrow when tomorrow came. There was one thing he would say over and over, *'Don't worry about a thing.'*"

Her brother's disdain for the nine-to-five world was accompanied by a penchant for the mysterious. He was an avid reader of books exploring the covert worlds of such as Robert Vesco and the CIA. He would play his cards close to the chest even where his own family was concerned. If they asked him what he was up to, he would be likely to reply, "What are you doing? Writing a book?"

Ellen still muses over this quirk of her former husband's. "There was mystery to him," she says. "An intense privacy. I remember things that surprised me when we were first married. I remember, for no earthly reason, we couldn't put our name on the mailbox. People shouldn't know where we were! There was no reason for it." This streak of fantasy in Jack Tupper's makeup was to be exploited artfully by his murderer.

Tupper's elusive dream would become Buddy Jacobson's defense.

As it happens, though, Jack Tupper's name is notable mostly by its absence from the memoirs of the Donald Brown Organization almost until the end. Jack knew, naturally, about the business in which so many of his close friends were engaged, and which was paying them handsomely. Yet for five years—years in which he was scuffling hard to get by—he kept clear of it. The question hovers: Why?

The opportunity to join the gang, it seems, existed. At any rate, he told several persons that he had been approached. "They asked me in," he once told a friend. "That's very rare. They're making a lot of money."

His disinclination to join the group did not spring from a fear of getting caught. "He told me the Donald Brown Organization was insulated," the friend adds. "They didn't have to come too close. They could work through intermediaries." Brian Monaghan, Jack's last partner, says that his family was the decisive image. "He was too moral," he says. Jack Tupper believed he was headed somewhere else.

Nonetheless, Jack admired Brown and Al Seifert greatly. The machinations of the Airport Gang both intrigued the incipient wheeler-dealer in him, the *Fortune* reader, and impressed his darkly romantic nature. But he was positive he could make money on his own. His certainty would often annoy his friends. "If you're so smart," Donald Brown would bellow, "why aren't you rich?"

Donald Brown was glorying in his success. "I was a legend," he says. "People would talk about me in New York everywhere I went." But there was such a thing as being *too* legendary, he decided. So he moved to Los Angeles and bought a house that had formerly belonged to Raquel Welch. He now again decided to become a restaurateur, and opened a place called Chequers a couple of blocks off Rodeo Drive.

Brown had left a favorite possession behind him in New York, a strawberry Cadillac Seville, so he telephoned New York and offered Ivor Shaw $2,000 to bring the car. Shaw promptly agreed. "I wasn't doing anything else," he says. "And it was cold."

His progress was leisurely. He zigged and he zagged. He stopped awhile in New Orleans, spent ten days in Santa Fe, then popped over to Mexico. Customs men asked what was in the Cadillac's trunk on his return to the border, and Shaw said it was empty. They waved him on.

"By the time I got to California, Donald was crazy," Shaw says. "He thought I was going to drive straight through. He didn't know I was going to cross the border." There were a rifle and a revolver in the Cadillac's trunk. "I could still be doing time in Mexico," Shaw says.

The Airport Gang members had a thoroughly American affection for guns. They would acquire them as others acquire collectibles from the Franklin Mint. Brown had come to know a number of arms dealers. They fit neatly into the derring-do aspects of his life. One evening a man appeared in the bar at Chequers. He wished to discuss a deal. The man turned out to be in the Irish Republican Army, and the deal would have been an exchange of armaments for hashish, which would have been supplied by the Palestinian Liberation Army.

Brown was outraged. He talks in fulminating terms about terrorists who injure women and children. "I told him it wasn't my quarrel," he says. "I'm making it your quarrel," the IRA man said, patting a gun.

This threat was followed by a number of unfriendly telephone calls. The gist seemed to be that if Brown failed to cooperate, he should not regard himself as a candidate for a long and healthy life. Brown agreed to a meeting. It was to be held in the restaurant.

The IRA man arrived with a couple of aides: the doors were locked. They seated themselves at Brown's table. Donald had taken the precaution of having five friends, all armed, occupy a neighboring table.

Brown communicated his continuing reluctance, and the IRA man, who had been assuming that he had been ready to buckle, began growing choleric. "Get out of my life," Brown said, indicating his own weapon. "And if I don't get you," he added, nodding toward the neighboring table, "*they* will." That concluded his dealings with the IRA. But the episode did little to blunt the appetite of Brown and his cronies for sophisticated weaponry.

Al Seifert was now, in his phrase, "semiretired," the proprietor of a Hallmark greeting-card shop and a couple of Baskin-Robbins franchises. Not so Donald Brown. A terse DEA memorandum states that Billy Sharrocks had given him a copy of "the San Francisco Profile, which is an aid for Customs Inspectors when examining cargo." The memo added that Billy Sharrocks had also obtained a printout from the TECS computer.

An accompanying photograph tells the fuller story. It was taken at Caesar's Palace, Las Vegas, in 1979. It shows Donald Brown and his wife, Billy, and a girl friend, a cargo employee from Japan Airlines, and another man, the supposed source of the TECS printout. They are looking into the camera with the broadest smiles imaginable.

Behind the beams, in Brown's case at least, uneasiness was growing. "I was paranoid," he says. "I couldn't enjoy it." He was gambling large sums, partly so that his dope profits could be laundered, but he was losing more than he was winning. "I'd lose seventy-five thousand bucks," he says, "and think, shit! There goes my check."

Nor were the watching agents amused. "Our investigation is continuing," the DEA memorandum concludes, stonily.

Tom Myers was posted to the FBI bureau in Puerto Rico in 1976, and he and Dorothy took up residence in San Juan. It was soon afterward, that the first tragedy hit the close-knit Tupper family. Jerry, the youngest, had been doing well at the Burroughs Corporation. Indeed, in March 1977, they presented him with a plaque honoring him as their New York Salesman of the Month. But Jerry, like Jack, had grown interested in the bar business, and he ran a small place in Queens, together with a couple of friends, near St. John's, his former college. It was part-time for Jerry, but the bar was already grossing $5,500 a week. As Dorothy Myers says, "Jerry wasn't doing badly for a twenty-three-year-old kid."

Then Jerry fell deathly ill. The most athletic of the Tupper children had been struck by leukemia. Its progress was devastatingly swift. Jerry had been going out with a young woman named Dee-Dee Zuber, and she insisted they get engaged right away. Shortly after the party, he was in New York Hospital, and the deathbed vigil began.

"The three of us, being the siblings, had to go on the machines. They took the platelets out of us and gave them to Jerry," Dorothy says, explaining that platelets are a constituent in the blood. "That's one of the treatments of leukemia. It was a grueling procedure because each of us had to sit on the machine every third day, with both arms extended, for three, sometimes four hours. . . ."

Dorothy was as good as living in the hospital. "Jerry was a patient on the floor where I was in charge," she says. "It was a very moving experience, because the nurses taking care of him were all friends of mine."

At five one morning, she was awakened in the solarium where she had been sleeping. The night nurse was sobbing.

"What's the matter?" Dorothy asked. Her first thought was that something had happened to Jerry.

"I just can't take it anymore," the girl wept. "I just can't *cope.*"

The night nurse had been listening to Jack Tupper talking to his brother. That evening Jerry had been flaming with fever. Kevin and Dorothy had been there, and Jack, and Dee-Dee, and they had covered him with ice and wrapped him in blankets, and finally they had brought the fever down. That night, Jack stayed with his brother, taking his temperature every half hour and talking.

At first they had talked of future plans.

"We'll go into the bar business together," Jack said.

"I really want to do that," said Jerry.

"We'll open up a place in the city," Jack said. "We'll do *fantastically.*"

Later the fever began to burn again. Jack covered his youngest brother with his own body.

"You know something?" Jerry finally said, when the fever had abated, "I really love you."

"You're my baby," Jack said. "Nothing happens to my baby."

Strangely, he really seems to have believed this. Of all the Tupper family, Jack was the most determinedly optimistic.

"What's going to happen to him?" he asked Dorothy as they drove to the hospital one night. "What's going to happen?"

"Jackie," Dorothy said, "he's going to die."

But Jack Tupper still would not believe it. "If only we had a private plane," he said, "we could fly him to Houston, or West Germany." It was pathetic, Dorothy thought. "Jack thought that was the answer: money," Dorothy says.

When Jerry died, Jack decided he had to be the strongest. "He was the only one who could handle my parents," observes Dorothy. "I'm the daughter. But my mother often says the only one who could give her comfort was Jackie." He would sleep on the floor of his parents' one-bedroom apartment, and he gave Marie Tupper books to read. They included the autobiography of Rose Kennedy, another woman who had lost sons, and books dealing with life after death. She has them still.

Jack Tupper resumed his own life, but his gloom was profound. "He was destroyed by what happened," Dorothy says. "He wrote me a letter about how he was flying around the country, trying to make a living, and how depressed he was since Jerry died."

It was now May 1977.

It was now that Ivor Shaw got into a scrape. The man-about-town had always had an interest in cocaine; specifically, the best laboratory on the Upper East Side. "I dealt weight," he says. "Better than Merck—the best cocaine—no garbage."

There were always potential problems, working conditions for one. "The elements were volatile. Acetone, hydrochloric acid. It was like *The Wages of Fear* in there," he said, jiggling a melodramatic hand. "It would take out a city block. *Your* block, as a matter of fact."

In July 1977, Shaw successfully had eight ounces of cocaine paste brought up from Bolivia. It was converted into crystals and sold to an East Side bookmaker. He and his partners (they had formerly brought the stuff up from Chile disguised as imported wine) decided to expand their activities.

Two kilos of paste were duly delivered from Bolivia. And Ivor Shaw was arrested by DEA agent Curtis Filmore. This was a problem which was neither romantic nor amusing at all.

This same summer, Al Seifert did a little business with Buddy Jacobson. Buddy bought him his first horse, a brood mare, saying it cost $13,000. "I offered him a few thousand," Seifert says. "He wouldn't take it." Seifert was grateful, and impressed. "Buddy was a very smart individual. I became interested in breeding, not so much racing. And I did acquire a certain knowledge from him." It was now, too, that Buddy tried to talk Donald Brown, Billy Sharrocks, and Frank Natiello into backing him in a breeding farm in, yes, Old Westbury.

Something else happened at this time. The Brown Organization sprung a leak. "At the end of August, four big ones went bad," Seifert says. "There was a common thread. The jobs used the same methods of operation. And they were really big. Eight to ten thousand pounds each."

We are, of course, talking about a great many millions of dollars here, and the main losers were Billy Sharrocks and Jimmy Leonard. "They went broke," Seifert says. An exaggeration, perhaps, but Billy and Jimmy were understandably distrustful of the existing procedures and looking for new approaches.

Jack Tupper was in the midst of schemes. He had a new girl friend, Natty, whose uncle, it appeared, was an important man in Peru, and most of his schemes involved doing deals in South America. Especially, he would buy and sell machines of the larger or more intricate sort.

The money to be made out of obsolescent American technology became Tupper's passion. He was always talking possibilities. "That must have cost twenty-nine dollars," he once told Ellen, pointing at an electric fan "Down there, it's worth hundreds of dollars!" Jack would explain that "the machinery people in the States throw out is precious down there. It's *vital.*"

He began to travel to South America and taught himself some Spanish; his family was relieved that he seemed to be making money. On one occasion, Kevin says, he knew somebody in the States who wanted to sell some gigantic payloader, and a potential buyer in South America. "It was all done over the phone," Kevin adds. "He arranged to have the payloader shipped, and made eight thousand dollars."

In late summer, accompanied by Brian Monaghan, Jack flew down to Caracas, hoping to sell a secondhand computer.

Brian Monaghan is a tall man with black hair and the aggressive handsomeness of a shirt-and-tie model. He was now that one intimate friend to whom Jack would always unburden himself. Monaghan owned a bar in Queens—Ellen Gannon worked there—but had formerly been in the computer business at GAF. His role on the trip was to be the technical specialist; Tupper was to be the salesman.

Upon their return, Jack told Ellen that they had made a successful sale. They were to be paid in three installments. "I saw his first check," she says. "A Chase Manhattan check for several thousand dollars."

No sooner had Jack Tupper been done to death than Buddy Jacobson was diligently indicating that his money had actually been made by trafficking in drugs, and that it was among his fellow dealers that his true murderers should be sought. Since this was to be the leitmotif of Buddy's defense, the facts demand careful study. Jack Tupper had become a recognizable figure in the life of the Upper East Side. He had made friends, a different sort of friend from those his family in Queens had known. Sophisticates, they represented what Dorothy called "the glitter."

"It is a milieu where the occasional toot of cocaine is normal. Jack Tupper's inhibitions wore away. He would use coke from time to time, and, as do many, would sometimes support this expensive habit by selling small amounts himself. These are not remarkable doings on Manhattan's Upper East Side.

So when the opportunity beckoned, as it again did in the late summer of 1977, he found himself in a situation of extreme ambivalence. He had two main ambitions. One of these was to own a truly glamorous restaurant and bar on the East Side. The other was to make a home for his son. Paul was now seven, and Jack's love for him was extraordinarily strong. And he was always speaking of taking him to England or to Spain.

On both these grounds, common sense would warn Jack to steer clear of easy money. The various parental authorities are not happy if a person is caught in some legal offense, and the State Liquor Authority can be even stickier. But opening a restaurant costs money, as does providing for a son, and Jack was still haunted by his financial impotence at the time of his brother's death. He would talk of dying.

"It could happen at any time," he told Ellen Gannon.

"Don't be morbid," Ellen said.

Jack persisted, and began to talk of setting up trusts for Paul. Jerry's death, Ellen believes, was a turning point in her former husband's life. "His whole fabric was shredded. There was a fatalism under his bravado," she explains, adding, "of course, he never did set up those trusts. He procrastinated." It wasn't for nothing that Jack Tupper's friends nicknamed him "the late Jack Tupper."

But it was now, and for whatever complex blend of reasons, that Jack Tupper did decide to go for the big score.

Jack Tupper's involvement with the Airport Gang was brief, but came about at a time when it was being kept under the keenest scrutiny. It happened thus. Jack had become friendly with a young woman who worked with a company that handled freight at Kennedy Airport. The implications of her job were brought home to Jack by Jimmy Leonard and Billy Sharrocks: This was Jack's way in. Everybody would profit.

Jimmy and Billy are a couple of tough but friendly souls. "We put Jack in the business," Jimmy Leonard says. Together, they did two jobs that summer, successfully bringing in shipments in the name of Emerson Electric, a spurious company, but supposedly located at 251 West 32nd Street. The consensus is that Jack came away with $300,000.

But the shipments were now attracting the interest of the DEA. The first shipment to go awry arrived on an Air France flight from Beirut on September 3. It consisted of nine crates, which were addressed to Astro-Electric Components, 345 East 54th Street, and supposedly contained drilling equipment and Oriental gifts. One crate did, indeed, contain much Benares brassware. The others, the DEA found, held 2,525 pounds of hashish. But Leonard was too wily. Nobody picked up the shipment. Astro-Electric existed only on a DEA file. On September 12, a shipment of thirty-one cardboard crates left Bangkok, Thailand, aboard a Swiss Air plane, Flight 305, bound for Zurich. The next day, the spare-parts shipment was put aboard Swiss Air Flight 100, bound for JFK. The addressee was listed as Tudor Industries, 147 East 76th Street, New York, N.Y. The crates actually held 1,846 pounds of marijuana of the superior sort known as "Thai sticks."

At four in the afternoon of September 15, Henry Stokes, who was the import manager for Swiss Air, was telephoned by one "Dan Sutton," who said that he was with Tudor Industries and asked about his shipment. Stokes told him it had come in on the 13th. Sutton told him that the crates should be sent on to Houston, Texas, by way of Braniff.

Stokes was obstinate. JFK was the supposed address where

the cargo was bound. If Tudor Industries wanted to send it on farther he would need a letter. Sutton said that he would send a messenger with the letter right away. When Stokes mentioned that Eastern had more flights to Houston than Braniff, Sutton wasn't interested. He wanted to give his business to Braniff.

The DEA had, by this time, observed that 147 East 76th Street was a big building with a great many residents, none of whom was either Tudor Industries or Dan Sutton. It also had noted that this was the fourth recent shipment of supposed spare parts to be shipped through to Houston via Braniff. They staked out the Swiss Air office.

Shortly after half past five, a messenger arrived, handed over a letter signed by Dan Sutton, and was surreptitiously photographed. The thirty-one crates were now moved from Swiss Air to the Braniff Cargo Terminal, and DEA agents staked out Braniff.

At nine-thirty the following morning, Dan Sutton again telephoned. He asked Braniff to hold the shipment saying he was unsure of the whereabouts of the *S.S. Regency*, the ship awaiting the parts. This was not surprising. No such vessel exists.

At twenty to four in the afternoon, Peter Splain, the Braniff cargo handler, came over and had a look at the shipment. The agents' surveillance report describes Splain as a "major smuggling and theft suspect." But nothing else happened. Sutton's interest in the thirty-one crates had apparently lapsed. At seven the next morning, the DEA, disgusted, seized the goods.

But that was not quite all. On the morning of September 21, Dan Sutton of Tudor Industries telephoned once more. Airily saying the missing ship had been found, he asked that the thirty-one crates be sent to the Levingston Shipbuilding Company, Orange, Texas, by way of San Antonio. It was a Brownesque touch, since he plainly knew that the shipment had already been seized.

In this specific case, the jaws of the DEA trap had sprung with a disappointingly hollow clatter. But the jaws on its larger trap were closing more surely. The messenger was identified in due course as Eugene Leonard, a brother of Jimmy's. Dan Sutton was identified as Jack Tupper. Jack knew it had been a close call and resolved that his days with the Airport Gang were over.

His role had not been a considerable one. Some, like Jimmy Leonard, Billy Sharrocks, Donald Brown, and others of their cohorts, had made millions.

But for Jack Tupper, $300,000 was more than enough.

It was while Jack was looking for a bar to buy that Donald Brown reintroduced him to Buddy Jacobson. In January 1978 he moved into a fifth-floor apartment in Buddy's building and, soon after, found the All-Ireland Bar a few blocks away and bought it in partnership with Brian Monaghan. The All-Ireland was one of the last of the old Irish watering holes. The former Killarney Castle just down the block, for instance, was now an elegant spot called the Parma; similar fates had overtaken Geordie's and the Shamrock, which were now known, respectively, as Hoexter's and Oren & Oretsky, and were frequented by brokers, sportsmen, and models. The moving men from Morgan Manhattan and the orderlies from the local hospitals nowadays had few choices. Jack asked his former wife, Ellen Gannon, who had been tending bar at Monaghan's place in Queens, if she would help out. "It's not an East Side establishment. It's still a working-class place," he told her, indicating he was looking toward a starrier future.

The nature of that future was memorialized in his diary. Jack was a voluminous keeper of diaries, which he wrote up in a neat hand. "Everything was itemized," Brian Monaghan says. "Taxi fares, all kinds of expenses. If he had a meeting, he kept notes. Jack wrote down everything."

This diary was not a physical presence during the trial of Buddy Jacobson. It was never examined by either prosecution or defense. It has, indeed, often been referred to as if it were a Rosetta Stone which would instantly make this complex case clear as crystal. Ellen Gannon says this is laughable. "There was nothing in that diary I couldn't have explained," she says. "There was nothing that could have caused a problem."

The grand reopening of the All-Ireland took place in June. Among the well-wishers was David Silbergeld, from whom Jack Tupper was in the process of subletting the duplex on the seventh floor of 155 East 84th Street.

Buddy was not there, but the black jukebox which had formerly been at Mount Snow, then Nicola's, was. "It was a present," Ellen says. "John was impressed. To him it represented another move toward acceptance by the glittery people."

Tupper told Ellen that he and Buddy were even talking about buying a building together. This is the superbuilding deal, which would also have involved Al Seifert and Carlo Carrara, and Jack spoke of raising three million dollars. Ellen was skeptical, indeed, amused, but noted that Jack had gone into it in some detail. He talked of a loan from South America at ten percent.

She was to wonder later, with a chill start, if there had ever been any progress with this.

Buddy also found time to discuss a new horse with Al Seifert. "I just made this great buy," he said. "A steal!" He had picked it up in Florida at a hurricane-disrupted sale, he claimed.

Al discussed the horse with Donald Brown, who was visiting New York at this time, his Beverly Hills eatery finally having gone under, sucking some $400,000 with it. They bought the horse together for $52,000. "It was a gelding," Al Seifert says. "And a disaster. The legs were bad."

Buddy promised Brown and Seifert that he would restore the strength in the horse's legs, and charged them another $12,000 for his efforts. But the gelding was a goner. "Whenever he was ready to run, he broke down. He never ran," Seifert says.

The fiasco marked a turning point in the relationship of Seifert and Jacobson. "I got to not so much dislike him as not to like him," Seifert says, with his usual precision. On May 21, Brown sallied over to Buddy's barn and kidnapped the steed. He kept it in a back garden in Queens for a bit, then turned it over to Bob Wood.

The name of the horse, by the way, was Gallant Suspect.

That April 15, Claire Normandeau made a bust. She had been, as always, working undercover, at this time with a Task Force group. The man she arrested—the narcs had made a buy from him—looked at her and incongruously said, "Haven't I seen you somewhere?" Normandeau, who could recall no such meeting, put the remark out of her mind.

The man she had arrested was named Rudy Dehesa. It was this arrest that was finally to bring about the downfall of the Airport Gang.

Some weeks later, Claire Normandeau's superiors told her

that she should do some investigative work of her own. A change. Hitherto she had simply been put into situations. Now she was expected to build cases, develop contacts. Donald Brown came to her mind. She had always known that D.B. was involved in illegal enterprises, just as (she assumed) he had known that she was an undercover cop. But there are rules: Neighborhood is neighborhood. However, at the beginning of July 1978, Claire put Donald Brown's name into the computer.

Had she been planning on covering her tracks, she insists, she could have done so with little trouble. But she properly fed in her code number and asked for information.

Jackpot. It wasn't just Rudy Dehesa's name that appeared in connection with Brown, Claire says, but at least a dozen names from the neighborhood. Among them she saw the name of Jack Tupper.

Jack was a close friend. He had been, she says, "like a brother" to her. She was, moreover, a close friend to John Gannon, the New York cop, then still with the narcotics squad, who was now married to Jack's ex-wife, Ellen.

Normandeau says that she simply didn't believe that Jack Tupper was involved with the airport gang. As an old narcotics hand, she knew how easy it was for innocent names to turn up on a computer printout. But the information clearly presaged a coming storm, and Tupper would be caught up in it with the rest.

Things seemed to be breaking well for Jack Tupper, that summer of 1978, and on several fronts. His mind was as full of schemes as ever, and two of them, involving the sales of used computerware to Venezuela and South Korea, were looking good. So, at any rate, he told Ellen. He took her and John Gannon to dinner in Nicola's that June, and she was impressed by his high spirits. "Jack was jubilant," she says. Much of the jubilation had to do with his girlfriend, Natty, who was returning home to Lima. "He said if the right thing happened in Peru, he was going to make a million dollars," Ellen recalls.

They were at the bar. Jack, no less entranced with Nicola's than Buddy Jacobson, pointed out various celebrities. A small group was sitting at the front table, playing backgammon with the proprietor. The three moved to a table, ordered a bottle of

Verdicchio, and, as Ellen puts it, "stayed till the bitter end." They were continuing a discussion that had been proceeding for months. One of the strongest characteristics of this complex man was his love of children, and there was nobody Jack loved as much as he loved his son, Paul. He talked to others of gaining custody, and he wanted him to have the best education going. Oddly, he had even gone for advice to Buddy Jacobson.

Buddy had been dismissive. He told Jack he didn't believe in education. "Give them something practical to do. That's why I have David training horses."

Jack had been mildly shocked. Another person Tupper consulted was Ivor Shaw. He had known Shaw as a face around the East Side bars for some years, but he had come to know him well only in the late spring of this year. Shaw proved far more helpful. They talked about the city's private schools, and which were the best, and later Jack told his family that he was thinking of sending Paul to Buckley.

Buckley is on East 73rd Street, and primarily WASP. It is perhaps the most fashionable junior prep school in the city. Jack's own family made no demur, knowing only how strongly he felt about taking charge of his son, but Ellen disapproved of the plan. "When this whole Buckley thing came up, I resisted it," she says. "But John was very impressed. It was no longer money that impressed him, it was some sort of social aspiration. John knew that he could only be on the fringe, the outside, but he wanted something else for Paul.

"I resisted the change. I wanted to know more about the school. Paul's a regular kid. His mother clips out coupons for grocery sales. There are *chauffeurs* coming to collect these kids. John told me that I was wrong—all these people were regular. I would be amazed when I met them!"

Jack would especially talk about Ivor Shaw.

"You have to meet him," Jack would tell Ellen. "He's just a regular guy."

"I've met him," Ellen would say, a bit sourly. To her, Shaw was just a fellow in preppy clothes who would come into the All-Ireland. Jack, on the other hand, thought he represented something special. He was far righter than he knew. Jack Tupper had no idea when he made Ivor Shaw's close acquaintanceship that summer, that this tweedily elegant barfly even knew Donald Brown or Al Seifert. He was flabbergasted when he found that they had done serious business together.

But there was something that neither Tupper, nor Seifert, nor Brown knew. Soon after his misadventure with the Bolivian cocaine, Shaw had been recruited by the DEA. He was now, effectively, a government agent. It was, Shaw says, one of those offers you do not have the opportunity to refuse, but certainly there was something in the role that appealed to his nature. Ivor Shaw, Special Agent. "You know what they say about me at the DEA?" he asked me once. "Not even *we* know who you're really working for!"

He now speaks of those undercover days with nostalgia. The methodology would be properly covert, and Shaw would be picked up for debriefings in the DEA's Checker cabs. "I had a lot of Checker cabs picking me up," he says. He would revel in flashes of bravado, like the time he was dining in Nanni Al Valletto, a plush Italian joint on East 61st, with Donald, Al, and various cohorts, and nipped out to take a dish of shrimp and mushroom—"a great big boat, like a gondola"—to the agents, watching and waiting in the chill outside.

It was in the late spring of 1978 that Shaw had, as an official report expresses it, been "instructed by the DEA to get as close as possible to Jack Tupper." There seemed to be a new flurry of activity among the Airport Gang. Donald Brown was back in New York a great deal, for one thing. Late that May, Donald told Ivor that he had four thousand pounds of Pakistani hashish on its way and forty thousand pounds of Colombian grass waiting in Baltimore.

On June 28, Shaw had lunch with Robert "Rinky" Dancke and Al Seifert. Shaw told them that he had gone legitimate, and asked Al, "What about you? You're not doing anything now, are you?"

"Well, maybe," Seifert said cautiously.

"I just knew a big deal was going down," Shaw was to tell me later. "Because Rinky has come over to the States, and he's living in Al's basement. Rinky's not going to be living there unless something is on its way."

Shaw sounded out Jack Tupper the following day. With some awe, Jack described the Donald Brown intelligence network. He also observed that he knew the DEA was collecting information concerning the Airport Gang, and that such information was stored in CADPIN, namely the Customs

Automatic Data Processing Intelligence Network, which had recently been renamed TECS, for the Treasury Enforcement Computer System. Jack said that the Miami computer was in excellent shape, but that the New York machine "had a lot of bugs in it," and that the Donald Brown Organization had access to the information it contained.

On July 13, a darker note intruded. Tupper told Shaw that the Donald Brown Organization had become aware of a "leak." It was three in the morning, and they were drinking together in the All-Ireland. They had done a certain amount of cocaine, and Jack was talkative. "I've been offered another deal," he said. "I could make a hundred and fifty thousand dollars." But he was out of it, he told Shaw. He had made his nut.

"Anyway," he added, "Donald's hotter than a pistol." Jack had just heard about the list. This list, says Shaw, was a "super-top-secret list of twenty-one names." It had been drawn up by Group 22, which was the name of the unit the Federal Strike Force assigned to the task, after a meeting in its office on West 57th Street. Among the leading operatives in Group 22 was Curtis Filmore, the feisty Mormon who was now working out at Kennedy Airport.

Shaw knew about the list, of course, but he was startled to find that Jack Tupper knew about it too. "Remember what I told you," Jack told him. "They're all going to go."

He did not then seem to know that he was to have been a part of the fall.

It was as if 155 East 84th Street were coming apart. The success of Buddy's building, like that of all his ventures, had always been dependent on his energy, his brazenness, and his guile. But now he simply couldn't be bothered. "He always went from extreme to extreme, from being helpful to being hostile," remarks one long-term tenant. "At the beginning, he was quite a warm person. There was nothing warm about him at the end."

It was being borne in on Jack that his decision to move into David and Mel Silbergeld's duplex had been a poor one. The speed with which Buddy had thrown the building up, his disdain for conventional procedures, had left defects that were getting worse all the time. Whenever it rained, the seventh-floor penthouses leaked like a rotten tent. Buddy would try to patch the roof himself, but never with much success. The only real solution, a new roof, would have cost $18,000, and Buddy had no intention of diverting such a sum from the reconstruction of the Park East. So he would try to mollify his tenants with plastic pails.

Jack decided to leave, but not right away. He was working too hard at the All-Ireland. So he planted buckets under the leaks, left his belongings packed in stacks of cardboard crates, and did not reestablish service on Silbergeld's two disconnected telephones.

Curiously, he didn't hold these discomforts against Buddy. He didn't trust Buddy, but he had a considerable respect for him, and would often talk to Brian Monaghan about those famous parties in the Towne House. He admired the driven quality of the man, and described in detail the way that Buddy had extricated himself from some trouble at the building by digging up some obscure regulation that even the building authorities didn't know about.

Brian Monaghan was not impressed, and this was to provide a minor crux in Tupper's worsening business relationship with him. One night, Jack was having dinner with Ellen and John Gannon at One Station Plaza, a restaurant in Queens, and he talked about the situation. Young Paul was asleep, his head resting on the table.

Jack was somber about the future of his partnership with Brian. Their views were too often divergent. Brian found it impossible to understand, Jack said, what Melanie saw in Buddy Jacobson. "What does a little bastard like that do to rate a broad like Melanie?" he quoted Brian as saying.

Jack Tupper, though, like Seifert and Brown, had a keen sense of Buddy's complex power. "Whatever else Buddy may be, he's a hard-working guy. He gets his hands dirty, he takes his own garbage out, and he's a genius at what he does," Jack told the Gannons. "Brian has no conception at all that this girl might *love* him."

The differences were minor, but they accumulated. It soon became apparent that a rupture could not be avoided. One would have to buy the other out. At first they considered an open auction for the All-Ireland, between the pair of them, but after much heated dispute they agreed on two rules: (1) the bids should be sealed, and (2) they should rely on their own resources, rather than approach their various friends.

Tupper and Monaghan agreed that the auction should take place on Tuesday, July 18.

Jack and Ellen Gannon had discussed the amount that they felt Brian could come up with. He had, after all, been strapped to come up with money for the original deal. Each partner was somewhat suspicious of the other. Jack felt that, despite the rules, Brian might attempt to bring in Jimmy Leonard, and Brian wondered whether Jack was dealing covertly with Donald Brown. It was, as usual, a tangled tale.

On the auction day, Brian and Jack exchanged folded slips of paper in the dingy poolroom at the back. Ellen was out front in the bar.

Jack Tupper bid $42,500. Brian Monaghan bid $44,000.

Tupper strove to maintain his composure, but he was flabbergasted. "Both of us felt it was his place. We were crestfallen," Ellen says. Soon he found that his presentiment had been correct. Brian's partner, for once silent, was the effervescent Jimmy Leonard.

Late that night, he began to call his friends. "Jack was in a terrible state," Donald Brown says. "He was weeping." He telephoned Ellen, swearing that he wasn't going to go through with the deal.

Ellen reasoned with him. "You've made a twenty-thousand-dollar profit," she said.

She went back to sleep, not able to guess whether Jack would heed her advice. He called her the next day, saying that he and Brian had seen an attorney, and he had signed his half of the All-Ireland away.

He sounded glum, but calm. His relationship with Brian Monaghan continued much as before. A hope had been dashed; there would be others. Tupper was a resilient man.

Soon after the auction, Jack drove to pick up his parents at the airport. They had taken young Paul to stay with the Myers in Puerto Rico a couple of weeks before, and now they were coming home, leaving the boy on the island. Jack's relations with his parents, once tumultuous, were now far more serene. Marie Tupper has memories rubbed with use, like the last birthday party he gave for her that May. It had been at a pleasant French restaurant on East 61st Street, and he had presented her with a dozen long-stemmed Talisman roses.

When their son did turn up at the airport, his parents were alarmed at his appearance. "He really looked beat up," says his father. It was all to do with the bar. On the drive back, though, his spirits revived, and he and his parents talked about the future. "Maybe you and I will go into business together," he told his father. "You're the only one I can trust."

This was his last meeting with his parents. Next day Jack met Melanie, as he was walking out of the All-Ireland, and she told him that she was leaving Buddy Jacobson. It was Thursday, July 20.

- V -

Nineteen
Days

*T*here are several events, many of them events Melanie would just as soon forget, that are cut into her memory as though etched on glass, but dinner with Jack that Thursday evening remains a blur. Mostly she remembers drinking wine, picking at her food, and talking. She was, she supposes, in a sort of delirium, compounded of pleasure at being with Jack Tupper and relief that she had at last severed herself from Buddy.

They knew, of course, that returning to East 84th Street was out of the question. Melanie and Jack spent that night in the Plaza Hotel, that Edwardian eminence on the corner of Fifth Avenue and Central Park. They did not make love. Melanie still felt she could never do so again. But she awoke the next morning filled with elation. Over breakfast, Jack told her that he was going to take her to stay for the weekend with his sister Dorothy, in Puerto Rico.

It was a ludicrous situation. When Melanie had walked out, she had done so with less property than she had brought to the city as an eighteen-year-old. "It was this that really got to Buddy," she says. "Money was such a thing with him. But when I left, I left with my sneakers, my overalls, thirty dollars in my pocket, and zilch in my bank account." Freedom. It was a wonderful feeling. Melanie felt as if the last five years had slipped away.

That was the morning of Friday, July 21. They dropped by the All-Ireland, and Ellen Gannon met Melanie for the first time. Melanie asked for a Bloody Mary, and it was then that it truly struck home to Ellen that Jack no longer owned the place. "He put his money on the bar," she says. "I was shocked." But Ellen was struck by how happy Jack looked. A shadow had lifted. He and Melanie were laughing together, Ellen says, and he had his arm around her.

Jack called Puerto Rico from the bar and told his sister that he was bringing "a friend." Ellen noticed that he didn't say who. The pair finished their drinks, said goodbye, and drove off to Queens, where Jack was to wrap up the All-Ireland transaction with Brian Monaghan. The payment that he was to receive came in two forms: checks and ready money. There were two checks, one for $9,000 and one for $5,000, both made out to John Tupper, and there was $30,000 in a paper bag. During this piece of business, Melanie waited outside in a red Pontiac Phoenix that Jack had borrowed from his father.

Consequently, Brian Monaghan, who had seen Melanie together with Jack in the bar a couple of times but had thought nothing of it—"They were neighbors" he says—had no idea that she was with him. Jack, who was always secretive, now had a reason, and when he told Al Seifert that he was off to Puerto Rico for the weekend, he didn't mention Melanie, but added casually, "Don't tell Buddy."

It was now after three, and too late to bank the money, even had Jack Tupper decided to return his capital gains to the mainstream, but the Zubers, whose daughter, Dee-Dee, had been Jerry's fiancée, owned a safe; so, with Melanie counting the bills in the back of the car, Jack drove to the Zubers' home. Jack locked up the paper bag, and the Zubers drove them to the airport. They took a 747 to San Juan that same evening.

Melanie's arrival was unexpected, but Dorothy and Tom made her welcome, although it did not escape Dorothy's pragmatic eye that her female guest carried no luggage, suggesting something hurried about her departure. The Myers house had only a couple of bedrooms, and young Paul was staying, so, from delicacy, Jack and Melanie stayed first at the local tennis club, then at a hotel.

Dorothy was skeptical about the relationship at the beginning, suspecting that Melanie was merely a touch of the "glitter" her brother so craved. "I don't care if she's a cover girl, Jackie," she said. "Can she cook you dinner?"

"She's a great kid," Jack said, "and she was in trouble. She needed my help."

Like Ellen, Melanie was a "cause."

Dorothy began to warm to Melanie when they went on a picnic, and she saw that the "cover girl" was quite content to borrow a T-shirt and a pair of black shorts, several unbecoming sizes too large. But now a shadow fell across the weekend. There were two causes, the first being financial. Jack had paid

Dorothy back some time before the several thousand dollars he had borrowed; suddenly, in full, and without a word of explanation.

This had bothered Tom Myers somewhat. Tom, who liked and respected his brother-in-law, is with the FBI, after all, and the FBI likes tidy answers. "How had he come into money so suddenly?" he said to me much later. "How had he paid Dee back? I should have confronted him. I could kick myself again and again."

The other reason for the unease was that Melanie's story had emerged over the weekend, and Dorothy Myers had not liked what she had heard about Buddy Jacobson. Melanie, moreover, was becoming visibly more nervous as the weekend drew to an end. Originally, it had been planned that Jack would stay on with his son for a while. But Melanie had to return—she had important bookings—and Jack decided they would go back together.

Before they went, Dorothy spoke to Jack by the pool. She is an indomitable woman, with a bony blond handsomeness more Viking than Celtic, but she was fearful. "You know, I'm afraid," she told him. "I'm so afraid of what you're going back to. Jacobson sounds like a lunatic.

"You're fooling with male ego, Jackie. If you really care for this girl, let her break up the relationship on her own. Don't flaunt it. Please!"

Jack scoffed at her fears.

"What's wrong with you?" he said. "You're always worrying about something. I'm not afraid of him. . . ."

When he and Melanie landed at Kennedy, Jack telephoned his mother. She told him that Buddy Jacobson had called, looking for him. Buddy had said it was important.

When Melanie failed to reappear that weekend, Buddy's intuition stabbed like a knife. He *knew* she was with Jack Tupper. He first called Melanie's mother, who confirmed that her daughter had gone away, but she wasn't sure precisely where. Florida had been mentioned, and Puerto Rico. Puerto Rico! Jack would often talk about his brother-in-law. Buddy solicitously warned Jean Cain that Melanie had become involved with somebody who was in trouble with the police; he artfully left the word "Mafia" hanging in the air.

He called Brian Monaghan and Al Seifert. Neither had the

Puerto Rico number. He called Brian back and asked for the number of Jack's parents. Monaghan was reluctant. "Brian," Buddy insisted, "it's very important."

"I don't know whether I should," Monaghan repeated, but gave the number anyway.

Buddy told Marie Tupper that he was a friend of Jack's, and was perfectly polite. "He was very charming," she says. But she had to tell him, apologetically, that Dorothy's telephone was not in working order.

Buddy became more intense, asking whether she knew a neighbor's number.

Marie Tupper was a little scandalized at this. No, she said, she didn't. Privately, she added to herself that even if she had such a number, she wouldn't have divulged it. Finally frustrated, Buddy could only wait.

At the airport, Jack and Melanie learned about Buddy's telephone calls. This was troubling. They checked into the Drake Hotel, and were further disturbed when he called in the morning. This could only mean they were being spied on. He demanded a meeting with Melanie. Face to face.

At first, Melanie demurred.

But Buddy pleaded. "Then I realized I owed him something," Melanie said. "Yet all this time, *I* had always wanted to talk to *him*. And he had never had the time. But now I figured, okay, let's settle up the whole business!"

"All right, Buddy," Melanie said. "I'll meet you."

"Come over to lunch, babe," Buddy said.

She agreed, and he asked her to stop by such-and-such a delicatessen and pick up some corned beef. A siren of recognition screamed. "This was the deli where I always used to pick food up for him," she says. "He was trying to get me in a familiar environment, get me dependent on him again."

It seemed blindingly clear to her that seduction was what Buddy Jacobson had in mind. She had for the first time a clear sense of the way he operated. It was as though she were looking at the workings of a crystal-cased clock. "That *bastard!*" she said to herself—and started laughing; this was the first time she had ever laughed at Buddy.

Certainly she was not going to lunch. "At first I thought I'd call him and say I'm not coming to lunch. Then I thought, no! I'm going to be *mean*."

That afternoon, she was called at the Drake by her mother, who asked if she was all right. Melanie was surprised, until her mother explained that Buddy had called, complained that Melanie hadn't shown up for lunch, and had wondered aloud if she had become involved in some sort of trouble. Melanie, again, laughed.

Finally, though, she did agree to a meeting with Buddy, if Jack was near at hand and would join them later. She agreed to meet him at ten-thirty that night at the Sign of the Dove.

This was a favored second-string haunt of Buddy's; a brilliant strategic choice. It was here that she had so often watched tears come to his eyes as the pianist thrummed through standards from the forties and fifties. The place was impregnated with memories—a psychic trap. Buddy took the offensive right away. "What happened to you at lunch?" he asked. "I was worried. I thought you might be on drugs."

Melanie, who regards aspirin with distrust, was startled.

"You know, I thought you might be on Quaaludes, or"—a meaningful look—"cocaine."

When it became apparent that Melanie wasn't picking up on this, Buddy attempted a different approach. "You can't leave me," he told her. "You're my wife."

"I am not," she said crisply, but not looking him in the eyes all the same.

"Well, it's just *like* we were married. We just don't have the license."

"I'm not your wife, Buddy. You have to let me go."

Buddy's gaze was fixed on hers, his whisper implacable. "I'm going to get you back, not matter what," he told her. "I'll beg for you, or I'll wait for you. I don't care. *But no matter what, I'm going to get you back.*"

Jack Tupper, who had been monitoring the conversation from the bar, came over. "Jack's a family man," Buddy told her in an oddly chirpy fashion. "He'll understand the situation."

Jack and Melanie looked at each other blankly. Buddy's agitation grew. "You want a restaurant?" he asked Jack, in a strained, mumbling voice. "I'll buy you a restaurant. You want girls? You want money?

"Just give me Melanie back for twenty-four hours!"

"Buddy, it's not my decision," Jack told him. "It's Melanie's decision."

"Let's be friends, Buddy," Melanie urged. "I'll always be your friend."

Buddy listened, and one moment he was agreeing, almost smiling, but all the while he was shaking his head irritably, as though trying to wake from an unpleasant dream. They parted amicably enough, but neither Melanie nor Jack felt reassured by Buddy's performance.

She got up early the next day, which was the morning of Tuesday, July 25, and the beginning of a two-day shoot. It was a commercial for One for the Road, a hair dryer manufactured by Clairol, and Melanie joined a group outside the midtown offices of the producer, Jerry Andreozzi. The group was some thirty strong, including representatives from the ad agency, Foote, Cone & Belding, and the hairdresser, Tommy Baratta. Melanie, who had been friendly with Baratta and his wife for a couple of years, was the only model. The equipment was loaded onto a chartered bus, along with a packed lunch, and everybody piled aboard. By eight o'clock the bus was traveling toward the location.

This, by some unsettling fluke, was at Old Westbury. The exit was the one that Buddy and Melanie had always taken when visiting his horse farm. Melanie mentioned to Andreozzi that she knew the place, but Baratta was the only person in whom she confided details of her breakup.

"She was very upset," Baratta says. "She was telling me about her problems with Buddy. She said she had to meet him that night."

When work began, Melanie resolutely pushed her problems aside. In the sequence they were shooting, she was to plop her hair dryer into a carryall and move off briskly down a path, away from the camera, but with her head turned, so that, in leaving, she favors the viewer with a wide and gleaming smile. The take went off perfectly. The tape records a healthy glow, her walk includes a jolly Chaplinesque shuffle, and she is smiling as though Buddy Jacobson did not exist.

The shooting finished at three, and Melanie was driven back to Manhattan. The next call was for eight-thirty the following morning. That evening, Melanie had agreed to see Buddy alone. The meeting was to be in J.G. Melon. Jack had gone along with her decision, saying that he would be just down the street in another East Side bar, R.J. Bonds, and that he would join them at seven. First, though, Melanie decided to pay an overdue visit to Jimmy Wood.

Melanie and Jimmy were still friendly and both were paying regular visits to Dolly Robertson. Melanie dropped into his office and told him about her breakup with Buddy, and about Jack. Then she brought up the reason for her visit. Douglas Jacobson had just moved into Buddy's apartment. He was to help with rebuilding the Park East. Douglas was, quite obviously, not yet out of his teens.

Whenever she had mentioned the newspaper clippings about his age to Buddy, she told Wood, he had said it was a mistake—the stories were about his uncle, Hirsch. "I just have to know about Douglas and David," she said.

"Well, think about it carefully," Jimmy finally said. "And you won't have to ask whether David and Douglas are his kids or his brothers. You'll *know*."

Subtle Buddy. Smoothly he switched his meeting with Melanie to a different Third Avenue bar, Rusty's, where he could work on her without interruption. The main reason that Melanie was deserting him, he now thought, was his other women. He would give them up. He would marry her. "The way you're coming back to me," he told her, "is by way of a church."

"I won't marry you, Buddy," Melanie said. "I don't love you." She paused, then added, "I know how old you are, Buddy. I know that David and Doug are your sons."

Buddy digested this and said, "If I could prove to you that I'm thirty-four, and David and Doug are my brothers, would you come back to me?"

"No," Melanie said.

"Okay. If I can prove to you that they are my sons, and I am forty-eight, and I can explain to you satisfactorily why I lied about my age, will you come back to me?"

It was the old Buddy, Melanie realized. If one story didn't work, slide into another. But she now felt willing to duel with Buddy on his terms. "Of course I would," she said.

So Buddy launched into a train of reasoning that was both lengthy, as was his way, and beguilingly plausible, as was also his way, telling her that he had found it necessary to lie to get a trainer's license, and then had been forced to lie all over again to get a license for his son, David. "God, am I glad that's over," he told Melanie, with an air of contrition. "Now, are you coming back to me?"

"No, Buddy," Melanie said, pert as a schoolgirl. "I was only kidding."

Buddy was both angry and astonished.

"You lied to me," he said. "You *never* lie to me!"

"Now you know what it feels like," Melanie answered. "All you've ever done to me is lie. I played one of *your* numbers. I just wanted to hear it from *you*."

But Melanie's glow of confidence soon dimmed. For two hours they sat together, and it began to seem that there was nothing she could say to which he could not find the right response. If she was headstrong, he would draw back. If he saw her floundering, he could come on strong. Very soon, she was in a turmoil, and in tears.

It had taken two hours for Buddy to reach this area of vulnerability. It was as if he were playing a game fish, unspooling line when she fought, reeling in when she slackened, and now, surely, he had her.

"You belong to me," Buddy said intently. "I know you're coming back to me. And when I get you back, I'll probably slap the shit out of you."

Buddy was to claim he had intended a joke, and this may have been true, but, if so, it was a disastrous touch of over-confidence. Melanie grew suddenly afraid, got up with panicky abruptness, and said, "I'm going to see Jack."

Buddy raced after her, and there was a preposterous tussle on the sidewalk, with Buddy tugging at Melanie's green canvas carryall, trying to get her into a taxi and back to East 84th Street. But Melanie broke loose and began walking blindly toward R.J. Bonds. So surreal did the situation seem to her that she didn't even find it curious that Buddy was walking beside her, yammering, saying he had things of the greatest importance to tell Jack Tupper.

Jack and Brian Monaghan were sitting together, the angst of the All-Ireland auction now behind them, when Melanie popped through Bonds door, moist with tears, and told Jack that Buddy was waiting to speak to him outside.

Tupper walked back in a few minutes later, entirely dumbfounded. "Can you believe this guy?" he said. One moment Buddy had been telling him, "I've always liked you, Jack! If it had to be anybody, I'm glad it was you." The next he was offering $100,000 and his pick of the My Fair Lady models for Melanie's return. Jack affected amusement. Monaghan, though, was not amused at all.

"If a guy threatens to have your head broken," he said, "maybe he will, maybe he won't. But this guy is telling you how terrific you are. Maybe you should take care."

The second day of shooting on the Clairol commercial was at a studio on 25th Street and Park Avenue South. Today, a couple of "hand models" had also been booked, and Clairol brass on the set included Tom Hogan, who was supervising the whole of Clairol's advertising and who had arrived long before shooting began. "You can't decide you don't like the makeup, you don't like the hair, after the action's started," says Hogan. "If you blow a day's shooting, you're blowing a good thirty thousand dollars."

Melanie arrived on time, but not feeling well. All night she had been sleepless and distraught. Jerry Andreozzi noticed how wan she looked, but thought little of it. Models often look a bit ragged early in the morning. *Trop de disco*. "I just thought she'd had a tough night," he says.

Tommy Baratta knew better. "Just give me some extra time to pull her together," he urged. He let Melanie nap for a little, then spent an extra half hour with her makeup. She emerged looking as fresh as if she had just come from Naperville, Illinois.

The shoot began late, but was soon going well. It was now that the telephone calls began. The first time, Buddy was told that Melanie was in the middle of shooting. The second time, he insisted it was urgent and demanded that she be hauled off the set. She wouldn't take the call.

The telephone was to ring, insistently, harshly, all morning. Buddy had always said there was nothing he couldn't do on the telephone, but he couldn't get through to Melanie. Nonetheless, news of her dilemma spread around the set. "There was back-and-forth that she was upset," Tom Hogan says. "But it didn't seem to be anything she couldn't handle."

The calls got to her, of course. At one point, between setups, Melanie telephoned Buddy's older son, David. He was at the track, and she got through to him at his barn.

"David," she babbled, "please help me! Make sure Buddy doesn't do anything to me."

Then Melanie returned to the set, shook her shining, honey-colored hair, and reassumed her artlessly happy smile. So, interminably, the morning wore away.

Around noon that Tuesday, Buddy went to see Jack Tupper in 7C. This visit was prearranged, and Tupper was wired, which is to say he was covertly taping the conversation on a Pearlcorder, worn beneath his jacket. But the fact that he was committing himself to a cassette did not make Jack Tupper mealy-mouthed.

"Buddy," he said, "I want you to listen very carefully. First of all, I'm not going to have this girl sneaking around here, sneaking behind the cover of darkness, or being up the block, where I have to sit in a restaurant, just to make sure that nothing happens. All right?"

Jack's voice became strident: Buddy had better not touch one hair on Melanie's head, he warned. "I'll break your fuck-ing ass, and I'll throw you off your own building. And you'd better have two bodyguards if you do it. They'd better escort you twenty-four hours a day, and they'd better have big guns. And furthermore, because I love her, I'm not going to stand by and watch you playing mind games, and trying to fuck up her head. I'm not going to permit that either."

Buddy's reply was panicky legerdemain. In one rambling speech he promised that he wasn't "going to bother her any-more," even though "it's hard to keep from doing what I am doing."

Jack Tupper remonstrated with Buddy for telling Melanie's parents that he was involved with the Mafia, and denied that he had discussed Buddy's cheating ways with Melanie. He also said that Melanie was scared. "She claims you threatened her," he repeated.

Buddy back-pedaled, a string of denials, then advanced, seizing on Melanie's "problems."

BUDDY: Melanie is half an inch away from having a nervous breakdown.

JACK: She's very distraught. I'll tell you that right now. That's why the best thing to really do is to just back off for a little while.

BUDDY: I told you what I'm doing, didn't I? Did I tell you what I'm doing?

JACK: Because the more she gets harassed . . .

Buddy suddenly zeroed in on what he now perceived to have been one of his errors.

BUDDY: I never believed in mental stuff. The Dolly thing [*Referring to Dolly Robertson's mental breakdown*] is a big joke.

JACK: Well, Dolly apparently affected Melanie very much.

BUDDY: She's afraid that whatever happened to Dolly is going to happen to her. And she went around to get advice from everybody . . . and she said, "look, I'm nervous with Buddy. I'm afraid he's going to, he's going to run around on me. I'm afraid I'm going to get hurt like Dolly."

The irony was staggering. Buddy was suggesting that Melanie was heading for a crack-up, even as he thrashed around, refusing to face his loss.

BUDDY: You know my whole fucking life I had a ball, and I ain't kidding about it . . . but I mean it, as sincere as anybody can mean it, that I really am ready to stop. . . . I said to her last night, I said to her don't come back to me unless it's by way of the church. Now how much more sincere can you be? So, I mean, if you think I'm kidding around . .

JACK: No, I don't, Buddy. Look, I firmly believe . . .

BUDDY: She is as close to me as anyone in my family. Think of it as your own family. How you would feel if you had to separate from them?

JACK: I agree, I told you. I said that's heavy. I wouldn't want to be in your position right now. . . . I know what's happening. I know what you're going through. . . .

BUDDY: I mean, you've got nothing to lose.

JACK: In all honesty? Okay, the truth. I fell in love with her. All right? Now, whether it's real, you know—now I don't know.

BUDDY: But if it comes to a point that you think you might not spend a long time with her . . . [*Intensely*] Understand that what you're doing is fucking me up with this!

Melanie was moved by everybody's concern for her at the close of the Clairol shoot. "I don't know about this guy," the art director told her, referring to Buddy. "But judging by the way he's been calling, you're going to have a hard time." People were offering all sorts of contradictory advice, and Baratta, the most practical of them, suggested that Melanie stay with him and his wife.

But Melanie felt she had a grip on herself. Last night's memories had dimmed. "Thanks," she said. "But he'll get over it. Buddy's just that way." And she returned to the Drake Hotel, and Jack Tupper.

Originally, Melanie had intended to muffle the resonance of her rupture from Buddy by finding an apartment, and asking him to move her things there. "That way he would think he was still in control," she explains. His growing eccentricity had changed her mind, though, and, when Jack did find her a place (it was in the same East 74th Street building where he had once inherited an apartment from Donald Brown), she was eager that Buddy not discover where it was. Her lease was to begin on August 1.

She did need the rent money, though, and at five past two on the day after the Clairol shoot, a Wednesday, Melanie telephoned Buddy from the Drake, and taped the call. Buddy had always told her that she owned fifty percent of the model agency and that her earnings were being invested in his buildings. She had trusted him. Now, at Jack Tupper's urging, she wanted something more specific. It was Corinne, the booker, who picked up, but Melanie knew that Buddy would cut in, as he always cut in when she telephoned, which was just what he now did. What, she asked, was he planning to do with the agency?

"Since you're not coming back, selling the agency we forget about," he said.

"Oh," Melanie said, "so you're not selling the agency? Is that what you're saying?"

"Oh, no. Wait a minute. No, no, I'm not saying that. If you want me to, I will . . . or I will keep the agency any way you want, and have you take care of all the money that comes in. . . ."

At this, Melanie began to laugh.

"What are you laughing at?" Buddy demanded.

"It's such a joke. All the money in the agency. What's in the agency?"

"You'll have your own money," Buddy said. "You take fifty percent."

Melanie zeroed in. "So you're saying you're fifty percent of the agency, and I'm fifty percent. Right?"

"That's correct," Buddy said.

In fact, Melanie's fifty percent was to prove even more illusory than Bob Wood's twenty-five percent, but, satisfied, Melanie moved on to the next subject, which was the money that Buddy owed her.

"If I can handle it, of course I will repay you," he told her.

"You will pay me the money?"

"I mean, I can't write a check right now," he said. "I'm going to be making a lot of money soon. I didn't know money meant that much to you."

Melanie said she needed the money. She was planning to move into a different apartment on August 1. Now it seemed to be a new Buddy she was talking to, utterly unthreatening. There was nothing he would not do for her. "You want to go to Europe? You're going to Europe. I'll pay the way over there, give you money. I mean, whatever you want to do, you're going to do."

Warmly he asked, "How do you feel? You still tired?"

"No," Melanie said. "I feel fine."

"You get anything to eat yet?"

"Yeah, I did."

"You shouldn't starve yourself," Buddy said. "I went across to Nicky's yesterday, you know, with Doug."

"Yep," said Melanie briefly.

"And I ordered a plate of spaghetti and baked clams. I did eat the clams. And I had two spoonfuls of the spaghetti. And that's all I ate."

"Yeah," Melanie said.

"I've still not really eaten since last Thursday," Buddy went on in a conversational tone. "This is interesting. I'm not saying it about—our thing."

Melanie would not be touched.

"No," she said. "Well, once you don't eat for a while. . . ."

"You don't need to eat?" Buddy inquired, "Jesus Christ! That's really something. I'll tell you, I'm like *speeding*."

"Yeah, you're speeding. Your metabolism speeds up," Melanie agreed.

"I want to clean every place, and I walk fast," Buddy said, lost in wonderment, the weaknesses he had sneered at in others now being visited upon himself, "You know? I see myself *doing all that stuff*."

"Yeah, yeah," Melanie said, briskly unhelpful, "Well, I've got to go now. I'll call you back later." This she did, only a few minutes later. Buddy Jacobson's lawyer, in the time to come, would say that this was to "shake down" his client, and Melanie agrees that she wanted a firmer figure on what precisely Buddy felt he owed her. But, this apart, the conversation scarcely sounds like a shakedown.

"My mind is going crazy here," Melanie told Buddy, "and I'm thinking crazy thoughts. . . . While they're in my mind I want to tell you what they are."

"All right."

"Buddy, you know, I know, it's over. Right? But you know I don't hate you."

"I'm glad, babe."

"You know I could never . . . I could never hate you. Right?" Melanie said, and rushed on, pell-mell. She had never thought that Buddy was stealing her money, she said. She had thought they would be together forever. But now she did want her money and, by her calculations, the sum she was owed came to about $100,000. Did Buddy think that was high?

"I don't think anything. I told you I am leaving the entire thing up to you," said Buddy, filled with sad sweetness. "I believe you're the greatest broad in the world."

"Broad!" She began to laugh.

"Yes," Buddy said.

"*Broad!*"

Buddy mumbled how nice she was, but it was a misstep, so he launched into an anatomy of the Park East, the payroll, the $23,000 he had in the bank, the loans upon loans upon loans, the stream of payments for plumbing, the electricity, the elevators, the windows. The spiel was lengthy, and mesmerizing, and he added, almost casually, "So, if I take anything out of the bank . . . I mean, if you insist, I'm going to do it. I'm nuts! . . . But it does mean the Park East is going down the drain."

Melanie floundered. Could Buddy give her any money at all?

"Yes, Melanie. I *said*."

"Today?"

"Today."

She went around to East 84th Street. Buddy wrote out a check for $2,000.

The money came with strings. Buddy fixed her with his eyes. They were burning, and filled with reproach. "I'm a wreck!" he told her. "I know why you're leaving me. It's because Jack told you about my sons."

Melanie said that this was not a subject that Jack would discuss with her, and Buddy turned to that other grievance which, he imagined, once resolved, would bring Melanie back to him: those other women.

"I can give you a list of every girl I've ever been with," he promised. "I'll never do it again. Melanie, I'm *almost fifty years old!* I never admitted I loved you before—I would play a big shot around town. Now it's all changed."

All Melanie could do was shake her head.

"Buddy, it doesn't matter," she said. "For five years I've wished you would say all those things. Now it doesn't matter."

"I have to tell you something, Melanie," Buddy said. He looked infinitely sad. "I have cancer. . . ."

"Cancer?" Melanie was dumbfounded.

"They say I've only got a couple of weeks to live. Just stay with me through it. All right?"

"Cancer!" Melanie began to laugh incredulously.

"Forget it!" Buddy told her glacially. "Don't let's even talk about it."

This was his customary gambit, after Melanie had doubted some outrageous statement, and Melanie would ordinarily weaken and say, "All right! Talk! Tell me more!" But not this time.

"Okay," she agreed. "We won't talk about it."

This nettled Buddy. "Don't you want to hear about the cancer?" he demanded.

"No, Buddy. It's a crock."

She took the check and departed. With the useless clarity of hindsight, Melanie now realizes that these financial pressures were just one more turn of the screw.

Buddy began to step up the pressure. Jack and Melanie knew that they were under surveillance, and Buddy half acknowledged as much to me once, though in a characteristically lopsided fashion. "I always knew where she was," he said.

"I live in New York. Right? People call me up, and say, 'Hey! I just saw Melanie go in the Drake Hotel.' I said to her, 'Melanie, there's no reason for you to be living under cover. Running around!'"

The relentlessness of it began to wear away at her. She would catch herself drifting into a glassy state, unnaturally observant, yet not altogether there, like a convalescent. She called Corrine, and said she had to take a few days off. "I'm so *tired*," she explained.

Buddy telephoned Al Seifert, assuring him that the business propositions he was offering Jack Tupper were wholly serious.

"Tell Jack I'll give him a hundred thousand dollars," he said. "I'll build him a bar myself."

"Okay, Buddy, I'll pass it on. . . ."

But Buddy began to mumble. "Nobody steals my wife and gets away with it," he said.

"Buddy, did you *really* marry her? That's the first I ever heard of it."

"She lived with me for five years. That's like being married. Tell Jack to give her back."

"How can he make her come back if she doesn't want to?" Al asked.

"He can *force* her to come back, and I'll *keep* her here," Buddy said. He spoke as if it were the most obvious thing possible, and Seifert felt stirrings of alarm.

His call to Donald Brown in Beverly Hills introduced a new element. "You introduced me to him," he told Brown. "It's your fault." He asked Brown to put through the $100,000 on his behalf. "Otherwise I'm going to take care of him," Buddy told D.B., darkly.

Brown thought this was ludicrous. "I thought he was bullshitting," he told me. The situation merely piqued his peculiar sense of humor.

It was now that David Jacobson approached Melanie, and argued on his father's behalf. Melanie thought this was a curious move. She bore no ill will toward either David or Douglas, but could hardly ignore the fact that they had agreed to pretend to be their own father's younger brothers for the past several years. "He molded them," she says. "David is his clone."

"My dad may be a bit strange sometimes," David told her. "But whatever he does, he does for a reason." Almost fiercely, he added, "He's a wonderful man."

By Saturday, July 29, it was apparent that Melanie had been too optimistic on the Clairol set—Buddy was showing no signs of getting over it; the reverse. This was even becoming apparent to his tenants. Kirk Citron, an advertising copywriter who lived on the third floor and who had always been intrigued by Buddy's obsessive cleanliness—the thrice-weekly hosing down of the lobby and the sidewalk—found his behavior increasingly erratic. "He just came into the apartment one day and said he had to repair some fixtures," Citron says. "He hammered a hole clear through the bathroom ceiling, and just left it there."

"Do you want to know what Buddy was like during those days?" Melanie would say. "He was absolutely . . . totally . . . beyond himself. Of all people to act like this, my last thought would be Buddy. Here was a guy who I was with for five years, who had every bit of control over his emotions. You know, he never had any hang-ups, never was physically sick. He even used to pretend that he wasn't, you know, *human*. He was so *superior* to everyone else.

"And here was this guy, when I told him I wasn't coming back . . . he did not *eat*, did not *sleep* . . . he stood outside his apartment on the terrace, just staring. He was *constantly* on that terrace."

Buddy was, for instance, spending much less time at the Park East on 83rd Street. It was his absorption in this remodeling project that had, so he chose to believe, been one reason for his problems with Melanie. Yet just now, when he seemed to be making the project work, Buddy eased up. Corinne told Melanie that he would take his group of workmen across to the Park East, get them started, and then, as likely as not, return to East 84th Street. He would spend the entire day sitting in the office, or upstairs on his terrace, just waiting for Melanie to call.

When she did call Corinne, Buddy would intercept. "He would talk for any reason," Melanie says. "He was crazed. It was like he was on his knees. I mean, every time, he would start crying. Buddy just didn't act like that. Buddy, you know, just did everything his way. But now it was pathetic. It reached such a point that Jack and I felt sorry for him. I mean, really sorry!

"I was not in love with Buddy anymore, but he had been a part of my life, and I felt very guilty about leaving him. I wanted to help him."

Melanie saw no reason why they should not continue their business relationship. She told Buddy that she was content to remain at My Fair Lady, as, indeed, she was—"I *liked* the agency," she says. Indeed, her promises became more sweeping. "I'll come over a couple of nights a week, and we'll go out and have dinner with all the girls," she told him. "Buddy, I'll find you a new girlfriend! I'll set the whole thing up. We're going to be friends for years."

Jack Tupper, though, had become exasperated, and this led him to make a disastrous decision. Jack had begun to feel that his and Melanie's caution—the "running around," as Buddy contemptuously put it—was unmanly. Paul was coming back from Puerto Rico, and he would think it peculiar to find his father staying at a hotel. Additionally, Melanie, as a part owner of Buddy's property, presumably had as much right at 155 East 84th Street as Jacobson himself.

So, even though Melanie was scheduled to move from the Drake to East 74th Street on August 1, she and Jack moved back into his seventh-floor apartment at the 84th Street building on Monday, July 31. It was Jack's way of saying that Buddy would not push them around any more.

Claire Normandeau explains the action that was to destroy her law-enforcement career in this way. Tom, her brother, was to be married on August 13, and the bachelor party was to be Friday, August 4. There would, she knew, be a number of Tom's police colleagues there—he was with the 112th Precinct—and, doubtless, other agents from one department or another. Jack Tupper, Tom's roommate in the dismal days after the failure of the Sherwood Inn, had been invited, of course, but Claire had no idea which other old friends Tom might be inviting.

This, she says, is why she pulled a sheaf of printouts from the NADDIS computer a second time. The files that she examined included those on Brown and Seifert, as well as those on Jimmy Leonard, Billy Sharrocks, Carlo Carrara, Peter Splain, and others—including Jack Tupper—linked with what the DEA was calling the Donald Brown Organization. Claire also pulled the printouts on Joseph Margarite, Breck Dana Anderson, and, yes, Buddy Jacobson.

Jack Tupper's printout reads as follows: "Subject is involved in smuggling kilogram quantities of cocaine from

South America into the U.S. . . . Subject believed to be involved with four tons of hashish and four tons of Thai sticks that were seized in New York: Subject believed to be involved in large scale hashish/Thai stick smuggling organization through JFK International Airport."

Thus spake the computer. It seems worthy of note, though, that Buddy's file, which Claire had pulled, she says, because he came "from the neighborhood," mentions him only as the recipient of a shipment from a suspect. *"Shipment was clean,"* the printout observes. *"Involvement unknown."* Brown, Seifert, Leonard, Sharrocks and their comrades are convinced Buddy was clean.

Monday, July 31, was a wretched day. Melanie was in a state: drained, frayed, emotions quivering on the surface. She still suspected that Buddy's grief was a charade. After five years of being consistently lied to, Melanie was now prepared to find falsehood in everything Buddy said or did. "I wish I could have been more understanding," she says. "But I didn't *know*. I thought he was putting on a big show. Buddy has *feelings*? Buddy *cares*? I couldn't quite comprehend it. . . ."

Even so, Melanie realized that the move into Jack's apartment was greatly upsetting Buddy. "You're putting your slippers under somebody else's bed," he said bitterly. "Can't you see what your leaving is doing to me? I will do anything. Anything in the world. I will marry you. I know how much you love kids. I will get you pregnant so fast that we will have six kids. Six kids! Isn't that proof?"

Melanie was incredulous. "He was holding my hand. Begging me! He just had a wild look in his eyes." She thought, suddenly, of Charles Manson. "Buddy's eyes were just *flames*. I mean, if you didn't know him you would have thought he was on drugs. He was very thin and drawn, and he had that sort of stoned, *bright* look."

But the offer of fathering children was ludicrous.

"That's not love!" she told him. "I know you don't want children. You just want to get me pregnant so I won't leave. I don't believe anything you say."

Buddy began to ramble. His rambling took him into a nonsense world.

"We don't even have to live in the same apartment," he told her. "You can have an apartment somewhere else! You can have another boyfriend! You can mess around as much as you want. Only marry me!"

Melanie had no idea what there was left for her to say, but she made one more attempt to make the breakup palatable. "Things haven't worked out. We don't get along," she said. "We're complete opposites. But we'll still be friends. . . ."

Buddy rejected what she was saying so violently that Melanie grew blunt.

"I don't love you anymore," she said. "And not only don't I love you anymore, I don't even *like* you. I don't like the way you lie, and treat people. I just don't *respect* you anymore."

The put-down was purposely a hard one. "I thought, oh, he would be mad at me and call me a bitch, and throw me out," she says.

But Jacobson did not respond as she thought he would.

"I don't care," he told her frantically. "*Hate me*. I don't care, I'll put up with it. Doesn't that prove how much I love you?

"It doesn't matter if we don't get along. It doesn't matter if we're totally opposite. You can't leave me, because you know too much about me. You're like my own left arm." Intensely, he added, "I *own* you."

Melanie flared with indignation.

"You do *not* own me," she said.

Buddy backed off. "I don't *really* mean I own you," he told her. "But we're so close—we're like one person."

"I want to live my own life, and you won't let me. You've got to let me go."

It had been an unsettling conversation. Melanie was relieved when Jack returned, and glad to leave the building. That Monday night, she and Jack drove out to the airport, met the flight from San Juan that was bringing ten-year-old Paul back to New York. The three of them had a late, high-spirited meal, then returned to the 84th Street building, and Jack tucked Paul up in the bunk bed he had made for his son's use. It was already three in the morning when Jack and Melanie went to bed. This was to have been her last night under Buddy Jacobson's roof.

It was Melanie's new landlord's secretary who caused her to abandon the 74th Street apartment. "Mr. Jacobson asked when you were moving in," she told her the next morning. So much for those promises to leave her alone. Melanie, panicky now, afraid to be parted from Jack, resolved to find a place further removed from Buddy's prying.

Later this same Tuesday morning, Jack went to Buddy's apartment for Melanie's remaining possessions, some clothes and the few pieces of furniture that she had moved into Buddy's place earlier that year. He and his son shifted them into 7C.

Some hours later, Ellen Gannon, curiously asked Paul how Buddy had reacted. "What was he doing?" she asked.

"He wasn't doing anything."

"Not *anything*?"

"He was just . . . sad," the boy said. "He said, 'Take the sofa, take anything.' There was only one thing he wanted. He said, "Please leave that. For *me*.' " Buddy's request had been for a soft pink blanket, a favorite of Melanie's. When Melanie heard, she was unimpressed, but when she began to sort through her clothes, her composure was shaken once more.

There were stickers all over her clothes. They were cut out of masking tape, and Buddy had scrawled messages of love on them. They were everywhere. "I would look at my underpants, and there would be a sticker . . . *I Love you . . . I Love You, Melanie*. . . . Then I'd open my desk, or I'd open a book, and there were more stickers. There must have been a good hundred of them."

"She, Jack, and Paul left at one o'clock and walked to the All-Ireland. "The door opened, and there was this little streak," Ellen says. "I hardly recognized him. He was as brown as a berry." Paul spent that afternoon in the All-Ireland mastering the pinball machine.

Jack and Melanie spent a few hours looking for a new apartment, then returned to East 84th Street in the late afternoon, and Jack strolled down to see his son. Melanie was alone in 7C when Buddy walked in. "I just want you to know that I'm not going to bother you anymore," he told her. "But I need to know if you're going to stay at the agency or not."

Melanie was irritated, especially since he was still refusing to be specific concerning her earnings.

"What about my money, Buddy?" she demanded.

Buddy muttered something about having never taken advantage of a girl where her money was concerned, but he seemed no closer to a straight answer than ever.

They both lost their tempers. Buddy told Melanie that she wouldn't see a cent if she left him, and stormed out of the apartment.

Melanie told Jack about the incident when he returned, crossed to 7D, and knocked on the door. "Jack wants to talk to you, Buddy," she said.

Buddy came in. "Now let's talk about this like adults," he said, seemingly composed. But it was seven-thirty. The TV interview with Melanie and the other models was on a cable channel. They watched in a strange calm, and it concentrated Buddy's mind.

"Are you going to stay with the agency?" he asked.

"No," she said simply.

He was quiet, but stubborn. "You *have* to stay with the agency!" he told her. It was an order, not a plea.

"Buddy, you don't *understand!*" Melanie said.

It was now that Jack motioned to Buddy. They both went out into the hallway, and Jack firmly shut the door behind them.

Ellen Gannon had finished work. She drove up East 84th Street and double-parked outside the Jacobson building, waiting in the car while Paul went upstairs to collect the things he had brought back from Puerto Rico.

It was a longish wait. When Paul finally did return, he was carrying his bag and a tennis racket, and Ellen was surprised to see that he was alone. "Normally John would come downstairs, and we'd have a chat," she says.

The boy, moreover, seemed shaken. What was the trouble?

"It's all confusing up there. Screaming and yelling," Paul said. "There's a fight going on."

It was heated, he said, but not a fistfight.

"Melanie doesn't like Buddy anymore," Paul told his mother. "She likes daddy. Buddy doesn't want her to leave him. Daddy and Buddy are yelling."

The next morning, Jack and Melanie drove to Al Seifert's country house in upstate New York. It was a roomy place beside a lake—indeed, Al had a house party of ten—and Melanie felt freer of her sense of oppression than for several months. Al and Jack talked, and Al suggested that he be wary in his dealings with Jacobson. But Tupper seemed more irritated than alarmed. Melanie and Jack stayed there overnight, returning to 84th Street late the following day, Thursday, August 3.

Thursday was a busy day for Buddy. The broody torpor which had weighed him down, anchoring him to his terrace or beside his telephone, had passed away. He was brimful of energy. He called a realtor several times. "I was putting in an offer for him on a very important, terrific building," she says.

Buddy's other calls were to Millie Lewis and Jimmy Wood. Millie, the doyenne of the South Carolina modeling schools, was at her house in Hilton Head. Jacobson, sounding breezy, told her that he had "something very exciting" to discuss with her. "It was a business proposition," she adds. "But he never told me what it was."

Millie happened to be coming to New York that Sunday; they made a date. They were to dine at Nicola's on Monday night.

The call to Jimmy Wood at his jewelry office was more personal. Wood was mystified to hear the familiar voice again.

"Let's be friends again," Buddy suggested. "We had a good thing going for us with the broads. The Zzzyp brothers! Right? Let bygones be bygones."

Jimmy listened carefully. "Yeah, Buddy?" he said. His tone was questioning.

"So we'll be friends. I'm going to send you some broads," Buddy said.

He was going to send them over to the office the next day, he promised, and if there was one that Jimmy fancied, well, why didn't they all have dinner? Just like old times.

"Maybe Friday," Buddy suggested. "Or Saturday."

This proposed, a peevish quality came into Buddy's voice. He was being tormented by an appropriate instrument, the telephone. Persons unknown to him were calling, demanding money for the return of Melanie. "You know where she is *right now?*" they would ask. "You know what she and Jack are doing?"

In fact, Jimmy knew about the calls. Donald Brown has a wicked sense of humor.

Thus it was that Buddy Jacobson tore through the day, speeding out of control.

* * *

Dorothy Myers had grown even more anxious when she found that Buddy Jacobson had been attempting to track her brother down in San Juan. Her nervousness steadily increased. "I was petrified," she says. "And I called Jackie's answering service twice that week, asking him to return a call, because I was a wreck. I just didn't know what to do."

Dee-Dee, Jerry Tupper's former fiancée, happened to be with the Myers at the time, and the two young women would stay up late talking the situation over. Later, when Dorothy heard that Jack and Melanie had moved back into the building, the folly appalled her.

Dorothy was relieved when Jack finally called her back that Thursday. She asked how everything was going.

"Oh, I don't know," he told her, sounding a bit dispirited. "It's all messed up. But I know he's been sneaking into my apartment."

"That's terrible, Jackie. What are you going to do?" Dorothy said.

"I'm getting out of here," Jack told her reassuringly. "Just don't worry about a thing."

This was the last time that Dorothy and her older brother spoke.

It was on this same day that Jack Tupper removed a package which had obviously eluded Buddy Jacobson's searching, and concealed it in a safe place, a place known to him only, in the All-Ireland.

At six-thirty in the evening, Buddy had a visitor in his apartment. He was Noel Bernstein, the textile millionaire whose horses Buddy had trained. He was dropping in to confirm a dinner date with Buddy and Melanie for the following weekend.

Bernstein parked his car and looked casually up to the seventh floor terrace, where Buddy would often be standing. "He was always around," Bernstein says. "He was married to the place." He did not, on this occasion, see Buddy, though, but somebody unknown, and not entirely prepossessing. He says that he was wearing a "pimp hat," which is to say a dark broad-brimmed hat with a light-colored band.

Noel Bernstein went straight up to the seventh floor. Buddy's door was closed. He knocked several times, but decided that Jacobson might be in the middle of some "capture," meaning an amorous conquest, so he went back downstairs, crossed the street, and dialed Buddy's number from the telephone in the hallway of Nicola's.

From this telephone, the 7D terrace is in plain sight, and another man now came out and joined the first. Bernstein's seduction hypothesis deflated. "I only saw them for a fleeting moment," he says. The only thing he could remember later was that both of them were "swarthy-looking young men. One of them had a mustache, I think."

There was no answer to his call, but Bernstein returned to the seventh floor. His knocking again was fruitless, but now he distinctly heard music from within. Angrily, Noel Bernstein descended and drove home to Connecticut.

That Thursday night, Jack Tupper proposed while he and Melanie were sitting on his sofa in a cubist landscape of cardboard crates. Melanie promptly accepted. Buoyantly, Jack called Al Seifert and asked him to be best man, and after some hesitation, Seifert accepted. Jack and Melanie agreed to marry quickly, perhaps as early as the following week.

This decision was not something, though, that Melanie chose to tell Buddy when he started buzzing around her, like a wasp around jam, the following morning.

"I'm going away, Buddy."

"Well, *when* are you going away?"

"I don't know. I'm probably going on Saturday."

"*Where* are you going?"

He was repetitive, as though chipping away with a drill, but there was something new in his demeanor. She was to tell me later that "the man had a real crazy look in his eyes."

Buddy persisted in asking where she was going, and Melanie continued to refuse to say. The fact was, she hadn't decided. She had thought of going home, but doubted if she could face her parents. She had even thought of returning to Paris, and Jack and she had talked of spending a week in Los Angeles, possibly with Donald Brown. But all that she knew for certain was that she had to get out of 155 East 84th Street.

"I'm not telling you where I'm going," she said coldly. "Because you'll be calling, or flying there, or sending *singing telegrams*."

"Just tell me," he pleaded. "I don't like you playing secrets."

"I'm just not telling you," she repeated stubbornly.

About eleven that morning, she and Jack walked to the All-Ireland. Jack made a telephone call, and they talked with Ellen at the bar. It was typical of this secretive man that he did not tell Ellen that he and Melanie were to be married. Earlier, he had proposed dinner next week, the Gannons and Ivor Shaw, but had not mentioned Melanie.

He was also concerned that Ellen's job was imperiled, what with Brian's deciding to close the All-Ireland for re-designing. It was Jack, after all, who had brought her with him into Manhattan. He told her he had plenty of friends in the restaurant business, and he would telephone around. "I'll take care of it," he told her. "Don't worry about anything. Do you want me to call you tomorrow?" Ellen said she was going upstate that evening. "I'll speak to you on Monday," Jack Tupper promised. In this way, they parted.

Jack and Melanie now went to David Silbergeld's office building. It had been David that Jack had telephoned from the bar, proposing that they lunch together.

"So I came downstairs, and I was floored," Silbergeld says. "There was Melanie with Jack. They were smiling. It hit me like a ton of bricks."

"No kidding!" was all he said.

"Yeah," Jack said. "We're going to get married."

The three walked to the Plaza and lunched in the Oyster Bar. After the usual congratulations, Silbergeld had some words of caution. "You can't live across the hall from Buddy," he said. "That's rubbing his face in it."

"I'm not planning to," Tupper agreed.

"I've got a friend who owns apartments all over," David told them. "I'll call him up. But, listen, I can't do anything about it immediately. I've got to go play soldier this weekend. I'll talk to you when I get back."

Jimmy Wood was rather surprised. Three young modeling hopefuls actually did turn up in his East 47th Street jewelry office. Buddy truly was an extraordinary man, Wood thought.

They arrived at noon, clutching their modeling books, and they were fetching enough. One of them, as he was to remember, was Cheryl Corey. Ordinarily, it would now be time for the Zzzyp trick. Jimmy was supposed to ask them into his private office, scrutinize their photographs with a sagacious eye, indicate that the girls would be perfect for a new advertising campaign he was envisioning, and tout "Mr. Jacobson" to the skies. A dinner date would follow.

But this was Friday. It was Wood's custom in the summer months to close his office at one o'clock on a Friday and make for the beach. He was, moreover, with a client—a genuine client—so the three girls had to sit out in the anteroom until he was done.

It was almost one when Jimmy Wood walked out, and his spirits failed. There the three models sat, holding themselves slenderly erect while smiling brilliant smiles, compounding hope and anxiety. Wood's own smile congealed on his face. He just couldn't go through with the game. He felt a rush of fatigue.

"Sorry, girls," he told them. "Can you come back on Monday?"

He was just closing up when Buddy telephoned. It was almost exactly half past one.

"Did you like them?" he asked.

"Sure, Buddy," said Jimmy, who did not point out that he was now living with a woman, Melanie's friend Ingrid, because Buddy knew this and would not have thought it relevant.

"Come on over," Buddy urged. "You've got to help me. I don't know what to do about this Tupper situation." The young models, he added, would be around the whole weekend.

"I'm sorry, Buddy," Jimmy said. "I'm just leaving for the beach." He still felt perplexed at this show of friendship, but now it seems perfectly clear to him. Buddy wanted Jimmy around the building that weekend because he is licensed to carry a gun, and customarily does so. Because of the scenario he was planning, he wanted Wood in place as a distracting element for the police. "He didn't want to let bygones be bygones," Jimmy Wood told me. "He was setting me up."

Jack and Melanie hunted for an apartment all afternoon, then dined with Ivor Shaw in the Parma. Jack talked about Paul. "He said that Paul was going to come and live with him," Shaw remembers.

It was obvious that Jack's patience with Buddy had worn thin. The surveillance was wearing on his nerves. "He's such a low-life he has brought his sons into it," Jack said. There was also the matter of Melanie's vanished earnings. Jack Tupper was resolved to see her repaid in full, and there is no doubt that Jack was in possession of so much information on the inner workings of the Jacobson empire (he said as much to Donald Brown) that Buddy might have found him a more formidable claimant than, say, Con Ed.

They finished dinner. "Where shall we go for an after-dinner drink?" Jack asked.

"Shall we go into the lion's den?" Shaw suggested.

The "lion's den" was Nicola's, so described both because it was Buddy's favored haunt and because of the loyalty of its proprietor to Jacobson. They duly walked the five blocks to Nicola's. As they entered, Shaw glanced up at the seventh-floor balcony opposite. He was mildly surprised. It was empty. "Guess who's not on the terrace?" he said.

"He probably *knows* where we are," Jack said.

They had their nightcaps, and then a couple more, and Jack and Melanie left and went back to Buddy's building. It was about a quarter to two.

Saturday, August 5, promised to be both warm and wet. Jack and Melanie were up by nine, and as soon as Jack was reasonably sure they were not being followed, they resumed their apartment hunt. That morning they looked at three apartment towers, all of them with impressive security, a couple being close to each other in the lower 80s; but the place that took Melanie's fancy was the third, a sizable building with a lobby boasting marble floors and palms, called the Brevard. This was because the Brevard is located at 245 East 54th Street, in midtown, a longish way from Buddy's World. Melanie told the real estate agent, a woman named Georgiana Ioli, that she would drop by the following morning, make the necessary payment, and collect the lease. This began on September 1. Jack and Melanie again discussed the possibility of spending the next couple of weeks in Los Angeles, and Melanie's spirits lifted at the thought.

It was now about noon, and Jack drove Melanie to Queens. His first stop was at a Chinese laundry close to Paul's school. Melanie dashed into the laundry, and retrieved a brown paper parcel of shirts and sheets. From the laundry they drove to lunch in the former Sherwood Inn, which was now known as Regents Row, but was little changed. This was Melanie's first visit to Jack's former Queens habitat, and it was, for Jack, to some extent a sentimental journey.

After lunch, on an impulse, he drove to his parents' house, stopped, and called them from a telephone on the corner. But they were at Shelter Island, and would have to meet Melanie another day. He also telephoned Ellen at her Queens apartment. Her mother happened to be staying the weekend, and confirmed that Ellen had gone upstate. It was now three o'clock. (Ellen sometimes puzzles over Jack's reason for making the call. Did it mean trouble? Or did he just want to tell her of his marriage plans?)

He now drove to the house of an old friend, the attorney Bob Kronenberg. Jack and Bob spoke briefly, while Melanie remained in the car. Finally, Jack drove to the house of Jimmy Leonard. Jimmy is a family man, but his wife, Lorna, and the kids were at a wedding. Jimmy was alone. Melanie was feeling a little tired now, and suspected the onset of a head cold, so she went upstairs and took a nap. Jack and Jimmy, meantime, talked long and earnestly about the trouble to come. Jack now knew that he, too, was in the trap. He was mostly horrified, but it partly tickled his sense of fantasy. "They've got me down as one of the *chiefs*," he incorrectly said.

For Jimmy Wood and Ingrid, it had seemed pointless going to the beach in the rotten weather. They stayed in Manhattan. Nancy, a model, called that afternoon.

"Buddy's lonely," she said. "Why don't we go over and spend the evening with him?"

Ingrid said she would rather not.

Jack and Melanie returned to 84th Street in the early evening. Jack couldn't be bothered to put the car away in the Ardor Garage next door, but parked it on Lexington. Melanie bought some pizza and settled down to watch *Love Boat*.

Jack Tupper was restless. A couple of hours later, he and Melanie walked down to R.W. Bonds at Third and 77th and ordered hamburgers. It was now shortly after eleven. Dick Leslie, the owner, joined them, congratulated Jack, and the talk veered toward Buddy.

Jack told Leslie about the harassment, the persistent telephone calls. Gesturing at Melanie, he said jokingly, "Did you know this girl was worth a hundred thousand dollars? He's offered me that to leave town. I said, 'Make that a quarter of a million, and we can talk about a deal.' "

Dick Leslie decided that Jack was taking the situation rather lightly. Seeing that Melanie was more concerned, he offered to let her stay in his place. It was only a small downstairs room, he said, but it would do for the time being.

"What about me?" Jack asked.

"You can have a set of keys. You can come and go." It was now that he said Buddy was "tough as a gun."

But Jack was still inclined to be dismissive and they finished their drinks and walked home. It was well past midnight, and August 6 had begun, when they finally went to bed.

Jack Tupper had been half asleep when Melanie left Sunday morning to sign the lease for the Brevard. Afterward, he got up, shaved, and prepared himself a light breakfast of an English muffin and a cup of instant coffee. He had business to transact that day, a meeting with Donald Brown's father, Irving, at which they were to settle the last of the paperwork concerning the old Sherwood Inn.

Nobody knows just how Jack was induced to enter Buddy Jacobson's apartment, but the time is thought to have been about eleven-thirty. Jack was certainly not prepared to leave the building: His keys, his address book, and his diary with the Mark Cross pen, all of which he usually carried with him, remained beside his bed. Nor, come to that, do we yet know just how many people were lying in wait for Tupper, but, apart from Jacobson himself, there were at least two others and, quite possibly, three. Their weapons included two handguns, a sledgehammer, and a knife.

It has often been pointed out that this killing was sloppy and crude, and that is true. It has also been theorized that the killing was too sloppy to be the work of somebody as "brilliant" as Buddy Jacobson. This writer has no idea precisely how Jack Tupper's murder was planned, or performed, but a combination of material evidence and plain common sense suggests that in concept, the murder was perfectly sound, and not unintelligent at all.

The plan seems to have been this. Jack Tupper was to be lured into 7D, and then either killed in as soundless a way as possible, or, possibly, rendered insensible and taken away to be disposed of elsewhere. He would then be burned beyond recognition. Jack Tupper, with his secretive manner and his penchant for travel, might not be missed for days, or weeks, except by Melanie, and Buddy had always been able to handle Melanie. By the time Tupper *was* missed, it would be too late.

Tupper, whether unconscious or already dead, was to be taken out of the apartment in the hefty crate that Buddy had been hammering together for that purpose a few nights before. Nobody in the building would find it remarkable to see Buddy moving a storage crate. He had always acted as his own janitor; that is the one quality his tenants most remarked on.

If Buddy was seen at all, that is. Younger people, the sort of people who lived at East 84th Street, rush for the ocean on August weekends, leaving Manhattan deserted. As for the seventh floor, Melanie was to say in court that she hadn't seen anybody in the corridors for several days.

It was Buddy's first stroke of bad luck that the weather was so wretched that several people decided there was no point leaving the city that weekend. Another problem was that Joe Margarite, whom Melanie had not seen for weeks, was there that day, and in his apartment. The worst bit of bad luck, of course, was that the murder itself was, apparently, botched.

What went wrong we do not know. Did a hammer blow fail to fell Jack Tupper, a powerful man? Did Buddy's paralyzing Taser malfunction? (His two Tasers, like his handgun, have never been found.) What did occur was a frenzy of clubbing and shooting and stabbing, a brutish carnage in which Jack Tupper was as good as killed several times over. He was then dumped into the crate and taken downstairs in the elevator. The crate was put in the back of a yellow van, which was driven off at high speed just as Beth McKay and Kelly Lougee walked back from the building from which Cheryl Corey had fallen to her death.

Buddy Jacobson remained behind, of course. He planned to clear the signs of the crime away and then spend the rest of the day working in the Park East. But as he left the building at three o'clock, he ran into Melanie, who was both alarmed and suspicious. This seems to have affected his time-table. That Melanie had been out of the building during the slaying he knew, and that she had seen things which troubled her he also knew. What she *had* seen he didn't know.

Buddy was probably not really worried. He had always been able to talk Melanie around, coax her, and cajole her. With Tupper gone, he must have felt that he would easily prevail. So Buddy talked to Melanie. But she seemed immune to his persuasion. Indeed, she sounded distinctly threatening.

A sense of urgency seized him, and he insisted they have coffee. Buddy had her by the arm now, and was tussling as if ready to tug her into the G&M Luncheonette by sheer force. But Melanie resisted, and at last his grip broke.

A tiny episode, but it seems to have alerted Buddy to a hazard. If his accomplices left a recognizable corpse, he could not rely on Melanie to keep silent.

There is no doubt as to what happened next. Buddy abandoned his plan of working at the Park East. Instead, he drove Sal Prainito's yellow Cadillac out to the place where the blackened crate was still smoldering in the Bronx. It was his most dangerous folly.

It was such folly, in fact, that many people refused to believe Buddy could have been so sloppy. "Buddy's on the borderline of genius," mused Irwin "Win" Klein, one of his former lawyers, in a characteristic reaction. "He's a general. You don't find generals on the firing line. Now, driving to the Bronx like that, that was dumb. Buddy's not dumb. There's something incongruous. It doesn't fit. Right?"

Wrong. Buddy's whole picaresque history—the racetrack, the discos, the buildings—can be read as a sequence of brilliant schemes marred by slovenly, hurried execution. Invariably he had too little time, a stubborn insistence on doing things his way, a sense of contempt for others. If something didn't work—tear out the page. There was no situation out of which Buddy felt he couldn't talk his way.

At the time of his arrest, the case against Buddy Jacobson seemed overwhelming; he had the means, the motive, and the opportunity, to say nothing of the knowledge that the opportunity might soon be out of reach. He was as good as caught with the body, and there were bullet-holes all over his apartment. So straightforward did it seem, in fact, that Detective Sullivan of Eighth Homicide did not, at the beginning, believe Buddy would even make bail.

Yet within weeks he was managing to cast doubts on his guilt. It is true that Buddy Jacobson had manipulative gifts of the most extraordinary sort, but it is also true that he had the richest material with which to work. Consider the cast of characters. Jack Tupper and Melanie had spent time with both Al Seifert and Jimmy Leonard shortly before his death, and they would soon find themselves on opposite sides of a massive narcotics case. Donald Brown, Billy Sharrocks, and Carlo Carrara, who were also well known to him, would find themselves involved in the same brouhaha. Simple: It was a "dope rub-out."

Where such simple scenarios didn't work, Buddy would prove resourceful. He would suggest that there was significance to the fact that John Gannon was a narcotics cop and that Tom Myers was with the FBI. He told this writer that David Silbergeld was a member of a "hit team" of former Green Berets working for the Mob, and other curious plots were invoked to involve Ivor Shaw, or the IRA by way of Brian Monaghan. Buddy soon realized that the fact that these scenarios were lacking in proof, were absurd and contradictory didn't matter a whit.

He had allies in the press, of course, but there is no question who his best ally was: Jack Tupper. The mystery that Jack Tupper loved came back to haunt him in death. "He always played that secretive 007 role," Kevin Tupper says. "My brother only trusted one person at a time. He would take one person into his confidence, and tell that one person everything about his life.

"Everybody else would be locked out—that was the way he dealt. He would confide in that one person for a year, two years, and then. . . ." He shrugged, indicating finis. "Earlier, he had been very close to Brian Monaghan. But at the time of my brother's death, I don't think anybody was in my brother's confidence. Why, I don't know."

Monaghan concurs. "About six or eight weeks before Jack was killed, he closed the door on his past life, on everybody he had known," he says. "But Jack liked to talk with somebody. He always needed a friend." In the end, he believes, this role was taken by Melanie.

But many people, including some close to Jack, were still plagued by the sense of something missing. The phantoms which most bedevilled the case were the following: *The Missing Money; The Missing Diary; the Missing Packages; the Missing Cassettes; the Missing Joe Margarite;* and *the Missing Element.* They all deserve examination.

The Missing Money is the haul that Jack Tupper made from his forays with the airport gang: an estimated $300,000. This has not turned up, and many participants in the drama have pointed accusatory fingers in as many different directions. It should be borne in mind, though, that the money had been made in 1977, and that Tupper had been sustaining expenses ever since. Ivor Shaw, at the time that Jack was talking of buying a bar, believes that he had access to no more than $100,000.

The Missing Diary would solve this problem, according to Monaghan. Its disappearance is strange, he says: "Jack wrote everything down. He wrote it down in code, but it wasn't hard to break. The money disappeared, but whoever has it, the name is in Jack's diary." Ellen Gannon disputes this. Jack's diary, at any rate in those last few weeks, dealt with business minutiae. Among the last few months' entries had been a notation that he had dined in the Parma—with Buddy.

My own information comes from one who has read the diary closely, who says that if there are secrets buried there, the pages refused to yield them.

The Missing Packages: It is certain that Jack removed at least one package, probably two, from his apartment a few days before his murder. One of these packages, by one account, contained C4 detonators. There is no suggestion that this was evidence of anything other than Jack Tupper's "Walter Mitty side."

The Missing Tape Cassettes: Attorney Jack Evseroff, arguing Buddy's defense, would make much of the fact that the only tape cassettes in evidence were those of Jack and Melanie, respectively, talking to Buddy. There must have been other tapes, he argued. Where were they? What had they recorded?

Plausible. Jack had taped tricky business dealings in the past, on the advice of Claire Normandeau. But the facts don't support Jack Evseroff. If there were other tape cassettes, Melanie never saw them.

The Missing Joe Margarite: The presence of Margarite in the building that day—he told somebody close to him that he had heard the shots—was another stroke of bad luck for Buddy Jacobson, but one that he turned to his advantage. What passed between Buddy and Joe was not known but, as a convicted dope dealer (he did time in Tangier) he could hardly have been enthusiastic about getting involved in a murder trial. "I guess he just thought—let's get out of Dodge," observed his friend, Breck Dana Anderson.

Joe Margarite was still at large as the trial opened. He would bob up here and there, and disappear, leaving the cops flailing in his wake. The *New York Post* speculated that Margarite might have been given a new identity, as a federal witness on an entirely different case. Another puzzle, or so it seemed.

The Missing Element: The most tantalizing of the phantom clues. Cocaine is a subject upon which the DEA files on Jack Tupper are brutally explicit: *Subject reportedly is head of group that smuggles cocaine into U.S. from South America.* The qualification "reportedly" should be noted, though, and whichever "group" is being talked about, it isn't the Donald Brown organization, with which Jack Tupper had no cocaine dealings whatsoever.

Some believe that Jack Tupper, in the months before his death, had made a cocaine connection, and there were wildly varying rumors after the murder, concerning a "missing key [kilogram] of cocaine." In one version, related in *Newsweek*, a couple of heavies from Montreal had been looking for Jack the night before his murder and in another, related to Evseroff by a lawyer, Jack had a meeting scheduled with a Cuban drug trafficker on the day of his death.

This writer believes the truth to be as follows. Jack Tupper had, indeed, been interested in cocaine, and on those Latin American trips, during which his endeavors to sell computers and machinery were real and energetic, cocaine might certainly have looked like an appealing option, especially since Brian Monaghan believes the attempt to sell a computer was "a bust." It is said, indeed, that Jack Tupper financed a man to scout for him in Colombia while he was in New York.

The scout failed. All he found (this source says) was leather suitcases and tropical fish. Jack lost interest. This was months before his death.

Both Al Seifert and Ivor Shaw maintain that Jack was clean. Tupper knew of the Donald Brown indictments and he was not a foolish man. He knew about the list of names, and he knew he was on the list himself.

There are other factors which have to be considered in assessing the probability of the various tales that have Jack

Tupper involved with rococo transactions on, or around, the date of his death. He was set, for one thing, on opening a bar, and the State Liquor Authority looks sourly on persons with a record. At the same time, he was set on making a home for his son, Paul, and sending the boy to a good school. Also, there is Melanie, whom he was marrying and who did not like Jack's even using cocaine. She believes that Jack was utterly clean.

The autopsy on Jack Tupper was performed at the Manhattan Mortuary on August 7 at two in the afternoon. There was, as yet, no inkling of the celebrity of this affair, so it was carried out not by Michael Baden, then the chief medical examiner, but by a junior colleague, Dr. Josette Montas. The report describes the body as being that of a "well developed, well nourished white male, measuring 6'1" and weighing approximately 170 pounds."

The autopsy lists the causes of death as follows. "There are two circumscribed round markedly depressed fractures . . . of the skull—the largest diameter of which is 1½" and the greatest depth of this depression is ½"." These fractures, which damaged the brain, were caused by a hammer-like object, and the prosecution was to contend that they had been caused by the hammer found in the trunk of Sal Prainito's Cadillac.

Also: "There are multiple lacerations and stab wounds mainly over the left side of the face, the left side of the head. . . . The skin is very dry around them and they are superficial. . . . There are approximately fifteen such wounds." These wounds, although listed among the causes of death, suggest both frenzy and a hunger to hurt; meaning torture.

Also: "Stab wound of the abdomen." This reached the liver.

Also: "Multiple gunshot wounds (7) of right ear, chest, back upper extremities, left buttock."

I should like to feel that it was with a tremor that Dr. Montas observed that the dead man was wearing a "burnt, ragged blue jockey-type brief with the trade mark 'LIFE.' "

A laboratory report, which was appended, stated that the liver, blood, stomach, bile, and urine had been examined, and no trace of acidic drugs, basic drugs, or opiates had been found.

Buddy Jacobson and Salvatore Prainito were duly arrested,

and charged with Murder Two. Salvatore Giamo, who had been with Buddy in the Cadillac, and who Buddy had said was a "hitchhiker" (though he had, it turned out, been on the Jacobson payroll at the time), was never charged. Peter Grishman, the assistant district attorney who was in charge of the investigation, says there was inadequate evidence.

It was now that the process began, both in the courts and out of them, that was to warp a great many lives and drive Melanie to the brink of a breakdown. And the man twitching the strings would be Buddy Jacobson.

- VI -

Waiting

Dick Huebner had been calling My Fair Lady without success all morning. Now he was growing anxious. Huebner is with Shirley Polykoff, the advertising agency, and wanted to confirm a booking with Melanie. It was a commercial for a Bristol-Myers shampoo, a two-day shoot, starting early the next day. But Huebner couldn't get through to the agency.

He was puzzled. He had worked with Melanie before and knew her to be reliable. They had done the tests with her, and a storyboard had been assembled from the stills. He tried again, this time letting the phone ring, and ring.

Somebody picked up at last. "Speak!" said whoever it was. The voice was female, but hard.

"I'm sorry," Huebner said. "I must have the wrong number."

"Who are you calling?"

"My Fair Lady."

"This is My Fair Lady."

Huebner was surprised, but said, "I want to confirm Melanie Cain's booking for tomorrow."

"This is Melanie," said the voice.

"My, aren't we rude today!" Dick Huebner said lightly.

"I'm sorry. I can't do the job," Melanie said, with the efficient intonations of an agency booker. "My ex-boyfriend just killed my fiancé." Dick Huebner, flabbergasted, said that he would postpone the shooting.

It was the early afternoon of Monday, August 7. Melanie was back from the Bronx, accompanied by her father, and numerous cops whom she had let into Buddy's apartment. The cops, headed by Bill Sullivan and Mary-Beth Abbate, the assistant district attorney, set to their business, which was the gathering of evidence.

They had cautioned Melanie not to answer the telephone. This advice she ignored totally. The next caller was Noel

Bernstein, making a second attempt to confirm dinner with Buddy and Melanie the coming weekend.

Melanie said she was sorry, but they couldn't make it. "Buddy just killed a man," she told him, in what he calls a "wooden" tone. Bernstein just didn't believe what she was saying.

George Cain had also done some telephoning. Cain, who was as disturbed as his daughter appeared to be composed, had telephoned a lawyer to whom he had been recommended, one Martin Pollner, told him of Melanie's situation, and asked to see him that day. This first call had been from the DA's office in the Bronx, but Cain called the lawyer several times from East 84th Street, bringing him up to date on events as they happened and complaining that his daughter was being pestered by the media.

Meanwhile, the police investigation was trundling methodically forward. Three lead slugs and a Smith & Wesson .32 shell casing were found in the apartment in a garbage pail. A pair of spectacles, smeary with blood, was on a counter in the kitchen. The blood-spotted plaid rug was found underneath the staircase that led to the upper floor, and there were slivers of shattered mirror in the vacuum-cleaner bag. "Seven years of bad luck!" Melanie had thought to herself as she glided through this new Crazy-Alice-Through-the-Looking-Glass world. There were a couple of bullet holes in the apartment door, and one of them still held a slug. This was the door that led out into the hall, and it had, the cops noted, been carefully wiped clean. No writer of detective stories would have scattered clues around as lavishly as this.

Buddy now had a lawyer. "Rita came to my office and retained me," Sidney Sparrow says, referring to Rita Costello, Buddy's sister. Sparrow is a veteran Bronx attorney. His offices are in the Silver Towers, where Buddy used to live, and where so many of his family still do. Sparrow was acquainted with them, as he had also been with Jack Tupper.

Kevin had already talked to the cops that morning and mentioned he wanted to get into his brother's apartment. "They said fine," he told me. "But 'Don't try to enter the apartment until we turn it over to you—it's sealed.' "

Kevin and Tom Myers arrived at East 84th Street in the

early afternoon. This was the first visit for both of them. Kevin explained his business to a cop, but the man could not have cared less. "He said he was relieving somebody who had gone to dinner," Kevin says.

They were both shocked to find that Tupper's door was not only unguarded, but open. At this moment began the Tupper family's unhappiness with the way the authorities were handling Jack's murder. Kevin and Tom then noted a group coming out of what they quickly learned was Jacobson's apartment. The group included Melanie, Mary-Beth Abbate, detectives Sullivan and Moreno, both of whom were in plain clothes, and Lieutenant Powers.

Powers told Kevin he did not want the responsibility of Jack's apartment. "Since it wasn't the scene of the crime, he wanted his men off the post," Kevin Tupper says. "The detectives talked back and forth. Abbate was there. Everyone agreed, and the apartment was turned over to me and Melanie Cain."

He and Melanie went into Jack's apartment together. This was their first meeting, and it was not pleasant. Kevin blamed both Melanie and Jack for having stayed under Buddy's roof, but Jack was dead, and Melanie lived. Anger and grief surged within him, and Melanie felt them, in palpable waves. Tom Myers was "really nice to me," she says, but even Myers began with a reproach.

"How could you be so stupid as to stay here?" he asked her.

"Oh, Tom!" Melanie said. "Stop! I'm not about to discuss that with you. . . ."

Tom had two messages. "The family would appreciate it if you don't come to the funeral," he told her. "But it's really up to you. . . ."

"What do you think?" she asked.

Tom gave an honest answer. "If I were you, I'd go," he told her. The second message was that the Tuppers wanted her to get her things out of the apartment that same day. They would be moving Jack's things tomorrow. They didn't want to see her.

Melanie took the news in her stride. She was moving through a world where the light was luminous, the colors very bright, the edges sharp. She was, she knew, looking for something important. Her eye fell upon Jack's briefcase, propped against the butcher-block bar. She looked into it, and realized what had been at the back of her mind. Those telephone conversations: Jack, Buddy, herself, preserved on tape.

She found something else. A couple of cashier's checks, made out to Jack by Brian Monaghan. One was for $9,000 and one was for $5,000; they were the balance on the All-Ireland. Melanie kept the tapes but handed the checks to Kevin and Tom.

Kevin's anger at the DA's office and the cops was growing. Sullivan appeared to be okay—logical, at least—but Abbate seemed to him to be just standing there "like a bump on a log," and there was another detective who was theorizing about what Kevin felt was crystal clear. "I thought I was going crazy," he says. "This guy was talking strange . . . there wasn't a steady flow. He kept going from one thing to another. . . . I was totally unimpressed with the whole situation."

He and Tom collected a stack of Jack Tupper's personal papers and departed. But he now felt a slight sense of foreboding, as if a hot breath were fogging a clear mirror.

It was Mel Harris Silbergeld who presided over the supposedly final dissolution of My Fair Lady. Wilhelmina, Mel's own agent, had promised to interview all the models to see if any suited her agency, so Mel spent much of that day passing on this news by telephone.

George Cain was in the My Fair Lady office downstairs when Martin Pollner, the lawyer, arrived. It was about a quarter to five, and Pollner was with his secretary, Donna Loughlin. Cain, a tall man, was looking rumpled, his gray hair disheveled and his tie still tied but hanging loose from his shirt collar. He closed the door on the mess in the street: the cop cars, the spectators, the swirling journalists, and asked about Pollner's credentials.

These were impressive. Then forty-four, Martin Pollner had grown up in a Jewish household in the Bronx, dispatching cabs as a teenager for his father's small fleet. He had considered journalism, but sensibly chose law. His first important post had been as an aide to Byron "Whizzer" White, the deputy attorney general in the Kennedy administration's Justice Department, who was to end up on the Supreme Court. In 1966, Pollner joined the Wall Street outfit Mudge, Rose,

Guthrie & Alexander, where he was soon on excellent terms with a new partner, Richard Nixon. When Nixon returned to Washington as President, so did Pollner as head of his Advisory Council on Crime and Law Enforcement. Eventually, he joined the war against narcotics.

In 1973, Martin Pollner was interviewed by the *New York Post* under the headline BIG BRASS IN THE WAR ON DRUGS. He had just been nominated to the American seat on a United Nations agency, the eleven-member International Narcotics Control Board. He told the interviewer he would be backing "a computerized program . . . to get at the nation's top drug traffickers." This was the program called TECS. And by this time its pincers were tightening on the Donald Brown Organization—which, as we have seen, nonetheless found ways of discovering what was clicking away within the computer's innards.

Pollner gave George Cain an abbreviated version of this, and Cain pronounced himself satisfied. He told the lawyer that Jacobson was "a dangerous, diabolic person," and said that he was gravely afraid that if Jacobson was released on bail he would injure or even murder Melanie.

That encounter, and what followed, impressed itself on Pollner's mind. The following weekend he described it on tape. "The scene that I would like to convey at this point was that the agency was a rather small room . . . I would say ten by fourteen. . . . It was very hot, because the door was closed, and there was no air conditioning. . . . the telephone was ringing. . . . Cain apparently had no sleep the night before. He was very distraught. . . . He continued to talk . . . glaring, transfixed into the distance, as if he was talking to somebody else. . . ."

After a while, Pollner suggested that he should also talk to Melanie. Her father went upstairs to get her. "And Donna and I sat there, waiting for Melanie to appear. The phone continued to ring, and the room was still unbearably hot. . . . My first impression of Melanie Cain was of a frightened little girl. . . . She was wearing, as I recall, green boots, which were not the type of tight boots, but very loose boots that one would wear in the snow. Which was incongruous to the hot August afternoon.

"She had a pair of baggy pants on . . . a long-sleeved check shirt . . . her hair was dirty-blonde, and long . . . a very thin and bony face, which was as white as snow . . . and she, too, walked in a transfixed manner.

"After our introductions, she sat on a stool, which was by the counter of the front desk . . . turned to the three of us . . . and we began to talk. . . . She told a story that was so bizarre, and . . . so complex that it is difficult for me, right here and now, to describe it all. . . .

"She impressed me greatly in one way. The facts that she recounted to me were so accurate and so specific that it was difficult, if not impossible, for me to believe that she had just gone through the experience that I am about to describe, with no sleep, with a former lover now being under arrest for murder, and a present lover dead. . . . and she sat there and recounted facts, as cool, and as coldly, and as unemotionally, as if I were describing a suit of clothes.

"After a few minutes of listening to her, I did recognize that she was in a state of shock, and asked her to stop . . . that we would adjourn, that perhaps we'd have some dinner, or a drink, and that when she was more . . . comfortable, it would be easier. But she insisted that she tell the story, because she wanted to get it out. She wanted to explain to someone whom she knew would be friendly to her, and she did not want even a glass of water. . . . During the next half hour, she told the story, and during that period, the telephone was ringing, and ringing, and ringing."

Pollner observed that Melanie "recounted these events as calmly as I am right now, but during the time she was talking, there were *twinges* in her face."

In due course, Mary-Beth Abbate came down and Cain began to speak, somewhat loudly, concerning his daughter's well-being. And Pollner realized that relations between Cain and the authorities were none too warm. "It subsequently develops," he observes, "that during the time in the station house, George Cain was naturally upset, and the police and the detectives were annoyed with him. . . . In my opinion, Melanie herself was feeling the wear and tear of his presence."

Pollner and Abbate tried to reassure Cain that Melanie's safety was also a priority of theirs. "Mary-Beth Abbate then told me the evidence they had," Pollner says. "It seemed to both of us to be overwhelming . . . and, of course, Melanie's testimony was extremely significant—putting it all together."

A grand jury would be convened, the assistant DA said. Melanie would probably be called on Friday.

It was now about six, and Heather Bernard was breaking the Jacobson story on NBC on Channel 4. Millie Lewis, the South Carolina modeling school owner, happened to be watching in her hotel room. She realized that her dinner date with Buddy was off.

Melanie at last decided that she needed a break. She crossed the street to Nicola's with her father, Martin Pollner, and Donna Loughlin. She had scarcely eaten for two days but was still unable to, and contented herself with a soda.

The long day was not yet over; in keeping with the Tupper family's wishes, she still had to move her things from Jack's apartment. Melanie had telephoned the Silbergelds and Jimmy Wood, asking for help. Meanwhile, George Cain had rented a van, arranged for Melanie to stay with family friends, and, pacified at last, left for home in Virginia. A couple of journalists now appeared in Nicola's: a female, laden with cameras, and a spry, wrinkled male with a boyish, silvery crewcut whose name was George Carpozi, Jr. They were from the *New York Post*.

Pollner told them that now was not the time. "Perhaps tomorrow," he said.

This was naive. When the group returned to the apartment house, the duo was waiting outside, and the photographer clicked away like a cricket. The encounter was more momentous than anybody then guessed: this was Carpozi's first scent of a story which he was to pursue with singular inventiveness.

Martin Pollner and Donna departed, but the Silbergelds, together with Jimmy Wood and one of his employees, helped Melanie get her things together. On an impulse, knowing Buddy's artful ways, she also went down into the My Fair Lady office and took various files giving the details of money she had earned but had not, as yet, been paid.

The five loaded until dark and drove off. She had finally left 155 East 84th Street. But she was nowhere near to leaving Buddy's World.

That same evening a council took place in the house of the Zubers, whose daughter had been engaged to Jerry Tupper. All the Tuppers were there, as were Ellen and John Gannon, and young Paul. Kevin, who had the papers that he and Tom Myers had removed earlier that day, proposed that they rent a truck and remove the rest of Jack's possessions the following day.

The family parted. Later, Paul came into Ellen's bedroom. His father's murderer, he had been told, was an intruder.

"What is it?" she asked.

"I don't know," the boy faltered. It was as if he had some special knowledge, but was afraid of what he was thinking.

"What is it, Paul?" she insisted.

"Do you know Buddy?" Paul asked.

"I know about him," Ellen said cautiously.

Paul finally blurted out his thoughts.

"Buddy's crazy enough so that if he got real mad *he* could kill Daddy!" the boy said.

Ellen gasped inwardly. "I was stunned," she says, "that Paul had put it together. In his own mind, he had decided that the killer wasn't a stranger—it was Buddy. I wrote it down, because it was such a striking statement, and I stuck it on top of the refrigerator."

Because she had not completely cleared her belongings from East 84th Street, Melanie went around early the following morning, before the Tuppers were to arrive. Jimmy Wood was there with a couple of fellows, and David Silbergeld tooled along in his nail-polish-red two-seater Mercedes. He was wearing a short-sleeved army shirt, and altogether looked like a mercenary after a successful coup. They took what remained of Melanie's possessions down to the van.

Melanie kept asking questions aloud.

"Why did he do it?" she would ask. "Why would Buddy do a thing like that?"

"Don't *ask* why," Wood told her.

He spoke nervously. Melanie's demeanor was entirely altered—the brittle calm of yesterday seemed on the point of fissuring like a windshield struck by a rock. "Don't think about it," he urged.

Silbergeld was more confident of Melanie's strength. "She's not going to crack up," he assured Wood. "She's asking logical questions at this point."

A couple of men were hovering around downstairs, and several young women whom Silbergeld recognized. "There was this little redhead from Buddy's agency," he says. "And she's screaming at the top of her lungs: 'I know who it is! I know who it is! *It's the Mafia from New Jersey!*' "

The men, who were journalists, approached Silbergeld as he was about to leave.

"I didn't catch your name," one said.

"I didn't give it," Silbergeld said.

"What comment can you give us?"

"It's a beautiful day," Silbergeld said, and drove home.

Half an hour later, though, the telephone rang.

"Hello," a voice said, "is this Mel Harris?"

Silbergeld recognized the voice as being that of the reporter.

"No," he replied.

"I *know* this is Mel Harris."

"Believe me, I'm not Mel Harris," Silbergeld said.

"I'm from *Time*," said the voice.

"I already have a subscription," Silbergeld said, and rang off. But this was just the beginning of the press coverage. George Carpozi, Jr.'s first article on the case appeared that morning. It occupied page one of the *Post* and much of page two. Buddy was described as living in a "luxurious 7th-floor penthouse," and the "link" was explored between the Tupper killing and "the 'accidental' 17-floor balcony death plunge of model Cheryl Corey." Carpozi also quoted an anonymous person in Saratoga as saying that his daughter had told him My Fair Lady was "nothing but a high-priced call girl operation." This exuberant piece set the tone of much media coverage to come.

The journalists waiting outside had been Bob Zeline of *Time* and Michael Daly, of the *Daily News*. Two of the young women had been Beth McKay and Kelly Lougee, the recent roommates of Cheryl Corey, and the garrulous redhead was somebody new to the agency, Terry McCart, also known as Sandra Lynn Atkinson.

Bob Zeline managed to get into the building, and roamed the corridors awhile. Later, he and Daly talked with the girls across the street in the G&M luncheonette.

Beth and Kelly were about to leave New York and go home. Zeline says they were "nice little Southern girls," but they were "pretty distraught" and, with two deaths as close as Cheryl Corey's and Jack Tupper's, they had reason. They told him what they knew about Buddy, which wasn't much. "He worked real hard," they said. "He was always worried about his real estate deals. And he was always popping into our apartment to fix something at real weird times."

Zeline asked if there was anything odd about My Fair

Lady, meaning the call-girl angle. "They denied it up and down," he said. Indeed, this "angle" soon disappeared from the press, as did the Tupper death's "linkage" with Cheryl Corey's.

Terry McCart impressed the two journalists differently. Zeline decided she was "real blowsy," but she was, in Michael Daly's judgment, the prettiest. "She said she liked Jacobson. She put a lot of sugar in her coffee. That surprised me, her being a model," Daly says. It was obvious that Beth and Kelly were outraged at the things Terry had been saying. They told her to keep quiet, but without effect. "Go fuck yourselves!" she said. "I'll tell people what I want."

But what she wanted to say was circuitous, her accusations insubstantial. One thing struck both journalists. "She told us that Melanie worked the My Fair Lady telephones," Zeline says. "That way, she got all the good bookings for herself." She was resentful. This was odd. McCart had arrived at the agency some time in July. A photographer had found her on the beach, taken some photographs, and recommended that she drop by and see Buddy and Melanie. She was a waiflike creature, and Melanie rather took to her. She showed her how to apply makeup, and took her to dinner. "She was my baby," Melanie says.

"She would listen to everything I said, and she would say, 'Yeah! . . . yeah!' in this thin little voice. I thought she was sweet, but Buddy saw through her right away. 'She's a junkie!' he said."

Buddy's street smarts served him ably. Born in Philadelphia in 1957, Terry McCart was adopted at the age of three. At thirteen she was in a foster home, and at fifteen in an institution.

Her first adult arrest, for trying to get drug prescriptions by fraud, occurred when she was eighteen. She was convicted. In March 1976, she was arrested in East Rutherford, New Jersey, for using forged prescriptions. Again convicted, she was put on two years' probation.

On August 28 of that year, the State of New Jersey recorded her probation had been violated. On October 10, she was arrested in Las Vegas. She was with a man and another girl, and had in her possession stolen credit cards and a stolen checkbook. She had foisted $589.58 worth of bad checks upon Wonder World, Smith's Food King, and Mr. B's Clothing, a store in the Circus-Circus Hotel.

Terry McCart spent five days in the Clark County, Nevada, slammer, and was released on her promise to face trial in due course. Terry, who had been arrested under the name Sandra Lynn Atkinson, later explained her predicament thusly: "At the time, I was running on my own and naive. I feel I was influenced by a bad man."

Terry still had not been tried for the Vegas offense on July 27, 1977, when she was arrested in New York City for disorderly conduct, and pled guilty. Nor had she been tried by the time of the murder of Jack Tupper. This was the young woman whom Buddy Jacobson was to use as a weapon against Melanie.

It was irritating. Dee-Dee Zuber had the combination, but Jack's door wouldn't open. It was now ten in the morning. Melanie had been and gone. Now they heard a telephone ringing in a nearby apartment.

Dorothy walked over and banged on the door. As she knocked, it came to her that this must be Buddy Jacobson's apartment. The door was opened by a slight young man with dark eyes and sallow skin.

"Is Melanie there?" Dorothy asked.

"No," the man said, "she's not here."

"Who are you?"

"I'm Buddy's son," David Jacobson said.

Dorothy reddened, as she still reddens when she thinks of the incident to this day. "I said, 'Oh! You're the one that helped after your father killed my brother?' "

"He said, 'No, that was my brother!' He just came out and said it: *'That was my brother.'* So then I came out with a very stupid comment, threatening! I told him to give that message to his father from me.

"He said, did I care to tell that to the DA? I said, 'No, just tell your father.' And he said again, 'Well, it wasn't me. It was my brother.'

"And that was the end of it. We went back to Jack's apartment and tried again. And this time we *did* get in, and started packing Jackie's things. . . ."

Besides the cardboard crates that Jack had never bothered to unpack, there was Paul's bunk bed, Jack's own bed, which was king-sized, a brown sectional sofa, a giant fish tank, and all manner of odds and ends. Kevin now came with Tom

Myers. Myers, who had formerly been with the New York office, brought along four friends, all off-duty FBI agents. They set to work. But the elevator was tiny. It was going to be a long day.

No more was seen by the Tuppers of David Jacobson. Indeed, the seventh floor seemed to have been abandoned and remained so, creepily, the whole day. Jack Tupper's apartment, on the other hand, was to become quite crowded. During the trial, Jack Evseroff, Buddy's lawyer, was to characterize the goings on as a "convention."

John and Ellen Gannon soon arrived, bringing with them young Paul. The sight of Paul was a special agony. He was standing there, wearing his father's sweatband and watch, and he looked on, wide-eyed, as the closets were emptied. "He was saying, 'Do you see that cup? My father and I used that cup,' " Kathy says. "Everything was a memory to him."

Some ill-feeling had always existed between the Tuppers and Ellen Gannon. It now began to smolder fiercely with the Tuppers resenting Ellen Gannon's refusal to help. "Nothing could be more frustrating," Kathy says, "than to be trying to carry chairs downstairs, and Ellen is just standing there—"

"Looking around, while we were hard at work," Dorothy adds.

"Drinking Amaretto," Kathy says. "A whole coffee cup of Amaretto."

It wasn't so much the Amaretto, though, as the direction of the conversation. Ellen was talking about Jack's money and his insurance policies.

Ellen, who knew that Jack had received money and checks from Brian but not that the family had them, does not deny that she was anxious to see Jack's business affairs settled. She also felt that the entire move was overhasty, and foolish. "I'd be running around with a pillow," she says, "thinking 'What am I doing here?' "

Kevin, meanwhile, would be saying, "Do you want to take Paul's bed? Do you want Paul's encyclopedias?" And Ellen would be thinking: "It all belongs to Paul, all of it." The clouds darkened further above this unhappy family.

The atmosphere did not improve after lunch, when Brian Monaghan arrived with Jimmy Leonard. They, too, appeared to be looking for something. "I heard them say to Ellen that Jack was worth three hundred thousand dollars," Kevin says. "I almost fell off the balcony."

The moving continued, but the search intensified. Jack's laundry bag, his preferred hiding place, as both Ellen and Brian knew, was empty. The refrigerator was torn from the wall. Every nook was checked. Tom Myers eyed Monaghan and Leonard with growing suspicion.

Not only was no money found in Jack's apartment, but Ellen discovered a sad irony as she searched through the former insurance man's papers. "I found the newspaper reprints he used for his spiel," she says. "FATHER OF THREE TRAGICALLY KILLED! That kind of thing. But he hadn't a dime in policies when he died." So the day passed.

Sharon Churcher, who had shared a by-line on the story with George Carpozi, Jr., in that Tuesday's *New York Post*, was also assigned to follow up the story. She visited 84th Street with a photographer, and saw some men moving crates and furniture into a U-Haul truck. They looked nothing like workmen—most being in business suits.

Nobody was telling her anything, so she entered and rode up to the seventh floor. Yes, it was Jack Tupper's apartment that was being cleared. She approached a couple of women, who ignored her; a young man was so distressed by Churcher's questions that he walked up and heatedly warned her off, saying that the men doing the moving were with the FBI.

This did nothing to dampen her curiosity, and the indignation of the young man, who was, of course, Kevin suddenly turned to a sort of despair. "For some reason, he had a change of heart," Churcher says. "He took me aside and thrust a telegram into my hand." The telegram was smooth, as if taken from a file. It was addressed to "Dear Melon,"— Buddy's pet name for Melanie, and dated July 29. It ran as follows:

SORRY FOR THE PAST WEEK AND FOR THE ABUSE I MUST HAVE PUT YOU THROUGH FOR THE PAST 5 YEARS. YOU ALWAYS HURT THE ONE YOU LOVE. JACK IS A GOOD GUY AND WILL LOVE YOU AND BE HONEST WITH YOU. YOU'RE RIGHT, I WOULD ALWAYS BE A BUM. BELIEVE ME WHEN I TELL YOU THAT I HAD NO IDEA, IN SPITE OF ALL THE HINTS YOU GAVE ME, THAT WE WOULD EVER PART, BUT IT IS BEST. EXCUSE ME IF I SLIP AND THINK OF OLD TIMES ONCE IN A WHILE, BUT IF I DIDN'T CARE, WOULD I FEEL THIS WAY? SOUNDS LIKE A SONG.

A scoop. The Tupper group piled the last of Jack's belongings into the U-Haul and left in the early evening.

Sidney Sparrow's tenure as Buddy's lawyer ceased next day. He had been about to leave and see his client in the Riker's Island jail. "The harpies had been to work," he told me. Actually, Frank Pagano and Bill Levin had been gloomily discussing the forthcoming trial with the Jacobs clan, and had recommended the short, bald, and ebullient sports world lawyer Irwin "Win" Klein.

It was Klein who had represented Buddy in the matter of the discothèques, and was still unpaid. Nevertheless, he decided, after a conversation with Gene Jacobs, to accept the case. He went to Riker's Island and conferred with Buddy, who agreed to a $25,000 retainer and gave him a $5,000 check. "It bounced all over the lot," Win says. He took the tempting case, all the same.

It was now that a police sergeant, the acting division chief of the Narcotics Division's strike force, sent a memorandum to his superior, concerning the continuing investigation of the Airport Gang.

"It has come to the attention of the undersigned that several subjects of said investigation are personal friends of Police Officer Claire Normandeau," he wrote. The Internal Affairs Division began its investigation that some day. Subject: allegation of corruption.

Such complications were still unguessed-at by Bronx DA's office, and, at half past three that afternoon, detectives Bill Sullivan, who was in charge of the investigation, and Charlie Moreno arrived in Joan Jacobson's driveway. Buddy's former wife now lived in Hampton Bays, and the cops were at last picking up her son Douglas. Joan Jacobson told them that they had been expected, and said she would follow them into New York in her own car.

Douglas sat in the back seat of the police car, and as they drove in Sullivan told him that his father had been arrested. He asked Douglas how long he had been living in East 84th Street. "About two weeks," the youth said.

"Did you tell your mother about the murder?" Sullivan asked.

"I told my mother everything," Douglas said.

"Do you want to tell me about the murder?"

"No," Douglas said. "I want to talk to my attorney."

They waited in the office at Eighth Homicide until Win Klein arrived. He talked with Douglas but said he couldn't represent him: conflict of interest. Klein recommended another lawyer, who duly arrived, and on his advice, neither Douglas nor his mother would answer questions concerning the case. Both were served with subpoenas, instructing them that they would be called upon to testify before a grand jury.

Jack Tupper's funeral was planned for Thursday, August 10. Kevin called Melanie in Martin Pollner's office, asking that she not attend, and, miserably, she agreed. "I was trying to be as diplomatic as possible," Kevin says. "The press, that's all they wanted. They would love to have a TV camera there, and my mother would have a scene with her."

The wake was on Wednesday. Most of Jack's friends were present, Jimmy Leonard, Brian, Ivor Shaw. But there was an ominous quality to the gathering, a sense that the dead man was not to be allowed to rest in peace. "That's the tormenting part about it," Dorothy Tupper says. "When Jerry died he was like a hero. People poured into the funeral. You know, the church was packed.

"When Jackie died, there was just a picture, because the casket couldn't be opened. Here's our brother, whom we loved very much, and I see people whispering in corners. I mean, you didn't know who to trust. It wasn't fair. Jackie had a lot of love in him, and really cared about people. This wasn't something he deserved." Nor would her despondency have been less had she known that both the funeral and wake were under photographic surveillance by the DEA.

It was on this same day that Rudy Dehesa, the man arrested earlier by Claire Normandeau, was sentenced to four years for trafficking in cocaine. But he served no time. In exchange for his liberty and that of his German wife, Edith, Dehesa began to give evidence against his former associates, and the Feds had their first major break in their pursuit of the Airport Gang.

On Friday morning, Melanie was to testify in front of the grand jury. She set off for the Bronx courthouse on the Grand Concourse with Martin Pollner in a black Cadillac. Pollner warned Melanie that they might expect something of a "cir-cuslike atmosphere with the media," but even he was startled by the several dozen photographers, reporters, and TV camera-men in front of the courthouse. Eventually Mary-Beth Abbate guided them to a side entrance, but Melanie was badly shaken.

The interior of the building was a poor sanctuary. The grand jury convenes on the fourth floor, and this floor, Poll-ner observes, "suddenly became alive with clerks, secretaries, and police—all trying to see Melanie Cain." She was put in a small office, with a couple of detectives at the door, and given a cup of coffee. Though she regained her composure, some-thing was becoming plain: Melanie was in the public domain.

Mary-Beth Abbate took Pollner aside, then asked Melanie about the rumors that Jack was involved with cocaine, that My Fair Lady was a front for a call-girl operation. Melanie said that neither tale was true, and volunteered to take a lie-detector test. Detective Sullivan also spoke to Pollner. He said he felt that the information was "bullshit." Melanie went in front of the grand jury at eleven, and she testified for two hours.

Martin Pollner, meantime, had a fine escape exit worked out, but the DA's office urged him to reconsider. The report-ers and cameramen had been waiting for hours, and the DA's office needed their goodwill. Pollner relented, knowing that he and Melanie, in turn, needed the goodwill of the DA's office. So they faced the cameras, then drove back to Manhattan. Melanie was left off at East 75th Street, where she was staying with Mel and David Silbergeld.

At four that afternoon, Pollner was called by John Powers, the lieutenant heading Eighth Homicide. He wanted to talk to Melanie. The lawyer, angered by the chronic press leaks, wouldn't give out her number, but asked Melanie to call him. Minutes later, Melanie telephoned Pollner, puzzled: Powers had been telling her that David Silbergeld had some sort of problem concerning guns. She had not told Powers where she was staying.

Pollner thereupon decided he had to tell Powers, who "got extremely upset, and said there was a major security problem." He wanted to see Melanie right away. She took a cab all the way back to the Bronx and sat in Powers' office while Powers called Pollner to say "there was no way in the world she could go back to that apartment."

Donna Loughlin, the lawyer's secretary, a slim attractive young woman, agreed to take Melanie in. Powers drove Melanie back to East 75th Street, where they picked up some of her things, and David Silbergeld grew understandably indignant—"Melanie was looking at me as if I was somebody *weird*"—and then they drove on to Donna's apartment.

Melanie enjoyed ten hours of sleep that Friday night. Waking refreshed, she felt that a measure of tranquility had returned to her life.

On Saturday they gorged on pizza and went to a movie; and Melanie, for the first time since the murder, turned to her journal:

> I want to express in writing now my feelings and emotions about these past horrible exhausting days. And yet I so want to cry for Jack . . . Nothing matters in life, Jack, you always said, but that you live each day and hour like it was your last. Because you never know when fate chooses you.

She wrote only one page, and stopped.

On Sunday evening, between seven and eight, Gail Moore, the brown-haired model from the fifth floor, went into Joe Margarite's apartment, 7F. She knew the combination; until about a year before, she had helped make ends meet by cleaning the place up. But she hadn't seen him for about three months. She hadn't even seen her boyfriend, Joe's buddy Breck Dana Anderson, who had been out of town for weeks. Now she wanted to retrieve some cooking things she had lent.

The TV set was on. A coffee cup was knocked over, on the rug. Another cup was encrusted with mildew. Gail noted the signs of hasty departure without too much surprise. Joe Margarite was not a man who led a very orderly life.

The following day, Rudy Dehesa was let out of jail and set about his work of betrayal.

While Buddy had been in the holding cell at Eighth Homicide, Melanie had been afire, and he had seemed a defeated man, a mechanism with a broken mainspring. The facts were so blatant, the account of the crime so irrefutable. Here were truths that could not be smoothed away. But this, of course, was to underestimate Buddy's talents.

Already, the previous Friday, he had given an interview to Channel 7, which had been as sweet as sugar and directed at Melanie. She was a wonderful person, Buddy said. He loved her. She had the inside information that would make him a free man. Channel 7 newsmen were enthusiastic and telephoned Pollner over the weekend, saying that Buddy wanted to meet with Melanie. The lawyer said no. The TV people said Buddy knew that Melanie was staying with the Silbergelds, and that Buddy had given them the Virginia telephone number for Melanie's parents. They also said (because Buddy had likewise given them this information) that he was being moved from Riker's Island to the Bronx House of Detention because there was "a contract on his life."

A few days after the murder, Brian Monaghan searched the All-Ireland, soon to become Chequers, very thoroughly, and found a letter from Natty, Jack's Peruvian girlfriend. It had been opened, and was grubby with much reading.

He sent it back to her. It was the least he could do, he felt.

Buddy's first attempt to get out on bail came some ten days after the murder. But the Bronx district attorney's office claimed his life would be in danger if he walked the streets. This news, the authorities said, came from a "reliable informant." The conduit seems to have been the DEA.

Buddy insisted, much against the advice of Win Klein, on making a personal appeal to the court. It was a tangled recitative, dwelling on the precarious state of his property empire: If he wasn't allowed to tend it, he would be ruined.

The judge denied him bail anyway. This was only the first of several bail hearings in front of several different Bronx judges. Often, Buddy insisted on making long attempts at self-vindication, concluding with a tirade in which he complained that he had asked for a paraffin test within an hour of being captured, but had been refused. This was not brilliant. Paraffin tests are administered to determine whether someone has fired a gun. One hour after Buddy's arrest, not even the cops knew Jack Tupper had been shot.

It was at the conclusion of this particular hearing that Win Klein put in a sanity plea. "Buddy didn't want a sanity hearing, but I asked for it anyway," Klein told me. He did not yet know it, but he was well on the way to becoming Jacobson's next ex-lawyer.

Remarkably, even in jail, Buddy continued to take care of business. On August 21, he sold the Park East to the Argentinian group that had previously approached him for $1.7 million, a profit of $800,000.

The police investigation, meanwhile, continued on its stolid way. On the morning of August 23, Leslie Hammond, the blond stockbroker, telephoned Bill Sullivan. She told him that the week before she had found a bullet on the counter near her kitchen sink. Sullivan and Charley Moreno collected the bullet, and noted a bullet hole in the kitchen wall. This is the wall that separates the Hammond and Jacobson apartments. The tenants had always complained about the flimsy construction of Buddy's walls.

Steve Dunleavy, the brash, genial metropolitan editor of the *Post*, got the first post-murder interview with Buddy, and, he remarks, "it was a bit of luck." Dunleavy, an Australian like his publisher, Rupert Murdoch, is a pro, with a penchant for the full-blooded. He was telephoned by a man with whom he had sometimes enjoyed a few in a South Street tavern, who was now in the slammer on a murder rap. The message said that Buddy was willing to be interviewed. This was just before Buddy left Riker's Island and, unfortunately, just after the start of a lengthy newspaper strike. Dunleavy, an optimist, went to see Buddy anyway, now in the Bronx House of Detention.

Dunleavy was shocked. "This was the jet-setting wheeler-dealer Buddy Jacobson?" he says. Buddy's appearance was woeful, his T-shirt ragged, his chin unshaven, his hair cropped to the scalp. (Few were aware that Buddy himself had asked for the drastic haircut, presumably to create confusion in the event of a lineup.)

His conversation was murky. Yes, he had once been in love with Melanie, and she had the information that could free him. He even proffered a suspect: David Silbergeld. "Tupper owed him money. That is where Melanie is right now—at Silbergeld's apartment. You check out that guy for me, and the whole story will come into place."

Steve Dunleavy questioned Buddy closely for an hour and a half, then left, unsatisfied.

David Jacobson now began to call Dunleavy, often at home: had Steve come up with anything that might help his father? "As politely as I could, I informed him I was not a private detective agency," Dunleavy says.

Dunleavy did set up another visit, but Buddy rambled on about rifled files and bounced checks, Silbergeld still being his target; and that was that.

It was now that I interviewed Buddy Jacobson, with an assignment from *New York* magazine. The interview took place in a small cell on the ground floor of the Bronx House of Detention. It was noon, August 23, and Buddy was in better shape. True, his skin had acquired that greenish pallor which is the coloration of Caucasians in metropolitan prisons, but the gruesome stubble on his skull was turning into hair. He greeted me with an odd, ironic smile; his dark eyes were alert. We sat. The cell had pinkish tiling and canary-yellow bars. He was quick to make an offer. I was not the first to hear it, nor would I be the last. "I am willing to cooperate with any reporter who really goes all out," he said.

What would this involve? Simple. "You get Melanie," he said. "I just want you to bring Melanie . . . to the district attorney! Whatever! So long as she and I talk on a tape recorder, so that I can use it . . . I don't want a lawyer sitting next to her . . . I want to talk out in the open. . . ."

His obsession was self-evident: *Melanie* would save him. "My interpretation of her character," he said, "is that she's a very honest person. . . . I think she always tells the truth. If I sat with her right now, and I said, 'Melanie, what about this? What happened on this day?' I think she would answer exactly what happened. If I asked her ten questions, I would walk out of here the next day."

He went on to say that Melanie was "extremely naive." But she was an "honorable girl—not a bouncing-around kind of a girl." Melanie had the evidence that could help him, Buddy said, but she didn't know she had it.

But he was thrown off balance when I told him I was to interview Melanie, and suggested that I put some of his "ten questions" to her. He muttered that I should ask Melanie if he had ever threatened her, I should ask about her hypoglycemia, and, most important, I should ask what it was Jack Tupper actually *did* for a living.

His questions bristled with dark hints of "revelations" to

come. Yes, he agreed, he had offered Jack Tupper $100,000 to stop seeing Melanie. She was "a nice, a really nice sweet girl," he said, with some sanctimony, "and she didn't belong in what she was getting into. . . .

"And that's what my discussions were with him . . . that we really do a nice thing—we *both* do a nice thing—we both leave this girl alone. That I'll work something out with him. And it's worth $100,000."

What did Jack say? "At one point he said no," Buddy conceded. "We had many conversations on this. . . ."

Buddy talked of his time behind bars with a degree of stoicism. "They use different sayings here in prison," he said. "One of them is 'Hang it up!' "

What does "Hang it up" mean?

"Hanging yourself," Buddy explained. "That's what it means. The prisoners talk about it all the time. Not me. They can keep me here till hell freezes over, but there's no way in the world that I'm going to give up fighting this thing."

How was he sleeping? Did he have nightmares?

Buddy, brusquely: "No. I've never had a nightmare in my life."

He paused one reluctant moment, and added, "I would say, when I wake up, my first thought is—Is this a dream?

"And then I get a feeling inside of me when I realize it's reality."

His thoughts reverted to Melanie.

"The thing I want to say to you," he told me, "is that you could do me a favor. Get the point across to Melanie: How will you face yourself if you do find that this guy at no time was doing anything but looking out for you? That he is not responsible for the crime that he is being charged with? Even if he was a *stranger* to you . . . if you saw someone hit by a car, a *dog* hit by a car, you wouldn't turn and walk away.

"Tell Melanie: 'He's not asking you to lie. But why not, for your own peace of mind, why don't you go *talk* to him?' " So he rambled on, in rococo squirls of innuendo, until I noticed a sheaf of papers sticking out of his pocket, covered with Buddy's distinctive scrawl, and asked what it was. "A letter to Melanie," he said.

A letter, I asked? Win Klein arrived as Buddy was explaining.

"The one thing I don't want is to make money on this

thing," he said. "I guarantee not a dime would come to me, whether it's to go to Melanie or . . . the Cancer Fund." He gave a dry rattle of a laugh, and went on. "If I can sell a series of letters and be able to do something nice with the money, I don't know what's wrong with that. Tell me?"

There was an uncomfortable pause. "You're writing to who?" Klein asked, carefully.

"Melanie," Buddy said, briefly.

"I don't know if it's right, Buddy."

"Well," Buddy said, without inflection, "I'm doing it anyway."

At a quarter to two on August 28, two agents from the DEA task force conferred with Bill Sullivan in his office at Eighth Homicide. This meeting took place because the cops had found that the names of both Buddy and Jack Tupper were on the DEA computer. Were there any arrests or indictments on the way? asked Sullivan.

"No," the agents said.

This was accurate, but not for long.

Even from within a cell, Buddy tirelessly reached out for Melanie. He had at the beginning tried to work through his son David. This tactic was impeded by Martin Pollner, who sent a letter to Bill Quinn, the assistant DA who had taken over from Mary-Beth Abbate, warning that David had been "attempting to locate Miss Cain, calling her friends and business associates."

Resourcefully, Buddy next tried to contact Melanie's parents. When they wouldn't speak to him on the telephone, he sent a letter. It starts, "Dear Mr. and Mrs. Cain," and covers two and a third pages of a yellow legal pad.

His words are at once ingratiating and ominous. "There are no comments made by me that could be detrimental to her," he says of Melanie, "but factual stories . . . may implicate her in other things. At this time, you must think I am nuts. My credibility is zero, but the big story has yet to come out. . . .

"How will you and Melanie feel when you find I did nothing wrong?" Buddy asked. "New York can be a big bad city. I left Melanie alone for the last few months while the building was being built. This was a terrible mistake. It appears that she still does not know what was to happen to her."

He made a semipromise. "If I get out, there will be no attempt to contact Melanie, but situations may develop that would make it necessary for her to call me. I am still her only real friend in New York," he went on, adding incongruously, "Being in jail is a great experience. You learn to appreciate the small unimportant things in life."

The Cains gave the letter to Martin Pollner, who sent it on to Bill Sullivan.

Melanie, who was not shown the letter, was still in a glassy state of shock. Her next entry in her journal takes the form of a prayer:

> Dear God,
>   If you do really exist—then help now to do justice. Please take away a very bad person's life—Buddy's.

With anguish, she asked one of the oldest questions in theology:

> Why do you give Buddy life? And then take away such a good person's life—Jack's?

She was back with Mel and David Silbergeld. Martin Pollner had decided the charges that David was trafficking in mines and machine guns were cloudy, unproven, and owed much of their circulation to Buddy Jacobson. Melanie had joined the Wilhelmina agency, but found it harder to resume work than she had, at first, supposed. The Polykoff agency had waited a couple of weeks, then had used another girl.

There was also the matter of the Clairol commercial. Their executives had read the stories in the papers, and blanched at the talk of call girls and cocaine. "There was real fear of the gossip columns," observed somebody on the campaign. "You know, 'Murderess Stars in Commercial.'"

"I got a letter saying they weren't going to continue with the footage about three weeks after the murder," Melanie says. "It was a very formal letter. They didn't say why."

That September Bill Quinn was replaced by Peter Grishman, a slight, mildly portly assistant district attorney with dark, thinning hair, who would be in charge of the investigation, and Bill Kelly, who would try the case in court.

The "war room" out of which the investigation worked was set up in Grishman's office on the fourth floor of 215 East 161st Street. An oblong room with a dirty gray carpet, it was bisected by a long table, in fact, two tables end to end, around which stood more than a dozen orange-upholstered chairs. Pinned to the walls were relevant materials, such as photographs and a large map showing the scenes of the crime, with notations referring to soil and blood samples, together with sheets of white paper listing the material evidence (spent bullets, burned underclothes, etc.), plus the names of the officers who attested to the evidence.

Grishman's first job had been to sift through the separate reports of the forty cops who had, at one time or other, worked on the case. He, Kelly, and Sullivan continued to interview witnesses, sometimes directing them to look through a large book of photographs of persons who might be connected with the crime. Ivor Shaw, for instance, who visited the office in a tailored blazer and an Allen Solly shirt, was nonplussed by the close interest of the authorities in Donald Brown, Al Seifert, and Carlo Carrara. "I've no great interest in being subpoenaed," he told me dolefully. "I want nothing more to do with the demimonde." He spoke longingly of foreign parts. "I'm cutting off my telephone number next week," he said. "As far as anybody is concerned, I've gone abroad."

Jimmy Wood was even more mutinous. He had flipped the book open, and there his own face stared up at him. "I was going to help," he said. "But then I realize they're treating me as a suspect."

The prosecution had its disappointments. Noel Bernstein was unable to identify the "swarthy" men he had seen on Buddy's balcony that Thursday evening before the murder. The woman in the apartment building opposite who usually kept the goings-on in Buddy's apartment under close, censorious scrutiny had, on that wet Sunday, been persuaded by her husband to go with him to the movies.

There was a greater annoyance. Joe Margarite was still at large. On September 14 he had checked himself into Bellevue, using his own name and his wife's Blue Cross. An appendectomy was performed, and he checked out four days later. By the time the cops learned he had been there, he was long gone. Peter Grishman could not help but be impressed. Despite Margarite's name on both the DEA and the NYPD computers, in terms of solid data—fingerprints, credit cards, and so forth—he was, as Grishman put it, "a ghost."

Buddy's efforts to get out on bail continued. He had a new lawyer, Otto Fusco, given to wearing patent-leather shoes and a flower in his lapel. He was not highly touted as a trial lawyer, but his political savvy in the Bronx was famous. "Don't worry about it," he told Buddy in the corridor, "the boys down in the Appellate Division will see things the right way. I *know* those guys."

In September, Fusco argued in front of Justice Louis Cioffi of the state supreme court, this being Buddy's seventh try and Cioffi the third judge. "There are various people I have in this file, not one . . . not two . . . who had a motive to kill the deceased," Fusco said, somberly, revealing that the number of persons with cause to frame Buddy was, in fact, five. He did not name them.

"I cannot deny this man bail," Cioffi told the courtroom, which included the glumly impassive Bronx district attorney, Mario Merola. Bail was set at $200,000. Buddy insisted he was low in funds, and Fusco successfully sought to have the bail cut in half. The $100,000 was paid by cashier's check, and Buddy walked out of jail, unshaven and disheveled, but exultant. It was October 17. The DA's office was enraged. "We feel one of two things can happen," Mario Merola predicted. "He can flee the jurisdiction, or someone out there has a number on him, and he'll get it."

Buddy, who had laughed off this "contract" while in the slammer, now found it a convenient scenario. "I don't dare go back to my place because I know that they're after me," he told George Carpozi, Jr. "They want to kill me."

He was in danger, he added, because of Jack Tupper. "There were other people who had far more compelling reasons to kill him," he said, moving into full gear. "He was a front for the Mob. The restaurants Tupper owned were used to launder underworld money. He was a heavy cocaine trafficker. He was mixed up in many rackets. His number was up. They killed him, and made me the fall guy."

The circus was about to start. "All I want is to find Melanie," he told Carpozi. "She's the only person besides those who killed Tupper who knows what happened. I'm going to start looking for her first thing in the morning."

* * *

The detective finally came out with it. "What is it you're hiding?" he asked Melanie.

What was it she was hiding? Melanie simply had to laugh. This was Buddy's line. Melanie's hiding something! She's leaving something out! You've only heard eighty percent of the truth!

It was just as Buddy had always told her: Repeat something often enough, and people will start believing it.

"It's just a bunch of bullshit," she told the cop. "He wants to know my testimony. So he can cover up."

"Yeah?" the cop said, skeptically.

Melanie was growing increasingly irritated by the police.

"They really don't know what they're dealing with," she told me that winter. "They're treating this murder as if it's just another street crime.

"When Buddy got out of jail, I said, 'You *know* he's going to call me. I think I should have a tape recorder here, so I can tape him.'"

She mimed a bovine cop.

"What? What? He wouldn't call *you*. That would be dumb of him. He would go back to jail."

"I told them, 'You don't understand. Buddy has no shame. Buddy has no embarrassment. Buddy doesn't listen to anybody. He won't listen to his lawyer. Anybody! Buddy will get into contact with me, because I am his only hope.

" 'He will, because I am the one he has manipulated and, he thought, brainwashed for so many years. He will. He will definitely call me. There's no doubt in my mind!' "

Buddy now moved back into the 84th Street building. Little more would be heard of the threat to his life. Rose Marie Taylor of Model's Mart, who called a couple days later to ask about that still unpaid $1437.75 bill for the model books and tote bags, was astonished to hear Buddy's voice.

"Hi, Rose Marie," Buddy said. He sounded as if he didn't have a care in the world.

He was back in business right away, selling off the two movie houses—that dream was over—and launching a brand-new agency, Polly Modeling, named after a young woman from Queens who had flown with TWA. Soon he had a new batch of models going on go-sees and was making plans to pull off the sort of coup that John Casablancas had done, but in a reverse direction: he was going to buy a *Paris* agency.

The news would reach Melanie in ripples of gossip. "Some agency in Paris was supposedly going under," she says, "and Buddy was going to buy it. He could hardly raise the bail money, and now he's going to buy an *agency*."

Melanie continued to worry. "Buddy can sidetrack anybody," she says. "His attitude is that everyone else is stupid, and he's the smartest person in the world. He'll mix half-truths with truths. He was definitely feeling he still had a power over me." On October 24, Otto Fusco was served with papers informing him that at nine-thirty on the morning of November 2 a motion would be heard in the Bronx courtroom directing that Buddy should have "no direct or indirect contact with Melanie Cain." But Melanie awaited his first, inevitable approach.

This came by way of her former "baby," Terry McCart. Buddy, who had formerly dismissed the redhead as a junkie, was now cultivating her. He gave her a job answering phones, and talked incessantly of his innocence. He even took her to the dump site in the Bronx, swearing it was his first visit.

McCart left a message for Melanie at Wilhelmina. When Melanie returned the call, Terry McCart asked for a meeting. Melanie, who had not been pleased at the remarks attributed to McCart in the press, was nonetheless eager to remove another fledgling from Buddy's influence, and agreed to lunch that very day at a restaurant on Lexington Avenue and 34th Street. This was Tuesday, October 30.

Terry McCart had a simple but important task: to persuade Melanie to meet Buddy. He had drilled her rigorously that morning for two hours, "What to do if Melanie responded that she wouldn't meet him," McCart was to tell Peter Grishman. "How to almost make sure that she *would*."

There were also specific questions: "He wanted to know . . . why was Melanie so positive that he was the murderer. . . . He wanted to know where Melanie was living. . . . He wanted to know her time schedule the morning of the murder."

Buddy paid Terry, handing her $1,000 in $50 bills, and she took herself downtown.

At the table Melanie leafed through Terry's model book, but it was soon obvious that this was not the purpose of the meeting. She had been on her guard, because the Silbergelds had been violently opposed to her coming. "No way!" David had told her. "Don't meet this girl!"

"Why?" she had asked. Replied David, "Suppose somebody just scoops you into a car? You disappear, and who'll be the wiser? They'll just think you ran. And you won't be the witness for *anything*." Melanie had dismissed this as a fantasy, but was wary.

"Are you still dancing?" Terry asked her. "Are you still dancing in the same place?"

There was no reason why McCart should know that Melanie had been taking dancing classes at all, let alone the location: suspicion blossomed into certainty.

"Have you been talking to Buddy?" Melanie asked.

Falteringly, McCart said she had. Melanie now wanted to know if she was wearing a tape recorder. McCart said no—Buddy had wanted to wire her, but she hadn't dared. She even told Melanie about the $1,000. They talked and talked. Her meeting with Terry McCart lasted for hours, but of what they talked she could later scarcely remember a thing.

Finally, Terry telephoned Buddy. She had, she said, no success to report. Melanie, listening on an extension, heard Buddy, impassive as ever, say, "Keep her as your friend, keep her as your friend," before hanging up.

The following morning, McCart went to see Buddy who asked where Melanie was living. "Melanie told me she's living with a girlfriend," McCart said.

The uses of Terry McCart were not exhausted. Buddy urged that she enroll in the same dance class as Melanie, and promised to pay her fees. Subsequently, she explained to Peter Grishman that Buddy had wanted her "to become better friends with Melanie, and gain her trust."

This was just one strategy. Jacobson's next assault was more frontal. On the morning of November 2, the Silbergelds' telephone rang. Melanie picked up the receiver. It was Buddy, and he affected to be surprised, saying he had wanted to speak to David.

"He was very clever," Melanie says. "He knew he was being taped. For five years, I had spoken with him every day. No matter where I was, where I was traveling. Now for three months I had not spoken to this man. But once I started talking to him—it all started again. He *drains* me so." She remained glued to the telephone all the same. "I didn't mean to call you about the case," Buddy said, paused a fraction and added, ". . . babe."

"Don't *babe* me!" Melanie snapped. "*You* know what happened, and *I* know what happened! I will never—"

"Don't talk—"

"I will never—"

"Listen!" Buddy said. "I would *never* take part in hurting anybody."

"I will *die* before I change my feelings. I *know* what happened," Melanie said, her voice blurry with tears.

"I don't want you to change your story," Buddy said. "I'm searching for more information, that's true, but—"

"If you're so sure that you're right," Melanie interrupted, "you can wait till we get to court."

"There's a problem with that," Buddy said. By then it would be too late for him to do his "investigating."

"It's really pathetic that a human being like you is in this position," Melanie said. "Because I wouldn't want to wish this on *anybody*."

"I feel the same way—"

"I would be the first person, I would be the *first person* to want to clear you."

"I don't believe that," hissed Buddy.

"Oh yes, I would. Oh yes, I would," Melanie was talking at a breathless rate, through her tears. "But I know the truth! And I know you did it."

"I—"

"I know you killed Jack! *Yes!*"

"I didn't—"

"You will even justify in your own head that you didn't do it," Melanie said, adding that Buddy had no reason to talk to anybody, except to bribe them for information.

"I'll do anything to find out about the case," Buddy said. "But bribe? No!"

"Buddy, don't insult my intelligence any longer."

"I'm not—"

"Oh, yes you are. You've done it for five years. So don't insult my intelligence."

Smoothly, Buddy glided into a different track. "How do you feel?" he asked solicitously.

"How do you *think* I feel?" Melanie cried.

"Do you think you feel any worse than me?" Buddy asked.

"*Yes,*" she replied, gulping the word out. "*Yes.* I think I do."

Buddy hinted that Melanie was being manipulated by the police. "Even they can't put words in my mouth," she said, enraged. "I know what I saw that day."

"I'm not implying you're not telling the truth. I don't know *what* you are saying."

"You want to know because you want to talk your way around it. For five years, Buddy, that's the way you talked to everyone. If something was white, you'd tell them it was black. You'd try to get your way. I *know!*"

Buddy was self-righteously indignant. "Oh, I'd love to ask you a whole bunch of things," he said. "Do you know that eighty percent of this story is far from—"

"Listen to me!" she shrieked.

"Where—"

"You listen to me!"

"I'll listen to you," Buddy said, with resignation.

"I'll tell you something you used to say: 'Melanie, you know how to convince people you're telling the truth when you're really telling lies. Start believing that lie yourself.'"

"I'll say for the rest of my life I am innocent," Buddy protested.

"But you did it!" Melanie finished, her voice shrill.

So it went on. When Melanie became feisty, Buddy would be subdued, lulling, confidential. When he had her weepy he would take hold. And, when Melanie seemed to have weakened, perhaps terminally, he struck with a question.

"Did you see anybody else around the floor that day?" he asked. His inflection was altogether casual.

"I don't think I should really tell you," Melanie said, "and I'm not going to tell you."

"I think you should tell me. But I'm sure the district attorney wouldn't want you to tell me."

"I only do what I want to do, Buddy," Melanie said, "I don't want you to know what I know, because you will completely twist the whole story around. And you will try to cover up for the times I said I saw you."

"Will you stop insinuating that I want to twist or change what you say," Buddy said, patiently, "I only want to know a *time* . . . because there are some very big important gaps in this thing. With what there is now, I'm not going to be convicted. I mean, you don't have—"

It was too much. Melanie burst into peals of merriment. "You think so, Buddy? Okay." She said, at length, "all right."

"Isn't it funny?" Buddy groused.

"Wait till we get to court! Okay?"

"All right. So we'll make a big joke out of it."

"So what are you worried about, Buddy?"

"Well, I've found out that when you go before twelve guys on a jury, you can be damn worried. It's a horse race."

This conversation, in its tortuous entirety, had gone on for forty-five minutes, and it had been a debilitating experience for Melanie. Buddy had seemed more than ever possessed of the idea that the world had no reality that could not be reshaped by the exercise of his will.

One week later, Buddy and McCart were in court. McCart's testimony finished thus:

GRISHMAN: Did he [*Buddy*] say anything to you, what he would do in the course of the trial?

MCCART: He said he wants to go to trial, and if, in fact, the trial looks devastating to his freedom, he might start over again in Europe—in Spain.

GRISHMAN: Terry, is there anything else pertaining to your dealings with Mr. Jacobson?

MCCART: I don't want to deal with him anymore. I don't want to ever see him again.

At the end of the short hearing, the judge ordered Buddy "not to contact Miss Cain or have others do so," warned him that if he tried to intimidate witnesses, he would be returned to jail. Immediately after the hearing, Terry McCart was arrested. Among the charges was the fact that she had violated her parole in New Jersey. While being booked, she began twitching like a marionette and was checked into Manhattan's Beth Israel Hospital, suffering from heroin withdrawal.

Buddy, who appeared in court in a somber striped suit, tie, and unstylish spectacles, looked wonderfully unruffled, wholly in control. It was only Melanie who was not deceived. "He'll send letters," she told the cops. "He'll start sending letters."

Now she began to fear that Buddy might go free.

Melanie was not alone in this. The Tupper family was also beginning to fear that justice might not be done. They were rocked by the stream of accusations that Jack had been smuggling drugs. Even if he had been, Kevin and Dorothy reasoned, what had that to do with the crime for which Buddy was charged?

Their doubts regarding the police investigation, which had begun the Monday after the murder, had multiplied. "I thought Sullivan was decent," Kevin Tupper subsequently said. "I didn't like him, but I thought he was the most logical. He worked toward an orderly solution. Jacobson had motive, he had opportunity, and he got caught with the box. It was done in his apartment. Explain how he *didn't* commit the murder.

"But everybody else was saying, 'Oh, yes! And what about this?' And they would go off on a tangent, and down a dark alley, and get frustrated. And start accusing other people.

"I thoroughly believe the police and DA's office can handle people who shoot each other on the street. They can process people like that through the court. But I have a feeling that when they come up against a real attorney . . ."

Kevin's voice died away. The resentment and anguish of the Tuppers was all the greater in that it seemed to them that they themselves were under a shadow. Jack Tupper, Sr., for instance, had signed his own name to the two certified checks that Brian Monaghan had given his son, and paid the money into the bank account for his grandson, Paul. The DA's office saw something sinister in this. One of the assistant DA's even asked Kevin what right he had to move Jack's belongings out of the seventh-floor apartment.

Kevin was incredulous. "Jerk!" he shouted. "Ask Mary-Beth Abbate! She was there when the cops turned the place over to me. Ask her!"

The atmosphere was poisoned. "The police act as if they think I'm hiding evidence. Like I have some personal vendetta against Jacobson. If he *didn't* kill my brother, why would I want to have him convicted? I had never met the man in my life. If he *didn't* kill my brother, who did? I'm after the truth! Just as much as they are!"

It was only the elder Tuppers who seemed tranquil, willing to trust to the course of justice. But the tranquillity had a fragile skin. Marie Tupper now found herself reading the obituary columns in the newspapers. The first thing she looked for was the ages of the dead. "I'm not interested in the old ones," she explained, with a stark and moving veracity. She would look for those who had died young—seeking company, if only in the coldness of type, for her loss and her pain.

Buddy was a dynamo. "After the murder, he had a new nickname in the building," says Gail Moore. "He was Everybody's Buddy." Again and again, he entreated Gail to put him in touch with Breck Dana Anderson or Joe Margarite—as if *she* knew where they were. He tried to ingratiate himself with Al Seifert, who was dourly uncompromising. He got in touch with Mary, Brian Monaghan's girlfriend, but failed to arrange a meeting with Brian. He reached out for David Silbergeld, giving one of David's sons a message for his father—"Buddy sends his regards."

"I went berserk," Silbergeld says. "I was going to go and get him with a baseball bat."

The cops calmed him down and issued a warning. "Sullivan tells me that if anything happens to Buddy, I'm the first one they arrest," Silbergeld says.

Buddy took to telephoning former models, denying his guilt. The tenants began to find it wearisome. "He's always bringing people into his apartment to look at the bullet holes," one complained. "And telling them he didn't do it."

Also, in the weeks and months after the murder much of the physical evidence at 155 East 84th Street underwent unsubtle changes. The intercom in Jack Tupper's apartment was wrenched clean away from the wall. Wooden boxes, burlap-lined and not dissimilar to the crate in which Jack Tupper's body was burned, sprouted in his apartment. Bullet holes appeared in the walls of Joe Margarite's apartment (where Buddy claimed the deadly fracas had taken place). Also, after coming out on bail, Buddy changed the letters on the doors of the seventh-floor apartments in a surreal attempt to create confusion.

Melanie's second prediction now came to pass. Buddy's letters to her were unsigned and written in the third person, but his style was inimitable. The first was written on November 3, the day after he and Terry McCart had their day in court, but was not posted until the 20th. It was addressed to Wilhelmina Models, attention Melanie Cain.

"Melanie," it began, "no longer can you use the excuse the criminal justice system will work. What has happened to Teresa"—meaning Terry McCart—"is unconscionable." The

DA was keeping Melanie away from Jacobson "because a combination of your facts and Jacobson's will destroy his case." She should "stop letting yourself be controlled by others." Concluded the letter: "Melanie, before it's too late, meet with him. Jacobson is as innocent as you are."

The second was posted December 6. "I watched what started with one of his flings grow into the most beautiful love story. One who knows Jacobson knows you must read between the lines."

In closing, Buddy painstakingly negated the "revenge" motive. "Jacobson has harmed no one in his whole life. Even if his love and affection for you may have dwindled this past year, he always took care of you and looked out for you. I know he wants only the truth and the trial which will be many months from now may be too late."

More followed, and the impact of the telephone calls and the letters on her mood was profound. He was, she told me, trying to make her feel guilty: " 'If it hadn't been for you . . .' That's what he's saying." His strategies were beginning to tell. For instance, it had seemed an excellent omen when she heard from Clairol again. "I got more of a personal letter," she says. "They told me 'We're sorry for everything that happened, and we're glad to tell you we're going with the original footage, and you're still the principal.' "

"We checked the situation out," Tom Hogan, creative director of Clairol TV commercials, says. "And the decision was, why penalize the girl for something that wasn't her fault?"

But the Clairol response, which should have been encouraging, did little to lift Melanie's spirits. Immediately after the murder, she had thought she would be back at work in a couple of weeks. She had trod briskly through life, as though shock-proof. "But when things started settling down, that's when they began to hit me," she says. With the renewed incursions from Buddy, her defenses were crumbling. She was dreaming, for instance. Her dreams were continuous, repetitive, and lurid.

In one dream, she saw the killing. She was on the other side of the closed door. "I see the way they must have tied Jack up, or had him against the wall. I see *images*." Buddy is never actually assisting in the murder, in Melanie's dream. "He is standing by the phone, *glaring*," she said. "The Italians are pumping bullets into Jack, hitting him, stabbing him. Buddy is standing there. He has his glasses on. He's swearing."

In another dream she saw the burning. Melanie has, in reality, never visited the dump site in the Bronx, but in her reverie it was a garbage landscape, foul and reeking. Below her, and shielded from the eyes of all except Buddy, the Italians, and herself, was a small gully. In it, a wooden box was burning. Inside the box, she could see Jack. He was still alive.

The dreams began to occupy more and more of Melanie's waking life. "I can be walking down the street, or talking to somebody, and I'll just phase out," she told me during those grim weeks. "I can't be alone too long. I try to concentrate on other things, read a book, keep myself busy. But after that I can stare out of the window for hours."

Waves of emotion would slap at her. She would sink into troughs of guilt—"There are times when I wish Buddy had killed me and not Jack"—followed by hatred, pity, and plain puzzlement. "What is in your head, Buddy?" she would ask herself. "Why did you do it? Why don't you admit that you did it? I'm really trying to understand. . . ."

Often she would think about revenge, working out improbable scenarios. In one borrowed from a mystery read long ago, she was going to buy some brownies and send them to him laced with arsenic. "I guess he wouldn't eat them anyway," she told me wistfully.

In another, she would go up to the seventh floor and confront Buddy in his apartment. "I knock on his door," she said, "and shoot him right between the eyes."

The violence of her imagination perturbed her. "Is it normal?" she asked me. "I hope so. I've *never* hated. I don't know if I *really* hate him. But I hate what he did."

The tension became more and more wearing. Melanie became increasingly listless. Some friends recommended medication. "I won't take drugs, I won't take sleeping pills," Melanie said. She did, though, agree to see a shrink. The psychiatrist was recommended by a friend. He had a mustache, gray hair, and a sober suit. "What are you coming to see me for?" he asked.

"Well," Melanie said, "if I knew that I wouldn't be here."

She began to talk. "I gave him a synopsis," she says. "Who I am, what I do, what I'd been through in the last five years, what I'm going through now. I talked to him for forty-five minutes, and he only asked me one question."

She assumed the shrink's voice, rich with Viennese solemnity.

"Well," he asked her, "why did you live with a man as terrible as this Buddy Jacobson for so long?"

Melanie would still explode with a mixture of anger and laughter at the memory. This was precisely the dumb question everybody asked. "Well, it wasn't *that* bad," she said.

Melanie returned to him with some reluctance. The problem was her pragmatic nature. "I said, 'What are you going to do for me?' I wanted an answer in the first two sessions. But he said, 'There is no answer—you must talk it out.' Well, I wasn't about to talk to this guy for three years."

A third session never took place.

Her next attempt at self-improvement was in a less conventional direction. She ran into her cousin Lindsay, who lives in Greenwich Village, and Melanie noticed that she seemed "very up." Lindsay, it turned out, had become enthusiastic about Werner Erhard's est, and asked Melanie to accompany her to a seminar. She permitted herself to be coaxed, and went along to a four-hour presentation at the New York Hilton. There the est instructors explained to the several hundred potential disciples that the four-day course would cost $300, and that, by the end of the course, they would have "got it."

Melanie was cautious. What qualifications did these instructors have? "Are they psychiatrists?" she asked.

Lindsay couldn't tell her.

"I think that's dangerous," Melanie decided. Also, she suddenly realized that the seminar was almost over, and she still didn't have the remotest idea what the "it" was that she was supposed to be "getting."

"You can't explain the gift verbally," the instructors told her. "You'll *know* when you get it."

Melanie decided that est was not for her.

Buddy Jacobson was not allowing the outside world to imagine that his legal problems were having any inhibiting influence on his way of life. Almost immediately after gaining bail, he was again seen around the East Side with his usual bevy of beauties. One evening in Nicola's, he sat with a young woman with straight brown hair, a milky skin, and large eyes. He introduced her as Audrey.

Later, as we stood by the jukebox, the same one that had formerly graced the ski lodge, I complimented him on his dinner date.

"Seen one, you seen 'em all," Buddy said impassively. Same old Buddy.

But Audrey Barrett was occupying a larger role in Jacobson's life than he was ready to concede. Audrey, who comes from Long Island, had met him within a couple of weeks after his release on bail. She was a "clothes horse," a model who shows off garments to buyers on Seventh Avenue, which is steady work, but neither as profitable nor as glamorous as photographic modeling, and so she had decided to make the rounds of the agencies. The first she visited was My Fair Lady.

The interview took place in Buddy's office, which happened at this time to be his apartment. There was another model there, and a girl answering the telephones. Buddy, shoeless, was watching television.

He switched his attention to Audrey, telling her that he had just been watching a TV program which dealt with the problems models encounter, and all their "terrible stories." He asked her if she truly wanted to go into such a rough business. As if trying to dissuade her. "I was fighting with him, saying I *want* to be a model," Audrey told Guy Hawtin of the *New York Post*. "He seemed to be very concerned, but I just wanted to go up to him and hug him."

Buddy asked her to dinner that evening, so that she could meet some models. On the next night, she had dinner with Buddy and just one other girl. "Then, by the third time, it was just the two of us," she said.

Soon Audrey was in love. It was "chemistry," she says. She and Buddy would talk. "He was very strong on being able to figure out why people act and think the way they do," she told Hawtin, untroubled by any suspicion that Buddy's grasp of psychology might have been applied to herself. She observed that Buddy "would look after anybody that he felt concern for. He has given so many breaks to so many people. Even if you hate him, he wouldn't do anything to stab you."

Audrey, who was brought up by her mother and stepfather, is a religious girl. She was, indeed, formerly engaged to a young man studying for the ministry. At the time of her meeting with Buddy, she was twenty-one, and she would never have dreamed of going out with a divorced man. Buddy told her that he was thirty-three, and that Douglas and David were his younger brothers.

It was a reprise of his earlier technique with Melanie. But Audrey's mother was skeptical. "She's been out to dinner with us a few times," Audrey says. "And she said, 'Audrey, I don't think he's thirty-three. The next time you look at him, look at the lines, compared to somebody that you know.'" But Audrey didn't care. She *trusted* Buddy. She had absolutely no idea that the apartment where she spent so much time in his company had been the scene of a brutal murder, and that he was about to be tried for committing it. Nor did she have any idea what strange stratagems were swirling inside her talkative, altruistic boyfriend's head.

In early December, Bernard Rome, a prominent New Yorker then locked in a power struggle with the New York Racing Association, was sent a package containing some interesting items. One of them was a photograph of Rome, clipped from the *Times*, upon which had been stuck a piece of paper, like a cap. Written on this were the words "Dunce, Schmuck," and two drawings of the Star of David.

"Berny takes on more than he can chew. You must be kidding," read the accompanying letter. "Do you think you can do battle with the system? Don't let your wife see this picture—she'll go into hysterics. She already knows you are a simpleton."

This letter, which was signed "Melanie Cain" in a scratchy hand, never reached Rome. It had been incorrectly addressed, so it was returned to the address that the "sender" had helpfully left on the envelope—Melanie Cain, c/o Martin Pollner, 277 Park Avenue. Only Buddy Jacobson knows how many such eccentric attempts to sully Melanie's reputation may have actually found their targets.

It was now also that Buddy was, at last, sued by Jim Edwards of Audley Farm. The Virginia breeder claimed that he had never seen more than the $5,000 front money of the $275,000 that Buddy had agreed to pay for the twenty-one horses he had bought from him in March.

Privately, Edwards was not optimistic that he would ever see the rest of the money. "I doubt I'll collect," he told me. "I think Jacobson's made himself practically judgment-proof." As to the murder indictment: "It couldn't happen to a nicer man."

Toward the end of December, Melanie decided she was ready to go back to work. "I was very eager," she said. "I went to see people. I didn't even call for an appointment first. They had been my regular clients.

"They would say, 'Oh! you look *wonderful* . . . uh, we'll let you know. . . . Okay?' "

Melanie soon got the picture. "There were people I normally worked for who wouldn't touch me with a ten-foot pole," she said. "They were afraid. The photographers themselves, they didn't care, but they were afraid to suggest me. Maybe the client would say something. The client doesn't necessarily care, but he's worried about the *public*."

The brushoffs were discouraging, but Melanie persevered. She even agreed to start going on go-sees. Go-sees are the fashion world's equivalent of the show-business cattle call, and they are tiring and humiliating. Established models do not, as a rule, bother with go-sees, leaving them to the kids hustling their way up the lower rungs. Returning to go-sees was not something that Melanie, who had been at the top of her profession for years, relished. But it had to be done all the same.

Her first go-see came after three weeks without a single booking. It was with a small advertising agency in the East 70s, and Melanie was up for a raincoat account. She began to suspect it would be an unpleasant experience when the creative director kept her waiting for twenty minutes. "Just to show me that he was important," she says. She sized up the man at once. Pushy. "I didn't say anything," she says. "I just showed him my book."

The adman plied his way through the book, but every so often his gaze would flick to Melanie, like a viper's tongue. "How's business?" he asked suddenly.

"It's okay."

"It can't be too great for you," he said, with meaning. When Melanie remained silent, he went on. "First, let me say that you're looking well after everything you've been through."

"Thank you," Melanie said.

"Can I ask you one question?"

"No," Melanie said. "There's nothing to ask. I'm not going to discuss anything. I don't see why you should be interested."

"*Please* let me ask one question."

"Well," Melanie said, exasperated. "What is it?"

"I would like to know how you could be so ignorant, and so stupid, as to live next door with another man when you've just broken up with your boyfriend! Let me tell you, I *know*

Buddy Jacobson, and the guy has absolutely no class. I just don't *understand* you!"

Melanie just sat there, stunned. "I could have defended myself," she later told me. "But I was up there for work—no other reason. What did I owe this guy? Why should I bother?" She sensed, moreover, an underlying message: "You *play* with me, sister, and I'll give you work."

Melanie boiled over. She picked up her heavy model book and snapped it shut, a few inches in front of the adman's face. "You talk about class? I'll sweep the streets of New York before I work for someone with as little class as you." She stormed out, and because she felt she had been properly strong and stern, she was both surprised and mortified when, in the sanctuary of the elevator, she fell into a fit of weeping.

These swings of mood were becoming characteristic. Some days after her encounter with the obnoxious adman, Melanie and I dined with David and Mel Silbergeld. The evening had begun on a note of bravado, with the decision that we go to Nicola's; a rash plan, since Buddy was still a habitué, and the owner a Jacobson partisan, was balefully disposed toward his enemies. But Melanie agreed to the choice of venue. She had frequented the place in the past, didn't see why Buddy should prevent her from going there now.

We sat at one of the small round tables in the front room. Hanging immediately behind Melanie was her *Cosmopolitan* cover. This was the table at which she and Buddy had sat together so often. At first she had refused a drink. Now suddenly she asked for wine.

We ordered pasta, veal, and a bottle of Verdicchio. Inevitably, the conversation turned to Buddy. Mel told Melanie that the Park East hospital had been sold, and at a sizable profit, but Melanie seemed dispirited, rather than indignant. She complained of the renewed need for bodyguards, and worrying about the progress of the case. "I think they're going to make some little mistake and Buddy's going to walk away free," she said.

She paused for a few moments, and then added, "Buddy's trying to get to me. And you know something? *He is getting to me.*"

Memories lay about her too thickly in Nicola's. It had been an error coming, after all. We agreed to go for a nightcap to Elaine's, and Melanie's spirits revived as soon as we were out on the street. She looked across at 155 East 84th Street, and saw that Buddy's lights were still on. The sight rekindled her defiance.

"Let's set his garbage on fire," she proposed. Suddenly she walked into the street, lifted her head, and began to shout. "Come and get me, Buddy!" she yelled. "I'm here! It's *Melanie!*"

There was no response. We took a taxi to Elaine's, where David and Mel continued to talk about Buddy, dismissing him with scorn. But Melanie's mood now veered again, and she flared at them, weeping, defending her former lover.

The squall died away. Soon Melanie said she had to leave. Tomorrow she was working early. A catalogue shoot: ski pants.

"Probably the back view—so people won't recognize me," Melanie said with a dark, note of humor.

A new prosecutor was appointed to the seemingly moribund airport case. Douglas Behm, the son of a famous Nebraska footballer, and an assistant U.S. attorney in the Eastern District, was a tall, youngish man, with the angular handsomeness of a G-man on fifties television. He was approached by John Cipriano, an agent who worked at the airport with Curtis Filmore, and who proposed a new strategy. The group should be charged not on separate cases, but together, as members of a "continuing criminal enterprise." This charge—"C.l"—carries not the marijuana penalties, but a minimum of ten years, with no parole, a maximum of life.

It's tough, and hard to prove. "We're attacking without any maps on this one," Behm said to Strike Force head Tom Puccio, but began to assemble his list. It included Brown, Seifert, Jimmy Leonard, and Carlo Carrara, who had just had a hung jury on the car bombing charge. (It had been eleven to one for acquittal, but the embittered Nassau County Feds swore to retry anyway.) It also included—as an "unindicted co-conspirator"—Jack Tupper.

Buddy Jacobson presented himself at Behm's Brooklyn office that December. The prosecutor doubted that he had much to contribute, but gave him a hearing. Buddy, in his old green army-surplus jacket and sockless, talked and talked. "He never looked me straight in the eye," says Behm, who gained two strong impressions. "I was thinking of Charlie

Manson," he says. "And I was thinking, this is *one shrewd dude.*"

Buddy's gains were meager. Behm told him that if his drug prosecution turned up anything relevant to the Jacobson case it would, of course, go to the Bronx district attorney.

The first meeting of the two groups of investigators took place soon after the Jacobson prosecutors journeyed from the Bronx to Behm's turf, the U.S. Court House in Brooklyn. Present were Peter Grishman and Detective Sullivan as well as Doug Behm and three DEA agents—John Donohue, John Cipriano, and Curtis Filmore.

The meeting was somewhat ill-tempered. Grishman and Sullivan were less than happy that the federal drug investigation, with its posthumous naming of Jack Tupper as an unindicted co-conspirator, showed every sign of muddying their own case. The Feds were obdurate. Jack Tupper was part of their business. Jacobson was not their problem.

That very day, Buddy made another move. "After the letters, he'll send me presents," Melanie had said. His Christmas present to her was an album by one of her favorite singers, Barbra Streisand, with one song on the jacket underlined in ballpoint: "You're My Buddy."

"A sentimental touch, no doubt!" she wrote in her diary. "I must say, though, it's a great record and, of course, the only Xmas present I ever did get from him. Very ironic it is." But then her sardonic humor failed her, and she recorded that the approach of Christmas served mostly to remind her of the loss of Jack Tupper.

Mindful of her depression, Melanie's friends tried to keep her occupied. Betsy Fitzgibbon suggested that Melanie join her in selling Christmas trees at an Upper West Side site leased from the city by a young entrepreneur, Billy Collins. Melanie agreed. Her journal entry for Sunday, December 24, shows the improvement in her spirits:

> My depression has been altered by the selling of Xmas trees. I really had a great time—probably the best therapy I've had during the past few months . . . I felt like a part of "life" again.

A conversation with a fellow worker briefly made her spirits droop:

Only when [he] asked me what my last name was did I feel a twinge in my stomach. . . . I hesitated, at first, and then I said, Melanie Cain, with an attitude—so, what of it?

In the end, the young man only asked if he might have her telephone number. Melanie was pleased. Perhaps she was part of "life" indeed.

After work she drove off to join her family. They had a more pleasant Christmas than she would have believed possible.

And so Christmas passed. In the case of the Tupper family, grief was in their company, while Buddy Jacobson did his best to ignore the holiday. Audrey Barrett, who had been telling her stepfather about her new boyfriend, probably had the most eventful Christmas. "I told him that I had met this guy, Buddy," she says. "And my father said, 'Is that Jacobson? And was he a horse trainer?' And I said, 'Yeah, how did you know?' I was surprised. And he started to explain the apartment building, and Melanie and Tupper. . . ."

Her mother and stepfather merely told her to be careful. "They didn't take it very seriously. . . ." Audrey, though, says it was "a shock."

At four o'clock on December 28, Claire Normandeau was telephoned in her office, which was then at Police Plaza in downtown Manhattan, and ordered to report the following morning to the 76th Precinct. Moreover, she was instructed to be in uniform.

Claire did not have a uniform. Undercover agents believe that wearing a uniform, even for a day, forces them involuntarily to give off police "body language" for weeks afterward.

Claire Normandeau arrived at the 76th Precinct in jeans. She now learned that her relationship with Jack Tupper was being investigated, and she was advised to take a two-week vacation. "Today you were going to get your gold shield," she was told as she left. The implication was that her chances of making detective had been destroyed.

Next day, at a quarter to four in the morning, a DEA agent who had been cruising Margo's, a discothèque on East 45th Street, spotted somebody who looked like the elusive Joe Margarite. But by the time his police backup arrived, Margarite, as indeed it was, had disappeared.

Melanie's Journal: New Year's Eve

Mel & David, I'm very sorry to have disrupted your lives, and those of your children & friends, but I can't fake my emotions at the present time.

Mel, I'm not as strong as I thought I could be. . . . When will it all be over? . . . Thoughts of Buddy flow in and out of my head. He's so bad! Why does he have to live still?

The trial of Buddy Jacobson had originally been announced for January. It was, to nobody's great surprise, postponed. Perhaps it would take place in June, but already the cognoscenti were talking of September.

In early February, I had my first meeting with Al Seifert. His home was in Queens, with a raised swimming pool in the back and electronic surveillance gear in the front. At the time, Seifert knew, as I did not, that he was under investigation as a leader of the Donald Brown Organization, and would probably soon be under indictment. He had agreed to see me, nonetheless, because, as a friend of Jack's, he was growing fearful that the murderer was going to walk out of the courtroom a free man.

Al, who dealt in real estate, had been working through the realty section in last Sunday's *Times*. "I find this," he said to me, and started reading an ad: " 'Investors wanted. Upper East Side. Bavarian village shopping mall, consisting of fifty prestigious shops. Already have more than half of needed capital. This projects over twenty-three percent profit. Call . . .' "

"This ad seemed like a come-on to me," Al said. "But I call anyway. I'm bored, I'm calling everything in the *New York Times*. And I get Buddy's voice on the phone!" Seifert laughed. "I go *uhhh!* I hung up. What amazes me is that in the midst of getting ready for his trial, Buddy can be running ads in the papers talking millions of dollars. You're talking fifty shops. That's a ten-million-dollar project!"

Jacobson's Bavarian shopping mall did not get off the ground, but it was shortly followed by a second scheme. The following ad ran in the *Times* on March 4: "Financing for Manhattan Renovation (1st or 2nd mortgages) available. 861-1700." Buddy's number.

The news traveled fast. "Real estate on the East Side is a very small world," one realtor told me. "There are the big boys, Harry Helmsley, Sulzberger, Sam Lefrak—and there are the rest of us." He approached Buddy himself, and found him "cagey." "He was talking about lending two hundred and fifty thousand, five hundred thousand. But he was very wary. He wanted twenty-four percent interest, and he also wanted collateral."

This particular deal foundered, but the realtor persevered. Buddy also seemed to have buildings for sale. "I knew somebody, and tipped her off. She telephoned, and he said, yes, he had a string of eighteen to twenty buildings.

"She went over to see Jacobson, and went over the list, and asked which ones he actually owned. But he wouldn't be pinned down. She came back totally baffled."

So, indeed, was the real estate community. "There's a certain coloration," another agent told me. "Perhaps Jacobson wants to liquidate? Does he want to move his funds into Swiss francs, and jump the country? I just don't know."

No loans were ever made anyway. Bob Wood believes that Buddy's offers were a ruse. "I think he just wanted to find out what was on the market," he says.

Tension continued to build inside Melanie. In the five months after the murder she had talked about the case constantly, and to anybody. No longer. "I don't talk about it to my mother," she told me. "I don't talk about it to my father. I don't talk about it to Mel. I don't talk about it to Ellen Gannon. I'm keeping everything inside. I'm dancing, running three miles a day, working to keep myself constantly busy. But how long is this going to go on?"

It was a chill spring morning. I had met Melanie on Park Avenue. She was dressed for jogging and was looking rested—pink and sleek—but this was deceptive. Her dreams were worsening. The dreams were always about Buddy. She would see his hard eyes, his tight mouth. He would be killing Jack, or her family, or her friends.

"Am I going to be strong enough?" she asked.

A few days later, she went to Florida. Originally this was to have been a working trip. The trip had been canceled, but Melanie had decided to go anyway. She filled a sports bag with books: the *Gulag Archipelago*, *Are You Confused?* and *Mega-Nutrients for Your Nerves*. She took very little clothing, and she was, of course, alone.

The weather in Coral Gables was spectacular. She went scuba diving and decided she was having a good time. Then, sitting at a table in her bikini, she began to write her journal. But each time, within a line or so, she found herself writing about Buddy. She cried, and pushed the journal aside.

One day, she went running. She ran through one of the most turbulent sections of Miami, as though she were in a trance. She ran for about twelve miles, and she so badly blistered her soles that a doctor told her that he had never seen such abused feet. He forbade her to run or dance for at least two weeks.

I saw her when she returned to New York. Mel and David Silbergeld had separated, and Mel and Melanie now were sharing an apartment in River Court, on 52nd Street and the East River. I arrived about noon.

Melanie was painting the kitchen cobalt, and I couldn't help remembering her hatred for the blue walls in the Bronx precinct house. "Everything in this apartment is white," she explained. "I *hate* white. It makes me think of hospitals."

She was deathly white herself, with dark half moons beneath her eyes. She had, she said, stayed up the whole previous night. At first she had drunk red wine with Mel and talked. Later she had begun painting, while eating a box of milk chocolates, shaped like miniature turtles, brought back from Florida. She was wearing white painter's pants, and a white T-shirt that bore a familiar legend: *My Fair Lady Models*.

The shirt surprised me. "Yes," Mel Harris agreed, "why *are* you wearing that?"

Melanie agreed the action was a little peculiar, and giggled. She made some coffee, and put an album by Samantha Sang on the record player. One of the songs, she told me, perfectly articulated her emotions. It was called "I Don't Wanna Go," and Melanie echoed the lyrics, in a light, high voice.

All last night, she said, while brushing vivid cobalt on the kitchen walls and gobbling chocolates, she had been thinking. Up till now, the situation had been plain. Jack had been murdered, and Buddy was to be punished. But now she realized that the attendant publicity was having an indelible effect on her life. "I don't want to be a . . . freak," she said.

Preparing to go out, she put on her puffy green windbreaker and, at the last moment, jammed a brown hat of Mel's onto her head. "I want to look *strange* today," she told me. We lunched at P.J. Clarke's. "The police think Buddy's going to run away before the trial," she said. "What if he gets on a plane and goes?"

Then, I said, they bring him back.

"What if they can't find him? What if he gets plastic surgery?"

She became more animated. "There's another thing that bothers me," she said. "Buddy's been *quiet* for so long. For the last two months—nothing! No letters, no presents, no *nothing*.

"Something is going to happen. What's he trying to do to me? Something is going to pop up. I just *know* it. That's the way he works."

Again, she was close to tears, but her talk spilled on. She was drinking a second Heineken, but her filet of sole was untouched. "I used to think that once I left Buddy all my problems would be solved," she said.

"I couldn't kill Buddy now. I couldn't kill *anybody*. But I'd like to ask him how he could do what he did. But I don't think he'd know how to answer."

We left the restaurant. "I can't actually think ahead about anything," she said. "I don't know what I'm going to do *next week*. So—fair warning! You might have a crazy lady on your hands."

In the middle of March, the Bronx district attorney's office tried to squeeze Buddy's alleged accomplice, Salvatore—Sal—Prainito, in an effort to persuade him to testify against Buddy. Prainito was brought to trial on a charge of statutory rape; the victim allegedly was a fifteen-year-old girl named Vivian Torres.

The authorities had, unfortunately, a few problems. The first was Vivian Torres herself, who announced on the stand that she didn't want to press charges. The second problem was Vivian's mother, who, when asked about Sal, said she "loved him like a son."

The third difficulty was Prainito's appearance. He looked very young—he was born in Borghetto, Sicily, in 1955—and his apparent youthfulness was further bolstered by a schoolboy height of five feet two. Even the prosecution lawyers agreed, despondently, that the jury might be puzzled. "The jury's going to think here's this young guy, screwing this young girl," one of them told me, "and she wants to marry him. And that's bad? We should put him in jail for that?"

Up in the press office, Ed McCarthy of the DA's office was coming under attack.

"You're really putting the screws to this guinea," said Pete McLaughlin of the *News*, with abrasive bonhomie. "What are you doing it for? He's only trying to make a living."

"All we want is for him to tell us what went on down on 84th Street," McCarthy said.

"Sure. And then he lasts two hours on the street."

"We'll offer him protection."

"Sure," hooted McLaughlin. "Change his features, give him a new identity."

Down in the courtroom, there was tranquillity, the jury being out to lunch. Salvatore Prainito was sitting in a shaft of dusty sunlight, reading *Il Progresso* and studiously ignoring a couple of cops from the Jacobson investigation. He was wearing a navy-blue suit with sharply flared trousers, high black boots with pointy toes and Cuban heels, and a plain white shirt open at the neck. The sun caught the gold chain that glimmered around his throat. Only his thickened fingers, coarse-skinned with worn-down nails, suggested the manual worker.

The trial resumed. Toward the end of the day I saw Prainito, his black eyes unreadable, unbending a paper clip. I took this as a sign of stress, until he began using the clip to clean his nails.

When the jury brought in the expected verdict of innocent, the Bronx prosecutor told me that he wasn't overly surprised. Now plan two of Operation Prainito came into play: Sal was to be charged with grand larceny.

Specifically, grand larceny in the third degree. It seems that Prainito, while an illegal alien, had collected unemployment insurance for some sixty-five weeks in 1974 and 1975.

The grandly larcenous total was $6,175, and this second trial was set for April 3.

It happened just as Melanie had feared. She fell into a bad time. She felt that she was without substance, with nothing solid to hold on to. She looked back at her years with Buddy, and they seemed stifling, friendless. The brief support that Jack Tupper had given her was gone, and the realization of her loneliness swept in on her like a chill wind.

It was now that her family and a handful of friends became overwhelmingly important. Mel Silbergeld, of course, and Billy Collins, whose Christmas trees she had sold a few months before. Self-effacing and in his mid-thirties, he was an entrepreneur who, besides running the tree business, was involved in a couple of truck stops. A fervent outdoorsman—a rock climber and a distance runner—he had been trying to school Melanie in the proper disciplines of running. "I'm teaching her the Oregon Method," Collins explained. "A hard run . . . an easy run. But she wants to run as hard as she can. She wants to run till she *drops!*"

About this time, Melanie went to a new psychiatrist. We will call him Dr. Sklar. He talked with her at length, and prescribed Valium. Shortly afterward, Melanie began a brand-new journal, and it makes for painful reading. It opens on a day in March.

Wake up at 8:30. Took valium—5 mg. When I woke up I felt anxious, hyper, paranoid. Feel pretty good now.

10:30 Billy [came over for a run] went home to do paperwork.

11:00 Mel left to go on appointment. Dad called. Great talk! I feel fine.

11:35 Regina called. Friend from dance. I still feel in good spirits. Now I'm alone but feel OK. Have to iron, paint, clean.

12:00 Noon. Talked to Lisa at work.

1:00 Talked to Mel. Lunch w/David. Talk to Sue at agency. Trip: Rockfield AGA [a studio] March 18–25. $750 a day. Plus booking Monday, definite with Pringle & Booth.

1:05 I feel uneasy now—maybe because I'm alone. I can't think who to call right now. I'll paint now—finish that project.

I will then go outside for a walk to the store alone. It's about time I do it ALONE!

1:15 paint kitchen—crying so hard I want help. But no one understands. I call Dr. Sklar. I do so like myself! He said I didn't.

1:30 Left message with his service—Where is he?

2:10 I'm OK. Not crying. Finish painting.

3:00 Jerry came to fix the tub. I'm normal now. No more tears. I feel almost catatonic. Emotionless.

3:15 Dr. Sklar called back—I'm in control—no more tears.

3:26 taking valium—5 mg. Now that makes 10 mg. so far today. Felt a little better—back to real world. Still haven't gone outside though.

4:00 Mel's home. Talk to her about crying but couldn't remember why. She listens so attentively to me. If only she could understand my deep anguish. She stayed for a while then left. I'm so anxious to get to the doctor.

Melanie went to see Dr. Sklar. On her return that evening, she wrote an additional half page in a scrawl which grew looser as she wrote, concluding:

The "friend" I thought would always be there is a murderer—and the other man, Jack, is dead. My family I had pushed out. I had forgotten what it was like to have friends. I hope Jane gets here soon.

The paranoid world is still here.

Thus the journal continues. Peaks and plunges of mood are recorded, as by a seismograph, in handwriting of wildly varying legibility. For a while, she would be in a blur of Valium, her dosage having climbed to fifty milligrams a day, and then, within moments, she would be crying. The tears would go, and she would be unable to remember the cause of her grief. Melanie began seriously to wonder if she was losing her mind.

Mel Harris and Billy Collins were similarly perturbed. Mel talked anxiously to Martin Pollner, wondering if Melanie should be hospitalized. Collins felt differently. He and Melanie were in love. Collins decided to take her away. Collins had been planning to visit two friends, Damian and Zanna Koch, in Fort Collins, Colorado. The three of them had talked of driving up to a log cabin in the Rockies and then skiing across the Continental Divide. At the last moment, Collins decided that Melanie should accompany them, and booked tickets for a Colorado flight on TWA for March 8.

Melanie's journal had now degenerated to a series of jottings, scribbled onto a file cover in several colors of pencil, ballpoint, and felt-tip, and in no particular chronological order. March 7 records that, in the morning, Melanie spoke to Ellen Gannon, and "Mel home—laughed a lot."

At 11:30 A.M., she took Valium, and describes herself as "relaxed." At 2:00, she feels "disorganized, but now I can't think what to do next." At 2:45, she takes ten milligrams of Valium, but feels "nervous and anxious." She went to bed at midnight, and "didn't take Dalmane."

March 8 was more scrambled yet.

6:30 AM—2 Valium (10 mg.). 1 hour later—anxious and nervous still.

8 AM–9 AM Normal.

10:30 AM—getting anxious again—mind wandering—going to see Marty to surprise him & Donna. 2 Val.

2:30—2 Val.—getting ready to go to Colorado. Frightened.

Melanie's Valium intake was, by the end of that day, seventy milligrams. It was in that state that she waited in a bar in the airport, drank white wine, and she waited for Billy. "Fantastic time," she scrawled on the folder; then, "Feel better," as she saw him arriving. So they boarded the plane and took off for the West.

It was early evening when the plane landed in Denver, and the air was feathery with snow. Damian Koch met them in his station wagon, and they set off for his house. As it grew darker, the snow began falling more thickly, and Melanie began to feel relaxed. She arrived at the house in a good humor. Next morning was perfect. From her window she could see snow, fresh and welcoming, like clean linen. Melanie decided to go for a run. This would be the first time she had run since Florida. She walked briskly through the Koch's kitchen and out the door, where—within seconds—she collapsed in the snow.

In the kitchen, she had glimpsed a rack of shining knives. It had taken a moment to hit her; now she could see Buddy stabbing Jack again and again. She sat there moaning, then got up and ran off through the snow. She had feared she might again run herself into the ground. The reality was more humiliating. She could scarcely run at all. Mastering her tears, she returned to the house.

After breakfast, they piled the Volvo with skis and back-packs and began the trip. It was a long ride. They arrived at the log cabin about five that evening. The air was pure, the light intense. It was a crystal world. Cleansing. Melanie suddenly eyed her emerald-green down jacket with revulsion. It had been a rare present from Buddy. She asked whether she could swap it for Damian Koch's down jacket, which was yellow. The green jacket was small for Koch, but he gallantly professed himself pleased with the exchange. Melanie took more Valium and, in due course, went to bed.

Next morning Damian pulled Melanie's leg. "Where's my wallet, Melanie?" he asked. It had been left in the jacket. She handed it back. "Melanie," he said, looking at her sternly, "where's my three hundred dollars?"

The joke misfired. Melanie, brimful of guilt, burst into tears. Billy began to realize what the Valium was doing to her. "You're up to eighty milligrams a day!" he remonstrated. Damian was shocked. "Don't take the rotten stuff," he told her. "You're going to get hooked."

The forthcoming ski expedition across the Continental Divide was in the forefront of everyone's mind. They had already decided where to head—a pass at eleven thousand feet. "Melanie was strong enough," Collins says. "Physically." Melanie was less confident. "Will I be able to keep up with the others?" she wondered to herself. "Will I hold them back?"

Before the trip, Collins took her for a drive. They traveled west, passing from Colorado into Wyoming. They stretched their legs in Cheyenne, then drove on and reached Laramie.

In Laramie, the sun shone on great sparkling mounds of clean snow. They drank strong local beer in dark bars, where the men were polite and nobody recognized Melanie. They strolled through the streets, quietly talking, and Melanie bought herself a cowboy hat.

On the drive back, she suddenly opened the window and tossed out the bottle of Valium. A minute later, she opened her handbag and took out one of Buddy's letters. She tore it into little squares and threw the pieces out the window as well.

"This is lovely country," Collins scolded. "You're littering."

"I've been carrying that letter for months," Melanie told

him. "I don't *need* to carry it anymore." It was like the green jacket—another bit of Buddy gone.

But the lucid moment passed. The car radio was playing and sometimes Melanie would cry. It got so that whenever Bill heard the opening bars of Barbra Streisand singing "Evergreen," for instance—a favorite of Buddy's—his hand would strike out reflexively and punch the "off" button.

"I felt I was at a breaking point and I didn't want to upset his friends," Melanie later scrawled, semilegibly, in a notebook. "I wanted to go home." Billy drove her to Denver, and she booked a flight to New York.

Melanie never did ski over the Continental Divide.

It was not an easy flight. The notion that she was dependent on Valium upset her. Yet she was grateful for the loose capsules she still had. "My psyche is so fragile, I need Valium at this point," she wrote. Melanie drank a bloody Mary, popped two of the pills, then drank some beer. She was met at Kennedy by a friend, an agency booker called Mimi. It was the evening of March 12.

Her diary for the next day, a Tuesday, ignoring the repetitions, underlinings, and crossed-out entries, runs as follows:

Valium intake

Morning	20 mg. at 9:30
Afternoon	20 mg. at 1:30
Evening	20 mg. 5:30
Night	20 mg. 9:30 plus
	2 Dalmane (calcium pantemanic).

Alcohol intake

½ Coors 1:00 PM
1 beer at 6:00 PM. Smoke joint.

Had dinner. Talked with Mel and Brian about living situation. Great understanding now. Opening up to one another.

2:30 AM. 10 mg. (90 mg. total) ½ glass wine.
Herbal tea—sleeping time

On Wednesday Melanie decided to get organized. She bought a number of yellow folders, one of which she labeled,

"What Is a Friend?" Within, she wrote pages of definitions, such as "A Friend is someone who accepts you for what you are," "A Friend is someone who is not jealous if you have other friends," and "A Friend is someone who understands why you like anchovies, even if they hate them."

The definitions had Billy Collins' name written after them, followed by a red check-mark signifying approval. Melanie then noted that she had five friends, and wrote, "Billy Collins is my friend because he gave me his nine-year-old Oregon track shirt." This was followed by a few more definitions and, in the largest letters of all, "Billy Collins is my friend because he accepts me for what I am!"

On March 19, Melanie went to Illinois. Her Naperville girlhood shone in her memory, a time of simplicity and happiness. She was going to see her friend Jane, and she would visit her brother, Chris. She arrived, wearing the Oregon track shirt, Damian's yellow jacket, and her newly acquired cowboy hat, clothing that had acquired almost totemic significance.

Melanie spent that first evening with Jane and her boyfriend, Bobby, and talked compulsively. Jane had prepared a turkey dinner of formidable size, but Melanie could only pick at it. After dinner, they were joined by some friends, and they settled down to watch *Gone With the Wind* on TV.

Melanie got up early the following morning and cleaned the kitchen before settling down to listen to the music on WCLR, a Chicago station. She was determined to decode the songs, which held, she knew, messages of help, so she wrote down song titles that appealed to her and snatches of lyrics, with comments of her own.

This occupied her for two and a half hours. Then she searched restlessly through Jane's video cassettes. "Hey!" she said, "Let's watch *M*A*S*H*."

Jane put the bilious comedy onto the machine, but this time Melanie saw no humor in it at all. Chris suggested a drive to look at the trees in a nearby arboretum. Melanie talked ceaselessly with Chris and Jane and Bobby while nervously switching the car radio from channel to channel, explaining "I have to find the right music!" It was clear to family and friends that Buddy Jacobson had pushed Melanie a whisker from the brink.

It was now that Buddy reached out for Tom and Dorothy Myers. Tom's tour of duty in Puerto Rico had come to an end, and he had been posted by the FBI to Fort Lauderdale, Florida. Buddy set to work in early April, calling the FBI headquarters in Washington and the *Washington Post.* He had, he said, "information" about Tom Myers. He declared that Tom had "destroyed evidence" by clearing out Jack's apartment. Myers had been laundering Tupper's drug money, Jacobson continued; indeed, Jack had gratefully presented the FBI man with a brand-new car.

Tom Myers was called to see his station chief in Miami. He pointed out that his only automobile was a 1970 Chrysler, which had formerly belonged to a nurse in Dorothy's ward. The nurse had decided to rid herself of the rattletrap because of parking problems. Dorothy had bought it for use in Puerto Rico for $450. "It's a joke," Myers says. "It's like an old cop car."

Nor did Buddy forget David Silbergeld. He told the Feds, for instance, that the "real" reason for the former Green Beret's honeymoon sojourn with Mel in the South of France was a secret rendezvous with Sam Cummings, a noted international arms dealer.

The tattle was not without effect. Silbergeld was telephoned by a Green Beret friend who had mentioned that the authorities had been to see him. The implication of their questions was that a team of former Green Berets might be acting as hit men for the Mafia. "They were jumping all over his ass," David Silbergeld reported indignantly. Absurdly, Silbergeld's photograph was even removed from Nicola's. He told me that army intelligence was interested in the weapon he was holding. "I don't even remember what it was," he said. "It was taken in 1976 at Camp Drum."

Buddy even reached out for Mimi, the agency booker who had picked up Melanie when she flew in from Denver. Mimi began to get telephone calls. "Don't befriend Melanie Cain," a voice would hiss. She grew alarmed, then panicky. She went to the police, but no sense of security resulted from *that.* At last Mimi had to tell Melanie she couldn't see her anymore.

On April 24, a Tuesday, the so-long-awaited event took place: The Donald Brown Organization—thus named on the indictment—was busted at last. This is to say that the Organized Crime Strike Force from New York's Eastern District, headed by Thomas Puccio, prepared to arrest sixteen persons as part of a "continuing criminal conspiracy," which, the Feds contended, had been afoot since 1970. Also, they threw in a number of individual, lesser charges, just in case they failed to make the big C.1. stick.

Donald Brown and Al Seifert were named as leaders. The other fourteen included Jimmy Leonard, who was charged with dealings in marijuana, hashish, and cocaine which totalled up to a possible thirty-five years; Billy Sharrocks; Carlo Carrara; Frank Natiello; Alan Finkelstein; Joey and Louie Ippolito; Neil Richards; Lou Prikas; and the red-headed cargo-handler from Braniff, Peter Splain.

Fifty-one people were named as "unindicted co-conspirators." And this was the list upon which, despite all the rumblings of discontent from the Bronx, Jack Tupper's name appeared.

The authorities decided that all sixteen arrests should be made simultaneously. But since Louis Ippolito and Donald Brown were both in California, they decided to make quite certain of them before moving in on the others. The arrest of the versatile Brown, they realized, might be a problem, although the agents didn't expect him to run. "He's the hamburger king," one of them told me. "Where's he going to go? Bogota?" Curtis Fillmore flew out to California to take charge of the Brown arrest personally.

The arrests were to be made as close together in time as possible. In the New York area, they were timed to take place at between eight and nine in the morning. Given the time change, this would mean rousing Brown out of bed in the early hours.

Fillmore and his colleagues resolved to keep Brown under the closest surveillance. They noticed, for instance, that early on Monday evening, he handed a paper shopping bag to a blonde woman, whom, they assumed, was his wife. (This was not so. The blonde was a realtor, and the shopping bag contained $200,000 in cash.) Brown then dined with a movie producer, and the two of them went to a roller skating disco in Reseda, and cavorted until two in the morning, with (Brown claims) a couple of the DEA agents wheeling around after them on the floor.

When Brown left the disco in his black Cadillac Seville, he was trailed by three cars, one of which, a rental, contained Fillmore. Brown dropped off the producer, then, as one agent reported, "took off like a bat out of hell." When he ran a stop sign, the Feds decided they would have to make a premature arrest.

Brown had turned left on Sunset, zooming into a side street. Fillmore forced the Seville to the curb, jumped out of his car, and pointed his gun at D.B.'s head. This firearm, incidentally, is a snubnosed .38, with elastic bands around the grip, because Fillmore doesn't like holsters, but can't risk losing his weapon down a pant leg at a time like this. A second DEA car blocked the Caddy from the rear. The third, of course, was still stuck in traffic on Sunset Strip.

Brown's thought was that he was about to be kidnapped; a career problem in his line of work. He plunged into reverse, somewhat to the Mormon agent's surprise, ramming the second automobile amidships. Only then did he realize he was being arrested, and by the Feds at that. "If it had been the Los Angeles police," he told me, "I would have been dead."

The others were picked up without incident. Alan Finkelstein, a thin, soft-spoken man, in his middle thirties, with show business interests—he was the angel behind a recently folded musical—had just returned from a birthday party for Halston, attended by Andy Warhol, William Paley, and Studio 54's Steve Rubell. Carlo Carrara, who was at home on Long Island, contented himself with describing Al Seifert as "a close personal friend." Told of Brown's arrest, he remarked they probably had to "slap that guy in the face" to stop him from talking. The only subject on which he was insistent was that "hard drugs" were repugnant to him. Which was correct. Brown's bail was set at a million dollars. It had begun.

A couple of weeks later, I visited Thomas Puccio in his office on the third floor of the Federal Building in Brooklyn. He has a soft handshake and a punctilious manner. The bringing of the conspiracy charge, he explained, was intended to send a clear message to dealers in grass and has. Heretofore such a charge had been brought only against dealers in hard drugs. "The word on the street is that the profits in grass are enormous and the risks minimal," he said. "What's the big deal? Five years if you get *maximum*." Originally, he had no idea of the scope of the Brown group's activities, he continued. "I thought they were making hundreds of thousands." His voice rose slightly. "But we're talking about forty or fifty million dollars."

Donald Brown guffawed when he heard this.

"We're talking about *a hundred million*," he said. *"More."*

Martin Pollner was perturbed. He was upset that neither Buddy's telephone calls nor letters had returned him behind bars, and he was growing concerned about the Bronx DA's office's conduct of the investigation; in particular, the failure to indict the Italians. Melanie had, after all, seen Salvatore Prainito in Buddy's apartment on the day of the murder. And it was Prainito who had rented the van in which (it was presumed) the corpse had been carried. As for Salvatore Giamo, he had been found, together with Buddy, leaving the dump site in Prainito's yellow Cadillac. Although Prainito and Giamo denied having ever laid eyes on each other, both had worked for Buddy, on and off, for many years. And both came from the small Sicilian township of Borghetto. Pollner fumed.

Matters came to a head on May 9. Melanie, Donna Loughlin, and Martin Pollner lunched with Peter Grishman and Detective Sullivan at David K's, a fancy Chinese restaurant on Third Avenue and 66th Street. The meal started amiably enough, with Pollner, Grishman, and Sullivan going through some of the ins and outs of the case while Melanie chatted with Donna. Only after forty-five minutes had passed did Pollner broach the question that was, for him, the object of the lunch: Why had the Italians not been indicted?

Peter Grishman, who had forked his way through his meal with every sign of enjoyment, did not respond. When Melanie joined in, Grishman, now a little less composed, still refused to answer Pollner's question.

But Bill Sullivan was more helpful. The nub of what he said was this: If Prainito wasn't indicted, he would resign. Grishman was shaken, but still found nothing to say. Pollner, at this stage, took Grishman off for a private talk. He told the assistant DA—emphatically—that he wanted to talk with somebody in Mario Merola's office. Otherwise, he would go public with his unhappiness.

A few days later, Pollner was confronting a senior person in Merola's office and emphasizing his disquiet that the Italians had still not been indicted. "It reminded me of the scene in *Serpico*, when David Durk confronted Arnold Fraiman," he told me later, with typically grandiloquent relish.

On May 31, Sal Prainito was arrested at a Memorial Day picnic. He was taken into custody by Bill Sullivan personally and was to be arraigned in court the following day. I dined at Nicola's that evening. Buddy was at the bar with Audrey Barrett and another girl, who was enjoying Buddy hugely. He was a *celebrity*.

"How's it going?" I asked.

"Smooth," he said.

As I sat down, he fed some money into the jukebox. "Makin' It" started belting out. Disco music. Buddy danced an awkward step or two on his way back to the bar.

By chance, Buddy and Audrey sat next to my table. I felt vaguely uncomfortable, an accidental eavesdropper. They were drinking the house red, and Buddy was anatomizing the case. "Pace is not the object, babe," he said. I left first, and he nodded as I got to my feet. "Well," I asked, scarcely expecting an answer, "what happens next?"

"You probably know better than me," he replied.

Buddy had, presumably, known that he was likely to see me in the Bronx courtroom that next morning, but it was, as far as he could have known, a routine appearance. A number of cases were being called before his own, and he was sitting, in the back, indifferent, as though the procedure did not concern him. He was disheveled in windbreaker and open shirt, and he was scanning the contents of a plastic file, which included various legal documents and some pages from the real estate section of that Sunday's *Times*.

He took the file with him when his case was called, and went to the rail. Sal Prainito was now produced, and here the district attorney's office showed a flair for stage management. Sal, who had been brought up the back stairs, was brought in through the door that the jury uses to enter the courtroom.

Prainito was wearing a blue workshirt and dungarees. His hands were cuffed behind his back. If the intention had been to intimidate Buddy, it failed. There was, perhaps, a momentary flicker in his expression, but it quickly passed. Thereafter, Buddy and Sal Prainito stood at the rail mere inches apart, but never glanced at each other again.

But Ida Libby Dengrove was far from fooled by Buddy's deadpan demeanor. "He looked so cocky when he was first arraigned," said Dengrove, who does courtroom sketches for Channel 7's Eyewitness News. "Now he looks pathetic. He's lost weight, he's aged. He seems so . . . out of it." She started a pastel and was generous with the silver when working on his hair.

During the luncheon recess, there was a gathering in the office of Mario Merola, the ambitious but unusually taciturn Bronx district attorney. Rick Pienciak of the Associated Press (another journalist whom Buddy had tried to enroll as an "investigator") had a question: If the case against Prainito was airtight, what with the bloody palm print in the elevator, why had it taken almost a year to indict him?

Merola smoothly tried to put the question aside, but Pienciak asked it again.

"We're not going to try the case here today," Merola finally answered.

Pienciak was frustrated. That was never the way he had known a homicide case to work. "They show you what they're holding in their hip pocket," he later told me. "What took you so long?" he persisted.

Mario Merola looked testy. "Why are you asking?" he said. "You *know* the answer to those questions."

Rick Pienciak had no idea what Merola meant. "Was he trying to say that they have a bad case?" he asked after leaving the briefing.

The courtroom was almost placid that afternoon when the new, or "superseding," indictment was read. This charged Buddy Jacobson and Salvatore Prainito, "acting in concert with each other and others," with murder in the second degree "by shooting John Tupper with loaded firearms, and by stabbing him with sharp instruments, and by striking the said John Tupper with blunt instruments."

Buddy was asked how he pleaded.

"Not guilty," he said. His voice sounded like a biscuit cracking.

The proceedings were over. As many of the press as could manage crowded around Buddy in the elevator. How are things? He was asked.

"New York's booming," he said.

But how are *you?*

He shrugged and said nothing.

In the press room, the cigar smoke was thick, the humor loud, the skepticism rampant. "I don't get it," Pienciak said, shaking his head. "Why are they being so easy on Melanie?"

"No wonder AP coverage has gone into the toilet," boomed McLaughlin. "All you guys are a bunch of fucking *lawyers.*"

"Oh, come on!" Pienciak protested. "It's a shady case."

Dan O'Grady, also from the *News*, agreed. "It's a shit case," he said, working the typewriter.

"It's a shit case," agreed McLaughlin. "So when Buddy's facing twenty-five, he can say: Otto Fusco told me it was a shit case."

"Do you think Buddy did it?" Pienciak asked.

"I think a couple of wise guys took Tupper to Buddy's apartment," McLaughlin said. "And they offed Tupper. Buddy's left there, holding his prick with his hands. So he gets these two Italians. And, being nuclear scientists, they try to burn the deceased."

The press room roars.

Pienciak was persistent. "Do you think Buddy did it?" he pressed.

McLaughlin paused, slowly shook his head.

"I don't think Jacobson knocked off Tupper over some broad," he acknowledged.

"Like I say, they should talk to Melanie," Pienciak said.

"I tend to agree with you," said Kevin Goldman of the *Times*. "Melanie has a lot of questions to answer."

"They're not going to lean on their star witness," McLaughlin said.

"Do *you* think Buddy did it?" Goldman asked Pienciak.

Pienciak thought it over. "I really want to maintain my objectivity," he said.

"I'll tell you one thing," Goldman said. "The day Melanie comes up to the Bronx you won't be able to get *into* that courtroom."

Very early in the morning on June 6, a plane crashed in Kanawha County, West Virginia. The plane, a DC6—a long-distance cargo carrier much used in the 1950s—had called the Kanawha Airport only four minutes before touchdown, had flown in low over Coonskin Park, and had, as instructed, begun to land on Runway 23.

But the pilot, for some reason, suddenly changed his mind, applied full power, and tried to lift off. The elderly plane wasn't up to it. She lurched off the runway, slewed over a hill, and landed on her back, a crumpled and shredded ball of aluminum. Two rental trucks that had been waiting on the outskirts of the airport drove off even before the wreckage had come to a stop.

The Kanawha County sheriff's office speedily discovered

that the DC6 had been ferrying in ten tons of marijuana from Nicaragua. The street value of the cargo, all of which went up in flames, was some $8 million.

Twelve people were indicted for their supposed parts in this venture, including the pilot, whom a police lieutenant found wandering down a nearby street called Barlow Drive soon after the crash. He had a badly cut face and a damaged eye, but, considering the state of his plane, he was a lucky man. The pilot's name was Breck Dana Anderson, lately of 155 East 84th Street. His address book contained several New York names and numbers. One name was Joe Margarite.

The Pot Plane trial, as the press called it, was to be the longest federal trial in West Virginia history, and one of the most publicized. Much of the notoriety swirled around Breck Dana Anderson. This was partly because of his outré glamor: The twenty-eight-year-old son of an oil executive, he had already done time for hash dealings in both Morocco and Colombia. The papers pounced on a DEA printout to the effect that while he was sailing from Lebanon to Cadiz, Spain, two Turks had disappeared from his boat at sea. Now this. "It hit the front page," Anderson says irately, "that I was involved in some love-triangle murder. They actually put me in as the one that did it. That's something I would expect in some foreign country that can get away with that stuff."

Later, despite his own problems, Anderson contacted Bill Kelly in the Bronx DA's office, asking whether the authorities wanted him to testify. "They weren't interested," he says. "The whole thing seemed to be some sort of circus gig by the defense lawyer for Jacobson." A new attorney, this. Otto Fusco had now followed Win Klein and Sidney Sparrow into the past. Buddy's new lawyer came from Brooklyn and his name was Jack Evseroff.

Evseroff is tough and brash. He had first met Buddy just before Prainito was indicted. At first he and Jacobson had considered his defending Prainito too (though not in the absurd larceny suit, which the state had wisely dropped), but this tactic was rejected as "too obvious."

Evseroff was paid a $25,000 retainer on a $150,000 fee by Jacobson, and promptly set to work. With him he brought Bennett Epstein, a lawyer who had himself once worked in the Bronx DA's office, and Dominic Barberino, a private investigator and former cop.

*　　*　　*

Kevin Tupper and I were in Regents Row, or, as it had once been called, the Sherwood Inn. Why had the *second* Italian not been indicted? Kevin stormed. He had seen Sullivan a couple of days ago, he said, and the detective had told him Buddy might have a war chest of some three quarters of a million dollars. There had been more talk, of Buddy's seeing a plastic surgeon. Kevin, like Melanie, was sure that Buddy was planning to make a break for it.

He had, he said, a wish, something he thought of constantly. "I want to go up to Buddy in the street. I don't want to do anything. I just want him to know I'm there. . . ."

Donald Brown refused to believe he was facing life imprisonment. Perhaps, he told me, the government might drop the big charges. "The little ones I can handle. One thing I can tell you. We're all going to stand together. Like a *rock*." He made his hand into a fist. We were walking into the Plaza. It was late August, and a sunshiny afternoon was waning into a tranquil evening. Donald Brown had a rendezvous with another former habitué of 155 East 84th Street—Carlo Carrara, who also had the misfortune to figure in the federal indictment.

Carrara was sitting in one of Manhattan's more elegant spaces, the Plaza's Palm Court, and looking expansively at home. He was wearing a business executive's dark-brown suit, a white shirt, a dark tie, and aviator glasses. But the sobriety of his attire emphasized rather than concealed the contractor's formidable bulk. Legend had it that three people had once tried to mug him in Central Park, and he had kept their wrist watches as souvenirs. He was a man I knew slightly from Nicola's, where he would nod amiably enough, and that would be that. He could not be described as talkative. Nor would it be accurate to say that he was, on this occasion, overjoyed to see me. He was there, after all, to meet Brown for a business discussion.

He had been drinking a Sambuca, and now tipped the last of it in his coffee. A waiter appeared in a twinkling, and Carlo addressed him by name. Donald Brown asked for his usual, a Red Label and water, and I also ordered a Scotch.

We chatted awhile about the Jacobson case. Carlo seemed surprised that Buddy's bail was a mere $100,000—he himself had been stung for $1 million in the aftermath of the Peugeot explosion in Nassau County. "And there isn't even a dead body in *my* case," he said, disgruntled by the inequity.

He was not surprised by the talk of Buddy's visiting a plastic surgeon. He was convinced that Buddy was smart enough to make a run for it while the going was good.

Another thing: Buddy had been sending him money, Carlo said. The story went as follows. Jacobson had discovered that Carrara now knew that it was he who had informed on him to the Feds, and it seems that this caused Buddy a degree of uneasiness. This unease was being alleviated by generosity.

"He's sent me a check for fifty-five hundred dollars—I don't know why," Carrara said, poker-faced.

"*We* know why," Donald Brown mumbled into his Red Label.

"Maybe for tilework," Carrara said.

I observed that Buddy had sent me no money. "Perhaps," I said, trying to be droll, "he didn't have my address."

Carrara leaned his massive frame over me and patted me on the arm. "Don't worry," he said with an amiable smile. "I'll *give* him your address."

I finished my Scotch and left the pair to discuss their complicated affairs.

In one respect, everybody—Melanie, Carrara, the cops, Kevin Tupper—was wrong: Escape was far from Jacobson's mind. "He never took the trial serious enough to think he would be convicted," Audrey says. She had completely forgiven Buddy for his lies. They had been a consequence of the pressures he was under. Buddy had explained it all. Now his troubles had only drawn them together more strongly. The critical moment had come in a dramatic fashion. Buddy had taken Audrey to look at a building that he was talking of buying. They had gone up to the roof and looked around. They were alone.

Suddenly they looked at each other with the same suspicion: *Are you planning to get rid of me?*

It was a moment of mutual paranoia. Buddy, it turned out, had been entertaining the notion that Audrey was a plant, an agent for the DA's office. Audrey's train of thought was more convoluted. "I was thinking, if this guy is a murderer, maybe he took me here to throw me off," she told Guy Hawtin of the *Post*. "You know, we were both thinking crazy." After their descent from the roof, Audrey was never to doubt Buddy again.

Acceding to Buddy's wishes, she began to model less and less in the garment center and soon stopped altogether. "He wanted to spend every second of the day with me," she said, adding that he was fearful that "somebody I would meet would take me away from him."

Instead, Audrey began working for Buddy in the realty business. (My Fair Lady was now moribund, though it still existed as a spectral entity under the name Polly Modeling in the Manhattan telephone directory.) This was a time when foreign money—Italian, German, French, British, Arab, Latin American—was gushing into the city, and property was undergoing an euphoric boom. Buddy sought to make the most of it.

That summer Buddy sold 155 East 84th Street—asking only for continuing access to the Margarite apartment—and bought three brownstones just off Fifth Avenue on East 63rd Street, numbers 9, 11, and 13. He paid $800,000 for them, and the deal was completed on August 1. The buildings have ten apartments. He moved into 13, and at first Buddy acted the good landlord, putting in new locks and installing washing machines and dryers in the basements. "He's very quiet," one tenant said. "He doesn't bother you." This tenant changed her mind about Jacobson's amiability when she found that he was planning to co-op all three buildings and, if he got the prices he was asking, would make $3 million. David Jacobson was listed as president of the company owning the property, as he was of Buddy's next building, 59 East 73rd Street.

All that summer, Audrey labored at Buddy's side. She would answer the telephone, make mailings, take potential clients around the properties, even carry bricks and slap on paint. There were times, she said, when she wondered what she was doing, as brick dust rose and walls fell. "I should be out at the beach," she would tell herself.

The drudgery was not unrelieved. There were occasional weekend jaunts, for instance, to Montauk Point at the remotest end of the Hamptons, and there were bicycling excursions around Manhattan. They played ping-pong, and joined a squash club. Audrey is of an artistic bent, and Buddy accompanied her to the Museum of Modern Art and the Met. They would browse through old prints in antique shops, and Buddy told Audrey that he knew just where to get such things, only better.

"He just had so many plans for after the trial," Audrey said. "He knew places up in Vermont where he could get things much cheaper. A lot of auctions up there. After the trial, we were supposed to do *everything*."

He and Audrey went out just about every evening, as had always been his way. Perhaps two or three times a week, they would go to a show, perhaps a musical of the traditional sort, like *Annie* and *Ain't Misbehavin'*. Almost nightly they would dine at some fashionable restaurant.

Buddy by no means confined himself to Nicola's. On one occasion he took Audrey to dine at R.W. Bonds. Owner Dick Leslie found out about their visit after they had gone and was incensed. When they came in again, laughing and apparently carefree, he had Buddy paged to answer the telephone. There was no call, of course. Very quietly, Leslie told Jacobson that he had been a friend of Jack Tupper's.

"I don't want to see you here," he said. "Now or ever."

Buddy was unmoved, as befits a winner. "He never really worried, because he knew, and everyone around us felt, that he was going to beat the case," Audrey says.

What she could not know was the reason for his self-confidence. He had set out to destroy the case against him, and he did not doubt he was succeeding.

Dom Barberino, Jack Evseroff's investigator, had joined the New York Police Department after being discharged from the marines (where he won a Purple Heart at Iwo Jima). He left the force to strike out on his own in 1958. He wears Cuban heels and tinted glasses, drives a white Buick Riviera, and one of his upthrust eyebrows is jet black, the other snowy white. He found Buddy an exacting client. "Check this out, check that out," he later said. "Every day something *new!*"

Buddy had already done what he could with the evidence, both tampering with the old, where he could, and creating new. There was now the matter of witnesses. On August 8, Barberino made out a list of several possible witnesses, which began with Leonard Finkelstein, the next-door doorman, and concluded, to my surprise:

> Anthony Guest. Reporter for *New York* magazine. Has spoken to Melanie quite a lot, is writing a book about Buddy Jacobson.

Two other witnesses turned up by Barberino:

Nancy Nelson (she is presently in Japan).

She runs the operation of the agency. She'll explain Melanie's condition.

She saw 1 or 2 pieces of the rug on Thursday, before the homicide.

This, incidentally, was the same Nancy who had invited Bob Wood and Ingrid around to "keep Buddy company" on the evening before the murder. The other witness was Rayna Spears. Dom's notes ran as follows:

She's a model in the office.

She cut her foot on the tacks where the rugs were picked up!

Oddly, nothing would be heard of either of these arguments for Buddy's defense, but the trial was yet again postponed, from the beginning until the end of September. Buddy told Jack Evseroff, that he had unearthed a crucial witness. "He says he got a very important guy," the attorney was to explain.

The guy was small and wiry, with reddish-brown hair, and about forty-five years old. He gave his name as Raymond Barnett and described himself as a former plainclothes cop, and he had a fine tale to tell.

He had visited 155 East 84th Street on the morning of the murder, he told Evseroff, because he was in search of a "cheater's pad,"—an apartment where a married man can entertain women other than his wife. Barnett went up to the seventh floor to see the landlord. There he heard and saw a fearsome struggle. "The gist of his story was that he didn't see Buddy there," Evseroff said.

Raymond Barnett seems not to have had the look of an ideal witness. "He was sitting and sweating," Evseroff told me. "I've never seen a guy so nervous." Barnett departed, and, although he left a supposed telephone number where he could be reached, he was never heard from again.

The next witness that Buddy produced was Anthony De Rosa, the former bartender at Nicola's, who was deeply in hock to him on the Norway ski lodge. This time Evseroff had Barberino do the interviewing. De Rosa said that he had driven in from Vermont on the Sunday morning of Jack Tupper's murder and that he, too, had decided to pay Buddy a visit on the seventh floor. He wanted, he explained, to complain about the lodge's plumbing.

De Rosa happened not to bump into Raymond Barnett, but the scene that he described was strangely similar. There was this struggle going on. Three people were involved, including Jack Tupper. Buddy was conspicuous by his absence. Melanie, though, was there. "Just yelling," Evseroff sourly said much later. Even at his worst, Buddy apparently never told Evseroff that Melanie had anything to do with the killing.

Barberino listened to De Rosa with mounting incredulity, then had a word with Evseroff. "Jack, let's get rid of this phony cocksucker. Let's not get boxed in, or we'll *all* end up in the can."

So much for De Rosa's evidence, but this was not the last to be heard of the phantom struggle on the seventh floor. Some weeks after, David Jacobson was approached at the race track by a man who identified himself as Big Al, and claimed he could produce a witness who would clear Buddy. His favor would cost $100,000.

David duly met this "witness." His name was Joe Toscanini, and he had retired from the NYPD three years before with a heart condition. He, too, was to say that he had visited East 84th Street, looking for an apartment, on that fateful Sunday morning. He had gone up to the increasingly crowded seventh floor, looking for the landlord, and had seen two men beating up a third. Buddy, he was willing to swear, was not one of them. David paid Toscanini $50,000 down, and promised him the rest after he gave his testimony.

But Joe Toscanini, sensibly, welshed. Buddy shrugged it off. One defense had failed—he had others. He was not to know that Toscanini was to reappear in the case, in a bizarre fashion, at a critical moment.

Out at Belmont Park, the Wolfsons were in their box. Blond Patrice, in beige, was demure. Lou Wolfson, wearing a Florida tan and a suit of battleship-gray twill, was a dashing figure. Though he would talk, and at length, about the Jockey Club, he had less to say about Buddy Jacobson. "I happened to marry his cousin, that's all," he said. "I just know what I read in the papers."

Elsewhere at the track, the impending trial was casting more of a shadow. I was standing with Frank Pagano when David Jacobson passed by. He was dark, drawn-faced, abstracted, just like Buddy.

"How's it going?" Pagano asked.

"I've got a few winners," David said carefully. "I've got a horse in the ninth race." He turned to go.

"Give my regards to your pop," Pagano said, and then repeated the message. "Make sure you give my regards to your pop."

It was a day of liquid sunlight. The sky was blue glass. Joe Finnegan drove me to the barn. There we saw Gene Jacobs. I had various questions about the Jacobs family, which he answered readily enough, then said, "Why are you so interested in my family?"

He stopped short, finally adding, "I was going to say none of us have murdered anybody. . . ."

Did he regard Buddy as part of the family?

"He's my sister's son. It's taken its toll. She worries."

A few days later, we learned that the trial had been put off yet again.

At the beginning of October, it became apparent to everybody in the Donald Brown Organization that Al Seifert had turned, and he was now helping the government put its case together. Al claims that the turning of Ivor Shaw and Rudy Dehesa left him with no choice. At any rate, he was now attempting to persuade his former colleagues that they too should make their deals.

He telephoned Billy Sharrocks on October 4. "You're going to come out of this trial a gray-haired man on social security," he told Billy. "You're going to be dumped on."

Billy was noncommittal. Both men spoke in the calm, dispassionate tones of those who know beyond a reasonable doubt that their conversation is being taped.

Sharrocks asked whether Al had complained that he, Billy, had threatened to "blow him up." He asked Al who had given him this information. He did not, much to the later dissatisfaction of his lawyer, Bob Kronenberg, actually deny having made the threat.

Sharrocks and Jimmy Leonard still refused to make a deal, cleaving to the hard old saying: If you can't do the time, don't do the crime. One evening I ran into Alan Finkelstein at the discothèque Studio 54. "I'm waiting to see Donald," he told me. "He hasn't shown up." He gave an ironic shrug, like an unspoken question.

* * *

Melanie was on the mend. Billy Collins was growing closer to her daily, and understood her ambivalence about Buddy. The area around 155 East 84th Street was at once abhorrent to her and a challenge. She refused to move her bank account from the nearby branch of the Chemical Bank, nor did it disturb her that her doctor was on 86th Street and Lexington Avenue. One day in late fall, she found she had a number of errands in the neighborhood, and Billy drove her there in his BMW.

First, she went into Gillie's, the health-food store on 84th and Third, to get some bran and dried apricots for Mel Harris. Many of the staff had changed, but a few regulars recognized her, and she imagined that she was picking up some hidden reproach: *This is Buddy's domain. What are you doing here?*

She straightened her spine—she had every right to be there, she told herself—and made her purchases. Then she and Billy strolled the couple of blocks to the bank. They returned to find the car had a flat tire.

Billy changed it, insisting the flat was an accident, but Melanie felt otherwise. Later they brought the tire into a garage to be patched.

"Somebody doesn't like you," the garageman told them. He was of the opinion that the punctures had been made deliberately. No, he said. He wasn't joking.

On October 9, Donald Brown telephoned. There was an odd timbre to his voice. He was insistent that I tell nobody of his presence in the city.

That evening I went into Chequers, where I happened to meet Billy Sharrocks and Jimmy Leonard. Sharrocks was gloomy. "Donald has turned," he said. "He won't talk to Jimmy or me. He won't answer our calls. And the Feds have come up with some stuff that could only have come from him."

How much time was Sharrocks looking at? "Fifteen, twenty years," he answered.

Would they make a deal of their own?

"We're going all the way with this thing," Leonard said.

As the trial approached, Buddy Jacobson was urged to improve his appearance. "We made him wear socks," Dom

Barberino says. "And Audrey took him to Bloomingdale's and got him a couple of suits."

On October 10, an article by Selwyn Raab in *The New York Times* was headlined: VICTIM'S ALLEGED ROLE IN DRUG CASE CALLED BOON TO JACOBSON'S DEFENSE, and an aide of Mario Merola's was quoted as saying that the allegation "certainly clouds the issue as to motive."

Jacobson's reaction was characteristic. A copy was received by Melanie's father in Alexandria, Virginia, addressed to G. Cain, and with "Raab, Times, 229 W. 43, NY NY" written in the top left-hand corner of the envelope. The painful, scratchy handwriting was plainly Buddy's. George Cain sent the article and envelope straight to the cops.

On October 22, Jerome Castle, Buddy's last major horse owner, was about to be sentenced in a suit brought by his former company, Penn-Dixie. (Among other things, they charged their former chairman with investing $5.8 million on Florida "building land" which proved to be mostly undrainable swamp, bisected by a geological fault, and sitting next to a Navy bombing range.) Castle got fifteen months, and little publicity.

It was now, and rather more spectacularly, that the Buddy Jacobson case finally came to court.

- VII -

Trials
and
Tribulations

The Bronx County Building, a chunk of lard-colored granite, is approached on all four sides by flights of steps and has a showy look, enhanced by the fact that each of the four main doorways is flanked by chunky neoclassical statuary depicting warriors, sages, and bare-bosomed maidens. It was constructed as part of the public works program during the Great Depression, and the *New York Herald Tribune* described the building, not in disapproval, as "a characteristic American example of the style developed under Mussolini." Mayor Fiorello La Guardia celebrated its completion by running New York City's affairs from the structure for three days in 1934, a symbolic act which might usefully be revived. Yankee Stadium is still in business a few blocks away, but the County Building now looks across at the boarded-up Concord-Plaza Hotel, streets of grungy shops, and a scabby wasteland still sometimes referred to as Babe Ruth Plaza. It was here that the Buddy Jacobson case was to be staged.

Most of the cast duly assembled, on the morning of October 22, outside the courtroom that would be presided over by the trial judge, Justice William Kapelman. "Billy Kapelman is the king of the Bronx," a lawyer told me. Kapelman was the Bronx's administrative judge, which is to say the most powerful. "I hadn't had a case since Son of Sam," he said later. "I thought I'll take a case. And I *got* one."

Things were starting on a fine, high note. Peter Grishman and Bill Kelly, the prosecutor, a youngish man, whose feisty manner concealed skills of which the defense were well aware, were both steaming at the first of the pre-trial motions, which charged that they had intimidated witnesses.

Nor was Evseroff slow in letting off a yet more resounding salvo. "We are going to prove that Tupper was not murdered by Buddy Jacobson," he said at an impromptu press conference in the corridor outside the courtroom. Jack Evseroff was whip-thin, with a skull-contoured face. He was wearing an extravagantly flared navy-blue three-piece suit, the first indication of a wardrobe larger than that of most traveling theater companies. Beside him, Buddy, in a decorous brown suit, looked like a workman dressed up for a job interview.

"If you're going to prove Buddy didn't do it, then who did?" Pienciak of AP asked.

"Come and see," the lawyer said invitingly. Evseroff, no less than Buddy, thought he knew how to handle the press.

When the proceedings did finally get under way, Judge Kapelman announced that he was imposing a "gag." This action would not bar the reporting of the trial, he said, but it was intended to prevent all concerned from outlining any theories or making any revelations that were not actually part of the court record. And though Evseroff and Epstein bitterly attacked the gag, the judge's ruling stood.

The hearing on prosecutorial misconduct was led off by Ben Epstein, and with his fuzz of hair, spectacles, and receding chin, he at first seemed soft and molelike. But the softness was deceptive—his bite was sharp. Epstein's manner contrasted with the bravura of Evseroff, whose voice could change from the soft confiding tone of a papal nuncio to a righteous, brutal snarl within microseconds. "I know you're an old shouter," Kapelman reprimanded him. But it was evident that the judge enjoyed his dramatics.

Rayna Spears, giggling and mugging as though auditioning for a sitcom, claimed that Bill Kelly while interviewing her had told his stenographer to stop taking notes when she said that Buddy was being "framed," and when she said that some tenants had heard shots, but not from Buddy's apartment. She added she had discovered a bullet hole and a bloody rug in Joe Margarite's apartment a short time after the murder. She had neglected to tell the grand jury this because "they didn't ask," and, she said, she hadn't thought to mention it to Buddy in the intervening year, though she had seen him almost on a daily basis. Very sensibly, Evseroff didn't ask her about the foot which (according to Barberino's notes) she had wounded with a tack, thereby splashing blood on the carpet *before* the murder. The Spears performance was well received by George Carpozi, whose article was embellished with a quarter-page photograph of the young woman, captioned: "A DEADLY COMMOTION, BUT NOT IN JACOBSON'S APARTMENT."

Bob Kronenberg, the lawyer for Leonard and Sharrocks, testified that he had moved to have the federal indictments against his client quashed on the grounds that prosecutor Grishman had been pushing for them to pursue a "tactical advantage." Grishman had told him this, Kronenberg said, at the meeting in May. The implication was that the prosecution had been selective, and not entirely forthright, in examining all the evidence against Jacobson.

Terry McCart reappeared as a witness for the defense and claimed that she had been badgered by the authorities and repeatedly jailed because she had information that would help Buddy.

Finally, the defense contended that "somebody" had come forward with evidence that would have put Jacobson in the clear, and that the DA's office had pressed this anonymous witness to change his testimony.

Such was the basis on which Buddy's lawyers were trying to have the case dismissed.

Jack Tupper, Sr., and Kevin first attended the trial on October 30, while testimony was being taken from the stenographer who had kept the record when Bill Kelly had talked with Rayna Spears. The Tuppers and I spoke in the corridor outside the courtroom during a recess.

"I came to look at him," Jack Tupper said.

He meant Jacobson. He had not yet seen his son's killer in the flesh. On his way into the courtroom, he noticed Sal Prainito, looking trim, cocky. "That little midget," Tupper said softly. "My son could have squashed him with one hand."

Buddy was already in the courtroom. Both Tupper men stared at him. His skin was sallow, his hair smoothed down and lifeless-looking, his arms were clasped across his chest as if he were trying to fight off the cold.

Afterward, the Tuppers and I went out for lunch to the Famous Yankee Tavern, one of the places with which we were to become depressingly familiar. We ordered pastrami and beer, and Jack Tupper submerged himself gratefully in the past. "We had a quiet life," he said. "We never knew any sadness. We knew hard times, of course."

About this time, Jacobson arrived in the tavern with Sal Prainito and some of their legal troupe. They sat a few tables down. Buddy was animated now, often smiling, and I wondered whether the dead-eyed waxwork in the courtroom was just one more ruse, calculated to arouse pity.

Jack Tupper, Sr., stared at Jacobson again, long and steadily. There was no vengefulness in his gaze, no rage. It was a direct gaze, full of contained grief and a sort of wonder.

What had he imagined about Buddy?

"A devil," he said simply.

What did he think now?

He answered only with a gesture. It indicated both despair and contempt. "There he is, supporting girls, and going to the best restaurants," he said. "And here we are. Suffering."

We walked back. Bill Kelly jogged over in his noisy checked suit. He was a-bristle, aggressiveness steaming off him. "They're trying to get my ass," he said. "They want me off the case." He moved off. "I hope Kelly doesn't blow his top," Jack Tupper observed, with a glint of humor.

At the hearing a couple of days later, Dave Greenfield, Prainito's attorney, now had the floor. Greenfield is a bulky man in early middle age, with dark hair and mustache, dark suit and tie, as though consigned by life to a permanent graveyard shift. He was attacking the authenticity of the "bloody palm print," which, he claimed, had never been tested to determine if the blood matched Jack Tupper's blood-type. In fact, he declared roundly, the palm print had never been proved to be blood at all.

This, if true, was the sort of blunder the Tuppers had feared. Jack Tupper, Sr., was sitting in the front row, next to Kevin. The courtroom had already taken on a fixed topography: Jacobson's supporters would occupy the right aisle, looking toward the judge, while the Tuppers, and others convinced of his guilt, would sit to the left. "It's hard to keep cool," the father told me. "When I hear them talking about blood, and I know it's my son's blood they're talking about."

Epstein summed up for the defense. Judge Kapelman denied the motion to dismiss point by point. Rayna Spears was wrong—the stenographer had taken down all the testimony that she claimed had been omitted. As to her claim that she hadn't told anybody about the blood-stained rug until a year later, Kapelman described this as "patently incredible." Bob Kronenberg's testimony was found irrelevant, Terry McCart was "not entirely truthful." As for the "somebody" with the evidence that would clear Buddy, he—or she—never could be produced by the defense.

But Jack Evseroff remained confident. "You think I can't

break Melanie Cain?" he said. He sounded in no doubt on the matter at all.

Indeed, the forthcoming cross-examination was much on Melanie's mind. "How big is the courtroom?" she asked me. "How many people does it hold?"

I told her that Evseroff was convinced that he could "break" her.

"He probably will," she reflected.

Nor was Melanie the only person preyed upon by doubts. So, too, were the members of the Tupper family. One morning, I breakfasted with a somber Tom Myers. "I think Buddy may get away with it," he said. "If I was betting on it, I'd give odds of fifty-fifty." The uncertainty was not helping his marriage. "The Tuppers are a very emotional family," he observed.

Even Audrey Barrett was having second thoughts, though of a different sort. Dom Barberino remembers sitting with her one day during this period. They were in the tiny kitchenette of the apartment at 9 East 63rd Street. Buddy was with David, off in the living room.

"How old is Buddy *really?*" Audrey murmured. "Is what they say in the papers true?"

"What do you mean?"

Barberino nodded in David's direction. "What do you think?" he asked. "Does he look like Buddy's *brother?* Or his *son?*"

"His son," she said dismally.

Only Buddy Jacobson seemed blithe. The failure of the motion-to-dismiss strategy did not discourage him. He had a hundred others.

On November 13, Estella Carattini received a telegram. Mrs. Carattini was a crucial prosecution witness. It was she who could put Buddy at the body's dump site in the Bronx. The telegram, which was delivered to her address in Co-op City, read as follows:

CONGRATULATIONS. THERE IS NOW A NATIONWIDE $25,000 CONTRACT FOR KENNETH, STEPHEN, AND STEPHANIE AFTER MRS. C'S PERFORMANCE WITH THE MAVERICK.

Kenneth, Stephen, and Stephanie are the names of the Carattini children, and the Maverick was the car Carattini was driving when they had stopped to look at the tricycles. The telegram continued:

> HOW WILL YOU ACT WHEN YOU ARE WITHOUT YOUR DIRECTORS, KELLY AND SULLIVAN. THEY WILL FINALLY LEAVE AND THEN WHAT WILL YOU DO. CHANGING YOUR ACT IMMEDIATELY OR TAKING LEAVE OF ABSENCE WILL CANCEL THE CONTRACT.

Estella Carattini refused to go into the witness box until her family received police protection, which was quickly forthcoming. An angry Peter Grishman demanded that Judge Kapelman revoke Buddy's bail, only to have David Greenfield ask for a change of venue. The prosecution, Greenfield said, had "tarred the defendants as senders of a death threat."

Kapelman refused both demands. The threat was a serious matter, he agreed, but there was "no evidence to connect these defendants with the telegram."

The following evening, I dined in Nicola's. Carlo Carrara was also there. "The first time since the murder," Carlo remarked.

Midway through the evening, I talked with him at the bar. He was indignant about Al Seifert. "He taped me on February twenty-seventh," he said, commenting on their ruptured relationship, "and three months later, *he's baptizing my daughter*." He sounded more incredulous than enraged. He also told me that I, too, was mentioned on the tape.

Melanie was now working hard, with several shoots for *Vogue* and plentiful catalogue work. But she still had the feeling that there were two people within her, and one was under Buddy's control. Billy Collins knew the signs by now, of course, and they were even becoming plain to Kelly in the DA's office. "I go in to the DA's office," she said. "And he tells me that sometimes I am very astute. And then my face will change, and I will be somebody else."

Her metamorphosis might happen even walking down the street. "People are all around," she said. "But I'm totally oblivious to them. I'm totally, completely alone. Trapped in my own world." Sometimes she would decide that she was a burden on her friends, and would wander the streets alone for several hours. She would even resent friendly overtures. She couldn't read and was no longer keeping her journal. "Even if I write a letter to somebody . . ." she said. "It's so morbid!"

She still could hear Buddy's voice: *People don't really like you, they use you. . . . Why do you want to have lunch with that girl? Why go shopping with her? She's nothing. . . . Why do you even talk to that guy? . . . The only reason people talk to you is because they want something from you. . . . You don't need friends, you don't need friends!*

It was as if the Buddy-manipulated Melanie was making a last attempt to exert control. One day Melanie found that she had finished a short photo session and had several hours free. It was a perfect opportunity to call some of the friends with whom she hadn't spoken for awhile.

Instead, she went for a walk. It took her to Grand Central Station, a favorite place. "I relate to the bag women just fine," she said, a sardonic flash. "I just sit there and sit there. I don't read, because I'd be looking at the page and thinking . . . Buddy, Buddy, Buddy. . . ."

Melanie was regularly commuting to Long Island to the place she shared with Mel Harris. One evening she was a bit late and had to make a dash for the train. Normally, she would remove her makeup before traveling, and often she would wear spectacles. But that evening she had no time. Everyone on the train seemed to be reading the *Post*. The threatening telegram to the Carattinis had just been published, and everywhere she looked she saw her own face looking back at her. "Everyone is sitting there with the *Post*," she said. "I mean, *everyone*. It was almost funny!"

The humor faded a bit when she talked to her parents. The threat to the Carattini children had made her mother fearful. "I wish you'd take it seriously," she told Melanie.

"I've been taking Buddy seriously for fifteen months," Melanie replied.

Dorothy Myers was feeling more and more frustrated. The news of Buddy's trial, as it reached her in Fort Lauderdale, was a bit late, and distorted. She would telephone Kevin and her parents. She would call Peter Grishman or Bill Kelly, and rail at them for the drug charges that were blackening her dead brother's name. "You're too emotional," Kelly would tell her. "I couldn't handle the case if I was that emotional about it."

Dorothy would acknowledge this truth, but she and Kevin

were nonetheless gloomily certain that what they perceived as a lackluster investigation by the DA's office—being embodied in the continuing lack of an indictment against the "second Italian," the "hitchhiker" Giamo—had no chance to succeed.

She received the first telephone call a couple of days before Mrs. Carattini received the telegram. The caller was female, purporting to be a phone operator, and she asked whether Mrs. Myers would take a collect call from New York. The caller's name was given as Tom Burns.

Dorothy declined to take the first call without further information. "Who is Tom Burns?" she asked the operator. "I know a lot of people in New York."

The "operator" hung up. Similar calls followed. Finally, she told Tom about them. He officially reported the matter on the evening of Friday, November 16.

Two events came into Bill Kelly's life that weekend, the triviality of the one mocking the horror of the other. On Saturday, he found that somebody unknown had bashed in the fender of his car. On Sunday, he learned his sister had been murdered. The body of Mary Kelly Schwartz was discovered by two little girls, sisters, who were playing in a dry creekbed behind the Futura Yacht Club in Sheepshead Bay, Brooklyn.

She had been brutally beaten, strangled, and shot once in the back of the head. It was no secret that she had been having spats with her husband, Fred, a customs agent. He immediately volunteered to take the most extensive lie-detector tests available.

Bill Kelly did not appear in the Bronx courtroom when the pretrial hearings were resumed on Monday. An assistant DA told the court of the murder and asked for a one-week postponement. This Judge Kapelman readily granted.

Next day, November 20, Dorothy Myers was alone in her Fort Lauderdale house. "I had a terrible throat," she says.

The call came at 2:20 P.M. It was, once again, collect, and from New York. This time, Dorothy, suddenly curious, agreed to accept it.

"Hi!" somebody said. "Is Dorothy there?"

The voice was female and sounded young, but Dorothy didn't recognize it and was puzzled. Most people she knows call her Dee. She is Dorothy only to her family.

"Yes," she said after a moment. "Dorothy Myers speaking."

"Your baby, Jack," the caller said. *"What kind of acid would you like thrown in his face?"*

Dorothy found herself floating, in some suspension of disbelief. It seemed forever, though it was only a couple of beats, before she even understood the threat. Nobody called her baby Jack. He was J.J., for John Jerome: "after my two brothers."

Later, when she discussed the call with Tom, their first reaction was to ignore it. They felt there was nothing they could say that Buddy would not twist to his own advantage. "When is it all going to end?" she asked. Tom Myers' FBI colleagues persuaded him differently. And Dorothy called Bill Kelly.

They spoke for about an hour. Kelly reminded Dorothy that he had warned her not to become too emotional. "When I heard about my sister, that was the first thing that went through my mind," he told her. He was certain that his sister's killing was "Jacobson-related."

"Bill Kelly is very basic," Dorothy says. "He's an Irish Catholic." They discussed faith, and heaven, and Bill asked Dorothy how long it took to get over a tragedy like the murder of a close relative. "Bill, if Jack had been killed with one shot, I would still have the grief," she told him. "But I would never feel this vengeful."

It was the manner of Jack's killing that obsessed her. "That's the toughest thing," she said. "The *way* he was killed. Not one of the shots was really fatal. Was it torture? How long did it last?"

Kelly described his sister's death in chilling detail.

"Bill, what do you *feel* when you think about it?" she asked.

"It gets me sick," he said.

"You go into a closet for a while," Dorothy said, trying to comfort him. "Then you come out."

But you never completely forget. "If justice does not take place, I am going to try Jacobson myself," she said. "I am committed to it. I could never let him walk the streets of Manhattan a free man. I couldn't live with that."

"I've heard you say that before," Bill Kelly said. "But I didn't understand you until this happened to my sister."

Kelly subsequently made a painful decision and took himself off the case. There were two reasons for this—both compelling. The first was that the defense would quite certainly try to make use of the incident on the grounds that Kelly's mere presence in court would influence the jury against *any-one* accused of homicide.

The second reason was personal. Kelly is a family man, with five children. The police officially declared that there was no connection between Buddy and the killing of Mary Schwartz, but Kelly's wife was in no way reassured. Finally, Kelly refused to continue with the case because he feared his marriage was at risk.

Not long after the second call to Dorothy Myers, there was a telephone call to Bill Kelly's sister-in-law, Mary Walsh, who lives in another city and has an unlisted telephone number.

This caller was a man. "You're next," he told her, and hung up. Another caller, equally menacing, threatened Kelly's aunt.

Kelly and his family were put under twenty-four-hour guard. Just like the Carattinis.

The hearings resumed on November 29. It was sunny and cool, the light was treacly through the courtroom blinds. Buddy Jacobson with hair and mustache both trimmed was standing with Jack Evseroff. "What about this case?" Evseroff said. "It's like *Alice in Wonderland*. It gets interestinger and interestinger."

When would the trial proper start?

Evseroff shrugged. "They don't even have a prosecutor," he said. "They need a new prosecutor."

"The fifth," Buddy put in, slyly.

Kapelman adjourned the hearings, but made it plain that he regarded Monday as a definite starting date. In the corridor, Buddy was asked, yet again, how confident he felt as to the eventual outcome.

"Who can read these things?" he said, adding, "I certainly don't want any more postponements."

Later, Evseroff came down to the press room and put on a splendid display of outrage. He had been bawled out by Judge Kapelman for telling CBS that he wanted to have Kelly taken off the case. "He wants to chastise me in his chambers," he said. "I'm going to have him do it in open *court*."

That Monday, the DA's office made a motion. It cited the letters and the threatening telephone calls, and demanded that the bail for both Buddy Jacobson and Sal Prainito be revoked.

Judge Kapelman once again refused, saying there was no proven connection between Buddy and these acts.

The mood in the DA's office was bleak, and Mario Merola gave a rare interview to Irene Cornell of WCBS. Cornell quoted Merola as irked by Kapelman's decision. "What is he waiting for? Another body?" Merola supposedly said.

Ben Epstein, Jack Evseroff's aide, scented in this comment a breach of the gag order and brought a motion against the Bronx DA, charging him with contempt.

Buddy Jacobson, meanwhile, was walking free.

The financial systems division of TRW Inc. has its New York headquarters at 666 Fifth Avenue—a glassy structure once described, unkindly, as the box the Seagram Building came in. This is where David Silbergeld worked, and it was here, at ten o'clock on the morning of December 4, that he was arrested by two federal agents.

It was not a private bust. "We were about to go into a meeting," Silbergeld says. The two agents arrested him with guns drawn, stood him against a wall, frisked him, and, just in case anybody watching still wasn't wise to what a desperate individual he was, snapped a pair of handcuffs on his wrists.

The charge was that he had once unlawfully cashed a government check. This had been an unemployment check that had been paid directly into his bank account some years back, Silbergeld says, just before he joined TRW, and he had repaid it. But it had gone into his account, nonetheless, and by post, which was worse.

Mail fraud. A heavy charge.

"They are deliberately putting the screws to him," Al Seifert told me. "And this is just the beginning. They don't want David. They want Carlo."

Now the stories went into high gear. They depicted David Silbergeld as a salesman of high-technology armament. In one exceptionally colorful variant, he was offering an A-bomb. *An A-bomb.* "I had to laugh when I heard that one," he said.

The same was happening to Silbergeld as had happened, posthumously, to Jack Tupper.

Even Tom Myers, an undemonstrative man, had now become possessed of a need to see justice done. "I'm going to take the offensive," he said. "We are going to visit Jacobson, Rayna Spears, and Terry McCart." By "we," it turned out, he meant the FBI together with the DEA. He was also going to have various phone records subpoenaed in the hopes of tracing the threatening calls.

The Feds did, in due course, visit Buddy at his apartment. He was mild and smooth.

"What purpose would it serve for me to have threatening phone calls made?" he asked, adding, "Friends have told me that Jack Tupper's money is being held by his sister. . . ."

Dorothy Myers now had an *idée fixe.* "I equate Jacobson with what is happening in the world," she said. Evil. "Whenever I see America going down to the pits, I think of Buddy Jacobson."

As Melanie's day in court approached, her self-doubt grew, and pressure intensified. Bookings dwindled, too, as always happened when her name began to pop up again in the press, and it was directly because of the trial, she was told, that she lost the cover of a fashion magazine.

Memories dogged her. Out jogging one morning, she passed some new co-ops, and Buddy's former telephone number, her former number, leaped out at her from a billboard. She worried that the first time she would have seen him in the flesh since the killing was to be their courtroom confrontation, and brooded on sneaking in for a preview, disguised in a wig. This plan, happily, was dropped.

Her appearance in court was to be December 10. A Monday. She sold Christmas trees for Billy all weekend, working till nine on Sunday night. She was staying with her friend, Barbara, and they talked for three hours. That night, succumbing one more time to the lure of Buddy's World, Melanie insisted on being driven past Buddy's buildings, including East 63rd Street, where he now lived. In the morning, she dressed smartly, but severely, in a skirt and blouse belonging to Betsy, having no appropriate clothes of her own, breakfasted on date bread and cottage cheese, which was something Buddy loved, and which Melanie hadn't touched since the day of the murder, and set off for the Bronx.

Electricity had been building long before Melanie's arrival. There was a full house, including Audrey, and David Jacobson. No fewer than six artists had sketchpads at the ready. Melanie walked in at half past ten. She was with Sullivan. Ingrown and intent, she acknowledged neither Barbara nor Billy Collins as she went to the back. Called to the stand, she took the oath and seated herself. She did not look in front of her and a bit to her left, where Buddy sat at a long table, flanked by Epstein and Evseroff. He was neat, bespectacled, a woebegone pitiableness wafting off him like a mist.

The questioning began, and Melanie told her tale.

She seemed controlled. Only her nervously twisting fingers, and an occasional shudder of her shoulders, betrayed the strain. She faltered somewhat when asked about the blood-stains, prompting Judge Kapelman to offer her a drink of water. (George Carpozi, Jr., did not let this slide by un-noticed, writing that the judge "had never offered such atten-tion to any of the more than two dozen witnesses who had preceded Miss Cain to the stand.")

She took a few sips from the cardboard cup and resumed her testimony. Melanie's eyes would now sometimes stray in Buddy's direction, but her face showed no emotion, and she walked straight past him when coming off the stand for a recess.

"This is good," Peter Grishman said. "She hasn't seen him for a year. This way she'll get used to seeing him."

What about David Silbergeld's arrest?

His irritation was intense. "What do I know?" he said. "That's the Feds."

Melanie returned to the stand. It was the defense's turn.

"You may begin, Mr. Evseroff," Judge Kapelman said.

Melanie sighed, quite audibly, and gave a tiny shrug. This was it.

Evseroff began with honeyed softness. This did not last. Soon he was deploying the Sarcastic Rasp, the Snarl, the Shout.

Melanie, somewhat to my surprise, showed no signs of crumbling. Evseroff's hostilities provoked not defensiveness, but attempts to be helpful. A sequence of loaded questions finally did provoke a flash of fire. Evseroff turned around and winked broadly at David Jacobson, as though to indicate that he was achieving just the results he wanted. But watching Melanie, her pallor replaced by a flush as she leaned forward in concentration, it seemed just possible that the combat would not be so one-sided, after all.

That same evening, Buddy's forty-ninth birthday was cele-brated with a dinner party at Claret's, a restaurant on East 60th Street. Thirty had been allowed for, but, as it turned out, eighteen showed. Other diners saw them only briefly as they were taken through and seated in the inner half of the long room, which, at Audrey's insistence, was shielded from public scrutiny by screens. Guests included Buddy's real estate lawyer, Jim Millard, and Nicola, who said that he could stay only a few minutes before returning to his own place uptown.

Buddy was still wearing the boxy black suit and nondescript tie that he had worn to court. He had been taken to Claret's by Audrey at eight-thirty. Supposedly they were to have dined alone. "But that was a surprise party that was no surprise," Buddy later told me. "I've become a bit of a *detective*." Yes, indeed.

There was rack of lamb, with salad, and a great deal of wine, and the dessert was a birthday cake, a foot across, from Dumas, a pâtisserie up the street. It was slathered with yellow icing, embedded with a single candle and inscribed *Happy Birthday, Buddy*, in chocolate. Buddy's presents included crayons and coloring books, and a number of bottles of booze, which were put away, along with quantities of red and white wine.

The toasts soon began to follow the wine. Most of those repeated, usually in a tearfully sentimental vein, the same message: "I hope we'll all be here together, next year."

Tim, the waiter, who happened not to be aware of the guest of honor's identity, scented business. "I guess we should book a table for next year?" he asked Buddy.

"By all means," Buddy told him. "Book the table."

The party broke up at about half past eleven, but Buddy showed no inclination to go home. He and Audrey, together with a last few guests, sat at the bar. They ordered some more drinks and stayed there, talking, till half past two in the morning. The check, picked up by Audrey, came to $847.50.

On Wednesday morning, Buddy Jacobson had more to say about the celebration. "I haven't had parties given for me since I was a kid," he said. "It was new to me." Nor the party only. "This was new to me, too," he added, looking around the courtroom. "Now it's getting old. . . ."

The courtroom, which Judge Kapelman had assigned to himself is on the ninth floor and, boasting 126 seats, is the largest in the building. The room has a look of lush austerity, with its demure neoclassical decor, and oak paneling the color of a sweet sherry. Before the trial was over, we regulars would feel that we were born here and had lived here for generations, side by side.

We would know each other by heart. The lawyers, with their quirks. The cops, obtrusive in their plainclothes. The shapes and sizes of court officers. The hard core of "court buffs," mostly retired people with time on their hands who prefer courtrooms to the TV soaps. And, of course, the press. Only Buddy seemed apart. And Melanie.

Melanie was off the stand. Her second day on the stand had been formidable. She had even addressed Buddy directly several times—"You remember that, Buddy? Don't you?"—forgetting Judge Kapelman's reproofs. Now the defense was trying to invalidate the search warrant that had allowed the authorities to go into Buddy's apartment. If they were successful, the evidence found in the apartment could not be used by the prosecution. Evseroff had subpoenaed one of the people who had sworn out the warrant: Al Seifert.

Al arrived, wearing a three-piece suit, the darkest of dark glasses, and a nifty brown trilby. His intention had been to conceal himself from the attentions of the press, but the effect was made-for-television-movie sinister. Artie Pomerantz, a *Post* photographer, snatched a few quick shots, and Seifert crossly flicked a cigarette at him. Pomerantz was outraged. "I told his lawyer I would have him arrested," he said.

Seifert sat in the courtroom, in the seats where the Tuppers would usually sit, and removed his glasses. Beside me I heard scratching from a female reporter and glanced at her pad. "Seifert sat in the front row with his lawyer waiting to be called," she wrote. "As soon as I saw him I thought he had the meanest eyes I've ever seen." I looked at Seifert again, but to me he merely looked weary.

Buddy was also looking at his former owner. "I hear you have talked with this guy," he asked me.

"Yes."

"I heard you both put your tape recorders on the table."

Yes, I agreed.

"We're all embarrassed by things we say on tape," he observed. "Sometimes we say things we don't mean. . . ."

Seifert took the stand, and questioning began. During a first recess, cautious as ever, he replaced his dark glasses and had a smoke in the tiny, but media-free, space between the outer and inner doors of the courtroom. Jack Evseroff came up to me in the hallway. "Am I too loud?" he demanded, indicating his suit, which was black with a vibrant pinstripe. A huge gold ring, a replica of the head of Michelangelo's *Moses,* glimmered on his pinky. "I don't wear my good jewelry in the Bronx," he assured me. "You could get mugged right in the courtroom."

He had other matters to impart. "I wasn't too impressed by Miss Melanie Cain," he said.

I observed that I thought she had stood up well under cross-examination.

"That wasn't cross-examination! Do you think I can't break her down? Get her on the stand for five days, and just watch." He turned to go, but swiveled and asked if I was staying. I said I wasn't sure.

"Stick around," he said over his shoulder as he stalked off. "You may find it interesting."

Seifert returned to the stand. Evseroff was trying to discredit the search warrant by charging him with perjury. Was it not true, for instance, that he had described himself as a property dealer, and the owner of a couple of Baskin-Robbins franchises, whereas he was, in fact, a narcotics dealer?

"He sells thirty-one flavors of marijuana," Greenfield observed.

It was now that Evseroff asked Seifert whether he knew Anthony Haden-Guest.

I grinned incredulously. The defense attorney turned and gave me not his Wink, but his Serious Look, and then asked Seifert whether he had a "deal" with me.

Seifert answered no, accurately enough, and Evseroff moved on.

"Did you see John Tupper on August sixth?" he asked.

"No," said Seifert.

"Did you participate in any way, form, manner, or shape in the killing of John Tupper?"

After asking the question, Evseroff pivoted around and looked directly for a moment, though without expression, at George Carpozi. Seifert paused a moment before replying, and spoke phlegmatically, but his voice seemed to resound through the courtroom.

"No," he said. "Only your client did."

He did not even glance in Buddy's direction.

We recessed, and I lunched with Seifert, his father, and his attorney on draft beer and corned-beef sandwiches. Seifert was unimpressed by Evseroff. "He's very antagonistic," he said.

We strolled back to court, and I bought a *Post* at the corner. BUDDY'S LAWYER TAPS MOB FIGURE. Carpozi's story began: "The alleged head of a vast drug trafficking ring has been . . . asked if he, and not Howard (Buddy) Jacobson, murdered John Tupper." According to the story, the gang was "headed by Mafia chieftain Simone (Sam the Plumber) De Cavalcante," and had brought in $1 billion worth of marijuana in seven years.

Al's reaction was amusement until he picked up on the Mafia howler. "It's just beginning to sink in," he said. "My son's friends are going to see that story. They're going to say: 'Did your father kill John Tupper?'" He returned glumly to the courtroom.

"I bet Al wishes he never opened his big mouth," David Jacobson told me, with searing intensity.

As the afternoon session began, Judge Kapelman addressed me.

"Mr. Guest, would you step out into the hall a moment, please," he said.

Jack Evseroff was waiting. Unsmiling, he slapped me with a couple of subpoenas. One was to hand over all materials relating to conversations I might have had with Melanie Cain. The other demanded materials relating to Al Seifert.

"Congratulations," Grishman said, as I returned to the courtroom.

Pete McLaughlin joked, "Don't sit next to me, Anthony."

Against my will, I had become part of the process.

On the night of December 14, Kevin Tupper dreamed about the murder. A man was at the front door of his and Kathy's house. He was unknown to Kevin, but he was carrying a search warrant, and his manner was authoritative.

The man accused Kevin of lifting Buddy Jacobson's fingerprints and planting them on a car that had crashed.

Kevin denied the charge vehemently, and tried to be logical. "That's an impossible thing to do," he said.

The man was inflexible.

"It *has* to be you," he told Kevin. Logic had nothing to do with it.

*   *   *

The attempt by the defense to overturn the search warrant of Jacobson's apartment failed, as did the motion to charge Mario Merola with contempt. The furor had been a far from empty exercise, though. Jack Evseroff had been enabled to peek at a great many of the prosecution cards, and much time had been gained. Time can dull both grief and memory. It had, for instance, been decided that young Paul Tupper's testimony would not now be of much use. Judge Kapelman adjourned for the holiday season, and declared that the trial would resume early in January.

But the pretrial motions had been an educational experience for Buddy. Right at the beginning of his steeplechase through the legal system, he had thought himself splendidly equipped to handle his own case. At the same time, though, he realized that his rambling performance at the bail hearings had not been a hit. "I wanted to defend myself at first," he told me. "I learned better. . . ."

It was not a lesson he ever learned completely. At the start of the pretrial motions, he had watched Evseroff and Epstein constantly and had been especially suspicious of the "sidebars" —the conferences between judge and lawyers—and all the private discussions in the robing room.

"You're deciding my life in there," he told Evseroff. "I want to see what's going on."

When it came time for the next conference, Evseroff told Kapelman that his client wanted to be present. The judge acquiesced.

The discussion was not absorbing, and Buddy did not ask for further participation. But he did keep his legal team under the closest observation. "Jacobson imagines himself to be a genius," Dom Barberino said. "When he was with me, he used to knock Jack. 'Who the hell does Jack think he is? All that *flair!* Why doesn't he do this or that?'

"And when he was with Jack, he would knock me. 'What does Dom think he's doing? He doesn't come back with the right information.' Sometimes I would go and see a witness, and they'd say Buddy was just here. I'd go to Buddy and say, 'What are you doing? You're good with horses. Leave the witnesses to me.' "

Jacobson had been watching Judge Kapelman closely, and with increasing sourness. During the motion to chuck out the search warrant, he had been angered when, as it seemed to him, Kapelman had leaned toward Melanie's explanation of the way she had found the correct combination to his door—through luck, habit, and jiggling around. Buddy broke into the conversation. "That's *totally impossible,*" he said. "There's ten thousand possible combinations."

According to Jacobson, he told Evseroff how to handle Kapelman. "If he decides against you, you cry like a baby. And, next time, he hands you one. And if he decides in your favor, you cry like a baby. Because he didn't give you enough. . . ."

"I told Evseroff what to do," Buddy said. "First he declares war on Kapelman, then he makes peace. Then he declares war again. Now things in the court are much better."

He spoke with assurance, as one who had everything under control.

Melanie went to spend Christmas with her parents. The Tuppers withdrew into themselves. Buddy had been in Manhattan. He had now resolved to turn the buildings on East 63rd into co-ops, and sell them off as quickly as possible. The price he had in mind was much higher than the going rate, the apartments being on the small side, but, as he would tell people, there were plenty of Arabs, Iranians, and Europeans in town who wouldn't haggle, if the location was right.

This would, however, mean getting rid of some tenants, and Buddy embarked on an imaginative campaign. For one thing, he would insist that rents be delivered to him personally. Then garbage bins disappeared, and were never replaced. One tenant was hauled to court. "Jacobson said that I had refused him access to the apartment and that I had refused him a set of keys," the miscreant said. Another tenant was one of several who received a legal document that read as follows:

Please take notice, that your landlord hereby demands access to your apartment on December 24th, 1979, at 6:45 o'clock in the evening of that day for the purpose of making an inspection thereof.

The inspection did not take place. Audrey persuaded him to spend Christmas with her parents on Long Island. They listened to Christmas carols, drank wine, and made as merry as possible.

*　　*　　*

Shortly after noon on December 30, I met Donald Brown in the Polo Bar of the Beverly Hills Hotel. This was the first time I had seen Brown since he had turned, and his mood veered from the rambunctious to the bleak.

"I didn't have any choice," he insisted. "I'm looking at twenty years. What kind of life would I have when I come out?" According to the terms of his deal, he now felt he might serve as little as two years, most of it in a minimum-security prison.

Gloom soon descended again, and Donald began to inveigh against those he would soon be facing in court. One of them had sworn to "get" him, Brown said, and that night somebody had fired a couple of shots into the wall of his mother's house. Another had robbed him. "He would say a shipment had gone bad," Donald blazed, staring at me with his pale-blue eyes. "He stole three or four million from me. You just don't *do* that. When you sit down at the table, the share has to be fair. That's *cardinal*."

But his guilt would not be so easily assuaged. He said that his testimony so far had been of little help to the authorities. "I haven't really hurt anybody yet. You follow me?" he insisted.

What else could he have done? he demanded. "I knew the indictment was coming down. I was advised to take a powder."

Is the drug charge an extraditable offense?

"Of course. I'd be gone tomorrow if it wasn't."

Donald Brown agreed, though, that his chances of lying low somewhere, even in the government's Alias Program, were, given his bravura personality, close to nil.

We ordered coffee, and he mentioned something else. A story had just reached him about Buddy. "I hear that the focus is going to switch to me," he said. "Buddy said, 'Next I am going to get Donald Brown.'"

On the morning of January 12, a young man named Ronald Norton—sometimes known as Scooter—was busted in apartment D4, the Thickett Apartments, Mount Pleasant, South Carolina. His offense was possession of five grams of coke, nine of hashish, 165 of marijuana, and a .38 caliber revolver. Together with Scooter at the time was Beth McKay, who explained that he was a friend of her fiancé's.

Beth McKay had, of course, been a My Fair Lady model,

and had been one of the small group that had seen the departure of the yellow van from East 84th Street on the day of the
murder. Later she had returned home to South Carolina, and
had been there ever since. She was working in a bank, and
was thought to be a sensible young woman. But the Scooter
affair would surface during Buddy's trial, and would do its bit
to confuse.

It should not be thought that Buddy never tried to explain
the events on the day of Jack Tupper's murder. And while his
apologia was to change and shift—both before and after the
trial—one version typed on his business stationery, runs in
part as follows:

During the prior year before the incident, much construction was done at 155. . . . Quite a bit of construction
material was being stored in the back yard, office, and in
the stair wells. I received a building dept. violation because of this, but until I bought the Park East Hosp. in
May, I had no place to store the stuff. . . . A part time
employee Sal Prainito borrowed his employer's truck on
at least two occasions and we moved supplies over. A
week before the incident I asked him if he could borrow
the truck again, but he couldn't so I gave him $ to rent a
truck, which he did. . . . We moved material on Sat.
Aug. 5th.

8 AM Aug 6/78—Models who lived on the 4th floor
and were with My Fair L. called to inform me that their
roommate, another model with M.F.L. had a terrible accident and was killed the night before. About 8:30 AM
Melanie knocked on my door and stuck her head in and
talked to me about Sherril Cory [sic]. I asked her to handle
the police questions and the family as I felt that a girl could
give our condolences better than I. Melanie returned about
a half hour later.

At 9 or 9:30 Leslie Hammond my next door neighbor
discussed painting her apt. and Doug and I walked around
the corner to the Park E. Approximately an hour later I
received a call from Melanie and in a hysterical voice she
pleaded with me to return to the apt. She said that something terrible had happened and it was all her fault. I said
what the hell are you talking about? She pleaded with me so
I whistled for Doug to tell him I was leaving, but he did

not answer. When I reached the lobby, Sal was stacking pipe. I asked him to come with me as I knew the bunch that Melanie was hanging out with was trouble. When I got out on the top floor of 155, Melanie was standing at the doorway of Tupper's apt. sobbing. She signalled me to follow her around the corner of the hall and entered my apt. The door was opened. Sal followed behind me. Tupper was sprawled out on the floor near the phone. He was grey in color and had blood on his hair line.

I said "Holy shit what happened, what is this guy doing in my place?" Melanie said "He's dead and it's all my fault." I grabbed her by the arm and pulled her back to her apt and I started yelling at her. She explained that Tupper and his bunch wasn't getting along with the Margarite bunch in the cocaine business, but when he caught her with Margarite he really blew his top. After a big argument in the hall outside Margarite's apt, a fight started, she heard shots and saw them drag Tupper into 7D. Margarite and his friends ran down the stairs. She begged me to help her. She said that she couldn't face the police as she was involved in the drugs.

I saw that helpless look in her eyes that I had seen so many times before and realized that I would do anything for her. I also knew that if a dead body of a drug dealer was found in my building, one who my ex-girl friend was living with and after Sherril had been killed the night before, the modeling business would be finished. I was about to get a loan . . . to complete the Park E. All of this was suddenly coming down around me. There in his apt was several boxes. I grabbed one of them and Melanie helped me carry it near the doorway of my apt. We avoided white paint that had been knocked over on the hall rug. I entered my apt and Sal was leaning over Tupper and saying something in Italian like Morte. I asked him if he had the van for the pipes and would he help me. He understood me and said are you crazy? But after asking him a few times he finally agreed to get the van. He returned a few minutes later with a dolly. He had helped me put him in the box before he left. Sal and me stood the box on end on the dolly and I helped him push it into the elevator, the door closed, and he was gone. I told Melanie to get in her apt and stay there. I cleaned my apt which had a little blood. A mirror was broken. There was slight stains on the cushions which I didn't know if it was blood or not. I removed the covers and burnt them in the fire place. I tried to clean the carpet in the hall with my shampooer but made it worse so I decided to throw it away. It was getting worn anyway. I put the glass from the broken mirror in a rubbish can which was kept in the stair landing and threw it and the rug in the container around the corner. There were no bullets in my front door at that time. It was now around 12:30. I went down to the lobby and did my normal chores which was to take the garbage out. I then left to go the Park E. Melanie was sitting on the bricks outside of 155. I told her that everything would be alright and that I would be back later. She was quiet and said nothing. When I returned to the Park E., I saw no one. I called Sal's house and spoke to an Italian lady who did not speak English.

At 3:30 Sal drove up in his yellow Cadillac. I was upset and said what the hell did you do with it? He said that he would show me, so I got in the car and we drove to a dump. We climbed a hill and I saw the box burning slightly. It was raining, so we ran back to the car. I told him to stop somewhere, that I had [to] get a drink. We stopped at a grocery and I got a grapefruit juice. Sal asked me if I would drive the car back to New York and he would take the van back. He stopped at where the van was parked. There was a guy standing there. I said who's that? He said "Gumba, it's okay, drive him back with you." I started back and was arrested.

This was Buddy's story.

On the morning of January 21, Buddy, Audrey, and I traveled up to the courtroom in the same elevator in the Bronx County Building. The trial was about to get underway.

The familiar group was re-forming. Besides the lawyers, Dom Barberino was there, as were Rick Pienciak, Pete McLaughlin, and George Carpozi, Jr. "Do you get a feeling of déjà vu?" asked Jack Evseroff. "It's like a reunion." He began talking about the Superbowl. "The Superbowl," Buddy said. "I don't know what it *is*. I was watching Bill Buckley." In the most casual of tones, he told me that he had recently spotted

Joe Margarite. He had seen him, he said, in Demarchelier, a restaurant much frequented by people in the modeling business.

"I walked in, and I saw this guy who's on the lam. I turned right around and went out."

He affected not to care whether or not Margarite was apprehended.

The new prosecutor was already sitting in the courtroom. He was a massive man with a broad bony face, and his name was Bill Hrabsky. "He's supposed to be a real hard-ass trial lawyer," Pienciak said.

Judge Kapelman made his entrance. He smiled a wide, rubbery smile, like the Duchess in *Alice in Wonderland*, and wished us "a very happy and healthy New Year."

The proceedings began. Hrabsky, on his feet, was at once impressive and ungainly. The trousers of his nondescript gray suit were an inch or two shorter than the norm, and were supported by both suspenders and a belt. He and Dave Greenfield, Prainito's attorney, began dueling almost at once. "There is to be no backbiting," Kapelman admonished. "Let's stop it."

During a recess, the reporters and the attorneys were speculating about Kelly's replacement.

"They call him the Mad Russian. What does that tell you?" said Evseroff.

"Where do they find these guys?" asked a TV reporter.

"They ask them all to run out of the building," Greenfield said, "and the last one out gets appointed."

"You know who he'd look like if he combed his hair a bit different and stuck a couple of electrodes in his neck?" demanded Evseroff. "Boris Karloff."

We crowded into the elevator. It was full of lawyers in chain-store three-piece suits. "Who've you got, Buddy?" one of them asked.

"Hrabsky," Buddy said.

"*Hrabsky!*" one lawyer said.

"Take a plea," advised another humorously.

"He can't control his temper," the first lawyer said. "Jack will get him."

Buddy was silent, only saying to me, "Do you think Kapelman included me when he wished us a happy New Year?"

* * *

The first flurry of interest came when Greenfield asked that Prainito be tried separately from Jacobson on the grounds that their defenses might be mutually "antagonistic." This Kapelman denied. Now began the process of picking the jury.

The pulse quickened. Buddy, giving one of his analyses in the hallway, affected to miss Bill Kelly. "I hear that he's honest," he said. "My theory is that's why he got off the case. Everybody wants this case until they look closely at it."

He discussed Melanie's nervous demeanor, adopting the fatherly tones of a family physician. "She was on something. She was flying high at the beginning. Later, she was more . . . sedate."

"She came across as a smart-ass," a reporter assured him.

"I looked her straight in the eye all the time," Buddy said, with a gleam.

"Buddy," said Pienciak earnestly, "just explain one thing. What were you doing in the car? In the Bronx?"

Buddy smiled, his most seraphic smile.

"If I was you, that's just what I would ask," he said, and did not answer.

Returning to the courtroom, Buddy gestured toward the black metal cylinder from which the jurors' names would be drawn: "That box is going to decide my life," he said. It was now that Buddy imparted to me some thoughts on jury selection, which Evseroff has described as anything from seventy-five to a hundred percent of a case.

"It's very complex," Buddy said. "Normally, you want low-income people, who may not much like the police." But he was beset with doubts. What would a poorly paid black guy think of a millionaire former racehorse owner? What would a middle-aged Bronx housewife think of a playboy who ran around with models? There was, moreover, the sheer complexity of the conspiratorial earthwork he was throwing up around the case. "This time," he said, "you may need people of above-average intelligence. And those are the sort of people who like to *convict*. But we may need people who can . . . *understand*."

It was Jack Evseroff's snakeskin cowboy boots that finally got to Buddy. He approached Ben Epstein, who agreed. It was too Brooklyn for a Bronx jury. So on January 28, the critical day upon which the selection was to begin, Evseroff's attire was pared down to a flared suit, Italian shoes, barely any jewelry at all. Minimals.

The courtroom was packed. It was time for the start of the questioning process the defense and prosecution use to accept or reject jurors, with each side allowed to veto up to twenty without explanation.

The media studied the first twelve prospective jurors closely. "That Archie Bunker guy," McLaughlin said, looking at a cheery blue-collar type. "He'd love a chance to send a millionaire Jew to jail." He soon was excused. A pretty girl was rejected, seemingly by both sides. Next came a computer operator, who revealed that he dabbled in writing—poems and short stories. He too went down. "Words are funny things," Evseroff mused.

After each side had asked its questions, the lawyers would cluster at the sidebar to approve a juror or use up a previous veto, with Buddy participating. Still nobody had been approved by both sides. Then it was the turn of a social studies teacher, a youngish man, unsmiling, with the sort of rectangular-faced handsomeness of the honest cop. Indeed, it turned out the man's brother was a cop in New York. A goner, I decided: Buddy would ditch him for sure.

Wrong. Dennis De Santis—that was the teacher's name—was chosen.

Five jurors, in all, were selected that day, all men, and they included the only black so far chosen. The choice of each and every juror was the end result of a sparring between the defense and the prosecution in which the weapons were, supposedly, logic and experience. Buddy's belief that what he called "low-income people" would not be disposed to look on him kindly was endorsed by prosecutor Hrabsky. Gail Jacobs, a young woman from the DA's office who sat next to Hrabsky throughout the trial, says simply, "We wanted those people."

Surprisingly, all remaining jurors were picked on the second day. They included three women. One of these, a young black woman working in the postal service, revealed that her husband had once spent six months in jail—unjustly, in her view. She claimed she bore the authorities no ill will, but the fact that she was consented to by Hrabsky caused a stir in the courtroom.

Three other choices aroused similar stirrings. They were all men, and they were all auxiliary policemen. Defense laywers will normally not let anyone connected with law enforcement near a jury. Letting these auxiliaries on the jury was a fateful decision, arrived at jointly by Jacobson and Evseroff. There was, first, Buddy's own feeling that he wanted jurors capable of picking up on some of the nuances of his defense. As for Evseroff, he was, after all, the Man Who Defends Killer Cops —as *New York* magazine had once described him. "Cops like me," he said, buoyantly.

Dave Greenfield was deeply hostile to the auxiliaries. "I immediately said I didn't want them on," he says. "But Buddy said he did. Sal went along with Buddy. Jack was lukewarm. Ben wasn't there. The vote was three to one." So it was decided.

The jury had now been picked. Dennis De Santis was the foreman. Harry Garrison, a bearded young Paramount analyst, was number two.

The others included Robert Coletti, a youngish man with a sort of macho restlessness. Bernice Faust, the resentful woman from the postal service, and the three auxiliary cops.

Michael Speller, a retired railroad employee, a black man with a broad face, was number ten, and he sat next to Frederico Velez, whose permanently attentive look contrasted strongly with number twelve, Rose Kovnit, an elderly woman who sometimes seemed to have wafted to some other place.

Four alternates sat in a row of seats a little removed from the jury box. That was it. The trial proper was ready to begin. Buddy Jacobson sat there at the long table, examining the jury that would be ruling upon his innocence or guilt.

He did not seem to find the sight satisfactory. "It's not exactly a jury of Buddy's peers," Audrey said petulantly, as we went down in the elevator.

"They don't look as if they know what a reasonable doubt *is*," commented Buddy.

One more coincidence, and a source of gnawing uneasiness in the Bronx DA's office: the trial of the Donald Brown Organization was to open in Brooklyn on precisely the same day as the Jacobson trial had begun in the Bronx. Among those cooperating with the government were D.B. himself, Al Seifert, Ivor Shaw, Natiello, and Rudy Dehesa. Among those on the block were Jimmy Leonard, Billy Sharrocks, Carlo Carrara, Alan Finkelstein, and Peter Splain. The prosecutor was Doug Behm.

It was the morning of January 30. The Jacobson trial was about to begin. Jack Tupper, Sr., was there, soberly dressed and silent, a Veteran of Foreign Wars insignia glinting in his lapel. "I'm a bit jittery," he told me. "I know I'm not going to like what I hear." Dorothy Myers stood beside him, her blond bangs and brown eyes belying the hardness of her expression. She had been banned from the courtroom, on the grounds she would be called as a witness.

"We will now proceed with the trial," Judge Kapelman said. "The people will make its opening statement."

The stillness as Bill Hrabsky got to his feet was broken when one of the court artists ripped a completed sheet from her sketch block. "I'm going to strike a very somber note with you," Hrabsky began, describing the case as "a picture puzzle." Soon his voice was booming, his finger pointing with righteous ire at Jacobson and Prainito.

He paused for dramatic effect. "Samples of metal strip were taken. Blood!" he intoned. "Samples of rug undermatting. Blood! A tile from the wall in the hallway. Blood! The very clothes that the defendant, Jacobson, was wearing at the time he was arrested. Blood! Blood! Blood! Blood! The eyeglasses in the apartment belonging to the defendant, Jacobson. Blood!"

Audrey, spectral despite the hooped earrings, the coral fingernails, savagely bit her knuckles. John Tupper, Sr., held himself in place, stiff as a waxwork. Buddy's eyes constantly scanned the jury. Never once did he glance at Prainito.

It was time for Evseroff to open for the defense. He had discussed his strategy with Greenfield and Epstein, and they had agreed not to show too much of their case. In the light of this, what Jack said was a bit of a stunner. "Howard Jacobson is the product of a frame, compounded by inefficiency and incompetence by the authorities," he intoned. "I submit to you that the evidence in this case will reveal that the architect and engineer of this frame was the Girl of a Thousand Faces, Melanie Cain, and that is what she was known as, and the evidence will so reveal it.

"I submit to you that the evidence will reveal that this Girl of a Thousand Faces, who was capable of appearing on a magazine cover as a sweet innocent thing on one hand, and of going to Paris and posing for pictures of the most sensual and exotic nature on the other hand, framed Buddy Jacobson . . . to cover up her own implication with respect to the murder of Jack Tupper, her lover."

Evseroff went on to say that it wasn't a "love triangle" but a "quadrangle"—and that "Jack Tupper was murdered because of Melanie Cain's involvement with Joseph Margarite . . . the reason that Tupper was murdered was because of a beef, a disagreement with respect to cocaine, drugs, and that Melanie Cain was right in the middle of it."

He could prove that "at the time Jack Tupper was killed, Buddy Jacobson wasn't there." According to Evseroff, Tupper was murdered by two men—in Margarite's apartment—and Melanie had abetted the conspiracy to frame "this forty-eight-year-old fool, who was in love with the Woman of a Thousand Faces." Now his voice was as loud as Hrabsky's. "We will show you who the true culprit is," he promised. "I know that by your verdict you will vindicate this . . . *fool!*"—and here he pointed a bony finger at his client, who quite plainly did not enjoy the description.

Recess. I was in the hallway talking to Dorothy and her father when Evseroff passed. "How did you like my opening?" he asked as he swept by.

"You shout when you lie," Dorothy said. "I used to do it with my mother."

She spoke loudly enough that Evseroff must have heard, but he gave no indication. He was still elated when his colleague Ben Epstein arrived. "I really wowed them," he told Epstein.

"What do you mean?" asked Epstein.

"Jack's blown the case," Dave Greenfield said. He was joking, but there was no mistaking that Evseroff had issued a challenge. The defense strategy now depended on the destruction of Melanie's credibility, and the tools that Evseroff would use, the information with which he had been supplied, had come from Buddy Jacobson.

At 2:25 P.M., Melanie arrived at the courtroom. She was just, suddenly, *there.* Her arrival was so speedy that she almost collided with David Jacobson in the doorway. The prosecution was leading with its main event.

Melanie had not known when she was to take the stand until Gail Jacobs of the DA's office had told her late the previous afternoon. Now she had just heard that the defense was claiming that *she* was responsible for Jack Tupper's death, and she was as white as a shelled egg.

During her testimony, the courtroom was hushed.

Melanie first answered questions about Cheryl Corey, pausing frequently to dab at her eyes. But when the plaid rug was produced as evidence, the rug stained by Tupper's blood, she stared at it fixedly—even as Buddy stared at her. Later, when she heard Jack talking to Jacobson on tape, she could not keep the tears from coming in earnest.

Though she tried to avoid Buddy's eyes, occasionally she would weaken, and sometimes she would even address him directly. "I *guess* he's left-handed," she told Evseroff in answer to a question, then confirming it with Buddy—"You're left-handed, aren't you?"—as a ripple of laughter spread across the courtroom. Evseroff had no intention of allowing Melanie to seem sympathetic. Jabbing and needling, he would veer from sarcasm to outrage as he hauled her again and again over nearly identical ground. On February 1, Melanie's third day on the stand, he broke into a provocative line of inquiry.

"Have you had any acting instruction?" he asked.

Melanie replied that she had been to a drama coach for three weeks some five years before, and that she had been in drama class at high school.

"Did you study acting somewhere else?" Evseroff asked.

"Yes."

"Where was that?"

"Lee Strasberg Studio."

When was that, asked the lawyer meaningfully.

"Last fall," Melanie said.

Lee Strasberg! Method Acting! There was a momentary buzz in the courtroom, and the jurors studied Melanie's face for signs of make-believe.

In her testimony, Melanie told Evseroff that she had left Buddy several times during their years together.

"During these periods, did you have other boyfriends?"

"No."

"Never?"

"No."

Buddy smiled, as though in utter disbelief, and shook his head. In case the jury might not have noticed his reaction, he slapped the table hard with his palm.

Evseroff persevered. Did *Buddy* have other girlfriends?

"Yes," Melanie said unwillingly. "I guess so."

"Would you say many?"

"I guess so. I don't know."

Had Melanie ever found Buddy in bed with another girl?

"Yes."

"Do you know the name of that other girl?"

"Yes," Melanie said. She was very pale, and the room was totally quiet. Buddy, she realized, had told his lawyers about Ingrid.

"What's her name?" Evseroff asked.

"I'm not going to tell you her name."

Evseroff began to utter a name when it happened!

"I'm not going to tell you her name!" Melanie wailed as she swiveled around to Kapelman and begged, "I don't think I have to tell him the name?"

"Just one moment," Kapelman broke in. "I don't see the necessity of disclosing that," he said to Evseroff.

The defense attorney backpedaled hastily, but the damage was done. Clearly Melanie was no vengeful bitch. Evseroff returned to the subject of Melanie's own fidelity, asking about her dance classes, and then about one of her instructors. Had he been a boyfriend of Melanie's?

"He was not. Buddy always assumed he was. Buddy was so possessive, he didn't want me to dance *anywhere*," Melanie replied.

"So Buddy was in error?" Evseroff inquired.

"Yes. He was!"

There was a note in Melanie's voice that sounded transparently sincere. Evseroff shot Buddy the briefest of glances. But he had eyes only for Melanie, like a snake trying to hypnotize a rabbit.

"The poor girl is going through an awful lot," Jack Tupper, Sr., whispered in my ear. He and his daughter Dorothy, although she had to wait outside, were now turning up in court every day. "This is a circus," Jack Tupper said. "I have to represent my son. He would expect that." Their earlier resentment of Melanie was now gone. "Just think. She could have been my daughter-in-law," Tupper said. "What a nice thing that would have been."

Evseroff continued to wear away at Melanie, coming back to a principal theme of his opening statement. He produced that Eugenia Sheppard column about her from January 1976, which had been headlined GIRL OF A THOUSAND FACES. Did this not mean, he demanded, that she could "affect many different poses and many different images?"

"Yes," Melanie agreed. "I was very animated."

"On the one hand, you could appear to be very innocent and very demure, and, on the other hand, you could appear very exotic, if that is the right word?"

Evseroff began to introduce a copy of the French magazine *L'Officiel* into evidence. This was evidently the source of the "exotic" photographs to which he had previously made reference. *L'Officiel* is such a proper magazine that beside it *Vogue* seems like, well, *Penthouse*. Melanie began to giggle.

"Excuse me," she said. "But this is so ridiculous. *Exotic!* That picture is from a fashion magazine over in France, and I wouldn't call it exotic."

"What picture?" Evseroff asked, again backpedaling.

"The picture on your desk," Melanie said. "I can't believe you play these games."

Kapelman reproved Melanie and granted a short recess, after which Evseroff did indeed introduce *L'Officiel*, which he pronounced to rhyme with "pal," into evidence. Melanie was shown a double-page photographic spread. The picture showed a female model. It was shot from the back, so the model was unrecognizable, but she was, quite unmistakably, nude. Melanie was asked if she recognized the model.

"This isn't me," she said.

"Pardon?" said Kapelman.

"This isn't me," Melanie repeated. She was in other pictures in the fashion story, but fully clothed. "It's the other girl," she explained.

At this point Jack Evseroff, fed one bit of misinformation too many, snapped his pencil and threw it down on the table, more or less under Buddy's nose.

During recess, Evseroff and Buddy would whisper together, looking like Faust and Mephistopheles, or vice versa. They then appeared before the press, framed by lenses, lights, and busy notebooks. "It makes you want to vomit," Jack Tupper said. "There's my son dead. And there he is, in all his glory." Jacobson affected to be unimpressed by Melanie on the stand. "I think she's actually helping us," said Buddy, getting in his message. "She's an old pro at this stuff." Nor was there a shortage of voices, such as that of George Carpozi, both in person and in print, to assure Buddy that Melanie was making a poor impression on the jury.

Others, like WCBS' Irene Cornell and columnist Murray Kempton, were of a contrary opinion. Evseroff's questioning had been spectacular, veering from grinding repetitiveness to actual mimicry of Melanie, but so far he had hardly dented her. Moreover, she was ignoring opportunities to score the sort of points against Buddy that his lawyer was trying to score against her. At times, this worried prosecutor Hrabsky. "In the courtroom she doesn't paint Buddy as this hyper guy," he complained. "The way she did to us." Generally, though, Melanie's lack of vindictiveness—at times, her obvious ambivalence about attacking Buddy at all—was perfectly clear.

But the defense had another strategy: the dope motive. Both Buddy and Evseroff were watching the tortuous progress of the Brooklyn trial with eager eyes, and the defense attorney lost no opportunity, always over the strenuous objections of Hrabsky, to remind the jury of the interesting friends Jack Tupper used to have. On February 4, for instance, Evseroff handed Melanie a copy of the Brooklyn indictment and asked Melanie if she recognized any of the names.

"A few of them," she agreed.

Evseroff moved in. Did Melanie know Donald Brown? Al Seifert? Carlo Carrara?

"Yes. She did. And she would add, whenever she could, "So did Buddy."

"And was Jack Tupper a business associate of Donald Brown?" demanded the lawyer.

"I don't think so. They were just friends."

"I see. And isn't it a fact that Donald Brown is a major drug dealer?"

Melanie agreed she knew this, "from reading the papers," as the Tuppers' rage grew. "These are boys Jackie grew up with," Jack Tupper said. "It's all association!" Next recess, Evseroff was again being interviewed in the lobby. They listended grimly.

"Can I say that Jack Tupper was indicted?" asked the columnist, Murray Kempton.

"I can't interfere with the freedom of the press," Evseroff said.

This was too much for Kevin, who exploded. "You *know* my brother wasn't indicted," he told the lawyer. "You can be as obnoxious as you want. But you're not proving it to the press! You have to prove it in court!"

I walked back into the courtroom. Buddy was by the rail. "You have to sympathize with the family," he told me, with all the earnestness at his command. "I see them sitting there. I know what they must think of me. I hope they'll think differently when it's all over."

Buddy's army of straw men, stooges—Seifert, Brown,

Jimmy Leonard, Carrara, Ivor Shaw, and the rest—were now deployed and, it seemed certain, about to be called into play.

"I think you can reasonably assume you will see Mr. Seifert here in connection with this case," Evseroff told me. He added that they were now looking hard for Ivor Shaw. "We'd put him on the stand in a moment," attorney Ben Epstein said. "But he's elusive." George Carpozi's headline that afternoon ran: YES, TUPPER HAD PALS IN COKE GANG, SAYS MELANIE.

The gist of the subpoenas with which I had been served was this: The defense lawyers wanted to see the notes of my conversations with Melanie. Otherwise I might be cited for contempt. I was working on a book, so was unprotected by Journalism's "shield law."

"I'm wondering how you're going to look in horizontal stripes," Dan O'Grady pondered.

"Go to jail," Buddy advised me.

But what would I have been trying to protect? *Melanie was telling the truth.* There was nothing in her notebooks or what she had told me that could possibly damage her.

Ike Sorkin, my lawyer, suggested that we propose a deal. The judge could read the material in my possession and then decide what part of it, if any, had relevance to the case. That part could go to the defense lawyers.

On February 1, I followed Sorkin and a clump of lawyers into the robing room, a dingy place, furnished mostly with a Westinghouse refrigerator, which, with some lack of trust considering the location, was padlocked. Judge Kapelman, to my relief, agreed to our proposal. Evseroff objected only to one provision—that he would have to read such notes as seemed relevant in the courtroom itself. He should, he said, be allowed to take them home for the weekend.

"I wish to have time to disseminate them," he said, paused, and corrected himself hastily. "I mean, *assimilate*."

"Freud is turning over in his grave," Ike Sorkin remarked.

Kapelman found that a twelfth of the material I had submitted covered the same ground as the cross-examination. Copies of this material were then provided to both prosecution and defense.

On February 5, I observed that a new image had been pasted onto the billboard which looks directly across at the Bronx County Building. This new advertisement—it was promoting a line of toiletries—showed the gigantic head of the model, Margaux Hemingway, blond hair shining, innocently parted lips a-glimmer. This apparition in the Bronx had seemed a good omen, but not for long. Court had been adjourned for the day. Melanie had the flu, we were told. There was speculation that she was buckling under Evseroff's grilling and was about to crack. That day's headline on the Carpozi story read: MELANIE STAYS HOME SICK AFTER BRUTAL DAY ON STAND.

Shaw and I dined in the Madison Pub that same evening. His buccaneer days were behind him, he had thought, and he was now working in the financial market. But the unceasing publicity was getting to him, and his customarily bland face was twitchy.

"Some days, you're crippled with paranoia, other days you feel fine. It's like arthritis," he said. Then he reflected, "No. It's like malaria. It comes back. . . ."

He felt in an agonizing quandary over the Jacobson case. "I think I have to testify," he told me. "Jack was *clean*. I can help bury Buddy."

The next moment, contradictory worries surfaced. "I don't dare take the stand," he said finally. "I've been working for the government longer than you think." Somehow I always ended with more questions than answers after my meeting with Shaw.

Certainly the pressure on Melanie was constant. "I had hoped to keep on running during the trial," she said. "I couldn't. I was too exhausted." She avoided the press, and if she chanced to hear a news bulletin on the drive home, she would quickly turn the radio off. "Buddy just sits there in court, staring," she told Betsy Fitzgibbon, and Billy, and her small group of friends. "He stares at me for hours."

Every night she would tell them that she couldn't face another day of badgering on the witness stand. "Stop looking at Buddy," Betsy would implore her. "That's what he wants you to do!"

Oddly, Melanie was finding another subject to concentrate on, as a way of combating the draining force of Buddy's stare, and this was Jack Evseroff.

It was true that Melanie accepted that Evseroff was an antagonist, but she was also, in a certain sense, a fan. She was fascinated by his balletic motions, and his baroque repertoire of smiles and snarls, the sarcasm-dripping courtesies—"Well, *Miss* Cain?"—and the howling rages. "I would *wait* to be questioned by Evseroff," she says. "Greenfield and Hrabsky were so boring!"

The bout of flu kept Melanie away from the courtroom only for one day. Upon her return, Evseroff renewed his attack. She knitted her brows, like a schoolgirl determined to do well, while he peppered her with questions about the tape cassettes that recorded her calls to Buddy.

Her answer rambled.

"I move to strike the answer as not responsive," Evseroff snapped. "Stricken," Kapelman agreed.

"*Miss* Cain," Evseroff said, "would you please answer the question that was asked of you?"

"I am trying to answer the question," Melanie answered. "You are trying to confuse me." She was a schoolgirl still, but bewildered by an unpleasant teacher.

Evseroff strove to correct this image, disastrous to his cause. "I move to strike the gratuitous statement by this witness. I ask your honor to direct her to answer the question," he said, "rather than try to elicit the sympathy of this jury."

"Objection," hollered Hrabsky, lumbering to his feet.

"Now look, Mr. Evseroff," Kapelman said. "I don't want you to make any comments about the purpose of the witness."

He now turned his attention to the $30,000 that Brian Monaghan had given Jack Tupper for his share of the All-Ireland, and that Jack had handed over for safekeeping to his brother Jerry's in-laws. It was his intent to make the money sound like the profits on a dope deal. "There came a time in July of 1978 when Mr. Tupper turned over thirty thousand dollars to somebody by the name of Zuber. Is that right?" he asked Melanie.

"Objection to that kind of statement in court, judge," Hrabsky said.

"Well, where should I make it?" barked Evseroff. "Out in the hall?"

"Preferably, your honor," Hrabsky agreed. "If it's going to involve innuendo and conjecture."

Kapelman ruled the question could be asked, if properly phrased.

Evseroff said, "Don't you know—"

" '*Don't* you know'?" queried Hrabsky, looking at Kapelman.

"*Do* you know?" Kapelman agreed.

"Do you know," Evseroff began, then interjected, "Judge, I

didn't go to the Lee Strasberg School, so I don't know how to say this"—a reference to Melanie's training in theatricals.

"Judge," Hrabsky said, "I object to the gratuitous statement. I assume counsel went to law school."

"You're getting a lot of smoke and damn little fire," Kapelman said. "So let's cut it out. *Both* of you."

The questions concluded, and Melanie, who had made no attempt to hide her amusement at the spectacle of the two attorneys locking horns, agreed that Jack had received the $30,000. It had been in a paper bag, and she herself had counted the notes as they drove to the Zuber home. Evseroff looked expressively at the jury, as though to fix this image in their collective consciousness, and Buddy was droll during recess—"Was it a Gristede bag, or D'Agostino?" he wondered.

The paper-bag line of questioning was followed by the playing of a tape. This was the cassette that contained Melanie's two telephone calls to Buddy, during which he had agreed that he owed her $100,000. An eerie silence settled on the courtroom. Buddy sat stiff and sallow, while Melanie was in a tearful reverie, swept back in time to a conversation that had taken place ten days before Jack Tupper's death.

MELANIE: I can only talk to you about business.
BUDDY: So I'm talking to you about business.
MELANIE: I know you well enough Buddy that you can do anything you want to do.
BUDDY: No, I can't, babe. If I ever thought so—
MELANIE: Yes!
BUDDY: Listen to me.
BUDDY: If I ever thought that before [*he laughed*] I sure as hell know that ain't true now. . . . If I ever tried anything harder in my whole life than what I tried to do with you, it's . . . and I lost. So don't tell me I can do anything I want. . . .

The tape held, to my ears, little of comfort for Buddy Jacobson, but Evseroff deftly homed in on Melanie's demand for money. The whole thing, he said, was a "shakedown."

"Didn't you take out of My Fair Lady all the records?" Evseroff asked her.

"No," she said. "Not all the records *at all*."

"I see. Some of them were missing?"

Buddy shook his head, noticeably, and gave an incredulous smile.

Evseroff continued his questioning, intent on proving what a prince Jacobson had been, financially, where Melanie was concerned. "Tell me, while you were working for My Fair Lady," he demanded, "clothes would be bought for you with respect to your work? Is that right, Miss Cain?"

"No," Melanie said.

"Well, did Buddy *ever* buy any clothes for you?" he asked.

"One time he bought me something."

"He bought you something *one time* in the five years that you were with him?" Evseroff said.

"Yes," Melanie said, matter-of-factly.

Evseroff promptly abandoned the subject of Buddy's largess.

Just after this, Dom Barberino was outside the courtroom with Audrey Barrett. His relations with Buddy were cool, but he was fond of Audrey, and she would confide in him, saying that her parents did not approve of her relationship with Jacobson. "You know what, Dom?" she had said. "They're *right*. But I feel sorry for him. And it's only for the trial. . . ."

On this occasion, Barberino was poking a little fun at Buddy's stinginess. "Hey, Audrey!" he asked. "How many gifts did this guy ever give you?"

"Nothing," Audrey said.

"Be patient," Barberino advised her. "Melanie had to wait five years before he bought her a dress."

Murray Kempton, meantime, had approached Buddy. Kempton is, by his own avowal, a "defense-oriented journalist," but he had been much impressed by Melanie's patient disinclination to tell helpful untruths. "If she's supposed to be a cold, calculating bitch, why didn't she stick a lie in there?" he had said.

"There's obviously an incredible emotional bond between you," he remarked to Buddy.

"Are you kidding?" Jacobson replied. "If it wasn't for this trial, I wouldn't remember her name."

Before going to court the morning of February 7, Melanie noticed that her bangs were growing untidily long, so she swept them back into a different hairstyle. It wasn't until she was actually on the stand that she fully realized the implications of what she had done. "Ah! The Girl of a Thousand Faces!" She expected the sneer any moment.

Evseroff, however, left the change unmentioned. He eagerly resumed his probing, delivering questions like a series of gentle and not-so-gentle slaps. He was wearing a Cartier watch —one of six timepieces he owned—and a gold ring with a seal denoting the Daughters of the American Revolution, a present from a client. Points of reflected light danced around the courtroom as his arms prodded and waved. He now brought up the building that contained the apartment for which Melanie had been signing the lease the day of the killing.

What was its name? Evseroff asked several times. Melanie said that she didn't know.

This seemed intolerable to the lawyer. "Do you have any recollection of the name of the apartment building on 52nd Street, that you tell us you went on August sixth to sign a lease on?" he shouted. *"What's the name of the building?"*

"I won't answer your question as long as you scream at me," Melanie replied.

This was not a good moment for Evseroff. Juries don't like bullies. He froze, his jaw dropping wide.

"If your honor please," he said, swiveling to Kapelman. "I respectfully ask your honor to direct the witness to answer."

"The witness is going to answer the question, but you're *not* to scream," Kapelman said.

"If your honor please, I respectfully object to the Lee Strasberg tactics," Evseroff barked.

"Now look here—" began Kapelman.

"On *his* part?" asked Hrabsky, getting to his feet. "Is he talking about himself?"

"I don't have acting training like the witness," Evseroff said.

Hrabsky turned his broad face toward the jury. "How do we know that?" he intoned.

"I so represent that I never went to acting school, Mr. Hrabsky," said Evseroff, his voice now velvety.

It was all too much for Melanie. With vivid spots of pink in her cheeks, she thrust her arm stiffly out in the direction of Jack Evseroff with two fingers extended, like horns.

"If I might inform you," she snapped, "I went to Lee Strasberg *for two days*."

Melanie's spurt of temper caused a buzz during the next recess, with Buddy's legal team determinedly looking on the bright side. "She *shouted* at you, Jack," a lawyer said.

"I love it. I love it!" Evseroff said. "I'm getting to her."

"Yeah," Buddy agreed. "We're getting somewhere."

Evseroff explained his strategy. "Hit them on the body . . . hit them on the arms . . . so when you get a chance for a punch to the face, the hands will be down." The zapping was, he believed, beginning to tell on Melanie. "I *want* her to volunteer things. Especially when you've got a jury of men. They're sitting saying, 'That's the way I've heard my *old lady* talking.' When they listen to her, they're hearing their *wives*."

His problem with Melanie, he said, was this: "You've got an articulate, good-looking, halfway-smart broad," he said, and talked about that flicker of emotion, when Melanie had refused to name Ingrid on the stand.

"You remember that expression Melanie had?" Jack Evseroff said. "I know that expression. It's the expression every one of my wives has had when they caught me cheating."

His expectations had apparently declined. No longer did he expect the jury to perceive Melanie as "the engineer of the frame" of his client. Now he would be happy if they found in her the nagging girlfriend, the shrewish wife.

Did Evseroff believe that Melanie was telling the truth?

"I still can't make up my mind," he said. "And if I can't, can those twelve people in the jury box?"

"Their minds aren't clouded by the fee," said a Dan O'Grady.

"Models," Evseroff said. "They're all the same. Do you know why Buddy chose me? Because I'm a male chauvinist pig *and* a good lawyer."

Back in the courtroom, the struggle resumed. Strands of hair were now straying from Melanie's coiffure, but she was otherwise unshaken. She even answered one of Evseroff's more scathing tirades by mimicking his rococo gestures.

The audience in the courtroom, the jury, the Tuppers, even Kapelman laughed, and I fancied that I saw an admiring gleam in the defense attorney's eyes. Only Buddy sat there in a stony silence.

The lawyers now were focusing on what they considered their "problem" jurors. Hrabsky didn't care for numbers five, six, and twelve. Especially, he disliked number five, a stout, youngish man, and one of the auxiliary cops. He customarily wore dark glasses and a discontented expression, and Hrabsky growled that he had "a hair up his ass. And I don't know what it is."

Bernice Faust, number six, also seemed sulky. She was the woman whose husband had done six months for assault. "I believed her when she said she didn't blame the police," Hrabsky said. "I wanted to get more women on the jury. Maybe I made a mistake." And number twelve? Rose Kovnit was the elderly woman with the dignified countenance of a Roman empress. "I don't think she wants to convict anybody," the prosecutor gloomed.

He also regretted that the jury had not been sequestered, especially given Buddy's skill at reaching out. "Just don't come to a decision and you'll find twenty thousand dollars on your doorstep!" Hrabsky said. "It's a crazy system." This thought was also much on the Tuppers' minds. "We talk about it every day," Dorothy said. "Twenty-five thousand dollars would change one of these people's lives. Everybody has their price."

Evseroff would admit to no such dark thoughts. How many jurors did he think were on his side?

"Six or seven," he said. "I think they like me." He began to walk away, but pivoted around. "Do *you* think they like me?" he asked.

So it continued. Again and again, Evseroff would take Melanie through the events of August 6. He dwelled with particular interest on the fact that when Melanie had returned to 155 East 84th Street after signing the new lease, she had seen a man, whom she did not know, in Leslie Hammond's apartment.

"What did you see?" he asked.

"A man standing on something, working on the ceiling in the kitchen," Melanie explained.

"And did you think that this man was Leslie Hammond's boyfriend?"

"That was one of my thoughts, yes," Melanie said. "Since she lived by herself, I thought it was probably a friend or her boyfriend." Though Melanie repeated that she didn't know the man, Evseroff hovered around the episode for some time.

He also showed great interest in the spyhole. Melanie had explained, in detail, how she had seen Buddy and Douglas cutting up the rug and walking in and out of Joe Margarite's apartment, partly through her door, which she had opened about three inches, but mostly through the door's spyhole.

Now Evseroff raised a startling point. It would simply be impossible to see as much as Melanie had said that she had seen, he maintained, either through the partially opened door or through the tunnel-vision spyhole. The angle was not wide enough. He produced a diagram, depicting the seventh floor to substantiate this, and demanded that the jurors be permitted to visit the scene of the crime. "A tearful Melanie was caught in a cross-current of contradictions today," wrote George Carpozi, and even the skeptical Dan O'Grady was impressed. "Melanie Cain may have been tripped up on an important detail," he wrote in the *Daily News*.

"Aren't I giving Buddy his money's worth?" Evseroff demanded. He had, he thought, struck a seam of gold at last.

By now, Buddy had become close to Evseroff and his colleagues. Barberino or Ben Epstein would pick him up at nine in the morning. He would already have been at work on one of his buildings for a couple of hours, with Douglas and David and, maybe, Sal Prainito, and he would have to comb the plaster out of his hair. They would spend hours in Buddy's apartment, an austere place furnished only with a sofa, a few plants, an exercise bike, a bedroll in lieu of a bed, and the black and white TV set that had formerly belonged to Joe Margarite.

Usually Buddy would take everyone to dinner. "We would go to Gian Marino or Truffles," Barberino says. "He would always pick up the tab. He even asked Jack and me to move into the building with him." Indeed, their closeness reached the point where Buddy began to make Jack Evseroff privy to the core of fantasy within him, relating that his apartment had once belonged to Jean Harlow, and telling of the time he had been with his father as a boy, and Sam Jacobson had been visited by his mistress, Marilyn Monroe, whose fur coat had slipped, revealing her nakedness.

But the relationship soon soured. "I'm not much of a handholder," Evseroff told me. Sometimes Buddy and Jack wouldn't even be speaking. "Jack would say, 'Tell your friend, Buddy, to do such-and-such,'" Ben Epstein recalls. "I was the Swiss Embassy."

Optimistic though Buddy felt about the outcome of the trial, he was unhappy unless matters were handled just the way he wanted. It was Buddy, for instance, who was responsible for the approach to Brian Monaghan. "I was *threatened*," Brian says. "They were going to talk about my dealings with

Jack. They were trying to get me involved with drugs. Buddy said he was going to talk about the IRA."

Brian heard them out. "Fine," he said. "Put me on the stand. I'll see that Buddy gets the *chair*."

Another attempt at procuring a witness favorable to the defense was more successful. Evseroff had said that it was important to show a connection between Tupper and Joe Margarite. "You remember this guy, Tony De Rosa?" Buddy asked his lawyer in early February.

"Sure," Evseroff said.

"He used to be a barman at Nicola's. He remembers seeing Tupper with Margarite a few times."

Tony De Rosa, consequently, was waiting in the wings. Other interventions were less helpful. There was the call that was made to Billy Collins' apartment. The caller said he was with Western Union, and he had a telegram for Melanie. But no telegram was delivered, and when the cops checked with Western Union, they found that none existed.

One afternoon, as Billy drive Melanie home from the Bronx, he realized that they were being followed. Later, he found an "intruder" in his building, a man who turned out to be a private investigator named Jorge Bermuduez. Nicknamed the Silver Fox, Bermuduez had occasionally been a visitor to the Jacobson group in the courtroom. Detective Sullivan had come around to sweep Melanie's place for bugs the day after the incident.

The matter was raised by Hrabsky in the privacy of the judge's robing room, also the following day, and Evseroff, patently shaken, agreed that Bermuduez had worked on the case, but that he was "under, as far as I know, nobody's instructions to investigate Melanie Cain, or anything of the like."

Hrabsky agreed that the incident was none of Evseroff's doing. "This man is still serving directions from Buddy Jacobson," he said.

The defense attorney agreed to keep Bermuduez out of the courtroom. "I want to get to the bottom of this," he said. "I'm really hearing it for the first time."

"I know when you say it to me it's so," Kapelman told him. They moved on to the next application, which was, again, Evseroff's request to have the jury taken to the East 84th Street building's seventh floor to see for themselves what Melanie could have observed through the spyhole and the crack in the door. Kapelman said he would not allow this at present, but that the application could be made again before the trial's end.

The next issue was, at least potentially, more explosive. It began with an application from Ben Epstein, and was based on what Melanie told this writer about seeing Joe Margarite on the day of the murder, and how, later, she had wondered if he might have had anything to do with the murder.

Kapelman was firm. He would allow Melanie to be cross-examined as to what she had actually seen, but not as to what she might have imagined. (Melanie, in fact, had wondered whether Margarite might have stumbled onto the murder and, sensibly, taken to his heels.)

This was not enough for Bill Hrabsky, who believed that Kapelman's fear that a guilty verdict would be reversed on appeal had made him into silly putty in the hands of the defense, so that he had allowed every sort of innuendo about dope dealing to be dragged through the case. Throughout the trial, so far, Hrabsky had groaned repeatedly about "hearsay," but this attempt to use Joe Margarite was, he complained, the worst yet, "an extreme—trying to bring in rumor, conjecture, gossip, and give it some sort of truth and validity through a witness."

Hrabsky now brought forward a threat. "Using the same theory, judge," he said, "there's no way this court can stop me from eliciting that Douglas Jacobson knew his father did it."

"You try," Kapelman said briefly.

"Judge, wait a minute now!" Hrabsky said. "What's good for the goose. Right?"

Kapelman said "I'm not—" but Hrabsky bulled on.

"I'm going to ask just the way Mr. Evseroff did. I heard his technique."

"Mr. Hrabsky," Kapelman said, "didn't you hear me?"

"You don't let me talk out there," Hrabsky complained. "You don't let me talk in here."

Now Greenfield asked that a mistrial be declared on the grounds of Hrabsky's behavior, and Epstein made a similar demand. This was by no means their first request that a mistrial be declared. It was refused.

The lawyers trooped back into the courtroom.

"You may continue, Mr. Evseroff," Kapelman said.

Evseroff's first move was an application that "Mr. Anthony

Haden-Guest be excluded from the courtroom, as he will be called as a witness." This was proper. I departed and, for the next few days, relied on the reports of my colleagues. Evseroff began to question Melanie about Joe Margarite.

"You didn't ask him if he saw Tupper anytime that day, did you?" he asked.

"I don't think so," Melanie said. "No."

He repeated this question, and Melanie said, "No, I didn't even know if he knew him."

Evseroff immediately demanded that the second sentence be struck from the record, but the jury had heard it. And so the questioning continued. The defense attorney returned continually to the subject of the dope motive in Melanie's last days on the stand, demanding, on one occasion, whether Melanie had ever heard Jack Tupper discussing a $150,000 hash deal.

Melanie said no, quietly, and smiled, as if at the idiocy of the often-repeated question. On the last morning of Melanie's testimony, Irene Cornell told her listeners that "it is the consensus of courtroom observers that Evseroff, a skilled trial attorney, has been able to act out his own disbelief of Melanie's story, but he has not been able to break her down in front of the jury." Melanie finished, Cornell said, "with her story pretty much intact."

Melanie said her goodbyes, to the Tuppers and to the DAs, and left the Bronx courtroom, never, or so she hoped, to return. It was February 13.

A dismal sight succeeded Melanie in the court's view, the black and skeletal remains of the crate in which Jack Tupper's body had been burned. This writer was not there to see it *in situ,* being still barred from the courtroom. But there was, of course, nothing to prevent me from frequenting the offices and corridors.

"I've got no objection to your being in the courtroom," Evseroff told me later. "I will withdraw my admonition. It's me who decides, not the judge. You understand that?

"I will withdraw it if you do one thing, which is sit down with me and a tape recorder, and go over your testimony. I don't want any unpleasant surprises. I don't want to have to throw any dirt at you."

Before taking the defense attorney up on his offer, I decided I would consult my own attorney.

At the end of the day, Evseroff paid his customary visit to

the press room. He was with Buddy, who was carrying the "schematics," the diagrams of the seventh floor.

"I support the freedom of the press," Jacobson told me. "I've got nothing against you being in the courtroom."

He looked covertly around the shabby room and beckoned me outside. We walked a few paces down the oyster-colored marmoreal hall. "All we want to do is go through your testimony," he said. "We want to know what you're going to *say!*"

I said that I was going to tell the truth.

"The truth can't hurt me. But up here"—Buddy motioned around the corridors—"the truth can be *bent*."

I repeated that I would talk to my attorney.

His warmth disappeared, like a suddenly extinguished match. "Okay, okay," he said rapidly, and left me.

Dorothy Myers had now been readmitted. She and her father were familiar figures in the courtroom, whereas Kevin's emotional turbulence at the sight of his brother's murderer had grown so great that he had all but stopped attending the trial. Not that father and daughter found the testimony much easier to bear. One morning, even the accident of passing Buddy Jacobson in the doorway to the courtroom, being close enough to him to touch, had proved too great a horror to Dorothy, and she had begun to cry.

As usual, she was deeply pessimistic about bringing Jacobson to justice. Despite Melanie's holding up on the stand, the official investigation, she was convinced, had blown the case. "He's going to walk, I tell you," she said. "The police department has screwed up the blood samples. Jacobson thinks the rest of the world is composed of idiots, and you have to wonder if he isn't right." She had taken to brooding. "Frontier justice!" she declared. "I could shoot him right here, and get away with it. After what he did, I'm obsessed." She paused, then added, "If he walks out of here, it'll be the end of my life."

But both Dorothy and her father usually were able to keep their inner life to themselves and present a reasonably cheerful face to the world. Dorothy was certain that her presence in the courtroom was helpful to their cause, and she ridiculed Buddy—whose defense, after all, had been that he was a love-maddened "fool"—for encouraging the daily presence of Audrey Barrett. "The jury are aware of me," Dorothy told me. "Every time I'm in there, I see some of them looking at me. Do I look like a drug dealer's sister?" Indeed, she looked anything but.

It was now that Bill Hrabsky called her to the stand. Jack Evseroff, who had unsuccessfully objected that the showing of the crate in court was "prejudicial," was able to prevent Hrabsky from cross-examining her concerning Jack Tupper's blood group, since this would have brought up the leukemia death of Jerry, which might have touched the jurors' hearts. Dorothy was able to establish, though, despite a rapid-fire series of objections, that her murdered brother had a bank account (so often denied by Buddy) and that the famous "paper-bag" $30,000, deposited in what Evseroff, his voice redolent of sarcasm, described as the "Zuber National Bank," came from no source more murky than the sale of his bar. She spoke warmly of Melanie, the girl who, according to Buddy's defense, had been responsible for the murder of her brother.

Dorothy was then asked whether she knew Donald Brown, Jimmy Leonard, and Al Seifert. She said that she had known Jimmy from childhood, Donald for twenty years, and Al for somewhat less. No, she told Evseroff, she had never known that they were "major dope traffickers."

The defense attorney, who had promised in his opening statement to unmask the "real" murderer, was not helped by Dorothy. This, in her view, explained what happened next. "Evseroff couldn't stand the pressure," she said. At another private conference in the robing room, the lawyer said that "in all probability" Dorothy Myers was going to be recalled to the stand, and asked that she be excluded from the court-room.

Hrabsky objected, and Kapelman, unhappy, asked if Evseroff was certain that he was going to recall Dorothy.

"My present intention is to call her as a witness," Evseroff said.

"I must tell you I don't think it's a nice thing to do, but I'm going to have to comply with your request," Kapelman said.

"Mr. Evseroff's present intention is to live forever," Hrabsky remarked.

The discussion moved on. Hrabsky handed out copies of a statement made by Nereida Torres, the mother of the young woman upon whose unwilling behalf the Bronx DA's office had brought its charge of satutory rape against Sal Prainito.

The statement of Mrs. Torres was startling, and Evseroff gloomily announced that if it was offered into evidence he would demand that Buddy's trial be severed from that of Prainito. He read out a passage:

QUESTION: Did Salvatore Prainito tell you who killed the man?

ANSWER: Not me. He was telling my daughter that his boss had killed a man, because he had taken the girlfriend away.

QUESTION: And when you say "the boss," you're talking about Sal Prainito's boss?

ANSWER: Yes.

At this time it was still not certain whether this testimony would be, or could be, used. Like the Douglas Jacobson phone call to Al Seifert, which was equally emphatic that Buddy had been the murderer, it was vulnerable under the rules of hearsay evidence.

Dorothy Tupper was duly asked, in open court, to leave. She refused, but she was coaxed into the robing room, where she exploded with rage. Kapelman was plaintive, asking if she didn't think he was being fair. Dorothy did not reply, but left, saying, with some vehemence, that they might have gotten rid of her, but they had by no means seen the last of her family.

Tensions were rising. It was becoming increasingly apparent that Evseroff was not in control of his client. "You're paying me a lot of money," he snapped at Jacobson during one recess. "Let *me* try the case." On one subject, in particular, speculation was becoming intense: Was Buddy going to take the stand in his own defense? "He has to," observed Peter Grishman, and most of the DA's office were of this mind.

The defense lawyers were, understandably, less explicit. Dave Greenfield said that Evseroff did not want Buddy to take the stand, but didn't think he could be stopped. "It's a matter of his ego," Greenfield explained. "His ego is so big that he'll *want* to take the stand."

"Can you imagine him *not* testifying?" Dorothy Myers asked. Dorothy, like me, was now condemned to haunt the offices and corridors, but her place had been taken by her mother.

Marie Tupper, who was severely dressed, was examining Buddy Jacobson in the corridor, and maintaining her composure with difficulty. "A little runt like that," she said. "I'd like to get my hands on him."

"Now, now, Marie," her husband said gently. "Are you looking for a mistrial?"

"Not here," Marie said. Her eyes were curtained.

On February 21, I met my lawyer, Ike Sorkin, outside the courtroom. He planned to attempt to force my readmittance on grounds that Evseroff's offer to allow me back if I would permit him to tape-record a dress rehearsal of my testimony amounted to coercion.

We went into the courtroom and thence into the robing room. Kapelman, who was looking incongruously civilian in a double-breasted blue pinstripe suit, with matching tie and handkerchief in dark red, heard Sorkin out, and denied the appeal.

"I don't want him in the courtroom! Period!" Evseroff announced. "I got to wash my hands." He stalked off, glowering.

"What would you do in my case?" Kapelman asked Sorkin. My lawyer replied that he would have admitted me. Hrabsky and Gail Jacobs agreed.

"You're a very pretty, charming girl," Kapelman told Jacobs. "But can I go by your judgment? Suppose there's a conviction, and I get reversed? *This* is the specter I face."

"You're the boss," Hrabsky said.

Sorkin and I left. "Well, at least we gave it our best shot," he said. "We pinned Jack's ears back a bit."

Actually, Evseroff recovered his good humor soon enough, and it was hinted that I would soon be readmitted to the courtroom. "You can take my place," Audrey Barrett told me. "*Disguise* yourself."

Audrey was seldom this lighthearted. Not even the departure of Melanie had relaxed her. Sometimes she would borrow a cigarette from Dom Barberino and go and smoke it in the women's room. If Dom offered her a pack, she would refuse, saying that Buddy would find it when he searched through her bag.

It was beginning to appear that not everything in this supposedly open-and-shut case was going the prosecution's way. "Some phases of the detective work on this case have been shown by the defense to be quite sloppy," Irene Cornell told her listeners. The cop who inspected the bullet hole in the apartment of the blond stockbroker, Leslie Hammond, was forced to admit, for instance, that he had carried out no tests on it, and that he had not gone into Buddy's apartment next door to check for a corresponding entry hole.

The prosecution also sailed close to disaster when Patricia Ryan, a lab technician in the medical examiner's office, testified that the spots on Jacobson's dungarees, which had been circled, and which Hrabsky had assumed to be bloodstains, were, in fact, not so. The only blood she had found was a small spot on the inside of his pocket. The trousers were hurriedly retested, using the ten-times-more-powerful benzidine method, and blood duly was found, on the legs.

Some of Hrabsky's witnesses, moreover, seemed to be having some trouble with their memories. The doorman of the building next door to 155 East 84th Street, Leonard Finkelstein, told the court that he had seen Melanie in the phone booth on the corner "for about ten minutes." She had then walked toward 155, looking up at it, as though "she had something on her mind." About ten or twenty minutes later, or so Finkelstein said, he heard a series of shots, and a "moan."

This was so contrary to what the doorman had previously told Hrabsky that the prosecutor did not bother to conceal his suspicions. "Did you talk to anybody about this case last night?" he asked, looking pointedly toward Buddy as he spoke.

"Not to my recollection," Finkelstein said.

"I'm asking for a recess, judge," Hrabsky said. "I have to talk to this witness."

He was rebuked by Kapelman for so speaking in front of the jury, but his point had been made.

On February 25, there was another prosecution stumble. A contractor, a man named Mazzurco who had formerly employed Sal Prainito, was called to the stand. Hrabsky wanted to show that Prainito was familiar with the dump site on Bartow Avenue because it was frequently used by Mazzurco. But when Mazzurco testified that he "could not say for sure" if Prainito had ever driven a truck there for him, Kapelman ordered his testimony stricken from the record.

That evening, Tom Myers called me from Florida. He was subdued. "I shudder at the thought of this guy getting off," he said. "It wracks me to the bottom of my soul."

The following morning, a woman juror asked to speak with Kapelman and spent an hour with him in the robing room. The pressure had been telling on her, and the judge emerged to announce that she had been dismissed. She was replaced by an alternate.

Gail Moore took the stand on February 28. Hrabsky proceeded to question the young model about the times she had seen Melanie on the day of the murder. She was also asked about her visit to retrieve the pots, pans, and casserole dish from Joe Margarite's apartment on August 13, exactly one week after the murder.

"Can you describe the condition of Margarite's apartment?" Hrabsky asked.

"Extremely messy," said Gail.

Messier than it had been when she used to clean it for him? Hrabsky asked. Both Evseroff and Greenfield screamed objections, but Kapelman allowed the question.

"It was normal," she said.

"While you were in the apartment, in the areas you were in, did you see any blood?"

"No."

It was now Evseroff's turn. Gail Moore had moved into the building in September 1977, he established, and, until July of the following year, when she moved down to the fourth floor, she had lived in 5B. For much of that time her next-door neighbor in 5A had been Jack Tupper.

Evseroff now sprung what he hoped was a trap. "Did you tell Buddy Jacobson that cocaine was being cut or prepared in Jack Tupper's apartment?" he asked.

"No," Moore said, her brow crisscrossed with puzzlement. Undeterred, Evseroff plowed on.

"Did you ever tell Buddy Jacobson that you smelled cocaine cooking in Tupper's apartment?"

"No. I said that there was a strange odor from the apartment."

"Did you tell him that you smelled cocaine cooking in the apartment?"

"I don't know what cocaine smells like," said Gail.

He moved on to more promising terrain. It had already been established that Gail had dated Breck Dana Anderson. "Do you know that Breck Dana Anderson has been arrested, and is under federal indictment in West Virginia for transporting eight thousand pounds of hashish by plane into the United States?" he barked. "Do you know that?"

Hrabsky boomed an objection. Kapelman upheld him, and granted a private conference. "This attorney is engaging in trial by character assassination," Hrabsky said. The smearing of Jack Tupper was "illegal, immoral, unethical, and unprofessional."

The conference grew more heated. Evseroff hammered away that his defense was that the murder had been committed by others, and Hrabsky retorted that he was dealing in "rumor and conjecture."

Evseroff interrupted. "I think—" he began.

"You've got to wait until I finish," Hrabsky said. "That's the rule."

"I don't have to do anything you say, Hrabsky."

"Mr. Hrabsky to you, shorty."

"Cut it out," Kapelman advised them, allowing Evseroff to pursue the line of inquiry.

They went back into the courtroom. When had Gail talked with Breck Dana Anderson about his hash problem?

"About four days after the crash, I guess," she said.

"After the *crash?*" bellowed an incredulous Kapelman. "What crash?"

Gail dutifully explained, and Evseroff pressed on, asking about Anderson, about Margarite, and about Jack Tupper, again and again, skillfully planting the notion that the three men all inhabited the same narcotics world.

The atmosphere during the next recess was electric. Buddy, his son David, Audrey, and Jack Evseroff were huddled in one complacent group while the Tuppers were huddled in a wounded silence only a few feet away. Buddy was doing his usually good job of briefing the press. "Gail had complained to me, in a kind of nice way, that there were terrible smells coming from Tupper's apartment," he said. "That she thought he was cooking cocaine or something. I just ignored it."

Again, he drew attention to the Brooklyn trial. "Every one of the defense attorneys has said that Al Seifert killed Jack Tupper," he said. "And that's why he turned government witness—to get protection from a murder rap."

Was Seifert to be the "real" murderer promised by Evseroff?

The sight of this congratulatory tableau was, at last, too much for Jack Tupper, Sr. Something within him overflowed, and he charged the Jacobson claque, his face full of anguish, and pointed a finger at Evseroff. "Listen, everybody," he shouted. "This man is accusing my son, Jack, of taking drugs! And it's a lie!" He confronted Evseroff, his face bare inches from the attorney's. "You're rotten, Mr. Evseroff!" he said loudly. "And you'll pay for this!"

Dorothy stepped forward. She took her father's arm very gently. "Come on, Dad," she told him as she led him away. "Jerry's dead. And Jack's dead."

They walked back into the courtroom, leaving Evseroff sputtering in their wake. "He threatened me!" Evseroff said. "I'm going to tell the judge! Mr. Tupper threatened me!" Buddy was silent, but Audrey said, "It's very hard for parents to accept what their children are involved in." As she should know.

I lunched with Al Seifert that same day. We had chopped steak and salad in the cavelike gloom of the Madison Pub. "I was with Stanley all morning," he said. This was Stanley Arkin, his lawyer. "He wanted me to bring him up to date on what I really knew about John."

Seifert nursed a Tanqueray. He was sporting a tweed jacket, emphasizing his pallor. "I never did a deal with John Tupper," he said. "Anything I know is hearsay. There's nothing I can say that will hurt him.

"Evseroff wants me to go on the stand and take the fifth. That way John would look bad. I'm not going to do that. I took the fifth before because I didn't want to talk about the Brooklyn indictment. I don't care now. I don't mind talking about stuff I'll be talking about in a couple of weeks anyway."

He rather hoped, he said, that he *would* be called. "I'll knock 'em out of their socks," he promised.

It did not seem that Seifert would fill the bill as the stooge the defense so badly required.

Buddy's attorneys continued to rack up small victories, though. A police officer testified that the "matted hair" found on the elevator door had, in fact, been a purple-blue fiber. And Kapelman refused to let Silbergeld be questioned about the time, some nine months before, that Jacobson had discussed gun clubs with him and asked him to register a Beretta .32, which happened to be one of the probable murder weapons.

Silbergeld did concede that he had once seen Jack Tupper having a drink with Joe Margarite in Nicola's—and Evseroff realized that he would not need to call Tony De Rosa to testify on this point.

That evening, the Joe Margarite "Wanted as a Material Witness" poster showed up on television. It had, of course, been leaked by Buddy. "Buddy, you're fucking crazy!" Barberino told him. "The judge will lock you up tomorrow."

Buddy didn't care. "Maybe the jury's watching," he said.

The incident, as a matter of fact, passed without comment from the bench.

On the last day of prosecution testimony, March 10, the focus was the attack on Jack Tupper, described in all its grisly detail. Hrabsky came up to me afterward looking eminently satisfied, "Sniffing around, I don't believe Buddy's going to take the stand," he said. "It's looking good! Some of the jurors have had enough of Evseroff. They're fed up with his games."

Buddy was later to say that the opening day of his defense was his best day. Kathleen Millard, who lived with her husband, James, beneath the Margarite apartment, testified that on the day of the murder she had heard bangs and "rough noises," and that they were apparently coming from Margarite's living room. Her husband, James, said that he, too, had heard bangs, but imagined they were "firecrackers" and coming from somewhere outside the building. Buddy sidled over to the press, during a recess, to express his contentment with the Millard statement. "Sure, they had connections with me," he agreed. "She was my secretary, and his father was my real estate lawyer, but they're substantial people. She's a magazine editor, he's a big real estate man himself. I hope the jury doesn't think people like that would lie for me."

Several persons were called to testify that the layout of the seventh floor made it impossible for Melanie to have seen what she had claimed to see either through the peephole or through a narrowly opened door, and Evseroff yet again demanded that the jury be taken to the scene of the crime. Kapelman again said he would postpone that decision.

Shelley Braverman, the author of the section on firearms in the *Encyclopedia Britannica,* a grizzled and irascible man, was carried in on a stretcher (polio) to testify that a bullet hole that Buddy had had the good fortune to discover in a closet in Margarite's apartment could easily have put the stray bullet on Leslie Hammond's sink.

On March 17, Evseroff called Dr. Thomas Noguchi, the medical examiner of Los Angeles. Noguchi is a man who appears not to dislike the celebrity that has come his way via his autopsies on Robert F. Kennedy, Janis Joplin, Sharon Tate, and Marilyn Monroe, and the fact that his career inspired a television series, *Quincy*. His function was to raise doubts whether the Stanley sledgehammer found in the trunk of Prainito's car had been used as a murder weapon—cast further doubts, I should say, since it had already been shown that there was no blood on the tool. Noguchi lifted the sledge with delicate hands and said, "This is a heavy weapon, difficult to control." Had this sledge been used, he said, Jack Tupper would have been more badly injured.

The following day, it was Hrabsky's turn. He hefted the tool lightly aloft with a hand like a saddle of beef. He could, he told Noguchi, "embed this whole sledge in your head and crush it down to nothing. Yet if I gave you a quick glancing blow, it would be a different injury. And if you were standing up and able to dodge my blow, it would create an injury still different."

Dr. Noguchi had no choice but to agree.

That evening in Nicola's, though, Buddy was elated by his star witness. "This Japanese, he's *great*," he said. He was dining with Audrey, and invited me to join his table. He was drinking Chianti Classico and seemed carefree. Audrey, who was subdued, was clutching a notebook, from which a few newspaper clippings protruded. On the cover she had written, "Mass Communication and Public Opinion." Buddy was full of minutely detailed contempt for the prosecution's attempt to dismiss the Type O blood traces on Margarite's kitchen counter —Tupper was Type A. "There was blood *between* the cracks. Even if I had put the blood there," he said, demonstrating with a patting motion of his palm, "it couldn't have gone between the cracks like that.

"The blood was spurted into the crack. It couldn't even have been a vein. It had to be an artery."

"Enjoy your dinner," Audrey said, wanly.

He continued to talk about the case, and I began to understand why he had asked me to join the table. "Melanie is lying," he told me. "At first, it was just like she was making mistakes. Now it's obvious she's lying."

He wanted, he claimed, to see the end of it. "I want to cut the action off right now," he said. He talked about the jury.

Buddy was happy with the auxiliary cops. I remarked that I was surprised Hrabsky had accepted the young woman who believed that her husband had been wrongly imprisoned. "We knocked out all the women and blacks," he said. "They thought we were going to knock her out."

Will you be taking the stand? I asked.

"Take the stand if things are going badly for you, that's what they tell me," he said.

He smiled and shrugged.

"Right now, things are going so *well*."

In the courtroom, I had always assumed that Buddy was trying to snow the jury. I now realized that Jacobson, truly a master of the charlatan's art, understood that the first person you need to snow is yourself.

Abruptly, his mood darkened. "After this is all over, what are some people going to do?" he asked. "Where will they go? Will they be able to say it's just a game? It's lost—that's okay. It's over!"

He gestured. "Do those people think that's all?" he demanded.

Should "those people" be compared to the government witnesses in Brooklyn? "That's different," Buddy insisted, "They have a lot of different things on them. It's not like that in this case. They have only one thing against me. Just this one time. . . ."

That Sunday, Evseroff and Ben Epstein were summoned by Buddy to his East 63rd Street apartment, where the principal decoration, an architect's drawing of the Norway ski lodge, had been reinforced by another decoration hung above the television: a Rand McNally map of the world.

Jacobson was sitting on his exercise bicycle, pedaling, when he told them, definitively, that he would not be taking the stand. There were three reasons a source discloses: He didn't want to involve his son, Douglas. He didn't fancy saying in public what he had been saying in private about, for instance, Seifert, Brown, and, most particularly, Carlo Carrara. And third, he thought he had a win.

Evseroff did not agree with his client's decision. "Buddy was going to take the stand. It was the key to the whole thing," he mourned much later. "It was the game plan from *day one*."

*   *   *

Next day was the first day of spring—mild and pleasant. "You can't be nervous all the time," Dorothy Myers said cheerfully as we walked to Fun City, a local coffee shop, for lunch. She poured scorn on the defense witnesses. "They were pitiful," she said.

She also had news. She had overheard Evseroff and Buddy, and it sounded as if I was to be allowed back. This was correct. I was duly called to the stand, and asked if I could vouch for the accuracy of Melanie's recollections on my transcripts. I explained that I could not do this. Melanie had been upset and barely audible at the time the early interviews were taped.

But, yes, I agreed, Melanie had wondered aloud if Joe Margarite might have been involved with the killing: "Along with Buddy," I explained. At this stage, Evseroff declared me a hostile witness.

Meanwhile, the poor luck that had left the wrong type of blood smeared on Margarite's counter was affecting much of Buddy's other evidence. None of the witnesses remembered noticing that the communications box had been ripped from Tupper's wall on the day of the murder suggesting a violent struggle, though this was certainly the state it was in some weeks later, after Buddy was out on bail. A defense ballistics expert testified that the gun which had fired the bullet into Margarite's closet had been only about two feet from the wall, which was decidedly odd. Then there were the other bullet holes in the Margarite duplex, which were yet odder.

These were two holes in the window of the upstairs bedroom. There were two holes in the pane, which was glass reinforced with wire mesh, and photographs taken by the defense in November the previous year showed that they were of the size that .32 caliber bullets might plausibly have made.

But on September 14, two months before, the cops had videotaped the same window. It was quite plain from examining the holes in relation to the mesh in the earlier picture that the holes were smaller, the size of holes that might be made by, say, a BB gun.

When Buddy's defense discovered that the police camera had been at the scene before them, they sensibly kept their own photograph to themselves. But Hrabsky remembered its existence and saw to it that both photographs were shown to the jury. "There are auxiliary cops on that jury," Hrabsky said later with satisfaction. "Do you think *they* don't know the difference between BB holes and bullet holes?"

Down in the press room, the typewriters clacked merrily away. Sal Prainito came in and gave a brown paper bag to Greenfield. "Here," he said. "I get this for you."

The lawyer peered into it cautiously. The bag held a bottle of Talisker twelve-year-old Scotch whisky. "Thanks, Sal," Greenfield said, adding jokingly, "it's not my brand."

Group attention switched to the small Italian. "Aren't you gonna write a book, Sal?" demanded McLaughlin.

'We're going to call it *What the Fuck Am I Doing Here?*' Greenfield said.

"Are you going back to Italy?" asked O'Grady.

"Yes," Prainito promised.

"You want to leave this wonderful country?" McLaughlin said. "Where things have been so good for you?"

Prainito nodded vigorously.

"Why not leave now, and save yourself a lot of trouble?" suggested Al Soschten.

"I leave next weekend," Prainito said, in a rare attempt at humor.

Buddy standing there, gray-faced, in his gray suit, did not join in the laughter. He wished to discuss the mystery of the expanding bullet holes. "Bullshit!" he hissed. "We never raised that point. We never put those bullet holes in evidence." It didn't seem quite the right time to say that this wasn't the point: Buddy had clearly manufactured evidence to suggest a shootout in the apartment of Joe Margarite. [I was later to find that Buddy had borrowed a handgun in November from a racetrack denizen, saying he had to make "ballistic tests."]

Are you really trying to find Ivor Shaw? I asked Greenfield. This was because I knew that no investigative ripples had been detected at Shaw's favorite watering holes.

"We'd love to put him on the stand," Evseroff said. "We'd put him on tomorrow."

Where were all the other mysterious witnesses?

Dave Greenfield made a gesture, as of birds flying.

Ivor Shaw never was called, nor was Al Seifert. Jimmy Leonard was called, and admitted that he was on trial on narcotics charges in Brooklyn and that, yes, he had been a friend of Jack Tupper's for many years. Leonard sounded at once cordial and sincere. "He looks just like a cop," Evseroff told me. Doug Behm, the federal attorney prosecuting the Brooklyn case, agreed that Jack Tupper was an unindicted co-conspirator in the case. No, he told Evseroff, he had never heard of Joe Margarite. The "true culprit" who was Tupper's killer seemed no closer to being unmasked than he had been during Evseroff's opening statement to the jury.

One evening, standing in the parking lot with Epstein and Evseroff, I asked whether they had heard the news: Margarite had just turned himself in. There was a frozen moment, until they realized I was joking.

"I'd love him to turn up," Ben Epstein said.

"I can see him in court!" Jack Evseroff improvised wildly. " 'Yes—it was me! Buddy and me! We did it!' "

But reality is more baroque than invention, as two dizzying twists now showed. It was at this late stage—too late, the defense howled—that the matter of the investigation of Claire Normandeau's relationship with Jack Tupper was unearthed by Dave Greenfield. The prosecution professed ignorance, implausibly, since N.Y.P.D. records state that ADA Quinn had been informed at five past three on August 23, 1978.

A new group of "recalcitrant and ornery" potential assassins—as Greenfield put it—had been found: killer cops. Jack Evseroff brought Claire Normandeau to the courtroom five days running, but never called her, realizing that she might do him more harm than good.

The killer cops were forgotten but the second twist was even trickier.

Georgette Bennett, a writer with connections in the police department, received a tip. Arthur Broughton, a police sergeant, supposedly had been approached the previous October by Joe Toscanini, a retired cop. Toscanini had offered Broughton $100,000 to put Buddy under false arrest.

Broughton hadn't gone for the offer. Instead he had reported it to the police department, which had wanted to wire him up and send him back in. Broughton hadn't gone for that either. The cops' Internal Affairs Division had investigated the affair and turned over a report. But nobody had told Jacobson's defense team.

The DA's office, fearing a mistrial, went crazy when Georgette tried to verify the story, so she went to Jack Evseroff, who became particularly excited when he found Broughton had once been a partner of John Gannon, now married to Jack's former wife, Ellen. The defense attorney demanded, and got, a sidebar, where he screamed that the withholding of the file on the investigation was grounds for a mistrial.

"I don't want a mistrial, but I can't abrogate the rights of my client," he told me. "The last thing in the world I want is a mistrial."

Buddy, at his side, looked sour.

"The second-last thing," Evseroff hastily amended.

The DA's office denied that any files existed. Kapelman refused to allow Evseroff to introduce the issue in front of the jury. He once again began screaming mistrial, but was now talking of the attempt to "arrest" Buddy with some ambivalence. And rightly. The truth, when it emerged, was that Toscanini had been the "third man" prepared to swear he had seen three men fighting on the seventh floor the day of Jack Tupper's murder. He was to get $100,000 and had gotten $50,000 in advance from Buddy for coming forward, but had come up with a scheme both to avoid the risk of perjury and to get the rest of the money anyway. He would have Buddy and himself arrested for bribery, by a third party, when he picked up the rest of the payoff from Jacobson. At the same time, the rest of Buddy's funds would be seized. This fake arrest is a frequent ploy used by crooked cops to shake down drug dealers.

There was no Gannon connection whatsoever.

Toscanini had been Broughton's driver, and approached him because he knew him to be a tough cop. What he did not know was that Broughton was honest. The Internal Affairs Division, incidentally, bungled its investigation of the case, which had, when it broke, looked so lethal for the prosecution, but which would only demonstrate one further time that Buddy believed the truth was something he could manipulate at will.

We were into April; the end was close.

Hrabsky was bringing his rebuttal witnesses to the stand, to disprove defense claims. They included Whittier Foote, who lived on the sixth floor of 155 East 84th Street and testified that the fish-eye peepholes on his floor had been taken out and replaced by less efficient tunnel-vision items soon after Buddy came out on bail. He had checked upstairs, and Jack Tupper's spyhole had been changed also.

There was scorn among Buddy's supporters. George Carpozi, Jr., showed some snapshots that had been taken of himself poking his head out of the Tupper apartment. "This is me," he said. "I couldn't even get my *head* through the door."

Buddy looked at the photos intently, but seemed dissatisfied. "It doesn't matter what shape the peephole is," he told me. "You still can't see sideways. It's all distorted at the edges. You have to *be* there—you can't see it on the plans. You have to spend an hour *explaining* to people."

Perhaps so. Perhaps Melanie had erred, and she had opened the door wider than she realized. If so, it had been the only time her memory had betrayed her on the stand, and it was Buddy's own tampering with the evidence that had prevented him from exploiting the lapse. The jury never were permitted to go and examine the scene of the crime. Buddy, one more time, had outsmarted himself.

Dr. Michael Baden took the stand. Baden is a former medical examiner of New York, and it was his job to reestablish the hammer as a murder weapon. He talked of the thirty thousand autopsies he had performed, and an eerie light flickered off his face as he slapped a sequence of slides into an X-ray machine. "The jawbone . . ." he said. "The nasal sinus arch . . . below are some teeth . . ."

Tom Myers put on his spectacles and stared hard at the slides, while Dorothy and Dee-Dee Zuber sat numbly at his side.

And that was it. Neither Buddy nor Sal Prainito was to take the stand. Defense and prosecution would sum up the following week. Kapelman wished us all a "happy and enjoyable Easter Monday."

"I think it's fifty-fifty," Ben Epstein told me. Evseroff was more sanguine. "We may still get an acquittal," he said.

"He's going to skip," Dorothy Myers suddenly said. She had been looking at Buddy. "He'll skip tonight. I think finally he's *realizing* not everybody is stupid."

I was not certain she was correct. Buddy was already dissecting the prosecution's case concerning the dreadful wounds to Jack Tupper's head and the instrument that had caused them, ruling out the hammer as a murder weapon. "This way would be crazy for a murder—a *premeditated* murder. That's one of the things I learned in the can. They all told me they knew the killing wasn't premeditated. You don't go after a guy like Tupper with a hammer like that. He would have made you eat it.

"And why leave it in the car? It would have gone . . ." He

paused momentarily, and finished, ". . . where the guns went." One of the newsmen began to hum "If I Had A Hammer." Buddy smiled, and walked away.

Evseroff had the beginnings of a cold, and looked terrible. "Buddy's a very mysterious guy," he told me. "He likes it to seem as if he has no compassion. I don't know what he's thinking. Sometimes I do for a while, and then it's gone."

Tuesday, April 7, was a fresh spring day. The courtroom was filling. Sal Prainito sat surrounded by a small group of his relatives. Jack Tupper, Sr., arrived. His handshake was firm. Marie Tupper was carrying a box of Easter eggs for Dorothy's son.

"Justice is going to be done," Dorothy Myers said. "In this court or out of it."

Dave Greenfield began his brief summation at 10:42 A.M. A blind was pulled up at the end of the court with a loud clap, as Greenfield poured scorn on the "bloody palm print" which had never been shown to be blood at all. It might, he said, have been anything, even horseradish. Buddy sat wringing his hands, in a rare display of tension.

Evseroff began at five minutes to eleven. His suit was dark, his shoulders tapered, his walk a springy crouch. The jury, looking suitably grave, occasionally swiveled curious eyes around the courtroom, but they looked at Buddy not at all. By 3:20 P.M., Evseroff reached the testimony of the doorman, Leonard Finkelstein, and by four he was back in the mainstream: Donald Brown, Seifert, Normandeau. "Jacobson had a model *agency* to protect!" he said ringingly. "Who needs a body on the premises?" He closed on his most operatic notes of outrage, while the Sicilians nodded their approval. Allowing for recesses, Evseroff had spoken for three hours.

Later he approached me coyly proud of his summation. His strength had been sapped by sickness, he said. "I was twenty percent below my best," he mourned.

Had he a sense of how things would end? "It's simple," he said. "If the jury believes Melanie, he goes. If they don't believe Melanie, he walks."

It was the following morning, and Audrey was sitting next to Buddy on the front bench, doing her nails. Around, there was desultory talk about the holidays. Buddy was disposed to be wry. "I may go away on a very long holiday," he said.

What did he think of his chances? "It's a horse race," he said dispassionately. He was, of course, used to winning races.

At half past nine, Bill Hrabsky walked into the courtroom, a dead cigar between his teeth, a cardboard box cradled in his huge arms. Behind him, the burned crate was wheeled in. "Holy God! It will be the first time my mother saw the box," Dorothy breathed. The array of "exhibits" was laid out from the box: the plaid carpet; the bloodied spectacles; the Stanley hammer; the glass wine jugs that had held the gasoline.

Hrabsky began his summation at five past ten. His trousers were, as usual, too short, his smile amiable, his manner mild. "Two tricycles caught two murderers in Bronx County," he said. The set speech (which Hrabsky had rehearsed, taped, and played back to himself early this same morning), rose in a crescendo. Buddy was not the Fool, he insisted. Buddy was the Fox.

When, at last, he stopped, it was as if an elastic band had snapped in the courtroom. There was a lull, an interlude. Even Buddy Jacobson stretched, and smiled, and sighed.

He and Sal Prainito were then handcuffed by court officers, as is customary. The Sicilian women surrounded Prainito, wailing, and Audrey, shocked, sprang to her feet with tears in her eyes and kissed Buddy as he was led away. Buddy had known he would be remanded, but had not told Audrey, for whatever reason.

The Tuppers looked on the scene unmoved. "We should weep," Jack Tupper said. "We should be the ones crying."

Marie looked at Evseroff stonily. "He's the bottom of the barrel," she said.

Nor was the defense attorney well disposed toward the Tuppers. "Why do they have to come here?" he demanded. "Why do they have to be here every day?"

Judge Kapelman charged the jury, who left for the jury room. The longest trial in the history of the Bronx, with eleven weeks of testimony taken from seventy-nine witnesses, had entered its final phase, which was the most grinding of all.

Evening brought an odd atmosphere to the Bronx courthouse. A buttery light filled the corridors. Small groups formed. The Tuppers departed to arrange for baby-sitters. Ben Epstein went up to the holding pen to see Buddy. "I tried to crack a few jokes," he said, but Buddy had something else on his mind, and asked him for paper. Epstein tore a leaf out of his address book. Buddy scribbled for a moment and handed it back. "Give it to David," he said.

Epstein gave it a glance. It was a small ad, written in realtor's code and intended for the *Times*. Jacobson was putting his buildings up for sale.

A regimen was established. We would be told that the jury was coming back to the courtroom. They had asked to have such and such a piece of testimony read back to them. We would enter the room, and Buddy and Sal Prainito would be brought downstairs and would sit at the table with their lawyers. The jury would file in and take their places. The court reporter would read whatever it was they wished to hear, then they would file out, and we would all disperse again.

That first night, I dined with Evseroff and a couple of journalists in the Stella d'Oro, one of Bronx County's better restaurants. The defense attorney was churning, like a machine that could not be switched off, even though its job was done. "The more I think that the jury left after my summation, the more I like it," he said. "They went to bed immersed in what I said."

"Eight was asleep during Hrabsky's summation," a reporter said.

"I know! I know! I *hated* number eight. I thought he hated me. But he didn't close his eyes during *my* summation." Gleefully. "I think Hrabsky missed the boat."

While the jury was out, Melanie, running out of ways to keep her mind from the Bronx, decided to balance her checkbooks. Sorting through her canceled checks, she reached a $300 check upon which somebody had written a message.

The scrawl read *"Buddy Is Guilty"* in letters of red.

On Wednesday, April 9, the rain was coming down in a black, drenching downpour. The highways were blocked by the stalled hulks of cars. Margaux Hemingway was peeling into drabness on the billboard, her lips tattering. I lunched with Evseroff. "It's like *Waiting for Godot*," he said. "It's like waiting for a baby."

Suppose the verdict went the wrong way for him? "After thirty-one years there is no trauma, no shock, no feeling, no nothing," he added, a bit sententiously, "I've just done my job to the best of my ability."

Later that day we heard the jury had reached a verdict. As

they filed in, Buddy turned and muttered, "It's me. And it's guilty."

He was wrong. It was Sal Prainito, and he was found innocent.

There was a volcanic whoop of joy from the sisters, brothers-in-law, mother—a waving of arms, stamping of feet, and clapping of hands—while Prainito buried his head in his arms and wept. There were more tears on the other side of the court, but these were shed by the Tuppers.

Dorothy Myers, now in her sixth month of pregnancy, left the courtroom and telephoned Tom. "There's no justice," she said. "I told you there's no justice. Prainito's walking, and Jacobson is going to walk."

She left the kiosk, and encountered Prainito in the corridor. The meeting moved her to do something spontaneous. She extended her index finger, like a child miming a gunman, and said, "Bang! Bang!"

"You do that to me?" Prainito sputtered.

"I do that to you," Dorothy agreed.

San ran to Greenfield, who complained to Kapelman. The judge, without naming Dorothy, issued a bilateral warning. There were to be no more demonstrations in court.

How was the Prainito verdict likely to affect Buddy's chances?

"We're alive," Evseroff said. "It can't *hurt*." Hrabsky disagreed. "I don't think it matters either way," he said. "But I've seen it before. Money talks. You get to be like the reporters, cynical."

On Friday, the jury announced that they were "hopelessly deadlocked." Kapelman ordered them to bring in a decision anyway. With each piece of evidence they requested for review, emotions swung. The defense brightened when the jury asked to hear once again the definition of "a reasonable doubt," and the doorman Finkelstein's testimony. "I danced in the corridor when I heard that," Audrey says.

Sitting in the courtroom on Saturday was like sitting in a classroom at the end of a long and grueling examination. All passion was spent.

Jack Tupper, Sr., sat next to his wife, reading *Geo*, no longer paying attention when a member of the Jacobson entourage brushed by. Audrey looked through fashion magazines. Beside her, slung over the back of the bench, was Buddy's clean suit—the dry cleaner's plastic bag reading HAVE THE TIME OF YOUR LIFE. David Jacobson talked horses. "I have two races today at the track," he said. "And one here." He spoke with something of his father's nonchalance.

Bill Hrabsky, leaning against the rail, as though his reputation were not in the balance, reminisced about his Air Force days as a troubleshooter on the missile program: the Atlas silos in a Kansas cornfield. "We tested them," he said, "and we found half our deterrent force didn't work." He seemed to enjoy his mordant gloom, but admitted the case had been getting to him, with his weight dropping from 232 to 210 pounds. "The system's got to work," he fretted, "it's got to work because he's *guilty*."

"Have you noticed? The jury hasn't asked for anything," Evseroff said. "I wonder what that means." He sounded authentically at a loss. Minutes later, there was a request to hear Leslie Hammond's testimony. "When I heard that, I thought we had a win," Barberino said.

We dispersed again. The light was lemony, the sky a pewter tray. Inside, the windowsills were accumulating cans of Pepsi and diet black cherry, containers of coffee, and crumpled paper bags. Evseroff sidled up. "I'm beginning to think we may not get a verdict," he said. It was nearly three. A game of Scrabble was under way. The players included Audrey, David Jacobson, and others of Buddy's supporters. It was a listless sort of game, continuing until a flurry of excitement drew them elsewhere, and it was during an absence that Dorothy Myers picked up some letters and embellished the board with a word of her own: GUILTY.

At 3:55 the jury made their second request, asking to have some of Melanie's testimony read back to them. It was the part in which she described the scene on the morning that Tupper was murdered—the man in Leslie Hammond's apartment, the clean-up in Buddy's, the shattered glass, the blazing fire on a hot August day. Then they filed out, and Buddy gave them one last, hungry look.

Five minutes later, we were told they had a verdict. The wait for the jury seemed abnormally long. Evseroff turned around, with an expressive shrug. Even Epstein was biting his knuckles. David Jacobson paced up and down, and the creak of his corded legs sounded like a cap pistol. Dorothy Myers fixed her eyes on an inscription on the wall. This reads

In God We Trust, in gold, and it seemed to her that it was flashing in her eyes like a strobe light. Buddy twisted in his seat, just once, with a searching expression. Audrey was not there. Now of all times she was out, getting a cup of tea.

At 4:32 P.M., the jury came into the courtroom. Judge Kapelman asked them for their verdict. Dennis De Santis, the foreman, rose to his feet. "Guilty," he said, quite clearly.

It was shocking to me that so little changed. Only David Jacobson gasped, a sudden "Ohhhh," as though he had been punched in the solar plexus. Buddy cast his eyes down for a moment, then reassumed his customary expression of stony watchfulness. He turned around toward the spectators' benches, met David's eyes, gave a half-smile, and lifted a clenched fist of defiance. David mimed encouragement. As the jury was being polled, Buddy stared each juror full in the face.

The Tuppers were sitting in a trance, like a sculptural group. Dorothy was clutching her mother's shoulder, and Marie was holding her husband's hand. The three looked so desolate that for several moments I wondered whether I had misunderstood, and Jacobson had been found innocent, after all.

Kapelman was droning on. The prisoner was to go to "Bronx County Detention or Riker's Island . . ." Buddy, oddly, was looking sharper, clearer-eyed. The uncertainty was over. He had solid objectives again, and he was already whispering busily into Ben Epstein's ear.

For Hrabsky, the prosecutor, the verdict had been a slight surprise. "I sat there emotionless," he said. "I felt very drained. I was still bitter about Prainito. But Buddy the Fox had finally lost to the system."

The trial was over. We began to leave. Evseroff's eyes were red. He smiled as he passed and patted me on the upper arm. "You were right and I was wrong," he said. "That's the way things go." Audrey was in the hallway, sobbing. The Tuppers were hugging each other, and now, for the first time, Jack Tupper, Sr., wept. "Let it all come out," his family told him. "Let it all come out."

The family was walking away from the courthouse when a car pulled up. Epstein jumped out and motioned to Dorothy. She hesitated for a moment, then walked toward him.

"No," she said. "I am *not* going to kiss you."

Epstein laughed, then said he just had one thing to tell her: The person he had felt the most admiration for in the whole case was Dorothy herself.

They parted, and she rejoined her parents.

"Justice has been done," she was thinking. "But Jackie is still dead."

Bill Hrabsky returned to his office. On one wall was a framed quotation from Kafka's *Trial,* reading: "The Court wants nothing from you. It receives you when you come, dismisses you when you go." On another wall was a large green board, upon which, with Prainito's acquittal, a score had been kept. With Buddy's conviction, the board could now be completely chalked in: GOOD GUYS 1, BAD GUYS 1.

At a quarter to five, he left to have a beer with another ADA in the Yankee Tavern. They were walking to the corner when a large green van pulled out of the courthouse, and approached. Hrabsky had a premonition, and watched. There was only one prisoner. As the van passed, Howard "Buddy" Jacobson stared directly at Bill Hrabsky. There was no expression on his face at all.

- VIII -

Aftershocks

Melanie was, she said, "on cloud nine" that Saturday evening. It was over at last. By Sunday morning, however, she had come down to earth. She had to tell herself, over and over again, that it wasn't she, Melanie Cain, who had closed the prison door on Buddy. It had been Buddy himself.

She knew, of course, that he would appeal. Buddy would never admit that he had murdered Jack Tupper—not if he stayed in a prison cell for the next twenty-five years.

The rash of headlines in the next few days confirmed her anxieties. JACOBSON LAWYER CLAIMS "IMPORTANT NEW EVIDENCE," the *News* proclaimed on Monday. BUDDY'S LAWYER ALLEGES JURY FISTFIGHT, ran George Carpozi, Jr.'s, headline in the *Post* that same day. A subsequent *News* story seemed even more ominous. JUROR THINKS IT OVER, DOUBTS BUDDY'S GUILT.

"He won't get out on bail, will he?" Melanie asked. Surely the whole dreadful dream could not begin again. Perhaps the dream could. Buddy's real estate machinery was humming away, apparently untroubled. The evening of the verdict, the real estate section of the Sunday *Times* carried the small ad that Jacobson had scribbled in the holding pen. He was asking $2.2 million for the three buildings on East 63rd. A woman buyer called Buddy's number, which was the one given in the ad, at ten-thirty on Monday morning. It was Audrey who answered.

"Mr. Jacobson's not here right now," she said. The woman gave her name as Mrs. Schwartz, and left a number. Buddy called her just half an hour later. He did not say that he was calling from Riker's Island. She asked for some details. Buddy told her that the buildings were 9, 11, and 13 East 63rd, saying they were "contiguous, and measure seventy feet across."

"Stairs or elevators?"

"One of the buildings has an elevator. The other two do not," Buddy said. Incredibly, there was the ring of another telephone.

"Excuse me," Buddy said. "I'll call you right back."

He did so, moments later, and they began to talk about money and mortgages. "It would have to be a million and a half cash," he said. "I have to pay off mortgages that are not transferable."

"Right," she agreed.

"We've got a minimal price on the properties because we're making a quick sale," Buddy said. "Because of some other circumstances."

He sounded almost airy.

Jury duty on a lengthy trial is always a wracking experience, and the Jacobson trial had been more so than most. Early on, there had been a certain consensus among the jurors: It was agreed, for instance, to discount all the testimony to do with drugs. So much for the "dope motive." Six of the jurors seem to have been persuaded of Buddy's guilt fairly early in the deliberations. They included foreman De Santis; number two, Harry Garrison; and the three auxiliary cops.

Hrabsky had been correct in supposing that Bernice Faust, number six, was not disposed toward conviction, and that number twelve, the elderly Rose Kovnit, was unhappy at the thought of convicting anybody.

The maverick at the beginning was number four, Robert Coletti. There was, it seems, no hypothesis so bizarre that he would not want to discuss it. One juror jokingly supposed that the fatality might have been suicide, and Coletti even wanted to discuss that.

By Saturday morning, nine were for conviction, and tempers were fraying. The recalcitrant three were called "bastards . . . morons . . . puppets." The climax came when Rich Lorino, one of the auxiliaries, grew so exasperated with Coletti that he heaved a heavy chair at an empty wall, narrowly missing Mike Speller. Lorino was sobbing, and shaking so much that he was taken out of the room to recover.

This had been at half past two. One and a half hours later, the jury had asked for that last piece of testimony—Melanie's —had sat quietly in the courtroom, filed out, and then returned with their verdict. Each of them had said "Guilty." Coletti and Freddie Velez, number ten, who had been adamant for acquittal, decided that the man up by Leslie Hammond's ceiling was searching for a bullet. "It was ironic," another juror says. "They changed in one moment."

Evseroff had known that there was dissension in the jury room. There is always dissension in the jury room. He even knew there had been a fracas. "I was sitting in the courtroom on Saturday, and I heard this bang," he said. "The door to the robing room was open, and I saw this court officer *run*."

Pete McLaughlin of the *News* initiated the next phase. On a hunch, he began to look up the jurors' names in the Bronx telephone book, and located Mike Speller. He went to see Speller, who told him, "I don't think we were right. If we had to do it all over again, I think it would go the other way." He added, "They wore me down."

It was now that Evseroff planned to send out Barberino to collect affidavits from any dissident jurors, but Buddy, who owed Barberino $12,500, would not settle. Indeed, he told Epstein he thought the investigator had been a waste of money. "So, Buddy, smart-ass, what do you think he did?" Barberino says. "You know who he sent to see the jury? Audrey!"

Audrey taped Mike Speller and took an affidavit, and she taped Bernice Faust. Author Dick Schaap got in touch with number twelve, Rose Kovnit, on Buddy's behalf, but she was reluctant to become involved. Bernice Faust, also growing reluctant, refused to sign the affidavit. It was a disheartening process, especially since Jacobson had not yet sold the 63rd Street houses, and they still owed Evseroff $28,000, even before the next round got under way.

On Sunday, May 25, Audrey told Dick Schaap that Buddy needed $10,000 for his appeal. The writer said he would try to raise the sum, but called on Friday, regretting there was nothing he could do. That evening Audrey dined with a friend out at Travers Island. Dropping her off at East 63rd, he saw that she had been met by David Jacobson and another man, who he lately found out to have been Tony De Rosa. The three began arguing.

Next morning, Ben Epstein called Audrey. He was off sailing in Long Island Sound, but felt he had to cheer her up. She had been supposed to meet Bernice Faust at Alexander's in the Bronx, but she had been fifteen minutes late, and Faust had not been there. Epstein told Audrey he would see her the following week.

At two that afternoon, Tony De Rosa walked into the Brooklyn House of Detention, where Buddy was now being held, and signed in as Buddy's lawyer, "Michael Schwartz." Guards ushered him to the visiting room, and left him with his client. After a couple of hours of conference, Buddy, now wearing the suit he was permitted to have for court appearances, simply walked out of jail.

This was discovered at four-thirty when "Schwartz" affected to ask where his client had gone, and was barely prevented from following Buddy to freedom. Soon all relevant agencies were being given the embarrassing news that Buddy Jacobson had broken out of a maximum security pen with the greatest of ease, and was on his way to parts unknown.

The trial of the airport gang, which had outlasted the Jacobson case, was drawing to a close, and there was a hectic, almost festive air in the courtroom, with defense attorneys for the eight defendants bouncing up and down like jumping jacks, and Carlo Carrara beaming as though it were a party, and he the host. I lunched with Jimmy Leonard, Billy Sharrocks, and various of the others, and only the quantities drunk were indicative of tension. "That's Donald!" Sharrocks said, as a car backfired on our return, "shooting from the bushes. . . ."

Indeed, it was the government witnesses who seemed not to be enjoying the proceedings, and the somewhat beleaguered Doug Behm who, in these declining days, noted a depressing detail and nudged John Cipriano, the DEA agent, at his side.

"One of the jurors was wearing a new piece of jewelry," he says. "A coke spoon."

Doug had a dire presentiment, and he was right. On April 23, the champion cigarette-boat racer Joey Ippolito was acquitted, and Alan Finkelstein followed him the following day. (The lean impressario soon aggravated the government further by posing for *People* with his model friend, Esme.)

That same day, though, Jimmy Leonard and Billy Sharrocks were convicted. Both managed something like a smile. The other four had hung juries. "I'm the jackass in this case," Behm grumbled, despondently. "I'm the savior of every drug dealer on the East Side." Soon, though, his verve returned, and he set to work preparing for round two.

*   *   *

Saturday afternoons are usually quiet affairs around the news services, and this one had been particularly placid. Richard Sisk, the city editor for UPI, would not normally have been in his Daily News Building office at all. "The mayor had a party at Gracie Mansion for Room Nine," he says—Room Nine meaning the media people that cover the city's affairs. "It's an annual thing. I was shit-faced. I came back to the office afterward, to work on some schedules."

The call came through from Channel 11 (WPIX) at about a quarter to five. Channel 11 often calls to check breaking news with UPI, and had picked up an emergency bulletin, much overlaid with static, on its police-band radio. The bulletin announced Buddy's escape.

Sisk assigned Ed Deitch, a young staffer who had covered the case, to follow up. "We were going crazy," Sisk says. "Then we started to pick it up on our own police radio. It was an APB"—an All Points Bulletin—"for Buddy." Deitch hastily called a friendly desk sergeant at the 84th Precinct, who confirmed the news. The story moved out at five-twenty-five.

The reporter now realized that he had mislaid Evseroff's home number. He left an urgent message with the defense attorney's service, and within minutes, Evseroff called him back.

Deitch told him the news.

"You'd better stop drinking in the afternoon," Evseroff said, adding, as Deitch repeated the news, "Oh, my God! I can't fucking believe it!" His disbelief, so often displayed in court for the benefit of a jury, was utterly genuine. "I'm absolutely stunned," Evseroff said. "We were coming in on Tuesday to bring in a motion." With customary braggadocio, he told Deitch that the appeal would have been a likely winner.

Peter Grishman heard of the escape while parking outside Edmundo's, a restaurant in Eastchester. He was taking his wife to a peaceful dinner. He was sufficiently alarmed that he considered asking that a squad car be posted by his house, but decided the fifteen-year-old babysitter was alarmed enough already.

They revenge motif was soon a popular one. COPS GUARD MELANIE CAIN, ran a banner headline in the *Post* that Monday. Melanie and Billy were living out of state at this time. The cop who was assigned to guard them was a state trooper, a callow young man who appeared on their doorstep and said that if they felt they needed him, they should call *immediately*.

The following day, Billy did call, and the state trooper's car wouldn't start. Melanie and Billy laughed a bit about that. But a few days later, somebody pulled a gun on this particular callow state trooper; the trooper shot him four times, dead with each shot, and then handcuffed him, as per regulations, so they decided he might not have been such a poor choice after all.

Hrabsky pooh-poohed the alarms. "Why should he be mad at Melanie for telling the truth?" he asked. "Why should he be mad at the judge for doing his job? As for being mad at me, I can't imagine why. I'm just another face in the crowd that tried the case."

One person who took it seriously was Judge Kapelman, who told Evseroff he was having round-the-clock protection. He suggested that the defense attorney do the same.

"I don't need round-the-clock protection," Evseroff snapped. "If I don't get paid my twenty-eight thousand dollars, *Buddy* will need round-the-clock protection."

"I think Kapelman is flattering himself," he told me later. "I think Buddy's only concern at the moment is how to put as much distance as he can between these people and himself."

Distance, yes, but in what direction? The immediate, and reasonable, assumption was that Buddy would have lit out for one of the fifty-nine countries that do not have extradition treaties with the United States. Gold and Merola, the Brooklyn and Bronx district attorneys, jointly announced that they were scrutinizing the flight logs at Teterboro, an innocuous airport in Bergen County, New Jersey. One early leak had Buddy already flown, in a chartered plane to "Canada, Mexico, or the Caribbean on the first leg of a search for a permanent, extradition-free sanctuary." LINK MOB TO BUDDY ESCAPE ran the headline in the *Post*.

But some who knew Buddy well doubted that he had left the country. He had once told Melanie that if he ever had to go into hiding, he would do so in Brooklyn. This theory appealed to Dom Barberino, and Ben Epstein, who knew how much Buddy had hated the modeling conventions in Puerto Rico and the Bahamas. "I'll tell you one thing," Melanie said. "Wherever it is he's hiding, it has television, and a telephone."

Frank X. Pagano, Buddy's ebullient former assistant trainer, had cheered when the news of Buddy's escape appeared on TV, secure in his belief that Buddy was innocent. "How could he have done such a slipshod thing?"—meaning the murder. "You saw how he walked out of the House of Detention? Buddy plans things." He, too, was of the firm opinion that Buddy was still in the United States. "To him, everything is a little game. He has to be watching TV, reading the papers. Otherwise—what good is it?"

Kapelman gave his message deadpan. "The court has been advised by the Department of Corrections that the defendant is not available for sentencing." There was a ripple of amusement through the courtroom, and Mario Merola, in a striking checkered suit, gave a discreet smile. The atmosphere was hectic, like a premiere. This was June 3, and Buddy was to be sentenced in absentia.

Kapelman, alluding to "the viciousness and brutality of this crime," lowered the boom. The sentence: "a minimum of twenty-five years."

Jack Tupper, Sr., told the press he was satisfied with the sentence. "The fox is on the run," he explained. "The fox is being hunted. He will never be happy. He will always be looking over his shoulder. And he will be caught."

Evseroff was less sure. "I think we've seen the last of Jacobson," he said. We were in the press room, which was teeming with both media and lawyers. Dave Breitbart, who came fresh from securing an acquittal for Joey Ippolito in the Brooklyn drugs case, told Evseroff, "I've polled thirty lawyers. This counts as a *win.*"

"We're going to make an appeal!" Evseroff crowed. " 'Come to your senses, Buddy. Come back and surrender!' " He jackknifed with glee. "Well, what do you want me to say? 'Good for you, Buddy! You screwed 'em all in the final analysis!' "

The question of whether we had "seen the last" of Buddy now became a matter of obsessive interest. Hrabsky tended to agree with Evseroff. "He's got friends out there," the prosecutor said.

"He's not stupid," Al Seifert added. "Right now, you wouldn't recognize him. Blond hair . . . I don't know what else. . . ."

Gene Jacobs, who had been at the races down at Gulf

Stream, Florida, when he heard about the escape, seemed to think the disappearance of his troublesome nephew would be long-lasting. "He seems to be able to accomplish anything he sets out to do," Jacobs replied.

The columnist, Earl Wilson, printed the rumor that Buddy was in Brazil. A night club comedian asked, "Will the real Buddy Jacobson stand up?" Four men did so.

Nobody came close to what happened. At ten-thirty on the morning of Saturday, June 7, Buddy called George Carpozi, Jr. "Wake up," he told Carpozi. "What's the matter, are you sleeping or something?"

"God! It's you!" Carpozi said, his voice awed. He was taping the call.

"Of course it's me," Buddy said. "I'm okay. Everything is fine."

Buddy explained the purpose of his call. Was there any way to make "serious money" out of his escape?

He suggested he might dictate tapes, with his first-person story. Carpozi asked that they be sent to his house on Long Island.

Buddy was cautious. "No, I'm not going to send you anything until I know what kind of money we're talking about," he said. He would call him again on Tuesday or Wednesday. "I'll tell you what it's like to be a fugitive," he said, and hung up.

Carpozi told Evseroff. This was not, perhaps, his most brilliant move. "I made George go to the DA," the defense attorney says.

Gold put a tap on the reporter's telephone, and for two weeks stationed a squad of detectives in his house, awaiting that second call. It never came. It is possible that the fact the *Post* on June 9 ran a large front-page picture of Buddy, with the heavy-type caption **$20,000 REWARD** **for any reader who provides this paper with information that leads to the capture of Buddy Jacobson,** had something to do with his change of heart.

Jacobson's unexpected telephone call indicated, first, that he was still in the continental United States, or perhaps Canada. Second, it suggested that he was, as usual, low on actual cash.

"I hate to see him at large," prosecutor Bill Kelly said. "He's been made into a hero! The Brooklyn cowboy. This man's a murderer!"

Kelly's complaint was justified. Buddy Jacobson was becoming a legend. It was transfiguring.

David Jacobson told me his life was "a big, bad dream" but met me on June 12, at the corner of 63rd and Fifth Avenue. He was dressed exactly as his father dressed; unpolished shoes, sloppy jeans, a checkered shirt. Only the smile seemed a fainter photocopy of the original.

He complained that the authorities were making it hard for him to do business, that they were trying to put liens on his property. Various people—Jim Edwards of Audley Farm, Ellen Gannon on behalf of young Paul, and Melanie herself —all had claims against the Jacobson estate. Was it a problem, I asked, taking care of both the real estate and the stables?

Not really, he said. "I'm only training two horses right now."

He looked at me with sudden intensity and added, *"Nothing's changed."*

The following day, all four buildings—the 84th Street property as well as the 63rd Street structures—were advertised for sale in the *Times*. Total price asked: $3,600,000. This was a plunge, and I was telephoned by an excited Bob Wood.

"Judging by the wording," he insisted, "this is Buddy talking, not the kid."

That same day, I lunched with Evseroff and Barberino in the Bronx. The lawyer was in a jovial mood. "You know what this Sunday is?" he said. "Father's Day."

Perhaps Buddy would be calling Douglas and David?

"A lot of people hope so," Evseroff said. "There are going to be a lot of ears on that line."

"A lot of fathers," snorted Barberino.

Ironically, David Jacobson soon afterward telephoned George Carpozi, Jr., saying that he wished to discuss his father's story, and suggesting a meeting at Truffles, a Madison Avenue restaurant around the corner from the East 63rd Street building. "I set up the meeting," Carpozi recounted later. "But first the Brooklyn DA taped a hidden tape recorder on me to pick up the conversation in a police car nearby."

David wanted to know precise details of the story that his father would have to tell, and how much money could be expected. Carpozi mentioned $50,000.

David never did call Carpozi back, though, and when Carpozi called him, denied that his father had been in touch.

The blue 1980 Dodge Aspen which David had used to drive his father away from the Brooklyn House of Detention was discovered on June 22. This automobile, the description of which had been so widely circulated that it had become known as "America's Most Wanted Car," turned up in Parking Field One at La Guardia Airport.

This is a big, active parking lot, and attendants check it every day, changing the tickets on vehicles that have stood there longer than twenty-four hours. That, anyway, is the theory. Buddy's getaway car had been sitting there since June 10.

Buddy-watchers took note of two facts. The Dodge had been rented in Queens, near La Guardia. By the time it was found at the airport, there was an extra 2,400 miles on the clock. Somebody had driven it 1,200 miles in one direction and somebody, not necessarily the same somebody, had driven it the same distance back again. The second fact: There are no international flights from La Guardia.

The presence of the blue Dodge in the lot was a clue, a false clue, or a dumb mistake. Nobody knew.

The fortitude that had kept Melanie going on the stand had gone, and the strange mood that had gripped her after she first heard the news of his escape—an almost triumphal feeling of I-told-you-so—had lapsed. She now again felt the tug of those pressures that had nearly destroyed her. Once again, she was preyed upon by nightmares, falling back into that netherworld where death scenes were played and replayed. She began to read again, more to conquer her insomnia than for reason of pleasure. For instance, Nietzsche. Driving with Billy, for instance, she declaimed aloud the German's thoughts on such subjects as Power, Insanity, and Suicide, with the jolly pleasure of one who has found something favorable in her horoscope. She would read Jacobson stories in the newspapers as carefully as though they were cryptograms: Crack them and his whereabouts would be luminously clear.

She thought it highly probable that Buddy had undergone plastic surgery, or was at least skillfully disguised. She remembered the time, long before, when he had shaved off his mustache. It had made him totally unrecognizable. Melanie believed him to be in Brooklyn, but she saw him everywhere. "I keep thinking I've seen him," she told me. "I turn around in the street." She was, incidentally, not the only person in her circle to have had this impression. Melanie's brother, Chris, lives with his wife in Palos Verdes, not far from Los Angeles. Chris's mother-in-law had become something of a Buddy Jacobson buff and, late that June, became so convinced that she had caught sight of Buddy that she telephoned Melanie's mother.

She had spotted Jacobson, she said, in a place not far from Palos Verdes called Manhattan Beach.

Within a few days of this call, Melanie flew to Hamburg. She had been booked for five days of work on a fashion catalogue. "I'll probably run into Buddy," she told me, trying to make a joke. She was miserable on the trip. Sitting on a set in the Hamburg studio, she began to think about Audrey, putting herself in the girl's place, and began writing her a long letter.

It was never finished. Just before she flew home she heard that Audrey had given herself up.

On Friday, June 27, a lawyer, Lewis Cohen—it is one more coincidence that his Brooklyn offices happen to be in the same building as Evseroff's—was telephoned by Audrey Barrett, whom he had never met. She told him that she had left Buddy and was with her family. He told her that it was essential she give herself up right away. Sobbing, she agreed.

The next morning, Cohen met her in Philadelphia and drove her to his house in Kings Point, Long Island. From his house, the lawyer called and left an urgent message for Brooklyn DA Eugene Gold. When Gold called, Cohen said he was with Audrey Barrett; he prevailed on Gold not to send a squad car, and arranged to take Audrey to the DA's office the next day.

As if unaware of Gold's relative magnanimity, and much to Cohen's dismay, Audrey subsequently spent two hours closeted with David Jacobson. Nonetheless, she was duly in Gold's office at the proper time—one o'clock on Sunday.

Gold announced that he intended to ask for $500,000 bail, and that Audrey would be charged with "criminal facilitation, escape, forgery, and criminal possession of forged instruments." There was also a charge of "escape in the first degree," which carries a sentence of up to eleven years. Audrey was duly arraigned, in such a sorry state that she had to be seated halfway through the proceedings. Bail was set at $350,000, and her relatives announced they would put up their houses as collateral.

"It was dreadful. They handcuffed me like a dangerous criminal," Audrey told Guy Hawtin of the *Post*. "At Central Booking they stripped me and did a body search. That's really demeaning."

There were soon reports that Audrey was "cooperating." She was, in fact, being interrogated by Gold's eager beavers, not in a prison cell, but in a sequence of hotel rooms. She was allowed the company of her cat, Pumpkin, and guards were sometimes dispatched to procure food for the pet. "We had some fun," she told Hawtin. "They took me to a disco. We played Frisbee in the park, and one night they even let me go roller skating." Guy Hawtin, a bearded and rumbustious Englishman, and the former Frankfurt-based correspondent of the London *Financial Times*, seemed a surprising choice, at first, to replace Carpozi on the Jacobson beat, but he was soon to play a colorful part in what was to unfold.

The thinking in the DA's office, until a few days before Audrey's return, had increasingly been that Buddy was not only in the United States, but probably in Brooklyn. "It's the dirtiest borough," Bill Kelly told me. But an insight gleaned from several tapped telephones had altered this belief. Buddy had been in California and probably still was. Even before Audrey's return, Gold had a squad of ten detectives alerted and ready to fly out to the West Coast. The search was now zeroing in on Southern California—specifically, Ventura County.

Audrey, now officially cooperating with the authorities, was asked to make herself the bait. This would have involved communicating with Buddy and arranging to meet him at a prearranged rendezvous in Oregon. She refused. Instead, a description of Buddy, based on Audrey's information, was issued by the police. He was said to be wearing a baseball cap, sometimes a wig, and traveling with camping gear. He had many false IDs, said the cops, and he was armed. He was clean-shaven, with no mustache, and he had short hair, neatly combed. On the basis of this information, Brooklyn alerted the state and federal authorities in Ventura County, but Jacobson slipped through the net, much to Gold's displeasure. "At this point, we don't know where he is," the Brooklyn DA's office conceded on July 4. Posters depicting Buddy, with both his supposed new face and his old one, were distributed to every state in the union.

It was now that the squeeze on David Jacobson began. Like those of other associates of his father's, his line had, of course, been tapped since the escape. He was now being followed, and in no inconspicuous manner. In the first week of July, he had stopped his car, got out, walked back to the plainclothesmen and said, "Why don't we all go in the same car, so we can save gas?"

David's jauntiness under pressure, though, was becoming frayed. The threat that he would be indicted for helping his father to escape was constant, and there was much talk about the indignities to which inmates subject young males in the U.S. prison system.

On Tuesday, July 8, David was summoned to Eugene Gold's office, which is on the fifth floor of the Brooklyn Municipal Building, and shown a sealed indictment. If this indictment were opened and he was convicted of the charges contained therein, David would be looking at seven years' hard time.

The next day he called Gold. He was expecting a telephone call.

The Great Jailbreak had been strange and wonderful, but not necessarily in the way the world had thought. It had confirmed friends and foes in the belief that Buddy was a modern Machiavelli, a coldly brilliant man, full of schemes, and this is true; up to a point. It is not, though, always easy to see when a strategy turns into a chimera, as the saga of the escape was to show.

Certainly, Buddy had thought about it long and hard, especially with regard to his final destination. Sometimes he had inclined to the conventional wisdom, which would be to put as much mileage as possible between oneself and one's pursuers. He had talked of Spain, and France, but Buddy had no foreign languages, and, at any rate, was repelled by foreign parts. It seems that one contingency plan was this: He would make his way to California, then to Latin America, as cooling-off stops, but would finally settle as a country squire in Ireland. "He would often say if I wanted to live anywhere but New York, I would go to Ireland," Melanie says, "It was green, and it was horse country. But it was only a fantasy."

He had another plan. He would just stay more or less where he was. "It's simple to disappear," he told Pete McLaughlin, "I could have stayed here in New York. I bet I could have walked up to any cop in the city and they couldn't have recognized me." He considered Jersey. Or, perhaps, it would be enough to move over to the West Side. He would "fade away." In a few years, he told intimates, he would be able to return to the East Side without trouble. Re-creation of his identity was, after all, his forte. Such were the dreams of invulnerability that possessed Buddy Jacobson.

There was one problem, though: money. Neither the small ad that he had written in the holding pen, nor its successors, had attracted buyers for his buildings, and time was running out on Buddy. The Brooklyn House of Detention stands on Atlantic Avenue, in the teeming borough where Buddy had spent his youth. But the day of his sentencing was looming. Afterwards, Buddy might find himself packed off to some maximum-security stronghold the very same day. Buddy decided to make his break for freedom just as quickly as he could.

The scheme came, unwittingly, from William Dickinson, one of Buddy's fellow inmates. Dickinson is a safecracker and a thief, specializing in jewelry and art. He is of the old school, which is to say he doesn't carry a gun, and the only reason that he was alongside Buddy on the maximum security tenth floor is that he has broken out of three separate jails. "Buddy never told me he was planning an escape," Dickinson says, "but he asked me a lot of questions." In one escape—this had been in Georgia—he had put on a suit of clothes, smuggled in by another prisoner's wife, sawn through his bars, and simply walked out. Buddy took this in, set to studying the workings of the jail, and began to assemble the elements of the plan.

Afterwards, he decided, he would go to earth in Brooklyn, so David Jacobson arranged for a hideaway with friends. The getaway car was rented, unknowingly, by one of David's hotwalkers. Buddy, a man who was on the telephone a great deal, worked out a telephone code, and it was typical of the insouciance of the scheme that Audrey showed this code to a friend four days before the escape took place. It consisted of a column of telephone numbers, written onto a leaf, three inches by six, taken out of a notebook, and the exchange (recorded by Michael Daly in the News) went like this.

"These are the phone booths he's going to call afterward," Audrey said.

"After he escapes?" the friend asked.

Audrey nodded.

Tony De Rosa, the former barman at Nicola's, was already part of the operation. It was Audrey who procured the forged legal identification which identified him as "Michael Schwartz," a real lawyer with whom Buddy had had brief contact in the past. Buddy shaved his mustache, and waited.

The day chosen for the venture was Saturday, May 31, just three days before Buddy's sentencing. He lunched on gumbo, liver, and mashed potatoes, washed down with cocoa. De Rosa signed in at twenty past two, and waited for his client in the visitors' area on the first floor.

Buddy was brought down to him by prison officers, according to the rules. Apart from the pair of them, the place was quiet, lawyers being seldom keen to work on summer weekends. The two men "conferred" for two hours. Much of their conference dealt with the matter that had brought De Rosa into the plot. He was deeply in debt to Buddy over the ski lodge, and Buddy had promised, in exchange for this favor, both to forgive the debt, and make over to him the stock certificate, which (Buddy claimed) would give him control. This Buddy now signed.

At twenty past four, shortly after new guards had come on duty, Buddy Jacobson walked out of the visitors' area in one of his courtroom suits, and made his way through three checkpoints. The guard at the outer gate, preoccupied with other business, waved him through.

A brilliantly conceived escape.

Well, yes and no.

It was characteristic that Buddy had neglected to take the "Michael Schwartz" pass from Tony De Rosa. A single challenge—even a look at their differing signatures—would have undone him. David seems to have had little confidence in his father's scheme. At any rate, he had parked a block from the jail, and Buddy was forced to run for it: a burlesque beginning to an increasingly bizarre adventure.

Audrey, also, had thought the escape plan far-fetched, but Buddy had been able to talk of little else, declaring that she was his "outside man." She had gone through the motions only, in her words, "to humor him, and keep him happy."

Anyway, in the unlikely event of success, she told Buddy that he was on his own. Yes, she loved him, but she also loved her family, and friends.

She had been fearful as the date approached, but mainly for his safety. It was her mother's birthday, so she called at three, and said she would be home at seven. Her mother was cooking dinner. In the Brooklyn hide-out, Audrey drank two large Scotches, and fell asleep; it would all be over when she woke up, with Buddy snug in his cell. Instead, he shook her awake.

There was a good deal of fuss, not all of it welcoming. Buddy's original plan, which had been to stay underground in Brooklyn until his money came through, was regarded with dismay by the owners of the "hideaway" who had no more believed in the break-out than had Audrey, whose only equipment was her pocketbook.

It didn't matter. Buddy felt too alive with nervous energy to stay put; he wanted to get on the move. The conflict now was that he wanted Audrey to come with him. Weeping, the girl refused. Disguised as an elderly man, and with $4,000 in his pocket, which was all that David had been able to raise, Buddy climbed into the trunk of the Dodge. David was to drive, and Audrey sat in the back, still sobbing, and talking to Buddy through the partition.

A second car followed. This was driven by the nervous owners of the apartment, who had agreed to follow Buddy wherever he decided to go, then ferry Audrey and David back into the city. The problem was that Buddy had no clear idea on his final destination, and was expending his energies persuading Audrey to go wherever it was with him. She wept, and argued and, while police and the FBI were checking airports, the most wanted car in America was weaving its way through the streets of Brooklyn.

Buddy, at last, decided to head for New Jersey. On the Queens side of the Whitestone Bridge, David waited by the phone booth, while the second car drove on, reconnoitering for road blocks. The coast was clear, so Buddy was again driven through the Bronx. This precaution was repeated at the George Washington Bridge, and every few miles thereafter.

It was hot, fiendishly so in the trunk. They stopped for cold drinks. "Please somebody stay by the car," Buddy asked. He was alarmed that it might be stolen with him inside.

They were now driving due west along the superhighway, Route 80. Somewhere in New Jersey, they pulled into the parking lot of a Howard Johnson's. Buddy clambered out of the trunk, and sat in the back of the car, while the others went inside to eat. Audrey quickly ate a salad, and brought Buddy a cold beer and a Reuben sandwich. Interminably, he pleaded that she accompany him. At last, worn to a frazzle, she succumbed. She would go with him, but for one day only. David returned to Manhattan in the other car, while Buddy and Audrey continued westward.

They passed through Pennsylvania in the night, reaching Ohio with the fishbelly light of dawn. By midday, they were famished and exhausted, so pulled into another Howard Johnson's, ate, and slept in a motel room till the early evening. Audrey then made the first telephone call of the trip, asking that a girl friend take care of her adored Persian cat, and they bought clean clothes in a K Mart. Audrey changed in the washroom in such a nervous haste that she forgot the clothes she had brought with her—green blouse, cord trousers, sandals—and wept all the more.

They were now headed for Iowa. It was always Buddy that drove, with Audrey navigating, and Buddy had now formulated some goals. The first goal was familiar. He would buy property; a motel, a ski lodge, a horse farm. He began stopping whenever he passed a realtor's office, and the car was soon awash with brochures. It was like a reprise of those voyages with Melanie, but more fantastic, because Buddy had another goal also. He had grown obsessed with Mount St. Helens, the volcano erupting in Washington State: He and Audrey would be married there, he said.

Audrey was not consoled. Life was becoming a sequence of motel rooms in nameless towns, and K Marts where she would buy fresh underwear, T-shirts, jeans. "God, I've got to get out of this," Audrey told herself. She envisioned a future of cooking hamburgers, cut off from family and friends. Buddy, oblivious, talked, and talked. He had made a discovery; he loved traveling. "I used to hate driving," he was to say, later, "I never drove when I lived in Manhattan. Yet, when I was on the road, I loved every minute of it."

They broke their journey in Des Moines, Iowa, stopping for several days. It was here they met the person who drove Buddy's hot car the twelve hundred miles back to New York, parking it at La Guardia, though Buddy had, apparently, instructed him to take it to Kennedy. Buddy then spent $700 on a 1970 Chevy Impala. His bankroll was slimming.

It is pleasing to think that while the cops were searching for leads in Ireland, Spain, and Brazil, Buddy was in Des Moines. Here he became youthful again, by means of a blond dye-job, which he kept partially hidden beneath a baseball cap. Here, too, they acquired new identities, visiting the Merle Hay Mausoleum-Cemetery, and copying down the names of children who would have been their ages, had they lived. They then rooted out the parents' names from the death notices in the local newspaper files, and applied to the County Clerk's Office for copies of the birth certificates: Cost $2 per copy.

Audrey became Rhonda Sue Guessford; Buddy was Lonnie Sherman Rumbaugh, and, under these names, they took Iowa driving tests, and secured licenses. Buddy was also to use other aliases from time to time, including Antony Zippolini. After all, this was the ultimate Zzzyp Trick.

"Rumbaugh" continued to look for property deals. His particular interest, he told realtors, lay in motels and roller-skating rinks. If his New York accent drew comment, he would explain that he had grown up in Miami. From Des Moines, they drove to Omaha. It was from there that he telephoned George Carpozi. Money was running low. The Carpozi deal souring, Buddy called David, who promised to have money waiting for him at his next stop, which was Teton, Wyoming.

There was $5,000 waiting in Teton at the Alphenhof Hotel, c/o "Ronnie Guess". It was charming—a real cowboy town. Audrey enjoyed it, and Buddy talked of buying a farm there. The journey had begun to seem timeless. Buddy did what he could to keep Audrey occupied. They would study Indian artifacts in local museums. In Omaha, they had ridden on a kids' choo-choo train through the Henry Doorley zoo. She would find yoga classes or dance classes to go to while he checked with the neighboring real estate offices. They would drink in a bar in the evenings, and every two or three nights they would dance in the local discothèque; and Audrey would roller-skate.

But it wasn't working. Audrey was increasingly miserable. She had told Buddy that she would like to see the Grand Canyon, so, eager to please, he broke his westward run in Wyoming, and plunged south.

"Is that all there is?" she said, miserably, when they got there.

"I drive you all this way," Buddy griped. "And *that's* all you can say?"

They passed from Utah, through Arizona, into California. In San Francisco, Audrey wrote a letter of farewell, after a Chinese dinner, but decided she couldn't leave Buddy alone, weary in a strange city. One last day. They drove north through the redwoods, Buddy talking about Mount St. Helens. In a small town, he stopped, and went to talk with the local realtor. Audrey was in the car. Studying the map, it seemed they were close to Eureka, a town with an airport. Audrey left the farewell letter on the driving seat, and hitched a lift on a logging truck. It is in keeping with the whole jaunt that the truck could only take her five miles. Eureka was fifty miles away. Audrey checked into a motel, and called her brother's house, in the Los Angeles suburb, Thousand Oaks.

Her mother and stepfather were there, she found, on holiday. She joined her family the next day. Audrey protected Buddy as best she could, saying she had split up with Buddy many days before. The family relaxed, going to Disneyland, and joining the audience for Johnny Carson's "Tonight" Show. This false calm was destroyed. A Long Island neighbor telephoned. Buddy had been calling, and calling. Audrey's parents now realized she had been less than candid. Audrey took the advice of somebody close to Buddy, and called the lawyer Lewis Cohen.

Audrey's defection had driven Buddy frantic. He guessed she was at her brother's house, and drove south to Thousand Oaks, his car bristling with camping equipment, and his hair dyed an interesting shade of pineapple. He called Audrey from a street kiosk, and found she had already gone. He began to bombard New York with calls, and the news was chill: Audrey was "co-operating."

From Thousand Oaks, Buddy drove to another Los Angeles suburb, Manhattan Beach, and checked into the Sea View Motel on July 5th. He paid $150, a week's rent in advance, and said he would be staying two or three weeks. The name he used was "Lonnie Sherman Rumbaugh." Which was known to Audrey, of course. He was a few hours from Mexico. Audrey believes that he, at this stage, wanted to be caught, but it is quite possible that he simply, as so often in the past, felt invulnerable.

"Lonnie" told people in the Sea View that he was a writer, and he would spend part of the day by the pool, scribbling on a yellow pad. At times, they would hear him in his room, pecking away at his brand-new Smith Corona. Also, he was trying to teach himself to roller-skate, a promise he had made Audrey, and would trundle up and down the ocean front with his shaggy orange hair. It was perfect cover: another freak.

He was, of course, telephoning New York constantly. He needed money, he said. He was in the middle of negotiations to buy a roller-skating rink. Often he would call from his regular hang-out, the Criterion, a diner popular with the inhabitants of Manhattan Beach, many of whom are young and female. Manhattan Beach is close to LA International Airport, and functions as a dormitory suburb for flight attendants, as stews are called nowadays. It would soon be like old times.

July 9th was beautiful: ninety degrees, and free of smog. At two-thirty, Buddy walked into the Criterion, and sat at the counter, in white T-shirt and blue jeans. He asked for a half order of fried zucchini, a dish upon which the place prides itself, and a coffee. "I'll order something else later," he told the waitress, Eda Allen, got up, and went to the pay phone at the back. It was now three P.M.; SIX P.M., New York time; time to call David. He had some trouble. "Something's wrong with this phone," he complained. "It's taking all my quarters, and I can't get my party." "Just call the phone company, and they'll send your money back," he was told.

He got through at last. David's instructions from the Brooklyn Attorney's office were to keep his father on the line as long as possible. This was not a problem. Buddy talked, and talked, while the New York Telephone Company's security office probed for the source of the call.

The trace was made after twenty minutes. Leonard Michaels of the DA's office called Sergeant Mair of the Manhattan Beach police, and told him where Buddy was. That's half a block away, Mair told him.

Buddy talked on, meandering, meaningful. He was still talking at 3:35 when Mair walked in, with six cops, armed with rifles and shotguns. Officially, Buddy was "armed and dangerous." A waitress said Mair "walked up behind Jacobson and stuck a gun in his back. The other officer stood nearby, with a shotgun cocked. Jacobson had a two- or three-day growth of beard, looked scroungy, and was wearing glasses. He seemed baffled for a moment, but didn't do anything."

They stood him up against the wall, searched him, and led him out to the patrol car. "He was very mellow," Sergeant Mair said. "It ran as smooth as silk."

It was over.

Epilogue

In the spring of 1981 I noticed gaily colored bunting outside 155 East 84th Street. The bunting was festooned around that ground-floor space that had once housed My Fair Lady, and a sign announced the grand opening of a new enterprise, a boutique for infants' clothes, called L'Amour de Bébé.

Other than this already defunct effort the changes to Buddy's building are few. The tenant who moved into Jacobson's seventh-floor apartment, the scene of the murder, laid Astroturf on the roof. Of all the models who lived there on August 6, 1978, only Gail Moore remains. She is still surprised at the number of tourists who come by and gawk upward at Buddy's former apartment. "It's as if it's part of some New York *tour!*" she says.

The Greek luncheonette where Melanie called and called that August night, trying to locate Jack, has been transformed into a pizzeria. Nicola's continues to boom. The photograph of David Silbergeld is gone, but the *Cosmopolitan* cover of Melanie still hangs there as I write, as, of course, does the photograph of Buddy with a winner at Belmont—thus affording some humorist the opportunity to paste a sticker, reading APPREHENDED, diagonally across Jacobson's face.

The glamorous Sarah Hall is out of racing. She says she does not miss the track. "It used to be so much fun," she says. "Now it's full of whores. It's a *business!*" Sarah will not allow Buddy's later troubles to affect her memory of him. "We had fun," she says. "He won a lot of races for me."

Frank Pagano, Buddy's longtime assistant, still trains for Bill Levin, another of Buddy's owners. Pagano runs the horse farm that Jacobson sold Levin out at Old Westbury, where Bold Reason stands at stud. This horse, probably New York's most valuable stud, was Buddy's greatest.

Gene Jacobs has stepped down from the HPBA presidency. Robyn Smith, one of the female jockeys Buddy brought to New York, married Fred Astaire in 1979, the actor then being seventy-nine and the jockey thirty-two. The Connecticut racetrack was seemingly stoppered the same year by the prospect of eutrophication, which is to say too much urine for the local water.

Mark Fleischman, the former owner of Mount Snow, where Buddy's ski lodge was located, subsequently sold it. In November 1980 he bought Studio 54, where the disco life achieved its brief apotheosis, from its creators, Steve Rubell and Ian Schrager, who were in an Alabama pen for skimming profits from the books. "It's fortunate that Buddy was living in New York," Fleischman muses. "He would have been a whole lot weirder living in the woods."

Jimmy Leonard and Bill Sharrocks lost their appeal, and went to jail to do their stretches of time. I lunched with Leonard on his last day of freedom; we ate steaks at J.G. Melon. "I'm going to a country club," he said, miming a golfer's swing. We strolled up Third Avenue and had a drink at George Martin's, which first was the All-Ireland, then Chaequers. The mirrors are few, the green carpeting has been stripped away, but otherwise the saloon is little changed. Jimmy had fallen out with Jack Tupper in the end, but he was glad that Buddy was getting his due. He and Billy Sharrocks surrendered themselves at the Manhattan Correctional Center the next morning. Billy went to Danbury, Connecticut, and Jimmy was fortunate enough to wind up at Lake Placid, the former Olympic Village.

Carlo Carrara collected five years probation, which comes to the same thing as acquittal. Exit grinning. Ivor Shaw laments the whole thing. "I was leading more lives than anybody knew," he said, "and suddenly it started unravelling like a bad sweater."

As to David Silbergeld, the charges that he was dealing in machine-guns and land mines were not made to stick. The feds contented themselves with convicting him for incorrectly collecting unemployment checks. He did three months.

Legal difficulties would not be over for Donald Brown, who spent several days testifying against his former colleagues. The course of events did not please him. He had returned to New York from a quiet time on a ranch in the West, and though he was looking tanned and fit, this was not reflected in his mood. "I'm in torture! Torture, do you hear?" he told me. "I don't *like* myself anymore. It's anguish. Do you follow? I was looking at thirty years. I'd be sixty-five when I came out. My life would be over."

He took a new tack. "I've thought of doing a book myself. I'll call it *The Stool Pigeon! The Rat*. I'd rather be in jail." D.B.'s mood turned to a depressed calm. "Let them do what they want," he said. They did. He got three years.

Joey Ippolito, his acquitted cohort, soon had a new problem. One foggy morning in September 1981, the Coast Guard (narrowly avoiding a challenge to Soviet intelligence craft off Montauk Point, Long Island) picked up Ippolito and others, allegedly while the group was removing twenty tons of marijuana—say $20 million worth—from a Colombian shrimp boat moored off the elegant resort, Block Island.

Eighth Homicide in the Bronx, the police division that had originally investigated the Jacobson case, went out of existence before the proceedings were concluded. Its premises, including the cubicle where a distraught Melanie had been questioned early in the morning on August 7, had been taken over by the arson squad when I last visited the place. A message on the blackboard read: "If something passes into oblivion sooner than anticipated—did it really matter at all?"

Irwin "Win" Klein still thinks that Buddy should have copped an insanity plea. "What a beautiful move that would have been!" he enthuses. A few years upstate, in some country-club institution, and Jacobson would have walked out, rehabilitated, a free man.

Bill Hrabsky has "subsided back into obscurity," he says. "I want to write a novel with a Dostoyevskian theme. The hero is a man who is bound to fail." The billboard outside showed not Margaux Hemingway but a brand of cigarette called, improbably, True.

The murder of Bill Kelly's sister remains unsolved. Kelly no longer believes that Buddy was involved in the killing, but is still certain that the telephone calls were his handiwork. Joe Toscanini, the cop whom Buddy tried to bribe, and who then tried a scam, was convicted of "attempted criminal solicitation . . . to false arrest" and given an unconditional discharge from the force.

Tony De Rosa, the former barman, was convicted of helping Jacobson escape, and sent to the slammer. The ownership of the Norway ski lodge is being contested in court by Buddy's former partners, so it remains uncertain whether De Rosa will profit from his action.

Sal Prainito, who was acquitted for his part in the Tupper murder, was arrested in January 1981 by the Italian police. He was on a train between Certaldo—a charming, inconsequential village—and the city of Florence. He was carrying a suitcase that contained three kilos of heroin. This would have fetched $8 million on the streets of New York. Somewhere, somebody evidently thought he acquitted himself well during the Jacobson trial.

Claire Normandeau now works at the Police Academy. I asked her how the Jacobson case had affected her career. "What career?" she replied. The inquiry had cleared her of corruption in March, 1979, suggesting only that her personal use of the NADDIS printouts had shown poor judgment, but she had become, she says, an "embarrassment" to the department, and was put into uniform for the first time in her career. Why is she staying? "I love being a cop," she says. "I was a cop's kid. I grew up on the job."

She says it is her belief that she was set up by someone within the DEA; sacrificed, presumably to save some operation or entrenched agent. Copies of the NADDIS printouts which she took became available to lawyers during the Brooklyn case, and

Normandeau is insistent that they had been tampered with since they left her hands.

Buddy's former wife, Joan, lives quietly on Long Island. His sister, Rita Costello, remains convinced of her brother's innocence. His sons, David and Douglas, are training horses.

Jimmy Wood remains somewhat obsessive on the subject of Buddy. "There are irretrievable things you can't bring back," Wood says. "There's Jack dead, and Buddy rotting away in jail. Buddy was a funny guy. He could have done great things."

Most law-enforcement people feel that Buddy is still dangerous. Says Peter Grishman, "As long as he's got a dime. Buddy will do anything and everything to get out of jail. What will he do to me? What kind of a wheeler-dealer is he going to be in jail? He won't *stop*."

Ellen and John Gannon run a restaurant-bar in upstate New York. "Paul knew his father, and the memory will remain intact," Ellen says. "He's got his tinful of pictures." The bitter feelings and the suspicions that were engendered after the murder between Ellen Gannon and Jack Tupper's family faded. The emotions are drained, or soaked up by Buddy.

"I never before had hate feelings in my life," says Dorothy Myers. "I used to think there was something wrong with me. But I hate Buddy, and my hatred has grown. I feel I know what he will do. Now that he's put away, he'll *reach out* for people. I don't think it's over. Now I think he's somebody who will just come back to haunt you. He's too bad to die."

Jack Evseroff's telephone had rung at half past five. He and his wife were watching the TV news while in Los Angeles on vacation. The caller was his secretary. "Did you *hear?*" she asked. "They caught Buddy!"

"Go on!" Evseroff scoffed. "You're nuts."

He soon discovered that Buddy had not only been captured, but was being held in Manhattan Beach.

Evseroff drove to the jail at ten the next morning, and was jolted by his first sight of Buddy. "They bring in Buddy in chains. I am shocked. He looked like he had aged twenty years. His hair was this dirty reddish-blond." An obvious dye job. "It didn't look like there had been any effort to conceal the dyeing. It was *childish*."

The interview room contained a long, narrow table, bisected by a see-through partition. "They manacled him," Evseroff said. "They chained him to the table, like you would chain a dog."

The attorney, who had never pretended to any personal liking for his client, felt an emotion for which he is not famous: compassion. "Well, Buddy," he said, "we meet again."

"Hello, Jack," Jacobson replied noncommittally. He struck Evseroff as depressed but lucid.

There was, they agreed, no point in fighting extradition. They would return to New York. Jack would take the appeal for a fee of $75,000.

Evseroff still regarded Buddy as a rogue genius, but there were details that did not jibe with this. Those telephone calls while on the lam, for instance. Buddy now began to ramble about Audrey. "I can't understand why Audrey did what she did," he fretted.

This also jarred. "Come on Buddy," Evseroff said. "You did this yourself. You wanted her to have absolution."

This was just what Evseroff had told me, but Buddy was vehement in denial. "He was hurt, almost broken," Evseroff says. He was nonplussed, but assimilated the fact that there was a side to Buddy of which he had known nothing.

Nor did he understand why Buddy hadn't driven a few hours more, and crossed the Mexican border. "They'd never have gotten him there in a million years," Evseroff said. He asked Buddy why he had come to Los Angeles. "Remember," Buddy explained, "Don Brown comes from here. . . ."

CBS and ABC both had sent correspondents from New York to cover the California arraignment, and Municipal Judge Barbara Johnson was startled to find her courtroom crowded with press. Evseroff took her aside for a few minutes in the robing room to fill her in on the "love triangle murder." A recent state law permitted the filming of court proceedings, if the defendant approved, but Buddy turned the media exposure down. He didn't want to come across as "a loser." The arraignment was brief. "Yes, your honor," Buddy answered, six times—and that was that.

Afterward, the defense attorney submitted himself to the television cameras with his customary willingness. Buddy, he said, had come to California to look for "the real murderer." Tupper's killer, he claimed, was Donald Brown. "My phone rang off the hook," Brown says. He didn't know whether to be more amused or outraged.

Three detectives from Brooklyn were in the courtroom. District Attorney Eugene Gold seems to have wanted to take no risks at all. Buddy was smuggled out of the California courthouse, and he and his escort flew out on the TWA redeye that same night. At ten past seven the following morning, Buddy was back in the Brooklyn House of Detention he had fled just forty days before.

Ben Epstein now came into the act, repudiating Evseroff's remark regarding Donald Brown. Buddy had never said it, he told the New York press.

Evseroff telephoned from California, livid. "Ben, don't speak to the press till I get back," he said. "On Monday we're going to have a *talk*."

Epstein walked into Evseroff's office that Monday and managed, just for once, to speak before Evseroff got his mouth open. "I want to say two things," he told him. "One, I'm going out on my own. And two, Jacobson is now my client."

At least, Evseroff says sourly, his Beverly Hillcrest tab was now tax-deductible.

Buddy was now back in a prison cell. He claimed to be fearful of vengeance, both from the Corrections Department, two of whose officials had been "reassigned" after his escape, and from his fellow cons, smarting because of the harsher security that had been brought in because of it. Indeed, a riot broke out in the Brooklyn jail shortly after his return; twelve guards and ten inmates required treatment. "Buddy was not involved," a spokesman said, "but he had a bird's-eye view of it."

Nonetheless his spring to the attack was as rapid as it had been after Jack Tupper's murder, almost two years before. Somehow he had unrestricted use of a telephone—the Department of Corrections was to ascribe this later to a "quirk"—and spoke to the press at length. He told the *Times*, in a report published on July 14, that he had escaped from jail only to seek evidence. He was reticent about the telephone call that had trapped him, saying only that he had been betrayed by "someone I had confided in, someone I trusted"—adding that his betrayer "had his motives and will have to live with them."

Shortly thereafter, though, Buddy struck a very different note talking to George Carpozi, Jr. "I know that my son David is targeted as the person who set me up with a trap that led to my arrest," he said. "It's true. But I don't hold it against him. He did the right thing. David knew I couldn't run forever. And I never intended to do that."

On the morning of July 16, Buddy was taken from Brooklyn to the Bronx in one of two black police cars, with sirens squalling; the vehicles were followed by a van filled with cops toting shotguns. Judge Kapelman now formally informed Buddy of his twenty-five-year sentence.

On July 23, Audrey, as had been expected, was released from custody. Buddy told Pete McLaughlin that this "tickled him to death." Apart from this, Buddy gave the reporter a melancholy interview. "The mornings are the worst," he said. "You start to wake up. Your mind clears. You realize it's not a bad dream. It's true."

Why had he gone to California? McLaughlin asked.

Buddy favored him with an enigmatic smile. "Maybe I was looking for Jack Tupper," he said.

On July 30, Buddy and Tony De Rosa met for the first time since the escape. They did not look each other in the eyes. De Rosa was on a hunger strike to protest the $250,000 bail which was keeping him behind bars. Buddy's tan had gone; his dyed hair looked even seedier as it grew out. A young assistant district attorney told the judge, Joseph Slavin, that his office was ready to prosecute Buddy for the escape, and De Rosa as an accessory. Slavin was brusque, and demanded to know why the Jacobson escape had to be tried before a slew of pending cases. "Other than the fact that this case helps sell newspapers, why should I grant a preference?" he snapped at the unhappy ADA.

Ben Epstein was already at work on the appeal. He set himself to a piece of work left uncompleted at the time of Buddy's flight— the tracking down of jurors who would be willing to say they had been "coerced" into their decision. Michael Speller and Bernice Faust, numbers ten and six, gladly signed affidavits.

A third was signed by Rose Kovnit, the elderly number twelve, who, Hrabsky had feared, "didn't want to convict anybody."

The DA's office affected a sublime indifference. Jurors cannot have second thoughts. That is the law. As to the "coercion," well, there is often sound and fury in a jury room. Kapelman duly refused Epstein's demand for a hearing.

Buddy, too, was hard at work. In early September, he complained of "stomach pains," and was taken to Kings County Hospital, Brooklyn. Here the examining doctors diagnosed merely a "voluntary spasm of the abdominal muscles," and he was rapidly removed to a guarded ward at Bellevue. He also continued with his legal endeavors. Jack Evseroff was now suing him for $377,000. Buddy countersued for around $5 million, the charge being "malpractice." "He thinks I should have won the case," Evseroff growled. Toward the end of September, I heard that Buddy had been talking with a new lawyer. This lawyer, supposedly, was none other than Roy Cohn. I asked Epstein about the rumor. "I would be very surprised if it were true," he said.

It was. Buddy had contacted Cohn, who had attempted to visit the prisoner on September 26. The lawyer didn't have correct identification, and the now overly vigilant security refused to admit him. Cohn later "reestablished contact" with Buddy and announced that he was talking about terms. That was the last heard on this matter.

Nor did Buddy neglect the press, giving several interviews to Guy Hawtin of the *Post*, who remains a true believer in his innocence. Buddy, he declared, was being given a "runaround." [This was true. A resentful Corrections Department, disregarding the court order, had switched him around three prisons within a single month.] WINE AND WOMEN ARE NOW JUST A MEMORY FOR THE PLAYBOY WHO HAD IT ALL, Hawtin wrote, in melancholic vein. Buddy would talk endlessly of freedom. "I used to believe in the American dream," he said. "Now the American dream has turned into a nightmare." Hawtin offered to get him some books. "I can't concentrate . . . I can't concentrate . . ." Buddy said, querulously. The clincher was the time Hawtin noticed Buddy staring at him, with a peculiar pallor. "I had cut myself shaving," Hawtin explains. The sight of the dried blood had upset Buddy so much that he had needed a glass of water. This incident, I pointed out, was open to more than one interpretation, but Guy wrote a five-part series, entitled *Does Buddy Jacobson Really Belong Behind Bars?* and his answer to the question was a resounding no.

Now a new lawyer appeared in court, much to Epstein's discomfiture. He was the former U.S. Attorney General, Ramsay Clark, and he had been brought into the case not by Jacobson but by Rita Costello, Buddy's sister, who felt he would benefit from Clark's "civil rights experience." "We couldn't believe it," says Gail Jacobs of the DA's office. "*Ramsay Clark!* Who would have believed what this case has turned into? A cause célèbre!"

Buddy Jacobson, as of this writing, is in Clinton, a fortress once known as the Siberia of the New York penal system, up on the Canadian border. Nobody has broken out of Clinton in its 136-year history, which didn't prevent Buddy from trying. In May 1981, he hired two fellow cons to dig a tunnel, starting in his garden plot. They'd gone six feet before the unusual quantities of earth in the surrounding plots were noticed.

He will not be stopped. Now he is writing a book. "He's got plenty of time," says his sister, Rita Costello. Leave to appeal was denied, but the game was not over. Around him lies the documentation of his trial—25 bound volumes. He can recite huge passages by heart. Letters written in that remarkable, scratchy hand bristle with arcane hints. He dreams of freedom, and he talks endlessly of finding "fresh evidence"; indeed, knowing his ingenuity, it is entirely possible that the weapons with which Jack Tupper was slaughtered will bob up in some unlikely spot.

It is impossible to believe that the dark, eccentric journey of Buddy Jacobson is over at last.

Melanie had a dream: Buddy was living among the woods and forests of upstate New York, and he was free from prison. He had asked her to visit him. She went, but took along Mel Harris.

Buddy owned a restaurant and a hotel, styled after the fashion of an English country manor. Around her, when she arrived, Melanie saw signs of frantic building.

Buddy was angry that Mel Harris was there, saying he didn't like her. She left, insisting that Melanie stay: "You know it's what you want to do," Mel said. Stay Melanie did.

Audrey was there, as were Audrey's parents. Audrey didn't relish seeing Melanie. "It's all right," Melanie told her. "Now we're only friends."

But then she realized she and Buddy *couldn't* be friends. She found herself explaining about Jack Tupper's murder to Audrey's parents, who didn't seem to have heard about it. "I *told* you about it, Mom," Audrey interrupted. . . .

Melanie awoke with a start. In bed with her, her husband Billy realized she had been revisiting Buddy's World.

She has lived through bad times. "There are days in the city when I get very weary," she says. Model bookings would be followed by sudden cancellations. "We went with a different model," one photographer apologized. "She's not as good as you are, Melanie, but the client didn't want you when he heard your name." This would happen each time another Jacobson story appeared in the papers, and his capacity for planting them, in the six months following his escape, was seemingly limitless. He had promised to ruin Melanie, and he was living up to his threat. "He'll go on," Billy told me in a despondent moment. "He's not an ordinary man."

But Melanie's will asserted itself, slowly, at first, then with gathering strength. Her work began to pick up. Soon she was modeling as hard as she ever had. One July morning in 1981, Melanie told me that she and Mel Harris would be working with a photographer on Fifth Avenue. I strolled out to watch.

They were on the steps of the Metropolitan Museum. The sun was full, the sky a vivid blue, almost cobalt. Melanie and Mel were rippling through their classic poses, and smiling bright, warm smiles. "Beautiful, girls!" exulted the photographer. "Beautiful!"

A knot of pedestrians had gathered, and the motorists, bicyclists, and roller-skaters looked on appreciatively as they scooted by. A cop wandered over, his handgun lolling alongside a paunch, but he, too, was smiling. "Okay, Melanie," the photographer said. "Let's see more of that shoulder."

Melanie pivoted, leaned into the camera, and gave a full, bubbling smile.

"Modeling can be crazy, a bizarre world," she said, later. "New York has the worst. And it has the best." She now, at last, felt that she could handle it. Melanie was continuing to run. Right now, she was running against herself, but she saw no reason why she should not be among the top female runners in the country.

But there is more to this than competitiveness. "I like to run early in the morning. The joggers aren't there," she said. "I love to run in the rain. I like the trees and the grass. It's as close to earth as I can get. It sorts out my thoughts. I get lost in myself. I make up stories in my head when I run."

She was taking classes in, for instance, acting technique, and voice. She was taking courses in English literature. There was, she realized, so much that she had missed. "Now I've got the confidence," she said, "I don't mind if I fail. No more depression . . . no more anxieties. . . ."

There is her family. And her husband. Buddy's World has receded, has become little more than a spectral memory. Recently, she told me, she had walked down East 84th Street, and it was only later, and with a bit of a start, that she realized she had not even glanced at the building, let alone looked up at those once so baleful and history-impregnated penthouses on the seventh floor.

Melanie still speculates on the circumstances that led up to Buddy's crime: "In the end, all he had was contempt for other people," she says. "And it caught up with him."

When she contemplates Jacobson's future, her ambivalence returns, and she says she understands that Buddy has books and television, and is not being treated too harshly. She sounds not displeased. She wonders how he will occupy the years that stretch ahead of him. At times, she will imagine him devoting himself to the case, bringing to the study of law that same intensity he had used to master the track and the property market. Again, she will see him scheming, dreaming up retribution for the individuals that brought him to this pass.

Sometimes, she wonders if Buddy will not simply cease functioning, like a watch with a broken mainspring. "I wonder how I would feel if Buddy committed suicide," she told me. "But then I think: No, he'll outlive me. He'll never die. He has control over that, too."

* * *

Books end. Like lives. And when it is a book that deals with real people, actual events, it is pleasant to believe that the end to the book also represents a natural end to the events it describes. It doesn't always happen. It does sometimes. Where the Buddy Jacobson story was concerned, no sooner had events seemed to reach a conclusion than there were fresh developments, unpredictable, but possessed of a certain bizarre symmetry. The Final Act. Or, at least, some last scenes.

Carlo Carrara, first. Tongues had begun to wag as soon as Carlo was convicted, but freed from the disagreeable obligation of actually spending time behind bars. One persistent rumor was that Carrara was "co-operating," which is to say helping out the authorities. Another was that he had somehow gotten at the jury.

Billy Sharrocks, simmering in the Manhattan Correctional Center believed the first story, and knew the second to be true. A female juror had been smitten by Carrara's charms, and they had enjoyed a rather public fling. He had taken her to Studio 54 and, yes, The Plaza. This is known as "tampering with the jury." Carlo Carrara was duly tried. Both Sharrocks and the errant juror testified.

Carlo Carrara faced up to the inevitable, and pled guilty. His lawyer, Frank Lopez, made a moving entreaty that the judge adjourn sentencing until the Little League team that Carlo had been coaching had their shot at the pennant. The judge acceded, earning the ire of the *Daily News*. Carlo's team did not win the pennant, and Carlo got eight years. Billy Sharrocks was taken into protective custody, and could look forward to a probable reduction of his sentence.

Another upset was the gradual reemergence of Joe Margarite. He had, in fact, been heard from, though rather obliquely, shortly after the end of Buddy's trial. Margarite had, it seems, been occupying himself on the lam by some profitable speculations in commodities. Gold, and such. He had used a front, a fellow called Burt Kozloff, the son of a Las Vegas entrepreneur, and had run up a seed investment of $100,000 to something like $3 million. He had been much around Manhattan at the time, sometimes soberly dressed in suit and tie, and using such names as "Arthur Amos" and "Ray Poli."

The problem was this: Kozloff had managed to lose most of this money in speculations of his own. Joe Margarite, still theoretically underground, contacted a lawyer named Stanley Drexler, and they sued Kozloff for $1.4 million. The lawyer had verified that Margarite was unwanted by the feds, and that his refusal to show up as a "material witness" in the Jacobson case had lost urgency after the verdict. "We were, we thought, very close to having Joe come in voluntarily," Drexler told me.

Some chance. In May 1980, Joe Margarite had been approached on behalf of an interesting group. The group was headed by some big-spending Lebanese, who had recruited a bunch of mostly American adventurers in the Caribbean. They had a boat, a freighter called the *Ulag,* which had taken on eighty tons of Lebanese hashish in Cyprus, and they required Margarite's expertise in docking it.

In the event, it was a fiasco. The boat was seized in the port of Perth Amboy, New Jersey. Margarite's name soon surfaced, and he elected to remain in hiding. Not for overlong, though. Life on the run had begun to pall. Working through his lawyers, he agreed to plead guilty on a couple of counts, and gave himself up in August 1982.

Yet another upset was the most unexpected of all. One Friday in mid June, that same year, I was telephoned by Brian Monaghan. He asked what I was doing that weekend. I said I was planning to go to Long Island. A weekend in Southampton.

"I'll fly you out," he offered.

There may be several of us, I said.

"I can take ten," he promised. It seemed a fine enough plan. We decided to leave that afternoon. But he telephoned again a few hours later, reporting weather hazards. "There's impacted thunderheads," he told me. "We can't get off the ground." The following morning was no better, and I made my way to Southampton by other means.

Brian Monaghan arrived, rather unexpectedly, at the house in the middle of that afternoon, accompanied by David Silbergeld. They were exuberant, the tall Irishman especially so, and we went into Southampton Village where we consumed quantities of whiskey in a local bar. Monaghan and Silbergeld were as full of suppressed, enigmatic glee as ever, but Brian was seemingly becoming more elated by the minute. We parted, and he suggested that we meet at midnight, at a Westhampton club, the Marrakech.

I never went, as it happened. But a young woman, who was of the party, later told me she had become uneasy, even suggesting to her husband that they might be being "watched." I spoke with Monaghan the next day, but it was still, apparently, not flying weather. Privately, I had begun to wonder if the airplane wasn't as chimerical as so much else in past events. I returned to Manhattan and, a few days later, left for Europe.

Ivor Shaw called me in London. Had I seen the New York papers? No. "It's all over the front page of the *Times*," he told me, fretfully. "Will this never end?"

The facts were these. On Monday, June 20th, a bit more than a week after our last meeting, Monaghan and Silbergeld had taken off from Suffolk County Airport, Westhampton, in Brian's twin-engine Cessna. Accompanied by a pilot and a copilot, they had flown to Florida, refueled, and had flown on to their rendezvous, a primitive airstrip in the jungle south of the Colombian capital, Bogota.

They here took on their cargo. Their cargo was 610 pounds of cocaine, with an ultimate value in the United States of some $200 million. It was contained in 300 packages, some cheerfully done up in gift wrapping, which were themselves stuffed into eight duffel bags. The load was so bulky that the seats had to be removed from the plane's interior.

Brian Monaghan was paying $10,000 a pound, mostly on credit, and the Colombians insisted that a "minder" return with them to the United States. The minder was a barman called Fernando Alzate, and a hefty piece of work, so hefty in fact that a hundred pounds of cocaine—say $3 million worth—had to be left behind to make room for him. Even so, the plane was so loaded that it struck the topmost branches of several trees on take-off, knocking a piece off its left wing.

They refueled at an airstrip on the Florida–Georgia border, and landed, following the pilot's suggestion, at Brookhaven Airport, Long Island. It was a quarter to four on Thursday morning. David Silbergeld was, yet again, attired as a Green Beret. He was armed with a nine millimeter machine-pistol, equipped with a silencer, and three extra clips; throwing knives; flare guns; a couple of tear-gas pistols; a couple of live grenades; a revolver; a switchblade knife; and a wire garotte.

It was David Silbergeld's dream, of course. Or the end of one. The pilot was a nark. He had informed on the operation from the beginning, and the Cessna had landed under the eyes of more than a hundred local cops and federal agents.

Monaghan, Silbergeld, Alzate, and the pilots, including the informer, loaded the cocaine into a rented station wagon, and then Monaghan, Silbergeld, and Alzate got in, and drove off, followed by a cortege of unmarked cars. They were forced off the road by a police car just fifteen minutes later, and looked out into the barrels of some fifty weapons.

"I put my gun right to the window," Detective-Sergeant James Thompson said. "I was screaming 'Don't move a muscle!' and 'I'm the Man!' If we'd been trying to rip him off there would have been a lot of shooting and a lot of people killed. We knew he'd be armed to the teeth."

Brian Monaghan, David Silbergeld, and their Colombian chaperon surrendered.

Disaster means opportunities. Buddy Jacobson's lawyer visited Joe Margarite, of course. Here is the key to that final door which might fly open, throwing light on those others, the Fellow Conspirators. The Buddy Jacobson case is over, at last.